Dialectical Imaginaries

CLASS : CULTURE

SERIES EDITORS

Amy Schrager Lang, Syracuse University, and Bill V. Mullen, Purdue University

RECENT TITLES IN THE SERIES:

Marcial González and Carlos Gallego, Editors, *Dialectical Imaginaries: Materialist Approaches to U.S. Latino/a Literature in the Age of Neoliberalism*

Sherry Lee Linkon, *The Half-Life of Deindustrialization: Working-Class Writing about Economic Restructuring*

Mark W. Robbins, *Middle Class Union: Organizing the 'Consuming Public' in Post–World War I America*

Marie A. Failinger and Ezra Rosser, Editors, *The Poverty Law Canon: Exploring the Major Cases*

M. Michelle Robinson, *Dreams for Dead Bodies: Blackness, Labor, and the Corpus of American Detective Fiction*

Benjamin Balthaser, *Anti-Imperialist Modernism: Race and Transnational Radical Culture from the Great Depression to the Cold War*

Clarence Lang, *Black America in the Shadow of the Sixties: Notes on the Civil Rights Movement, Neoliberalism, and Politics*

Andreá N. Williams, *Dividing Lines: Class Anxiety and Postbellum Black Fiction*

Liam Kennedy and Stephen Shapiro, Editors, The Wire: *Race, Class, and Genre*

Mark W. Van Wienen, *American Socialist Triptych: The Literary-Political Work of Charlotte Perkins Gilman, Upton Sinclair, and W. E. B. Du Bois*

John Marsh, *Hog Butchers, Beggars, and Busboys: Poverty, Labor, and the Making of Modern American Poetry*

Matthew H. Bernstein, Editor, *Michael Moore: Filmmaker, Newsmaker, Cultural Icon*

Lorraine M. López, Editor, *An Angle of Vision: Women Writers on Their Poor and Working-Class Roots*

Carole Srole, *Transcribing Class and Gender: Masculinity and Femininity in Nineteenth-Century Courts and Offices*

Pamela Fox, *Natural Acts: Gender, Race, and Rusticity in Country Music*

Clarence Lang, *Grassroots at the Gateway: Class Politics and Black Freedom Struggle in St. Louis, 1936–75*

Fran Leeper Buss, Editor, *Moisture of the Earth: Mary Robinson, Civil Rights and Textile Union Activist*

Dialectical Imaginaries

MATERIALIST APPROACHES TO U.S. LATINO/A LITERATURE IN THE AGE OF NEOLIBERALISM

Marcial González and Carlos Gallego, Editors

University of Michigan Press
Ann Arbor

Published in the United States of America by the
University of Michigan Press
Manufactured in the United States of America
Printed on acid-free paper
First published November 2018

A CIP catalog record for this book is available from the British Library.

Library of Congress Cataloging-in-Publication Data

Names: Gonzalez, Marcial, 1953– editor. | Gallego, Carlos, 1971– editor.
Title: Dialectical imaginaries : materialist approaches to U.S. Latino/a literature in the age of neoliberalism / Marcial Gonzalez and Carlos Gallego, editors.
Other titles: Materialist approaches to U.S. Latino/a literature in the age of neoliberalism
Description: Ann Arbor : University of Michigan Press, [2018] | Includes bibliographical references and index. |
Identifiers: LCCN 2018021269 (print) | LCCN 2018028474 (ebook) | ISBN 9780472124114 (E-book) | ISBN 9780472073955 (hardcover : alk. paper) | ISBN 9780472053957 (pbk. : alk. paper)
Subjects: LCSH: American literature—Hispanic American authors—History and criticism. | Capitalism and literature—United States—History. | Marxist criticism—United States. | Politics and literature—United States. | Social conflict in literature. | Hispanic Americans in literature. | Literature and society—United States.
Classification: LCC PS153.H56 (ebook) | LCC PS153.H56 D52 2018 (print) | DDC 810.9/868073—dc23
LC record available at https://lccn.loc.gov/2018021269

For all those engaged in the fight against social injustice and inequality—
and for those who dare to imagine an alternative.

Acknowledgments

First and foremost, we want to thank the individual authors who contributed essays to *Dialectical Imaginaries* for their patience and persistence in sticking to this project until its completion. Thanks also to Ben V. Olguín for taking part in our initial discussions about the collection and for helping us to imagine its possibility. We acknowledge our gratitude to LeAnn Fields, Mary Hashman, and Sarah Dougherty, the editors at the University of Michigan Press who worked with us on making this collection happen, the anonymous readers for their tremendously helpful feedback, and the series editors Bill V. Mullen and Amy Schrager Lang. We are also grateful to Maceo Montoya for his permission to use his artwork "La Inmensidad" on the cover of our book and for his commitment to working-class Latino/a art. The University of California, Berkeley and St. Olaf College provided much needed assistance for this project. Finally, we extend our most sincere gratitude to Rebecca S. Richards and Valentina Holquin González for their valuable input and endless moral support.

Contents

Introduction

Reading U.S. Latino/a Literature through Capitalism—and Vice Versa

Carlos Gallego and Marcial González

Class, as a legitimate category for literary interpretation, was slowly but effectively marginalized and delegitimated in the United States during the 1980s, especially after the fall of the Soviet Union. The neoliberal ideological euphoria that followed celebrated the global triumph of parliamentary capitalism and "the end of history,"[1] a slogan that was meant as a prescription for the end of class struggle and dialectical materialism. Critical approaches to the study of race and ethnicity during this period were not unaffected by these political developments, and the radical antiracist discourses of the 1960s and 1970s among creative writers, scholars, and activists eventually gave way to U.S. neoliberalist notions of multiculturalism and identity politics. Despite contemporary neoliberal claims that class warfare no longer exists, recent politico-economic events such as the 2008 financial crash have continued to demonstrate—and recent political movements such as Occupy, the Zapatistas, and Black Lives Matter have continued to confirm—that the sustained, violent oppression of racialized, working-class peoples in the Americas not only persists but, indeed, has intensified. The authors of some recent works of literary and cultural criticism[2] have recognized the need to study literature and culture by incorporating social class analysis in their work, and our aim is to contribute to this cause. To that end, *Dialectical Imaginaries: Materialist Approaches to U.S. Latino/a Literature in the Age of Neoliberalism* brings together eleven essays that interpret Latino/a literature by employing Marxist theory, critiques of capitalism, or materialist analyses of socioeconomic injustices, for we find this literary tradition to be unique in how it represents and addresses several of the aforementioned issues.

In this regard, we are indebted to those scholars who have effectively employed Marxist theory, to one degree or another, as a methodology in their approach to Chicano/a and Latino/a[3] literary and cultural studies for more than four decades. Rosaura Sánchez, for example, published a landmark book in 1983, entitled *Chicano Discourse: Socio-historic Perspectives,* which drew on Marxist social theory and sociolinguistics to study the relation between social organization and verbal interaction in Chicano/a bilingualism.[4] Seven years later, in his groundbreaking *Chicano Narrative,* Ramón Saldívar engaged with the dialectical theories of such Marxist scholars as Georg Lukács, Theodor Adorno, and Louis Althusser to formulate his own theory of the "dialectics of difference."[5] Rosa Linda Fregoso and Angie Chabram followed suit that same year with an essay entitled "Chicana/o Cultural Representations: Reframing Alternative Critical Discourses," which rearticulated Antonio Gramsci's theory of hegemony to make an assertive call for historical materialist approaches to the study of Chicana/o cultural production.[6] And, in 1994, José Limón's *Dancing with the Devil: Society and Cultural Poetics in Mexican-American South Texas* drew on the work of Fredric Jameson to propose a method for cultural interpretation based on the analogous relation between the formal conflicts in cultural representations and the class contradictions in a capitalist mode of production.[7] These and other scholars of U.S. Latino/a literature[8] who drew on Marxism, either in comprehensive or more narrowly-defined ways, during the 1980s and 1990s can be viewed as following in the footsteps of earlier politically-committed writers, such as Raul Salinas and Ricardo Sánchez. As Ben V. Olguín, a Marxist critic in his own right, has notably explained, the eclectic Chicano poet Salinas was a "local/global Tejano Xicanindio Marxist" who collaborated as much with "indigenous anarcho-communitarian Zapatistas" as he did with "communist Cuban and Puerto Rican revolutionary independistas."[9] Moreover, Sánchez, a renowned Chicano pinto poet of the 1960s and 1970s, was active in cultural nationalist organizations such as the Brown Berets, but he was equally involved, as Olguín points out, in "La Resistencia, the immigrant rights arm of the Revolutionary Communist Party."[10] Our main point is that critics and writers of Chicano/a and Latino/a literature in the United States have a well-established history of engaging with Marxist ideas and practices at varying levels of political and theoretical commitment. In this regard, *Dialectical Imaginaries* is not exactly aimed at breaking new ground, but rather at building upon and extending earlier efforts to bridge the divide between U.S. Latino/a literary studies and materialist methods of interpretation, particularly Marxism. By focusing specifically on materialist methodologies, we hope this collection will serve as an impetus to foster dialogue about how to continue developing this important interdisciplinary area of study.

The essays collected in *Dialectical Imaginaries* investigate the manner in which U.S. Latino/a literature accentuates (or has been influenced by) the class conflicts experienced by Latino/as during the neoliberal period. On the one hand, neoliberalism allows for the seamless flow of capital across national borders; on the other hand, it supports an intolerant political rhetoric of homeland security, deportations, and xenophobia that is currently at the forefront of European and American politics. Neoliberalism, while not the principal focus of this collection, is nonetheless an important and often used concept in several of the essays, thus a working definition will prove useful. From the perspective of Marxist economics, neoliberalism refers to a stage of capitalism, roughly from the mid-1970s to the present, during which capitalism moved drastically away from the welfare state associated with Keynesian economics and toward a deregulated or laissez-faire economy that emphasized free trade, tax cuts for corporations and the wealthy, cuts to social programs, the privatization of services, attacks on workers' rights, relaxed environmental protections, and a sharp increase in the mass incarceration of working-class men and women, especially Blacks and Latinos. The implementation of these neoliberal policies has enabled global capitalists to accumulate enormous wealth and power on the backs of workers and other disempowered people.

Neoliberalism also refers to the socioeconomic paradigm that prioritizes market logic as the guiding principle behind any and all sociopolitical practices, an idea that emerged after World War II and increasingly gained traction during the second half of the twentieth century. As David Harvey succinctly explains:

> Neoliberalism is in the first instance a theory of political economic practices that proposes that human well-being can best be advanced by liberating individual entrepreneurial freedoms and skills within an insti-

> tutional framework characterized by strong private property rights, free markets, and free trade. The role of the state is to create and preserve an institutional framework appropriate to such practices.[11]

As a philosophy, neoliberalism is known for reducing all social issues to economic problems that can be solved by market reasoning. Or, as Silvia Federici argues, "The neoliberal attempt to subordinate every form of life and knowledge to the logic of the market has heightened our awareness of the danger of living in a world in which we no longer have access to . . . our fellow human beings except through the cash-nexus."[12] One example of such neoliberalism is found in the corporatization of U.S. politics, which fortified itself as a new paradigm with the massive market deregulations of the 1980s, setting up the "institutional framework" Harvey describes. By the 1990s, neoliberalism was the dominant geopolitical paradigm, most noticeable in international trade agreements like the North American Free Trade Agreement (NAFTA) and the emergence of new economic-political entities like the European Union and the transformation of China into a capitalist superpower.

A major criticism against neoliberalism as an economic-political model is that, in marrying all social interests to market logic, whenever the market experiences instability, that instability necessarily impacts the nation-state and its citizens:

> In so far as neoliberalism values market exchange as "an ethic in itself, capable of acting as a guide to all human action, and substituting for all previously held ethical beliefs," it emphasizes the significance of contractual relations in the marketplace. It holds that the social good will be maximized by maximizing the reach and frequency of market transactions, and it seeks to bring all human action into the domain of the market.[13]

Some of the negative effects of neoliberalism were well documented in the economic crash of 2008, when the housing market collapsed and millions of American citizens lost homes, jobs, and pensions in the process. The "ethics of the market" in that particular case demanded secrecy and misinformation on the part of the U.S. government and major financial institutions as a means of maintaining the illusion of political-economic order.[14] The reality was one of crisis and panic, as the U.S. government (in a move that seemed to contradict its own laissez-faire principles of neoliberalism) was forced to bail out major banks or risk potential socioeconomic and political chaos. The intricate intertwining of market interests with the sociopolitical health of the nation became too obvious to ignore, giving rise to movements like Occupy, along with a general mistrust of the existing political-economic order. The "contractual relations" philosophy of incorporating "all human action into the domain of the market"—the cornerstone of neoliberalist thought—devolved into a historic crisis that was anticipated by Marxist scholars years, if not decades, prior to the actual crash.[15]

Neoliberalism's "ethics of the market," when translated into actual economic and sociopolitical policies, has been particularly cruel to Latino/as living in the United States. For example, a 2009 report written by Catherine Singley and published by the National Council of La Raza[16] indicates that, in 2007, 42 percent of Latino workers earned poverty-level wages compared to 34 percent for African American workers and 22 percent for white workers. Or as Singley states, "Two in five Latino workers do not earn sufficient wages to keep their families out of poverty."[17] Latino/as also tend to work in occupations that are on the lower end of the wage scale, with Latino men earning 68 percent of white male wages and Latinas receiving 77 percent of the wages of white women. Perhaps worse, Latino/as are more likely to serve time in prison than their white counterparts, and generally they have been perceived as foreigners and threats to American culture. The ideological perception of Latino/as as foreigners and threats often applies not only to undocumented immigrants but to U.S.-born Latino/as, as well. Witness, for example, the claims that were espoused by Donald Trump during his 2015–16 presidential campaign in which he blatantly and unabashedly described Mexican immigrants as criminals, rapists, "bad hombres," drug dealers and social threats to the American way of life. His words were not only aimed at the undocumented but implicated the documented, as well. Moreover, Trump's rhetoric and policies encapsulate one of neoliberalism's central problems—the accelerated polarization of wealth, which creates sociopolitical and economic problems domestically that find facile answers in the form of foreign threats. Such complicated realities, while difficult to comprehend and map individually, have been represented or alluded to in many Latino/a and Chicano/a works, including Tomás Rivera's groundbreaking 1971 classic *. . . y no se lo tragó la tierra / . . . And the Earth Did Not Devour Him*, which anticipates the emergence of neoliberalism by exploring the difficult local realities of migrant workers laboring invisibly within an indifferent geopolitical capitalist order.[18]

The literature discussed and analyzed in *Dialectical Imaginaries* continues in this literary tradition, as it counters ultranationalist and racist discourse by giving voice in the public sphere to marginalized populations that have been systematically silenced as a result of colonization, imperialism, class exploitation, racism, sexism, homophobia, and other forms of oppression. The various contributors to the collection analyze literary representations of subjects customarily deemed invisible, socially deceased, or nonhuman within capitalist societies—subjects such as the manual laborer, the service worker, the unemployed, the undocumented, the precariat, the immigrant, the victim of racial or sexual violence, the political refugee, and the prisoner. To support their arguments, the contributors analyze a wide range of literary works in fiction, poetry, drama, and memoir by an impressively broad array of writers, including Rudolfo Anaya, Gloria Anzaldúa, Daniel Borzutzky, Angie Cruz, Sergio de la Pava, Mónica de la Torre, Sergio Elizondo, Juan Felipe Herrera, Rolando Hinojosa, Quiara Alegría Hudes and Lin-Manuel Miranda, Óscar Martínez, Cherríe Moraga, Urayoán Noel, Emma Pérez, Pedro Pietri, Miguel Piñero, Ernesto Quiñónez, Ronald Ruiz, Hector Tobar, Rodrigo Toscano, Alfredo Véa, and Helena María Viramontes. *Dialectical Imaginaries* explores the ways that U.S. Latino/a literary works challenge the perception of Latinos and Latinas as threats to American culture, as socially disposable, or as permanently suitable for an easily exploitable, malleable working class. As a collection of different critiques surrounding the general problem of class oppression under the banner of neoliberal capitalism, *Dialectical Imaginaries* calls for methods of literary analysis that highlight the various forms of class struggle and capitalist critique represented in U.S. Latino/a literature, and it aims at reinvigorating a kind of materialist analysis that critically analyzes the infrastructural networks of capitalism that foster oppression and alienation in the first place.

Consequently, we find the need for this edited collection to be timely, especially when considered in light of developments in geopolitics and academia in recent decades. Global events since 2000—from the attacks on 9/11 and the subsequent wars on terror waged in Iraq and Afghanistan, to the financial collapse of 2008 and the recent immigrant refugee crises in the Middle East, Europe, and Central America—have compelled us to re-examine the political exigency of traditional interpretive models. This reexamination is particularly important when one considers that working-class Latino/a populations on both sides of the U.S./Mexico border have been disproportionately affected by the austerity plans and resulting migrations of neoliberal capitalism. Another timely reason for the publication of this collection is demographic. Since its inception in the 1960s, U.S. Latino/a literary studies has grown significantly as an academic discipline in American colleges and universities. The accelerated expansion of the discipline correlates with the growth of the U.S. Latino/a population, which has increased from seven million in 1970 to more than fifty-seven million in 2015, or about 17 percent of the total U.S. population.[19] Moreover, the U.S. Latino population, which is predominantly working class, is expected to double by 2050. Already, in California and New Mexico, Latino/as outnumber whites and constitute the largest single racial/ethnic group. Alongside this rapid population growth, we have witnessed an explosion of U.S. Latino/a literary production (fiction, poetry, autobiography, and drama) over the past four decades. The literature documents the varied cultural and class experiences of Latino/as living in the United States, and it has also expanded and enriched the American literary tradition generally.

It is important to clarify, however, that the scholarship exemplified in *Dialectical Imaginaries* positions itself in direct opposition to the neoliberal appropriation of identity politics and the consequential tendency of examining Latino/a literature strictly in terms of cultural identity and otherness. Stated differently, it opposes the view that such literature is simply giving voice to a specific demographic. Instead, the essays in this collection foreground the material conditions of existence and class struggles that underlie the experiences represented in Latino/a literature, thereby signaling a paradigmatic shift to a more politically oriented—particularly Marxist—form of literary analysis that can be applied across various canons, and transcending the limitations imposed by the demographic-representational model. We assert that studying Latino/a literature from a class-based historical materialist perspective allows literary scholars to form conversations across cultural and national borders, thereby presenting a larger picture of how capitalism perpetuates neoliberal ideologies and maintains class power on a global scale. This assertion holds true whether one is analyzing the imperialist capitalism of the nineteenth century (for example, the Mexican-American War) or the treatment of contemporary marginal populations that are displaced by the policies of neoliberal capitalism—such as the Mexican and Central American diaspora that followed the implementation of NAFTA and the Central American Free Trade Agreement (CAFTA).

In a limited sense, contemporary U.S. Latino/a literature follows in the tradition of the radical U.S. proletarian literature of the 1930s because of the importance it gives to representing the economic and social inequalities of capitalism—and because, like proletarian literature, it deliberately foregrounds the representation of racial, ethnic, and gender divisions. Latino/a literary works, however, also deliberately foreground the representation of racial, ethnic, and gender divisions. Ultimately, many of these works condemn the racist and sexist ideologies promoted by capitalism, and they do so in a way that illuminates (and sometimes imagines alternatives to) the forms of oppression that take place daily in the lives of Latino/as. To be clear, we recognize that many U.S. Latino/a literary works, including some of the works analyzed in this collection, do not represent class overtly, or that class is not central to their plots and themes. But we hold that, even in these cases, capitalism nevertheless plays a role in determining the conceptual or ideological logic of the literature and of its forms and themes. In other words, the literary works display the effects of capitalism, even when capitalism is not directly confronted in the work. Thus, we are interested not only in analyzing *representations* of class in the literature but also in scrutinizing the ways in which capitalism and social class antagonisms have influenced the *manner of representation* and the particular *kinds of representations* in these literary works.

Additionally, some of the essays in the collection address the frequently encountered misconception that the American working class is predominantly white and male, and that therefore a Marxist theory of class is inadequate for addressing issues of race, ethnicity, gender, and sexuality in ethnic American literature. But given the contradictions of global capitalism and the forced immigration of large sectors of the international working class in the latter half of the twentieth century and the first two decades of the twenty-first century, and given as well the dehumanizing effects of patriarchy and sexism, the American working class has increasingly become female, immigrant, Latino, African American, Asian American, and Arab American in addition to white and male. From this perspective, issues of race, ethnicity, gender, and immigration *are decidedly* working-class issues, and to overlook this fact in favor of an identity-demographic model is to rely on an anachronistic conception of the working class and, by extension, that which constitutes working-class literature.

We find it important to acknowledge that a Marxist approach is not the only possible way to study U.S. Latino/a literature—or any literature, for that matter—but we argue that it is nevertheless an essential methodology, especially for our contemporary historical period. We are also not suggesting that a literary work itself needs to be Marxist for it to be considered a good work of literature. However, we do argue that a Marxist interpretive approach, regardless of the political bent of the literary work, provides important advantages within the discipline of literary criticism. Similarly, we do not hold that, when employing this approach, the value or merit of a literary work should be judged by its political claims, that is, whether it is for or against capitalism. Rather, our position is that a Marxist—or more generally, an anticapitalist, class-based materialist—analysis allows scholars and students to investigate the historical conditions and ideological discourses that make a work possible in the first place. Further, the study of literature would be lacking without proper attention to the formal, structural, or stylistic aspects of literary works. We do find, however, that a literary work's form and style are always intertwined with the sociohistorical context of the text's production, and this interconnection is especially relevant for literatures that offer sharp critiques of class exploitation, racism, sexism, and other forms of oppression, as minority literatures generally do.

Literary critics have excelled in theorizing the uniqueness or difference of U.S. Latino/a literature, a task we hold as indispensable. But it is equally important to illuminate the aesthetic and social features that U.S. Latino/a literature shares with other literary traditions—that is, qualities that stem from engaging with social conflicts of various kinds in a global capitalist economy. Doing so could aid in averting the potential problems associated with fetishizing cultural difference; it could also potentially serve as a corrective to Marxist theory. One goal of *Dialectical Imaginaries* is to bring U.S. Latino/a literature into conversation with Marxist theory in such a way that it benefits both the literature and the theory. We propose to show that this project can potentially broaden the theory by addressing an area of study that has been sorely underrepresented in Marxist studies—specifically, the study of racial and ethnic minority literatures. Conversely, Marxist theory can greatly enhance our understanding of the class experience of Latino/as living in the United States during the neoliberal period, as well as the specific anticapitalist, class-based logic of U.S. Latino/a literary production.

A NOTE ON METHODOLOGY AND ORGANIZATIONAL STRUCTURE

As the subtitle to this collection suggests, our primary methodology is grounded in materialism, and particularly in the Marxist tradition of dialectical materialism. Because the concept of dialectical materialism has undergone such a wide array of interpretations throughout the last two centuries, we find it necessary to offer a basic definition that, while not perfectly aligned with the particular critical approach of each individual essay, nonetheless provides a framework through which one can better understand some of the general theoretical premises that bind these essays as a collection. An important premise to keep in mind is that our approach to dialectical materialism can just as easily be understood as a materialist approach to dialectical analysis, meaning that our inclusive use of this long-standing Marxist concept is as attentive to its philosophical qualities (theory) as it is to its political imperatives (praxis). Emerging primarily from Marx's critique of abstractionism in philosophy, specifically the influence of Hegelian idealism on historiography and political economy during the nineteenth century, the concept of dialectical materialism has always been focused on the material conditions that make human productivity possible, whether this production is intellectual or physical. One of Marx's main predecessors and intellectual influences, Georg W. F. Hegel (and, to some degree, one of Hegel's own predecessors, Immanuel Kant), complicated the traditional model of human consciousness—the Cartesian cogito ("I think, therefore I am")—to reflect the importance of material conditions and historical-intellectual paradigms (i.e., "I think, therefore I am—but mostly because of the ideas available during a specific time"). Marx famously turned the Hegelian dialectic on its head by emphasizing more than abstract historical-intellectual influence in the development of human freedom.

Using Hegel's powerful analogy of the master-slave dialectic as a model for class struggle, Marx reformulated Hegel's system to emphasize the immediate locality of lived experience—that is, the material conditions of existence—as central to determining the capacity for freedom and agency espoused by Enlightenment philosophy. Abstract reason and historical paradigms were no longer enough; Marx challenged philosophy to account for an individual's socioeconomic position within society (that is, either master or slave) as a factor in determining to what extent one was actually free enough to become self-conscious and possessed enough agency to express the freedoms of selfhood. Marx thereby revolutionized Hegel's dialectical system by foregrounding materialism over idealism, a position he explained emphatically: "It is not the consciousness of men [and women] that determines their existence, but their social existence that determines their consciousness."[20] In general, this is the definition of dialectical materialism to which the essays in this collection adhere. Simply stated, our Marxist understanding of materialism foregrounds the philosophical principle that material conditions of existence are crucial to how humans develop the capacity to think, reason, and understand their place in the world, which in turn allows for the possibility of changing the material conditions of existence to promote more freedom and, correspondingly, dis-alienation. Consequently, we hold that if one wants to transform alienating conditions of existence, a materialist understanding of how those conditions emerge and what allows for their continuation is vital.

Thus, while we agree with traditional critics like Georg Lukács when he writes that "the most important function of historical materialism is to deliver a precise judgment on the capitalist social system, to unmask capitalist society,"[21] we also take note of contemporary critics like Fredric Jameson, who states that "[m]aterialist thinking, however, ought to have had enough practice of heterogeneity and discontinuity to entertain the possibility that human reality is fundamentally alienated in more than one way, and in ways that have little enough to do with each other."[22] Dialectical materialism, as a methodology that has influenced the essays in this collection, variously and unevenly, aims at addressing both these perspectives: unmasking the contradictions of capitalist society in this historical moment, and engaging actively with heterogeneous communities and experiences of discontinuity—or what Jameson more generally terms the "postmodern condition of late capitalism."[23] As such, our approach keeps in mind the original Marxist idea of a flexible materialism that can adapt to rapidly changing capitalist realities, or as Roy Bhaskar explains: "The first step in the direction of a more general dialectic can be taken by considering the nature of Marx's (and more generally 'materialist') criticisms of Hegelian dialectic . . . [which] permits the multiple refraction of *dialectic* as *dialectics* to accord with the complexities, angularities, and nuances of our pluriversal world."[24] The allowance for multiple forms of methodological application in a "pluriversal world" is what facilitates the dialectical conversation we hope to promote between Latino/a literary studies and

Marxism. This is why the essays collected here reflect a wide array of materialist approaches as an interpretive register, from traditional works by theorists like Lukács and Marx himself to more contemporary interpretive frameworks that speak to the plurality that Bhaskar notes, represented in the works of scholars like Jameson, Harvey, and Federici.

It is important to note also that our conception of dialectical materialism is equally attentive to the politics of form in literary study. While actual representations of racialized working-class struggle are important at the level of content, we find that the material conditions depicted in literary texts can also be communicated through literary form. In this regard, *Dialectical Imaginaries* does not simply seek to engage works that only represent, at the level of content, the difficulties Latinos/as face within a neoliberal paradigm; we also seek to show the manner in which re-presentation itself is influenced by capitalism, and how writers and artists challenge the packaged realities of contemporary consumer culture by offering works that—through their material form—intentionally challenge readers to rethink how meaning is created in the first place. In this manner, the form of a literary text can contain as much—if not more—political critique than a text that commits to representing class struggle through traditional formats, such as literary realism. Consequently, the critique of form is an important dimension of how we approach materialist analysis. Similarly, some of the contributors in this collection expand the limits of materialist critique with their focus on speculative fiction. In the past, speculative fiction has sometimes been dismissed by Marxists as decadent and bourgeois, while realism has been privileged as the best imaginative mode to reveal class struggle. By analyzing the capitalist basis of speculative fiction, we recognize the importance of this literary tradition as integral for Latino/a cultural expression, and, by implication, we also push back critically against the conventional Marxist privileging of literary realism.

We have organized the essays in the collection to reflect a certain dialectical logic that seeks to maintain an ongoing conversation among the contributors. Thus, we begin with a general essay that sets the groundwork for the collection, followed by a series of essays that exemplify different materialist approaches to various literary and dramatic representations of the Latino/a experience in the United States. Moreover, we staggered the essays in a style that we hope promotes some intergenerational dialogue between established scholars in the field and younger scholars who are making significant contributions to materialist readings of Latino/a texts. Finally, the structure of the collection is intended to model the pluriversality of the authors, texts, genres, and situations that each essay analyzes.

THE ESSAYS

In this volume's first essay, "Marxism, Materialism, and Latino/a Literature: What Is at Stake?" Rosaura Sánchez and Beatrice Pita lay out the central tenets of a "Marxist inflected" approach for the study of Latino/a literature. They argue that the continued expansion of capitalism and U.S. imperialism globally, along with its devastating impact on racial minorities and the working class in the United States, makes an ever-stronger case for a Marxist analysis not only of late capitalism and globalization but also of the way that Latino/as and Chicano/as represent their class positions within society. For Sánchez and Pita, narrative analysis offers a way to understand history as both a representation of the past and an allusion to the possibility of a transformed future. In outlining their approach, they focus on five areas of critique: identity politics, enclosures and dispossession, ecology and labor, police violence, and imperialism.

In "'When the Union Movement Was Murdered in America': Neoliberalism and the Political Economy of Class War in Alfredo Véa's *Gods Go Begging*," Dennis López continues the methodological approach established by Sánchez and Pita. López argues that Véa's 1999 novel revolves around a fundamental concern with the present-day failure to imagine radical alternatives to the neoliberal regime of capital accumulation. Set against the simultaneous backdrops of the U.S. war in Vietnam and contemporary neoliberal America, Véa's novel calls into question the dominant ideologies and social relations of late capitalism. López examines the ways in which *Gods Go Begging* excavates the buried histories of class exploitation, racism, primitive accumulation, and violent labor extraction that serve as the social foundation of capitalist modernity and on which are built the racialized and impoverished modern urban spaces of the neoliberal city.

In "Quarantine Citizen: Latinx Poetry and the Matter of Capital," Michael Dowdy examines how Latino/a poets, writing in the aftermath of the 2008 financial crisis, have found a way of "routinizing, even bureaucratizing" the imagination. He argues that Latino/a poets such as Mónica de la Torre, Urayoán Noel, and Daniel Borzutzky test their poetic imaginaries through rigorous exercises, deliberate experiments, appropriations, and numbered series and sequences. Together, their satirical, parodic, grotesque, surreal, and absurdist modes within these processes enact materialist and class critiques of neoliberal capitalism. Dowdy argues that because Latino/a subjectivity has been generated in and through capitalist crises, with an attendant range of peculiar relationships to citizenship norms and thus to the U.S. body politic and to social class and racial-ethnic formations, Latino/a poets have developed a dialectical imaginary unique in the Americas.

In "Historical Materialism, *The Decolonial Imaginary*, and Chicana Feminist Theories in the Flesh," Marcelle Maese broadens the scope of a Marxist methodology by providing a "long-overdue overview of the engagement between Chicana feminism and historical materialism." Analyzing key works by Emma Pérez, Maese argues that, as a Chicana historian, novelist, and self-declared socialist *lesbiana*, Pérez provides an important link between Chicana feminism and Marxist literary theory, two interrelated yet distinct genealogies of anticapitalist thinking. Maese also examines the conflict between materialism and the nonsecular in the work of Cherrié Moraga and Gloria Anzaldúa, tracing the tension between the spiritual practices of Chicana feminist writers and the need for a materialist-based social revolution, evident, for example, in Anzaldúa's reference to herself as a "third world lesbian feminist with Marxist and mystic leanings."

From yet another perspective, R. Andrés Guzmán draws on a Marxist approach to analyze the dialectical relationship between ideology and form. In "A World Out of Whack: Criminal (In)justice and Financial Capitalism in Sergio de la Pava's *A Naked Singularity*," Guzmán argues that de la Pava's novel—without specifically focusing on financial capital, and though written before the financial crash of 2008—is nevertheless plagued by an anxiety of crisis that prefigures this historical moment. It is a novel that makes use of its length, formal experiments, eclectic themes, and narrative style to demonstrate the absurdity at the core of capitalist accumulation in contemporary society, where speculation displaces production in an idealist bubble, and where materialism is situated at the site of its immanent implosion.

Carlos Gallego's "Pornocapitalism and the Translucent Borders of Social Identity in *Deck of Deeds*" builds on a dialectical materialist tradition that understands market economies as inherently functioning on the manipulation of psychic dynamics, particularly desire and identity. Utilizing the concept of *pornocapitalism*—a term that describes how wealth in contemporary capitalist societies functions as an "obscenely excessive-yet-appropriate" form of existential agency—Gallego argues that the spectacle logic that characterizes postmodern capitalism succeeds by privileging lifestyles and identities that are defined by decadent public practices available only to the upper classes. Reading Rodrigo Toscano's *Deck of Deeds* (2012) as a literary case study, he examines how pornocapitalism arrests the desire of the other by using wealth as an entry point into publicly visible but highly restrictive spaces of obscene pleasure.

In "Bodega Sold Dreams: Middle-Class Panic and the Cross-over Aesthetics of *In the Heights*," Elena Machado Sáez investigates the manner in which Quiara Alegría Hudes and Lin-Manuel Miranda brought Dominican York to Broadway with *In the Heights*, winner of a Tony Award for Best Musical in 2008. The reception of *In the Heights* hailed it as a welcome change from a limited lineage of Broadway musicals about Latino/as, namely, *West Side Story* and *The Capeman*—that is, as a musical that challenges the racial borders and stereotypes of the Great White Way. By contrast, Machado Saéz reads the play not as countering but as potentially reinforcing a bourgeois ideology. She recontextualizes the play in such a way that complicates its reading as a more authentic, less problematic intervention into mainstream discourses about Latinidad.

In "The Dialectics of Presence and Futurity in the Contemporary U.S. Latino/a Novel," Mathias Nilges argues that working-class novels such as Rosaura Sánchez and Beatrice Pita's *Lunar Braceros* demonstrate that we are far from confronted with the universal contraction of time into omnipresence. Instead, our present moment is defined by a plurality of temporal structures that are in turn connected to particular socioeconomic and political structures of power and domination. The U.S. Latino/a novel's effort to trace material history within the current "end times"—and the attempt of authors like Sánchez and Pita to expose the link between postmodern conceptions of temporality and class-based racial domination—constitutes, for Nilges, a renewed commitment to dialectics and an effort to accomplish precisely what Jameson describes as the "re-insertion of time into history."

Despite inexorable migratory conditions, writes Abraham Acosta, Central Americans have become the fastest growing Latino population in the United States. Yet the Central American migrant has emerged as the most pervasive figure of precariousness. In "Crisis and Migration in Posthegemonic Times: Primitive Accumulation and Labor in *La Bestia*," Acosta argues that the intersection between global capital and migration is hardly coincidental. The recent and unprecedented surge of young, unaccompanied Central American children arriving at the U.S./Mexico border is the latest humanitarian crisis to foreground the violent and precarious living conditions in countries like Honduras, Guatemala, and El Salvador. Óscar Martínez's recently translated journalistic narrative *The Beast* (*La Bestia* in the original Spanish) documents the perilous journey Central American migrants face when crossing Mexico, and it offers an urgent accounting of global capital, primitive accumulation, and migration.

While "dystopian" has often been used to describe a genre of science fiction literature that speculates on the future of a postapocalyptic society, Edén Torres asserts that novelist Helena María Viramontes provides a scathing critique of capitalist dysfunction in "A Chicana Dystopian Novel and the Economic Realities of *Their Dogs Came with Them*." Torres explains that much of the criticism of *Their Dogs* has neglected its representation of working-class Mexican American neighborhoods where squalor, police repression, and constant surveillance abound. She argues that as the conditions of global capitalism in the late twentieth and early twenty-first centuries have necessarily placed us all in varying relationships to power, Viramontes's novel shows us the daily terror, environmental degradation, and punishments that her characters must endure, and the assumed perfection of a meritocratic capitalist system.

In the final chapter, "Mass Incarceration and the Critique of Capitalism: A Working-Class Viewpoint in Ronald Ruiz's *Happy Birthday Jesús*," Marcial González analyzes the politics and structure of Ruiz's 1994 antiprison novel to link the proliferation of prisons in the United States since 1982 with the needs of a neoliberal capitalist system in crisis. The staggering number of prisons built, and the number of people incarcerated, over the last forty years can be traced back to the need on the part of the capitalists to recuperate a fractured economy on the backs of the working class—a strategy that has only prolonged the inevitable recurrence of economic (and hence political) crises. As González demonstrates, all aspects of social life during the neoliberal period—and by extension, all forms of cultural production, including Ruiz's *Happy Birthday Jesús*—can be understood to one degree or another as formal expressions or contestations of capitalist crisis, or both.

To conclude, we believe that *Dialectical Imaginaries* is distinct from other anthologies of U.S. Latino/a literature in the importance it gives to social class as an essential analytical category, in its insistence on viewing materialism and Marxism as valid approaches for the study of U.S. Latino/a literature, and in its attention to the ever-present social foundations of the literature. Additionally, the collection's value lies in its conceptualization of U.S. Latino/a literary studies as a discipline that potentially can make an incisive intervention in critiques of capitalism, and it further represents an effort to think through the philosophical, as well as the social, basis of minority literatures. In so doing, we feel that it provides a much-needed alternative to critical approaches that underestimate the importance of social class and thereby minimize the effectiveness of their analytical frames. We have consciously included the word "dialectical" in the title of this collection because it negotiates and synthesizes the sometimes-strained relation between "culture critique" and "class analysis," or between ethnic studies and Marxism. In this regard, *Dialectical Imaginaries* serves as a bridge between U.S. Latino/a literature and Marxism, and as a form of "immanent critique" for each of the two fields. Students and scholars interested in theorizing social class as an inseparable materialist aspect of race, gender, sexuality, and literary form will hopefully find interest in this collection, which seeks to pave a path toward a critical comprehension of these categories as they relate to U.S. Latino/a literature.

Notes

1. Francis Fukuyama is one of the main intellectual champions of neoliberalism, which he outlines in his book *The End of History and the Last Man* (New York: The Free Press, 1992). See also Fukuyama, "America: The Failed State," *Prospect*, December 13, 2016, http://www.prospectmagazine.co.uk

2. See, for example, John Z. Ming Chen and Yuhua Ji's *Marxism and 20th-Century English-Canadian Novels: A New Approach to Social Realism* (New York: Springer, 2015); Kirk Boyle and Daniel Mrozowski's anthology *The Great Recession in Fiction, Film, and Television: Twenty-First-Century Bust Culture* (Lanham, MD: Lexington, 2013); Cheryl Higashida's *Black Internationalist Feminism: Women Writers of the Black Left* (Urbana: University of Illinois Press, 2011); Christopher Nealon's *The Matter of Capital: Poetry and Crisis in the American Century* (Cambridge: Harvard University Press, 2011); Mark Bould and China Miéville's anthology *Red Planets: Marxism and Science Fiction* (Middletown, CT: Wesleyan University Press, 2009); Ben Carrington and Ian McDonald's edited collection *Marxism, Cultural Studies and Sport* (New York: Routledge, 2009); and Gary Edward Holcomb's *Claude McKay, Code Name Sasha: Queer Black Marxism and the Harlem Renaissance* (Gainesville: University Press of Florida, 2009).

3. Although some of the authors in this collection use the terms "Latinx" or "Chicanx" in their respective essays, the editors have chosen to maintain the traditional—if problematic—denominations of Latino/a and Chicano/a for purposes of clarification. More specifically, because the important conversations and critical debates surround-

ing the signification of Latinx and Chicanx are still currently taking place, we found it to be outside the scope of this collection to define these newer, more nuanced but also more complex terms. While we understand and agree with the manner in which Latinx and Chicanx necessarily complicate the dominance of gender norms that tend toward oppressive binaries, we also know that some scholars see the change in denomination as more complex than gender disruption. The "x" that replaces gendered pronouns can also be indicative of an anti-identitarian politics, much in the manner of why and how Malcolm Little became Malcolm X. For some, the "x" is more inclusive; for others, the "x" renders inclusivity and exclusion moot points. As such, out of respect for these ongoing debates, which go beyond the scope of this collection's main focus, we have sided with traditional terminology that will be more familiar to wider audiences. However, we hope that this simple note does offer some insight into the various tensions and contradictions that these traditional terms carry, while also highlighting some of the important debates currently taking place around them.

4. Rosaura Sánchez, *Chicano Discourse: Socio-historic Perspectives* (New York: Newbury House, 1983).

5. Ramón Saldivar, *Chicano Narrative: The Dialectics of Difference* (Madison: University of Wisconsin Press, 1990). It should be noted that Saldívar employs other methodologies in this work, such as deconstruction and poststructuralism, as a means of highlighting the theoretical possibilities inherent in Chicano/a literature, and from this perspective *Chicano Narrative* might be described as making use of a poststructuralist-inflected Marxism.

6. Rosa Linda Fregoso and Angie C. Chabram, "Chicana/o Cultural Representations: Reframing Alternative Critical Discourses," *Cultural Studies* 4.3 (October 1990): 203–12.

7. José E. Limón, *Dancing with the Devil: Society and Cultural Poetics in Mexican-American South Texas* (Madison: University of Wisconsin Press, 1994).

8. In addition to the collection's contributors, other scholars who have employed either class analysis, critiques of neoliberalism, or materialist approaches in recent studies of U.S. Latino/a literature and culture include: Jonathan Dettman, Emma Pérez (see chapter 4 of this collection), Belinda Linn Rincón, Lysa Rivera, Elda María Román, María Josefina Saldaña-Portillo, Kristi L. Ulibarri, Ariana Elizabeth Vigil, and Patricia A. Ybarra, among others.

9. B. V. Olguín, "Caballeros and Indians: Mexican American Whiteness, Hegemonic Mestizaje, and Ambivalent Indigeneity in Proto-Chicana/o Autobiographical Discourse, 1858–2008," *MELUS* 38.1 (Spring 2013): 45.

10. B. V. Olguín, "*Barrios of the World Unite!* Regionalism, Transnationalism, and Internationalism in Tejano War Poetry from the Mexican Revolution to World War II," in *Left of the Color Line: Race, Radicalism, and Twentieth-Century Literature of the United States*, ed. Bill V. Mullen and James Smethurst (Chapel Hill: University of North Carolina Press, 2003), 132.

11. David Harvey, *A Brief History of Neoliberalism* (New York: Oxford University Press, 2005), 2.

12. Silvia Federici, *Revolution at Point Zero: Housework, Reproduction, and Feminist Struggle* (Oakland, CA: PM Press, 2012), 139.

13. Harvey, *Brief History of Neoliberalism*, 3.

14. See Michael Lewis's *The Big Short: Inside the Doomsday Machine* (New York: W. W. Norton, 2011).

15. See Chris Harman, *Explaining the Crisis: A Marxist Re-Appraisal* (London: Bookmarks, 1999); Robert Brenner, *The Boom and the Bubble: The U.S. in the World Economy* (New York: Verso, 2002); and Michael Perelman, *Marx's Crises Theory: Scarcity, Labor, and Finance* (Praeger, 1987).

16. Catherine Singley, "Fractures in the Foundation: The Latino Worker's Experience in an Era of Declining Job Quality" (Washington, DC: National Council of La Raza, 2009). http://publications.nclr.org/handle/123456789/1211

17. Singley, "Fractures in the Foundation," iv.

18. Tomás Rivera, *. . . y no se lo tragó la tierra / . . . And the Earth Did Not Devour Him* (Houston: Arte Público Press, 2015).

19. *Economist*, "Tu casa es mi casa," March 13, 2015, http://www.economist.com/blogs/graphicdetail/2015/03/daily-chart-5

20. Karl Marx, *A Contribution to the Critique of Political Economy*, trans. W. W. Ryazanskaya (New York: International Publishers, 1970), 21.

21. George Lukács, *History and Class Consciousness: Studies in Marxist Dialectics*, trans. Rodney Livingstone (Cambridge, MA: MIT Press, 1990), 224.

22. Fredric Jameson, *The Ideologies of Theory, Vol. 1* (Minneapolis: University of Minnesota Press, 1988), 105.

23. Fredric Jameson, *Postmodernism, or The Cultural Logic of Late Capitalism* (Durham: Duke University Press, 1992).

24. Roy Bhaskar, *Dialectic: The Pulse of Freedom* (New York: Verso Books, 1993), 86 (emphasis added).

CHAPTER 1

Marxism, Materialism, and Latino/a Literature

What Is at Stake?

Rosaura Sánchez and Beatrice Pita

Among the many functions that cultural productions carry out, not the least important of these is that they provide a textualization of lived experience, of the way we experience real or actual events. Through these encoded imaginaries readers process multiple contradictions and multiple temporalities. The events writers encode are the product of layered mechanisms, that is, of the multiple operating mechanisms of contemporary capitalism that play out in all types of imbricated relations. In the process of "reading" these texts—of decoding them—we may become aware of cognitive dissonance and the slippages between temporalities, or the intersectionality in dissonance, as Fredric Jameson terms it. A Marxist inflected critical analysis enables a recoding of the narratives, highlighting the disjunctures and contradictions in the texts.[1] Given our Chicano/a-Latino/a histories, the present state of affairs, and our lived experiences under late capitalism, a nuanced Marxist analysis of the way that we, as Latinos/as, view not only our location within society but also our experiences and consciousness of history continues to be productive.

Chicano/a-Latino/a literature often, although not always, offers an encoding of experience marked by class, racism, xenophobia, linguistic oppression, ethnicism, and marginalization. We need to bear in mind that critical discourses per se are not inherent in ethnic literature nor are capitalism and its correlates requisite referents of our literature. Yet despite the fact that our ethnic literature is not inherently leftist, in any uplifting, "revolutionary" way, and not necessarily antihegemonic and critical of contemporary dominant structures, norms, or practices, our literature is progressive[2] as it does address, in different ways, crucial, unresolved, issues that arise out of our social location and that continue to need to be brought to the fore and not elided.

What might be deemed outright "leftist" literature may be rare in Latino/a literature, but there definitely is a cohort of progressive writers who focus on rendering the present and rewriting the past to release literature's critical potential for analyzing the present and speculating on the future. These writers in their different ways counter dominant U.S. narratives of democratic origins and equal footing and opportunity for all by focusing on various forms of inequality, dispossession, imperialism, and despoliation of the planet, and by dealing in some cases with exploitation and the labor spaces of workers. These texts may implicitly, or even explicitly, lay out a call for reform and change in the existing social system, and while they might not call for a significant change in the political structure or for the end of the capitalist economic system, they do raise a number of issues confronted by Latinos/as in this country. They are therefore important as registers/encoders of the past and present.

In our chapter, we propose to analyze several contemporary Latino/a works of fiction with an eye to examining the dominant issues that are constructed, what the driving dominant ideological perspectives are, and relatedly, what role issues of time, space, and notions of place play in these texts. To that end, in what follows we offer a series of categories of analysis derived from a Marxist-inflected approach: (1) identity politics (demarcation processes), (2) enclosures and dispossession, (3) ecology and labor sites, (4) violence and police brutality, and (5) imperialism beyond borders and resistance. For each category, we provide a brief sampling of Chicano/a-Latino/a texts that focus on several relevant narrative contours and constraints. Despite assertions to the contrary, as we hope to show, a Marxist lens has much to offer twenty-first-century Chicano/a-Latino/a cultural critique.

THE POLITICS OF IDENTITY

Our literature cannot be other than affected by dominant notions in the field and "trending" topics. At this moment of postmodern neoliberalism, with its ideological correlate of multiculturalism, hybridity, and pluralism, what continues to predominate in criticism—as well as in cultural production—is what one might term a "new and improved" postmodern form of identity politics. The turn from the patriarchal cultural nationalist identity that characterized much, if not most, of the Chicano Movement (El Movimiento) at its onset has not led to a rejection of identity politics, but rather to a revised discourse of identity politics, now concerned with fluidity and indeterminacy and with relativized and shifting notions of individual identity. It is a focus that primarily centers on fluctuating identities of ethnicity and race, gender, sexuality, and even—sometimes—issues of class. What was once central to the Chicano Movement of the twentieth century, identifying as a Chicano/a and as a *mestizo/a*, has now, ironically, led some individuals to a different type of cultural nationalism: identity as an "American," as an ostensibly socially mobile ethnic minority distinguished in good measure by accommodation and consumerism with a Latino/a flavor. Also in vogue is the "performance" of identity, as in the case of essentializing indigeneity, that ignores the real social conditions of Native peoples across the Americas. Identity formation is thus carried out within the constraints and parameters of prevailing imaginaries. Breaking these imaginaries down and scrutinizing their constitutive elements will shed light on the different identities that result, as well as their political valence and utility.

Identity politics as performance has been increasingly critiqued as essentialist, fungible, and manipulable. The essentializing and fluid character of identity politics runs the risk of playing into the neoliberal appropriation of identity in the service of marketing niches to produce a commodified illusion of pluralism, inclusion, and equality that in the end is not at odds with the dominant ideology but rather is essential to it. Thus, while Latino/a music and Spanish language are now often interpolated in ads and frozen "Mexican food" is sold at all supermarkets, with media recognition now extended to Mexican filmmakers like Alejandro Iñárritu, Guillermo del Toro, and Alfonso Cuarón, racism and xenophobia in the United States have not, by any measure, diminished; presidential pronouncements and the daily news are evidence to the contrary, in fact. Ethnicity, then, in itself, is not the issue; language use alone is not the issue; culture alone is not the issue. Social location, that is, factors and biases that play into being identified as belonging to a certain class is by far the overdetermining factor in how a Mexican or Chicano/a is viewed. To put it in a blunter, more obvious form: a poor Mexican immigrant is clearly not as well received in this country as, for example, a Guillermo del Toro. The question remains: Has the so-called hybridization of culture and its "inclusionary" bent in any way circumscribed the power of the 1 percent that rule the national and (increasingly) global economies? It certainly has not put an end to, or even remotely constrained, imperialism, nor the processes of dispossession, the criminalization of immigrants, the substandard education of minorities, and the disenfranchisement via incarceration, racism, and class exploitation of people of color.

Identity politics of different types have long been criticized for being essentialized, albeit deployment of "strategic essentialisms" can at times be important and necessary instruments of ideological and political struggle. What is crucial always to remember is that identity is a social, not an individual, construct, produced by a collectivity, although all too often, as we shall see, the focus in Latino/a narratives is on the individual. The individual's positioning—that is, his or her social location—plays a role in identity formation, but so does positionality, or the perspective one assumes vis-à-vis identity. Identification by others, given one's positioning, plays a good part in how one sees oneself. An individual, for example, may not identify as being Black or Brown, but if he or she is so identified by those around him or her, then this identification will undoubtedly have consequences in how he or she self-identifies, whether accepting or rejecting the identity label. A case in point: how many times has one heard, "I'm not a Chicano (or Black) writer, I'm a poet." This desire to disidentify does not, however, put a stop to having a given identity ascribed to the desiring individual or to being labeled (or profiled) as belonging to a particular race or ethnicity. These processes have a great deal to say about how one views the collectivity with which one is identified, often by taking a distance from that group or adhering to another.

Cultural identity, however, continues to predominate in what is labeled Chicano/a-Latino/a literature, although the perspective is mutable. For some time now, there has been a steady increase in cultural production and literary critique marked by a tendency to argue for the recognition of Latino/a contributions to U.S. society across time, especially in regard to participation in the armed forces, labor, film, music, and system politics. In these texts, citizenship is the primary right to be asserted, recognized, and respected. Thus, whether we look at fiction dealing with the nineteenth century, like *Caballero* by Jovita González and Eve Raleigh, or Fabiola Cabeza de Baca's *We Fed Them Cactus*,[3] in addition to the idealization of the past and the boasting of upper-class status under a prior regime, there is also a marked effort to stress the recognition of the contributions of *tejanos* and *nuevomexicanos* to the settlement of the Southwest region before and after 1848. These novels also stress the ability of well-to-do families—the focus of these novels—to assimilate into and contribute to U.S.-dominant Anglo society.

In some texts, there is a clear move away from stressing the socioeconomic underpinnings of identity formation in favor of a view of cultural identity as constructed in what we could term narratives of affect, in which the body experiences identity through physical sensations. In some Chicano narratives, like "Hijo del Sol" by Genaro González, the main character, raised in South Texas as a working-class *mexicano*, travels to Mexico as a young man and discovers he is a foreigner there. His ostensible ethnic identity is shown to be an illusion, and, back in Texas, upon seeing his image refracted/fragmented in a store's window display, he becomes fully aware of his multiform/complex identity. Yet, when a fight breaks out against Anglos at a dance, what is really essential in him proves to be a spirit of violence that the story suggests is inherited from his indigenous ancestors. This irreconcilable disjuncture between his awareness of his fragmented identity and the suggested genetic—and thus inherited—predisposition toward violent responses (he pulls out a knife) is left unresolved in the narrative.[4]

Tomás Rivera's classic story "The Salamanders" also presents a sketch of a young Texas-born boy whose working-class positioning and his migrant farmworker family's inability to find work during the rainy season lead to his disidentifying with his family unit.[5] Sleeping in the car at night parked along a highway, he awakens to see them asleep but waxen-looking as if they were dead. Wishing to be other and elsewhere, he declares to himself that he is no longer a part of them and wants no part of them. When the family, however, finds a farm where they are allowed to wait out the rains, they decide to set up their tent and for the first time in many days lie down to sleep. Awakening to find the tent overtaken by salamanders, the family—literally—stands its ground and defends its terrain by stomping on the salamanders; it is in this act of solidarity, in this act of violence, that the boy rediscovers his ties to his family and rearticulates his sense of belonging to a collectivity. Violence here, as a reaction to hostile or threatening situations, or both, seems to play a large part in how we view our identity. This violence is not always outwardly directed against another species or group. In Américo Paredes's *George Washington Gómez,* for example, the main character, Guálinto, despite an upbringing marked by cultural adhesion to things Mexican, much like the character in "Un Hijo del Sol," not only abandons his roots but moreover turns against his own people and becomes an intelligence officer spying on *mexicanos* in the Rio Grande Valley.[6]

While more recent literary works often focus on assimilation and on being part of the national U.S. body in all its ostensible multiplicity, others focus on the effects of trauma and alienation. Stella Pope Duarte's novel *Let Their Spirits Dance* tries to unite several ethnic minority groups through a joint trip to the Washington, D.C. Vietnam Memorial.[7] While there are highly critical statements regarding war and imperialism pronounced at the Memorial, the novel instead focuses on the process of bringing Vietnam War veterans of different backgrounds together, as it sets out to produce a "healed" multiethnic national "American body." In Cherrie Moraga's play *Watsonville*, by contrast, the Chicana character Susana, faced with anti-Latino/a legislation and a long union strike, expresses her alienation and desire to escape to "some place not here. Some place that doesn't feel like a foreign country."[8] It is an alienation from the U.S. nation-state, yes, but not from the working-class women organizing the strike against the cannery. Thus, whether the individuals are citizens or undocumented immigrants, class, gender, sexuality, and national origin are identity characteristics that create a sense of solidarity rooted in class location. Positioning and positionality thus come together here in a fashion markedly different from what is at work in Pope Duarte's novel.

Whether Latino/a texts argue for assimilation or for biculturalism and a recognition of cultural difference, what is clear is that—except for narratives on farmworkers—few of our works of fiction as a rule focus on working-class characters. It is one thing to mention, in a sentence or two, that a character is a maid, a field hand, or a factory worker, but focusing on their sites of labor and noting how this is constitutive of their lives is another matter. Often, narratives are primarily marked by affect and focus on relationships and the feelings (hope, betrayal, frustration) provoked in different characters by their circumstance and struggles. While one has to acknowledge that there are Chicanos/as-Latino/as from all walks and stations in life, it is telling that even if a good number of Chicano/a-Latino/a writers might be from working-class backgrounds, our stories tend to center on protagonists who are lawyers, artists, detectives, writers, professors, teachers, and college students, as if those were the only "interesting" lives worthy of narrativization. Few of our narratives focus on the lives of gardeners, tile setters, construction workers, plumbers, cooks, dishwashers, janitors, maids, nannies, tree trimmers, electricians, machine operators, caregivers for the elderly, or truck drivers, even though these are occupations that define the contours of the lives of so many of us. Nevertheless, much of Latino/a literature demonstrably argues against racism and xenophobia, against sexism, misogyny, and homophobia in defense of particular identities; consciousness of economic location and the identity derived from that social location, however, are at best "backgrounded" in much of our cultural production. Often what is textualized is the struggle to leave the working-class status, a class condition to be left behind—significantly, as an individual—via assimilation and professionalization into the so-called middle class. Clearly, as history has repeatedly shown us, difference is constructed and certain differences, like race, like ethnicity, like gender, like sexuality, can be marshaled to divide the working class when it is convenient for capital to superexploit some and favor others. Thus, Black and Latino capitalists have no problem in exploiting working-class Blacks and Latinos, although, on occasion, despite being a prominent professional, a Black person can also be discriminated against, as occurred in the 2009 case of Professor Henry Louis Gates; class standing would elicit the intervention of President Barack Obama, whereas the all-too-frequent assaults and murders of Blacks and Latinos on our streets would not. Sifting through and unmasking these contradictions, their origins, causes, and consequences is where a Marxist analytical lens can offer much in the way of precipitating out what is in operation and what is really at stake.

ENCLOSURES AND DISPOSSESSION

The process of enclosure, whether of material spaces, populations, or even discourses, has much to provide us in terms of categories of fruitful critique. Still, it bears remembering that the issue of enclosures or "accumulation by dispossession," to use David Harvey's phrase,[9] is at the core of the accumulation of capital, and what makes this concept productive is that it is not limited to land, as one can be displaced, dispossessed, and restrained from multiple domains. In his essay "Separating the Doing and the Deed: Capital and the Continuous Character of Enclosures," Massimo De Angelis notes that enclosures are a fundamental tenet in Marxist economic theory because capital always encloses.[10] But what then are enclosures, and in what ways can this category be pertinent to the study of Chicano/a-Latino/a social location and the ideological imaginaries that derive from it?

As De Angelis has noted, enclosures are often studied as a historical phenomenon—as a form of primitive accumulation that jump-starts capitalist regimes of power and enables the transition from feudalism to capitalism. But as the Midnight Notes Collective and De Angelis both stress, we have to account for both new and old enclosures, since the process of enclosures is continuous, multiform, and evolving.[11] Marx himself noted that the difference between accumulation and primitive accumulation is not a substantive one. In the *Grundrisse* he remarks: "Once this separation is given, the production process can only produce it anew, reproduce it, and reproduce it on an expanded scale."[12]

In *Capital,* Marx explains how primitive accumulation gave birth to the preconditions of a capitalist mode of production, through the separation of producers (the serfs) from the means of production (the land).[13] In separating the workers from the means of production, two things happen: (a) the social means of subsistence and production are turned into capital and (b) the producers are turned into wage laborers. Force and laws, or the state, are required to carry out this separation, but in time this relation of expropriation is normalized and accumulation appears as a constant, ostensibly inexorable process. Thus, the privatization of land for new industries, the relocation of communities for roads, freeways, and dams, the privatization of public services and basic resources, the privatization of medications, and the privatization of common space are all contemporary examples of enclosures that have much bearing on the conditions that affect all populations, but perhaps Chicano/a-Latino/a and indigenous communities to a higher degree. The fact that it is an "ongoing feature of capitalist regimes"[14] means that the phenomenon is not limited to the United States. In the Americas, North and South, we have to recall that the most egregious "hostile takeover" was that of the land of native peoples. In the United States, this dispossession was based in good measure on military force.[15] But, as a rule, force was, more often than not, accompanied by legal measures and state policies that enabled the use of outright coercion, as in the case of the Removal Act of 1830 and the Dawes Act of 1887. New and improved mechanisms of dispossession and enclosure are at work today in our twenty-first century.

Historically, then, the various implementations and forms of enclosures lead not only to the destruction of the commons but also to that of communities, for as De Angelis notes "there is no enclosure of commons without at the same time the destruction and fragmentation of communities."[16] There are numerous forms of enclosures, numerous ways of privatizing commons, whether it be through water privatization, land enclosures, effects of debt enclosures through structural adjustment policies, and, for the present moment especially, through the toxic effects of gentrification on Latino/a communities. What theorists dealing with enclosures offer is a framework with which to study the "processes of identification, types and modes of enclosures" in the present historical conjuncture.[17] And, we would add, it is a framework that can address what we would like to call the "lived experience" of enclosures—which is what we often find constructed in our literature—that would in turn serve as a register of the trauma resulting from the violent enactment of dispossession. Thus, we argue that the destruction of communities across U.S. history that some works of Chicano/a-Latino/a cultural production explore suggests that the notion of enclosures can speak powerfully to a shared history of dispossession.

What we are pointing out is that enclosures and dispossession are not things of the past. They are, as previously noted, still ongoing, although now in urban areas, as products of urban renewal, gentrification, and eminent domain, and they continue to be configured in the work of Chicano/a and Latino/a fiction writers. Dispossession, for example, is the overriding topic in the play *Chavez Ravine,* in which the playwrights and performers of Culture Clash focus on a twentieth-century case of dispossessed barrio dwellers in Los Angeles.[18] Dispossession, as we shall see, can be effected by force or by legislation, or by both. Here it will be urban planning and eminent domain ostensibly for "public housing" that led the early 1950s Los Angeles City Council to evict and forcibly relocate residents from Chavez Ravine, an area of three Chicano communities: La Loma, Palo Verde, and Bishop. Residents were told that they could return after the public housing units were in place, but the plans for the housing development were ultimately cancelled in favor of the construction of Dodger Stadium, leaving the Chicano residents with no recourse against the destruction of their communities, no options other than to submit and leave. In the play, two distinct time-spaces intersect to bring the past into the present. In one scene, Chicanos/as-Latinos/as in the 1980s are filling Dodger Stadium watching Fernando Valenzuela pitch as another overlapping time-space is juxtaposed. The "apparition" of former residents on the same Chavez Ravine/Dodger Stadium soil in effect reenacts the process of their dispossession in the 1950s, while at the same time the play makes the unmistakable point of signaling the growing demographic (and now majority) presence of Chicanos/Latinos in Southern California.

On the other side of the country, in his novel *Chango's Fire,* Ernesto Quiñónez takes up the displacement of Puerto Ricans and other Latinos/as from New York's Spanish Harlem tenements through the owner-ordered burning down of the buildings with an eye to gentrification and enhanced revenue.[19] Dispossession and displacement are likewise key topics configured in Helena María Viramontes's novel *Their Dogs Came with Them*, which focuses on yet another Los Angeles instance of dispossession.[20] In this case the state again uses eminent domain to buy up lands in the East L.A. barrio, displacing many residents, for the construction of a metropolitan freeway system. The East Los Angeles Interchange, composed of six feeding freeway segments and connecting four different freeways (the Santa Monica Freeway I-10, the Santa Ana Freeway I-5, U.S. Route 101, and the Pomona Freeway SR-60), was begun in the early 1960s; this investment in infrastructure would displace a good number of Chicano/a residents of East L.A. Viramontes's novel is a wonderfully complex work with a fragmented structure, multiple temporalities, and different narratives that intersect dissonantly. If the "most valuable works are those that make their points by way of form rather than content," as noted by Jameson, then the form and structure of a number of Chicano/a-Latino/a texts, like Viramontes's novel, that offer fragmented narrative structures and encode a series of spatiotemporalities, best register and encode the multiple realities of what are now over fifty-eight million Latinos/as in the United States.[21]

Displacement of East L.A. residents is witnessed by Ermila Zumaya, a child who grows up viewing the four freeway crossings and interchange right across the street from her grandparents' home in a working-class Chicano/a community. As a teenager, she becomes increasingly aware of social location as she notes the daily work schedule of her neighbors. While still in bed, she hears the women walk by at 5:30 a.m. on their way to the bus terminal to take buses that will take them clear across the city to the Westside where they work as maids, nannies, and housekeepers. By 6:00 she hears through her window a second group of women walking to the bus stop to take buses that will take them to their downtown jobs in the garment industry. All of these women have long bus commutes ahead of them. Ermila, a high school student and part-time office worker, knows well this life on the city buses, on the streets, on the sidewalks, and the long waits that people have to go through at the roadblocks set up during the Quarantine Authority's curfew, both a spatial and temporal constraint in a primarily Chicano/a-Latino/a East L.A. At night, the entire community hears the constant noise of helicopters flying by and shooting dogs out on the street. The city's excuse for this surveillance is a rabid dog alert that just happens to coincide with the Chicano student walkouts of 1968. It is an inchoative moment of the Chicano Movement where students in several high schools walk out of classes to make their ethnic studies demands known and to stand in solidarity against racism, segregation, repression, and the Vietnam War.

Dispossession, displacement, and police harassment are key topics in Viramontes's novel, as it follows several characters across different moments in time. When these temporalities come together, dissonance and violence are generated. Issues of gender identity and its constraints, police violence, homelessness, dementia, gang identity, immigration, lack of health care access, mental health issues, gender violence and rape, as well as religiosity, are linked to issues of dispossession and displacement, from Mexico to Texas to California. An outstanding example of a complex work, the novel figures multiple temporalities and spaces and is richly rendered in all the contradictory, dissonant, and painfully violent lived experiences of its many and multiform characters. Viramontes's *Their Dogs Came With Them* captures the dissonant intersections not only of the freeway system built upon the material landscape and the fragmentation of communities, but also the intersection of characters and their individual experience of the social and economic processes at work.[22]

ECOLOGICAL CONCERNS IN THE LATE ANTHROPOCENE: INHABITABILITY AND LABOR EXPLOITATION

Human activity and the use of fossil fuels that are destroying the ozone layer have led scientists, like the 1995 Nobel Prize winner Paul Crutzen, to propose calling this geological epoch the Anthropocene Age.[23] Some scientists posit that the Anthropocene epoch began with large-scale agriculture (eight to five thousand years ago), while others trace it to the Industrial Revolution in Europe and the large-scale burning of fossil fuels. Still others see the year 1945 as the beginning of the Anthropocene, with the presence of radiation from human-initiated nuclear fallout. Finally, some Marxists scholars, like John Bellamy Foster, trace this new epoch to the rise of monopoly capitalism and the speed-up it entailed at the level of fossil fuel consumption to underwrite increased production.

Eco-socialist and eco-Marxist critics like Foster, Andreas Malm, and Jason Moore see an intimate connection between (a) monopoly-finance capitalism and the third technological revolution, and (b) the ecological destruction of the planet, establishing a linkage between Marx and ecology.[24]

Foster's contribution is central to these and other studies on Marx's materialist conception of history and nature. Particularly key is Foster's discussion of Marx's theory of social metabolism and metabolic rift. Marx used this concept of "rift" in the metabolic relation between human beings and the Earth "to capture the material estrangement of human beings within capitalist society from the natural conditions which formed the basis for their existence—what he called 'the everlasting nature-imposed conditions of human existence.'"[25] This rift began with the antagonistic division between town and country but also—importantly—extended to colonized peoples who saw their land and resources (natural and human) robbed to support the industrialization of the colonizing, imperialist centers. Foster notes that already in the nineteenth century Marx and Engels also—interestingly—addressed other ecological problems, including the depletion of coal reserves and the destruction of forests. He further discusses Marx's comments on enclosures and the dispossession of the serfs, the burning of their villages, the usurpation of the common lands, attendant to the development of large-scale agriculture. The genesis of industrial capital was a story that took the form of the displacement and exploitation of Europeans, the pillage of the noncapitalist world, and the creation of the triangle trade of the transatlantic slave system. In all of this, the alienation from the Earth is the sine qua non of the capitalist economic system. Hence from the 1840s on, both Marx and Engels insisted on the need to transcend this form of alienation from nature upon which capitalism rested.[26] Marx and Engels also saw that the working classes were disproportionately exposed to pollution and contamination and addressed as well the despoliation of the environment. For all these reasons, Moore finds that the Anthropocene age should more accurately be called the Capitalocene.

Issues of global warming, the buildup of greenhouse gases in the atmosphere, the threat posed by global water shortages, the contamination of rivers and oceans, and the increasing extinction of species all over the planet are ecological issues that have not been taken up much in Latino/a literature. Popular culture—with films like *Mad Max* and *The Book of Eli* and much writing in the vein of science fiction and speculative fiction—presents numerous instances of a postapocalyptic Earth destroyed by nuclear war and desertification. Science fiction narratives in Latin America, and especially in Mexico, deal with postapocalyptic scenarios where nuclear warfare has reduced cities to rubble, creating water and food shortages. But Chicano/a literature is not yet, at least, characterized by these dystopic postapocalyptic scenes.[27] What is registered, however, in the literature is a concern for natural resources and the impact of the earth's contamination on workers, whose social vulnerability more readily subjects them to the toxic effects of pollutants. These issues are in fact prevalent in the literature.

The contamination of agricultural fields and illnesses caused by pollutants and the spraying of fields and field workers with pesticides are topics central to Moraga's play *Heroes and Saints*.[28] Here a cancer cluster is discovered in the town of McLaughlin (a fictional version of McFarland in the San Joaquin Valley of California) that has an anomalously high rate of infant mortality and a high incidence of infant deformities. The play's main protagonist, Cerezita, has been born without limbs and is represented with an oversized head. Yet she becomes the one to organize the workers and their children to protest the use of pesticides in the fields, in the end serving as a martyr for the cause, dying a gruesome death, crucified by the growers in the toxin-contaminated field. Textualized denunciations of unhealthy work environments affecting the Chicano/a-Latino/a populations are also found, for example, in Viramontes's novel *Under the Feet of Jesus*, which narrates the case of a young boy from Texas working in the fields of California who is sprayed by pesticides.[29] He too is close to death when Estrella's family drops him off outside a hospital. Likewise, in Ana Castillo's *So Far from God*, set in New Mexico, women working for *maquiladoras* come into contact with carcinogenic substances that also lead to workers' death.[30]

Rudolfo Anaya's detective novel *Jemez Spring* broaches the issue of the risk of radiation poisoning from the nearby nuclear labs and the threat of a plutonium bomb on Jemez Mountain.[31] Raven, the personification of evil in Anaya's four detective novels, plans to detonate a bomb near Albuquerque. The threat, developed further in another novel from the same detective series, serves the interests of a right-wing militia group made up of high-ranking government officials who are ready to take over the government in Washington. In these novels, as well as in *Alburquerque*, Anaya deals at some length with the issue of water shortages and the dispossession of indigenous Pueblo people's water rights to serve corporate interests.[32] The still-farming Native Americans organize to fight the plan to dispossess them of their access to water—and therefore their livelihood and way of life—but some of them are ready to sell their land and their rights. Generally speaking, however, Anaya's work shows a tendency of focusing on interpersonal relations over ecological issues; habitat despoliation and crimes against nature are, nonetheless, highlighted.

LOCKED UP: POLICE BRUTALITY, INCARCERATION, CRIMINALIZATION

The years 2014 and 2015 were deadly for young African American men, whether in Ferguson, New York City, Cleveland, Chicago, San Francisco, Los Angeles, or Minneapolis. The *Guardian* reports that in 2015 "young Black men were nine times more likely than other Americans to be killed by police."[33] Rarely are the killers charged, but when they are, in most cases the police are found to have been "justified" in the shooting. Clearly the authorities are all too quick to use lethal force against African American men who are often unarmed. Sometimes these deaths are not caused by a bullet fired by the police, but occur while in custody, as in the case of Sandra Bland, arrested—incredibly—for not signaling a lane change.

Living while Black in the United States is clearly a high-risk occupation, but so is being Native American, Mexican, or Latino/a. In fact, half of all the people killed by police in 2015 (a total of 1,134) were minorities, although we make up only 37 percent of the overall population. In the case of Mexicans/Chicanos/as, they often are shot not only by increasingly militarized police forces but also by U.S. Border Patrol agents. While less publicized, Border Patrol agents carrying out these murders are also usually exonerated, as is evident in cases registered in El Paso, Texas; San Diego, California; Nogales and Douglas, Arizona. In 1997, another state agent, this time a Marine Corpsman, fatally shot a boy at the border as he herded his sheep.

These acts of police, ICE (Immigration and Customs Enforcement), or Border Patrol brutality, or what we could more rightfully call criminal action by the state, are not new. They have been used historically to intimidate and dispossess the population but also to lower the unemployment rates through incarceration, protect private property, and ensure profit for the prison industrial complex. Let us not forget too that during the colonization of the Southwest, thousands of Native Americans were killed by Spanish, Mexican, and later U.S. soldiers. The state, of course, always had a hand in the mob lynching of Blacks as far back as the nineteenth century. Lynchings were "tolerated" as expressions of the public will, and no one was ever charged.

It bears recalling that throughout the nineteenth and early twentieth century, Mexicans were the targets of lynch mobs as well. *Californios* were lynched after 1848 in California, and *tejanos* were killed by the Texas Rangers, the infamous *rinches*, who, unfettered, practiced necro-politics in Texas. Despite the fact that many of those killed were natives to the Southwest—and not new immigrants—the natives were met with xenophobia, or as put by Juan Seguín, they were treated as "foreigners in their native land."[34] At one level, these lynchings and acts of police brutality appear to be simply acts of racism or xenophobia, but closer scrutiny reveals these shootings to be closely linked to the class status of the victims and not just racially or ethnically motivated. Minorities, moreover, have been and continue to be blamed for economic conditions in this country, as hindrances to the Manifest Destiny of U.S. "greatness."

The impunity with which Blacks and Mexicans/Chicanos/as have been the object of violence repeatedly throughout the nineteenth and twentieth centuries, and as we are witnessing today, into the twenty-first as well, begs consideration of what is a layered historiography; we find ourselves encountering the past in the present. It's as if time were multilayered and the past were sedimented in the present, with the streets now still bearing "Strange Fruit," although clearly past cases of police brutality and lynchings are not identical to those of today, as they were a response to a different set of historical and material conditions. Yet what are distinctive temporalities can be seen to come together, not in a conjuncture, but in an intersection marked by dissonance.[35] In this period of global capital, marked by flexible modes of accumulation that allow for the incorporation of different phases or temporalities of capitalist production in different localities into the global market, past temporalities of state violence also intrude on the present.

Theorists, such as Massimiliano Tomba, posit that Marx's later writings already presciently noted that the capitalist market was able to produce the copresence of colliding temporalities. These are colliding or dissonant temporalities because they are not, as in a liberal pluralist model, harmoniously blended and coexisting.[36] We argue that a consideration of colliding and multilayered temporalities might help us better understand the continued violence against Black and Brown bodies by allowing us to see the numerous recent cases of police brutality as modern day versions of lynching, now practiced by police state agents rather than by a vigilante mob. Past temporalities that allowed for the lynching of Blacks and Mexicans survive in today's twenty-first-century law enforcement officer shootings, as does neoslavery through the carceral regime in which all too many people of color find themselves enclosed today.

How these multilayered temporalities are expressed, constructed, or textified in cultural production is what concerns us. If history is unrepresentable and only made accessible by being textualized or narrativized, then it is through narrative that the reader grasps the contradictions of multiple temporalities, be they explicitly figured or not, even when a particular text treats these shootings as individual and isolated cases, thereby focusing primarily on the singular experience of said events. We want to turn now—if briefly—to some concrete examples from Chicano/a literature, to see how these texts can be mined for treatment of these embedded issues.

Sometimes, cases of brutality by state agents are seen in literary texts as part of an ongoing regime of violence that takes multiple forms. Acts of brutality can be found in the narrative by Paredes, who documents one particular act of lynching by the Texas Rangers in his novel *George Washington Gómez,* written in the decade of the 1930s, but not published until 1990. Paredes configures this lynching by the *rinches* within the wider context of repression by police and Rangers—who were responsible for many lynchings—and of the subsequent *tejano* resistance in the seditionist movement of 1915–17. Rolando Hinojosa offers a different take. His novel *Generaciones y semblanzas,* from 1977, recalls the killing of the character Ambrosio Mora, a veteran of World War II, shot by a deputy sheriff in Klail City in the late 1940s, noting too that this deputy was, not unsurprisingly, cleared. This act, though not connected to other shootings in the novel, is viewed within a broader context of social, economic, and political transformations in the Rio Grande Valley that brought a new Anglo ruling class to Klail City and disempowered *tejanos.*[37]

In his 1983 play, *The Many Deaths of Danny Rosales,* Carlos Morton captures not only the killing of the character Rosales by a sheriff of Arroyo County in 1975—without cause or provocation—but also the subsequent metaphorical murder of Rosales by the state court system that found the sheriff innocent.[38] As Rosales's wife puts it, her husband was killed many times: once when he was born poor, once when he didn't get a decent education, once when he was shot by the sheriff, once when his body was buried by the sheriff's wife near the Louisiana border, and once again in the Texas court of law. As the character rightfully points out, these many deaths respond to multilayered economic, social, and political temporalities. It was not till the federal justice system intervened that the sheriff and his wife were found guilty, not of murder but rather, ironically, of "violating Danny Rosales' civil rights." The play—based on the actual killing of Richard Morales in Castroville, Texas, in 1976 by the local sheriff—makes a lucid connection between the lack of equal protection under the law for Chicanos/as and the social status of Mexicans in Texas, all of which speaks to the impunity with which Anglo lawmen can kill Mexicans.[39] A hundred years earlier in 1873, a Mexican Investigative Commission looking into the lynching of Mexicans in Texas had concluded that there was no justice for Mexicans in Texas.[40] In Morton's play, it is up to the audience to make the connection between the various temporalities, since it is still the case today that working-class, unemployed, or undocumented Mexicans can neither expect nor exact any justice from state agents, who are quick to shoot to kill when, for them, certain lives don't matter much.

Sergio Elizondo's 1984 innovative novel *Muerte en una estrella,* translated as *Shooting Star* in 2014, is, like Morton's play, based on historical events: the murder of two teenage Chicanos by the police in Austin, Texas.[41] The novel recalls events in the decade of the 1960s when two Camp Gary Job Corps trainees decide to go into Austin on their day off. One is nineteen and the other sixteen. Valentín Rodríguez, the bored nineteen year old, decides they should take a joyride in a car taken from a parking lot near the river where tents have been set up for a visiting circus. The two boys drive off in a stolen car, but they don't get far, only a few feet, because Valentín does not know how to drive an automatic car with power steering and he crashes into a light post almost immediately. The boys jump out and start running with the police after them, and both are shot in the back. What Elizondo has done in his remarkable novel is not only tell the story of this historical case of police brutality but also add depth to the lived experiences of these two teenagers, a depth, resonance, and even epic stature that dominant society would deny them. The narrative constructs a life for the two teenagers as they lie dying on the grass, figuring a subjective spatial experience of time as they recall their past and their families in their native South Texas. Elizondo also situates the murders within a historical context that includes the 1960s Chicano Movement, farmworker unionization, the impoverishment of the field workers, and the rise of Chicano culture in general that extends from Texas to California. The decade of the 1960s was in fact a deadly decade for Chicanos/as. It included the murder of other teenagers, and even a child, by the police in Dallas in 1973. If these Texas killings recall a past temporality of *rinche* killings, then this reconstruction in Elizondo's novel appears to be in dissonance with a new temporality of activism—not the armed sedition of Paredes's text but a temporality of protests and marches that were then emerging, as the novel testifies.

Other narratives, plays, or works of poetry may document lives of delinquency or crime (often with a focus on "redemption" and assimilation to the righteous rule of law and a law-abiding life), but few have reconstructed blatant and direct instances of state violence against individuals and communities as these authors have, and in so doing they contribute powerfully to making clear the various forms that state violence against these populations takes. In textifying acts of violence, these works force us to confront the ongoing intersection of multiple, dissonant temporalities and their deadly outcomes for communities of color, the consequences of which we are witnessing still today.

IMPERIALISM BEYOND BORDERS AND RESISTANCE

Another area in which Marxian approaches assist in understanding the particularities of U.S. Chicano/Latino lives and their representation in cultural production is in the centrality of the notion of imperialism. In his book *Imperialism and Global Political Economy*, Alex Callinicos discusses various theories of empire, including territorial and nonterritorial imperialism, that can to good effect be applied to Latino/a texts dealing with the global reach of capital and empire.[42] Like Harvey, Callinicos sees capitalist imperialism as constituted by the intersection of two forms of competition, namely economic and geopolitical.[43] Today capitalist imperialism involves the imperialism of free trade, the control of the international financial system, the dispossession of landowners in the Global South for privatization, all to clear the way for the free circulation of capital across a globalized market.[44] The establishment of free trade zones has brought on transnational migration to these sites where wages are low, thus furthering the influx of immigration, especially undocumented immigration, from the South to the United States, as well as Europe and metropolitan areas in the Global South. For particular spatial fixes, U.S. capitalists count on the cooperation of governments in the Global South, as in, for example, Latin America. Thus, the United States is infamous for its support of right-wing dictators like Rafael Trujillo, Fulgencio Batista, Anastasio Somoza, and Augusto Pinochet in the past and, more recently, for its reluctance to accept the left-leaning governments of Venezuela, Bolivia, and Ecuador. Through its influence on local governance and of governments that accept U.S. hegemony in world affairs, the United States need not, as in the past, resort to territorial control; the results, however, are equally onerous for the inhabitants of what used to be termed the Third World, who, in all too many cases, are obliged to migrate to survive.

The resulting dispossession and unemployment in the Global South, as well as warfare in the Middle East, have led to massive emigration north, whether to Europe or the United States, where precarity is also the condition awaiting these migrants. Their low-wage jobs in domestic work, sweatshops, field work, and the service sector constitute temporary and insecure labor conditions that are all-too-seldom represented in Latino/a literature—except for field work in earlier Chicano/a literature—especially if the focus is on "making it" in the United States. The onerous and dangerous trip north is, however, an issue that is frequently taken up in Latino/a literature that deals with Puerto Rican, Dominican, Central American, or Mexican migration to the north. Some literary works, like Graciela Limón's novel *The River Flows North*, deal with the actual trip, with brief sketches of people making the crossing on foot across the Sonora/Arizona desert.[45] The focus is on the individual as she or he faces obstacles; the narratives thus become paeans to individual strength, endurance, and personal fortitude in the face of seemingly insurmountable odds. The backstory, as it were, is that NAFTA has wiped out small industries and agribusiness has made it all but impossible for small farmers to survive, but also that U.S.-supported military regimes have pushed people out of their homelands to escape genocide, as in El Salvador and Guatemala. Here, too, a Marxist-inflected optic enables us to register and decode the reach of imperialism in these immigrants' lives. In Chicano/a literature, however, stories of immigration often skirt the issue of the workings of imperialism and focus primarily on *la migra*, the Border Patrol, and on the coyotes and drug dealers that take advantage of the immigrants—sometimes killing them—in the U.S. Southwest, as in *The Guardians* by Ana Castillo.[46]

Latino/a works of fiction do, however, bring into account acts of U.S. imperialism that may not be even acknowledged as such, nor are central to the plot, but are definitely marked as contextual in the works. A novel by Angie Cruz, *Let It Rain Coffee*, for example, is an exceptional text that deals with several temporalities, as evident in a fragmented narrative that represents different modes of production in the Dominican Republic: communal farming, squatter farming, capitalist agriculture, life under dictatorship, moments of resistance against dictatorship and U.S. invasions, and global capitalism with the arrival of U.S. companies and the installation of a free trade zone with a variety of sweatshops, and, toward the novel's end, what one character calls "socially responsible capitalism" with the creation of a garment industry collective.[47] Juxtaposed to these temporalities are those in the United States where immigrants toil in factories and the service sectors in a network of social and physical spaces that include banks, private companies, prisons, and barrios.

The issue of history, in this case twentieth-century Dominican history, going from the 1916 U.S. invasion of the Dominican Republic to the 1930–61 Trujillo dictatorship, which ended with his assassination in 1961 and led to the election of the left-leaning Juan Bosch, is not a mere backdrop to the novel but rather fundamental to the Cruz narrative. The U.S.-backed coup of 1963 against Bosch, only a few months after his election, will spark an uprising of Dominicans that will be repressed by a new U.S. Marine invasion and the installation of a new U.S.-friendly president, Joaquín Balaguer. This history follows the life of Don Chan Colón, whose memories of the past capture these temporalities that intersect with his life after 1991 when, recently widowed, he travels to New York City to join his son's family. Don Chan, significantly a Chinese survivor of the coolie indentured worker trade, arrives on the shores of Juan Dolio in 1916 at around the age of six, never knowing what became of his Chinese family. He will be taken in by the Colón family that moves inland, to Los Llanos, after the U.S. invasion in 1916. In Los Llanos villagers work land that is not theirs; they are squatters on the farmland, but in 1963, after a hurricane uproots a tree, Don Chan finds a pot with treasure that he uses to buy the land for the villagers. The communal farm that he sets up recalls earlier nineteenth-century communal farms in the Dominican Republic and allows for community interaction and solidarity. As Don Chan explains, those who work the land should own the land: *La tierra debe ser del que la trabaja*. The novel follows Don Chan and the villagers who call themselves "Los Invisibles" and resist the Trujillo dictatorship and later the military coup against Bosch. Key among them is Miraluz, a young girl who is the only woman who sits with the men in Los Llanos as they discuss village and national issues after farming the land all day. Years later, when Miraluz is working in San Pedro de Macorís in the neoliberal promoted free trade zone and finding herself unable to unionize the garment shop workers making expensive Victoria's Secret underwear for export, she recalls Don Chan's words about the rights of workers to own the land. She begins organizing the women and asks them to contribute to the purchase of sewing machines to begin a collective shop. Echoing Don Chan, she argues that those who work in a factory should own the factory. That will be the beginning of *El Secreto de la Victoria*, what Miraluz calls "socially responsible capitalism," a plan that follows closely what in effect happened in the Alta Gracia apparel collective in the Dominican Republic.[48]

The Cruz novel also captures contradictions as it focuses on those that accommodate to the Trujillo and Balaguer regimes. Santo, Don Chan's son, marries Esperanza, the daughter of an urban Trujillista with upper-class aspirations and a definite consumerist bent. She does not take to the communal farm and in fact dislikes the very idea of a communal farm. An avid fan of the *Dallas* TV series (which ran from 1978 to 1991), she above all things desires to go to the United States where she is convinced she can work to buy a ranch like that of the Ewings. In time, the couple and their son and daughter end up in Spanish Harlem in New York City, with Santo working as a taxi driver and Esperanza working for a senior caregiving agency. Unlike other texts that spend little narrative time on sites of manual or service labor, the Cruz novel takes us to the Bronx and describes the exhausting work Esperanza does, often on twenty-four-hour shifts. Meanwhile, surrounded by consumerist capitalism, Esperanza falls prey to credit card debt as she buys obsessively for herself, Santo, and the children.

Let It Rain Coffee addresses the issue of the Caribbean diaspora, labor exploitation, and the coping mechanisms of immigrants as well as their alienation. As the years pass and Santo is robbed and killed and Don Chan develops dementia, the latter begins to despair over the possibility of never seeing his homeland again. The sight of Don Chan crying one night convinces Esperanza to take him back to the Dominican Republic. Returning to their homeland some fifteen years later, they find that Santo Domingo is now full of U.S. stores, products, and sweatshops; there also are hundreds of deported Dominicans returning to the island. Going back to Los Llanos is what Don Chan wanted, and once at his old home he walks off into the sugarcane field to die on his own terms and on his own turf. The different temporalities come together nicely, and the novel provides a critique of neoliberal policies in the Dominican Republic as well as in the United States, recalling the two instances of U.S. invasions and the consequence of these factors in the lives of the characters who struggle with all kinds of displacements. In the case of Don Chan, who becomes afflicted by Alzheimer's disease, his alienation is multiple and stems from being displaced from both his homeland and from his memory/history.

Héctor Tobar's novel *The Tattooed Soldier*, like *Let It Rain Coffee*, at one level focuses on the effects of diaspora and migration, as it deals explicitly with U.S. imperialism, and takes up issues of genocide in Guatemala, making evident the U.S. complicity in these murders by training the government soldiers and providing military aid to the right-wing governments of Guatemala.[49] These, however, are not the main issues of the novel, as it operates more at the level of personal trajectories and individual vindication. Tobar's narrative focuses on the Guatemalan soldier who murdered the main character's (Antonio Bernal) wife and son and on Antonio's chance encounter with said soldier (Longoria) in Los Angeles, where the two find themselves living as part of the Central American diaspora. The novel also textualizes the increasing homelessness and precarity of life on the streets of Los Angeles. Serving as immediate context in the novel is the 1992 L.A. uprising after the court's failure to find the police guilty of the brutal beating of Rodney King. But Tobar does not dwell on the police brutality nor suggest reasons for the growing number of street people. It is Antonio's personal trauma and his failure to have confronted his wife and son's killer back in Guatemala that is centered in the novel. In the end his killing of the soldier in Los Angeles is said to free him from a life of failure. With the pending and handicapping immigrant baggage resolved, Bernal can now remake himself and "make it" in America. Contradictions are sidestepped and historical correlates and causations are sidelined. The narrative is at bottom not an indictment of the "American Dream," but a corrective, a call for an "even chance" and therefore reformist and inclusionary. Personal failure, handicapped masculinity, and individual redemption, as well as the chance for the immigrant to start anew, make the Tobar novel consistent with the "American Dream" narrative that has long been a mainstay of the U.S. imaginary.

CONCLUSION: REFORMATIONS VIS-À-VIS TRANSFORMATIONS

Issues that are at the same time constitutive and products of global capitalism, like state coercion, ecological devastation, genocide, racism, xenophobia, and class, are not always central to Chicano/a-Latino/a narratives, but their encoding and inclusion in the works allow for a decoding by readers. As noted by Callinicos, "unraveling the enigma of capital, rendering transparent what political power always wants to keep opaque, is crucial to any revolutionary strategy."[50] More often what is both detailed and woven together in these narratives is the individual trauma about family or socioeconomic success/failure, skirting for the most part the intersecting structural and economic and ideological contradictions at work.

Unraveling the cloth woven by narratives (as well as imaginaries and their attendant ideologies), turning it inside out and examining the warp and weft of it, to wrestle with its composition and its attendant contradictions—that is the task of the cultural critic who recodes the text to signal both the connections and gaps. It is in the decoding of these narratives through a nuanced Marxist lens that we can begin to unravel the narrative to decipher coded issues and perspectives in their historical specificity. These texts are the narrative sites in the Chicano/a-Latino/a cultural imaginary wherein the ideological work of both writer and reader takes place, and where there is much work to be done.

Notes

1. With thanks to Fredric Jameson, Roy Bhaskar, and Alex Callinicos. See Alex Callinicos, *The Resources of Critique* (Malden, MA: Polity Press, 2006); Fredric Jameson, *The Antinomies of Realism* (London: Verso, 2013); and Roy Bhaskar, *A Realist Theory of Science* (London: Verso, 1975).

2. We use the term "progressive" here to refer to politics that are concerned with social justice but are not necessarily an indictment of the dominant political-economic system. In our view, they tend to be reformist. Left politics, by contrast, offer an indictment of the socioeconomic-political structure and envision a transformation of the capitalist system as the sine qua non of that change. The latter are often (although not exclusively) underwritten by Marxist/Marxian thinking.

3. Jovita González and Eve Raleigh, *Caballero, a Historical Novel* (College Station: Texas A&M. University Press, 1996); Fabiola Cabeza de Baca, *We Fed Them Cactus* (Albuquerque: University of New Mexico Press, 1954).

4. Genaro González, "Un Hijo del Sol," in *The Chicano*, ed. Edward Simmen (New York: New American Library, 1971).

5. Tomás Rivera, "The Salamanders," in *Tomás Rivera: The Complete Works*, ed. Julián Olivares (Houston: Arte Público Press, 1991), 223–25.

6. Américo Paredes, *George Washington Gómez* (Houston: Arte Público Press, 1990).

7. Stella Pope Duarte, *Let Their Spirits Dance* (New York: Harper/Perennial, 2002).

8. Cherríe Moraga, *Watsonville/Circles in the Dirt* (Albuquerque: West End Press, 1996), 44.

9. David Harvey, *The New Imperialism* (Oxford: Oxford University Press, 2003), 137.

10. Massimo De Angelis, "Separating the Doing and the Deed: Capital and the Continuous Character of Enclosures," *Historical Materialism* 12.2 (2004): 57–87.

11. Midnight Notes Collective, "The New Enclosures," from *Midnight Notes* #10, 1990.

12. Karl Marx, *Grundrisse* (New York: Vintage Books, 1973), 461.

13. Karl Marx, *Capital*, vol. 1 (New York: International Publishers, 1974), 714–15.

14. De Angelis, "Separating," 59.

15. Anthony F. C. Wallace, *The Long Bitter Trail* (New York: Hill and Wang, 1993), 4.

16. De Angelis, "Separating," 58.

17. De Angelis, "Separating," 71.

18. Culture Clash, *Oh, Wild West! The California Plays* (New York: Theatre Communications Group, 2011).

19. Ernesto Quiñónez, *Changó's Fire* (New York: Harper Collins, 2004).

20. Helena María Viramontes. *Their Dogs Came with Them* (New York: Washington Square Press, 2007).

21. Jameson, *Antinomies*, 311.

22. The novel's title and its referencing of another instance of violent dispossession attendant with the Spanish conquest of Tenochtitlán, and both its short-term and long-term effects cannot go unremarked here.

23. Ian Angus, "When Did the Anthropocene Begin and Why Does It Matter," *Monthly Review* 67.4 (September 2015), http://monthlyreview.org/2015/09/01/when-did-the-anthropocene-beginand-why-does-it-matter/

24. See John Bellamy Foster, *Marx's Ecology: Materialism and Nature* (New York: Monthly Review Press, 2000); Jason W. Moore, *Capitalism in the Web of Life. Ecology and the Accumulation of Capital* (London: Verso, 2015); and Andreas Malm, *Fossil Capital: The Rise of Steam Power and the Roots of Global Warming* (London: Verso, 2016).

25. Foster, *Marx's Ecology*, 163.

26. Foster, *Marx's Ecology*, 172–74.

27. Additional examples of how these issues are taken up would necessarily include Alex Rivera's 2008 film *Sleep Dealer*, which is also concerned with issues of water enclosures and cyber labor on the border. In our own novel *Lunar Braceros* (2009), ecology, toxic waste disposal and disposable workers, and Amazonian deforestation are central to the narrative.

28. Cherríe Moraga, *Heroes and Saints* (Albuquerque: West End Press, 1994).

29. Helena María Viramontes, *Under the Feet of Jesus* (New York: Penguin, 1995).

30. Ana Castillo, *So Far from God* (New York: W. W. Norton, 1993).

31. Rudolfo Anaya, *Jemez Spring* (Albuquerque: University of New Mexico Press, 2005).

32. Rudolfo Anaya, *Alburquerque* (Albuquerque: University of New Mexico Press, 1992).

33. Jon Swaine, Oliver Laughland, Jamiles Lartey, and Ciara McCarthy, "Young Black

Men Killed by U.S. Police at Highest Rate in Year of 1,134 Deaths," *Guardian*, December 31, 2015, https://www.theguardian.com/us-news/2015/dec/31/the-counted-police-killings-2015-young-black-men

34. See David J. Weber, *Foreigners in Their Native Land* (Albuquerque: University of New Mexico Press, 1973), 177–81.

35. Fredric Jameson, *Valences of the Dialectic* (London: Verso, 2009), 543.

36. See Massimiliano Tomba, "Marx's Temporal Bridges and Other Pathways," *Historical Materialism* 23.4 (2015): 75–91; and Harry Harootunian, "Piercing the Present with the Past: Reflections on Massimiliano Tomba's *Marx's Temporalities*," *Historical Materialism* 23.4 (2015): 60–74.

37. Rolando Hinojosa, *Generaciones y semblanzas* (Berkeley: Justa Publications, 1977).

38. Carlos Morton, *The Many Deaths of Danny Rosales* (Houston: Arte Público Press, 1983).

39. In Texas, Chicanos are generally called *mexicanos* or *Mexicans*.

40. Weber, *Foreigners*, 182.

41. Sergio Elizondo, *Muerte en una estrella/Shooting Star*, trans. Rosaura Sánchez and Beatrice Pita (Houston: Arte Público Press, 2014).

42. Alex Callinicos, *Imperialism and Global Political Economy* (Cambridge: Polity Press, 2009).

43. Callinicos, *Imperialism*, 15.

44. Harvey, *New Imperialism*, 50.

45. Graciela Limón, *The River Flows North* (Houston: Arte Público Press, 2009).

46. Ana Castillo, *The Guardians* (New York: Random House, 2007).

47. Angie Cruz, *Let It Rain Coffee* (New York: Simon and Schuster, 2005).

48. See *Tejid@s Junt@s: Workers, Students, and the Movement for Alta Gracia*, https://vimeo.com/40438513

49. Héctor Tobar, *The Tattooed Soldier* (New York: Penguin Books, 1998).

50. Callinicos, *Imperialism*, 241.

CHAPTER 2

"When the Union Movement Was Murdered in America"

Neoliberalism and the Political Economy of Class War in Alfredo Véa's *Gods Go Begging*

Dennis López

> Under neoliberalization, the figure of "the disposable worker" emerges as prototypical upon the world stage.
>
> —DAVID HARVEY, *A BRIEF HISTORY OF NEOLIBERALISM*

> Thus only the slum remains as a fully franchised solution to the problem of warehousing the twenty-first century's surplus humanity.
>
> —MIKE DAVIS, "PLANET OF SLUMS"

"The bombs in Vietnam explode at home," intoned Martin Luther King Jr. during a speech in 1967.[1] Entitled "The Crisis in America's Cities," King's address established a direct link between the U.S. war in Vietnam and the widespread destitution and violence raging in Black urban neighborhoods. "The security we profess to seek in foreign adventures," King forewarned, "we will lose in our decaying cities."[2] For King, U.S. military campaigns abroad, fought in the name of "a spurious democracy," left working-class African Americans and other Americans of color doubly wronged, since poverty-stricken, racialized communities disproportionately bore the brunt of the casualties resulting both from the violence of war in Vietnam and from the violence of political economy at home.[3] The expanded social wage of New Dealism and the Keynesian compromise—whose benefits African Americans unevenly enjoyed in the first place[4]—quickly disappeared as Washington shifted ever more public resources toward the Vietnam War and away from the so-called War on Poverty. Law and order policies soon supplanted the lofty promises of President Lyndon B. Johnson's "Great Society" programs. "Our real problem," King stressed, "is that there is no disposition by the Administration nor Congress to seek fundamental remedies beyond police measures."[5] Impoverished workers of color, both in Vietnam and in the United States, were deemed a threat to and an enemy of the state—a consensus that would carry dire consequences in the ensuing decades. As King concludes, "To war against your own people, while warring against another nation, is the ultimate in political and social bankruptcy."[6]

King's analysis of the urban crisis in America offers a compelling point of entry for examining Alfredo Véa's *Gods Go Begging* (1999), which likewise traces the complex linkages between imperialist violence abroad and the domestic forms of violence afflicting poor, racially segregated U.S. neighborhoods. Véa insists that modern-day injustice, oppression, and inequality remain the product of—and are indissociable from—the long history of capitalist modernity, for which 1968 and the Vietnam War are seminal moments, at least in *Gods Go Begging*. From this vantage, King's criticism of U.S. political and economic decision making in the late 1960s anticipates many of the baleful policies, priorities, and positions that eventually became hegemonic in the contemporary neoliberal world that Véa's novel describes. Set principally in mid-1990s San Francisco and in Vietnam during the week leading up to the day of King's assassination in 1968, Véa's narrative weaves together these two historical times and spaces through a broad cast of characters and interrelated storylines that in the end reveal not only how densely "their histories had become entangled,"[7] but also the very nature of the overlapping social, political, and economic forces that forged "their histories" in blood and fire.

Gods Go Begging opens with the double homicide of two lovers, Persephone Flyer and Mai Adrong, as they embrace one final time on "a cold city sidewalk" in San Francisco's Potrero Hill.[8] The gruesome scene proves the consequence of a tragic string of coincidental and parallel events that lead back to a hill on the Vietnam-Laos border where U.S. Staff Sergeant Amos Flyer, Persephone's husband, dies in 1968 while embracing Trin Adrong, a North Vietnamese Army soldier and Mai's husband, at the moment he detonates the satchel charge strapped to his chest.[9] Jessie Pasadoble, a Chicano Vietnam War veteran and city public defender, straddles the time-spaces of the two hills and the multiple deaths transpiring on them. Assigned to defend Calvin "Biscuit Boy" Thibault, an eighteen-year-old African American man wrongly indicted for the coldblooded killings on Potrero Hill, Jesse soon realizes that he still carries with him the dog tag of none other than Persephone's husband, a close friend alongside whom Jesse fought in Vietnam and whose death, nearly thirty years ago on a hill near Laos, still haunts him. Relying on experimental narrative techniques, Véa supplies readers with countless more chance concurrences and admittedly implausible coincidences involving both plot and character. However, testing readerly disbelief is not Véa's intention, for as Brian J. Williams reasons, "[r]ather than simply asking us to believe his unlikely plotting," Véa's storytelling "makes a strong case that far more unlikely crimes and traumas occur every day," social and political "horrors" that all too often go unnoticed and unquestioned.[10] Véa disarticulates narrative time and space as a means to chart anew the social relations and political imperatives that constitute the historical geographies of violence and inequality depicted in the novel. In so doing, Véa calls attention both to the violence of political economy and to the political economy of imperialist violence subtending late-capitalist warscapes abroad and at home.

Scholarship on *Gods Go Begging* is scant, and most interpretations of the novel focus on questions of war, trauma, and masculinity, reading Véa's narrative alongside and against the grain of existing Vietnam War literature.[11] This chapter tacks differently, reading the representation of state-sanctioned warfare and violence in *Gods Go Begging* through Véa's explicit engagement with neoliberalism and its politics of economic and racist coercion, social neglect, and urban decay. In an interview with Jeff Biggers, Véa confesses that his novel "is less a war story and more a definition of war."[12] If so, his portrayal of U.S. imperialism in Vietnam alongside the Potrero Terrace and Annex housing projects in San Francisco suggests less an abstract and ahistorical definition of war than one centered on the class violence of capital accumulation in the age of neoliberalism.

As a theory for economic prosperity, neoliberalism ostensibly sets out to unchain from the intrusive and tyrannical restraints of the Keynesian welfare state the entrepreneurial abilities and potential of "free, possessive individuals," in the main by cutting down all impediments to robust free trade, financial innovations and investments, free markets, and wholesale privatization and economic competition.[13] Freedom and liberty are the catchphrases of neoliberals, by which they mean specifically absolute, unconditional free rein toward the universal marketization and commodification of every facet of global society. Rather than widespread affluence and liberty, however, in practice the neoliberal turn during the 1970s ushered in a period of utter immiseration and social disenfranchisement for the vast majority of the world. The foremost achievement of neoliberalization, Naomi Klein makes clear, has not been "a perfectly harmonious economy but turning the already wealthy into superrich and the organized working class into disposable poor."[14] Regardless of its theoretical and ideological claims, neoliberalism is best understood as a *counterrevolution* carried out against the minimal reforms and economic redistributions embodied in the Fordist-Keynesian compromise and the New Deal welfare state, as well as against the looming threat of social revolution put forward by the increasingly radicalized political movements of the late 1960s.[15] As such, it is primarily "a *political* project"—and, as we shall see, a fundamentally *racist* one—whose key objectives remain the restoration of unfettered capitalist class power and wealth, and the securing, at all costs, of optimal conditions for profitable capital accumulation.[16] Gérard Duménil and Dominique Lévy underscore the class foundations of the neoliberal turn: "Although it is true that neoliberalism conveys an ideology and a propaganda of its own, it is fundamentally a *new social order* in which the power and income of the upper fractions of the ruling classes—the wealthiest persons—was re-established in the wake of a setback," namely Keynesianism and its legal and trade-unionist restrictions on capital accumulation.[17] With the economic, political, and social dislocations of the Vietnam War serving both as catalyst and as justification, alongside the deepening crisis of the Fordist-Keynesian regime of accumulation, the neoliberal counterrevolution set out to dismantle the minimal working-class gains of the previous two decades.

To achieve these ends, neoliberalism in the United States implemented wide-ranging transformations of social life, normalizing a set of fundamental principles and practices crucial to its profit-making logic:

(1) economic and financial deregulation, alongside the intensifying privatization of the public commons and the extension of market values to all societal institutions and relations;
(2) the transition from a Keynesian welfare state to a neoliberal austerity state that abandons all responsibilities for the collective improvement and fulfillment of social needs and instead redirects the state apparatus, including institutions and agencies formerly aligned with

New Dealism, toward the dual goal of facilitating capitalist class consolidation and favorable conditions for capital accumulation;

(3) systematic dissolution of the social wage, of collective welfare provisions and social safety nets, and a turn toward austerity politics, together with the political disciplining of the working classes, labor unions, and unemployed masses under the new pervasive conditions of economic insecurity and precarity;

(4) a politico-cultural revolution rooted in the reconfiguring of the citizen-subject as *homo economicus* and in the propagating of radical possessive individualism and a racist ideology of "personal responsibility" that transfers all accountability for well-being to the successes and failures of self-investment in one's own "human capital";

(5) the codifying of force and punitive action as the singular response to each and every social problem and threat to capitalism—thus the proliferation of military interventions globally and of foreign and domestic policy campaigns such as the "War on Drugs," "War on Crime," and "War on Terror."[18]

The neoliberal counterrevolution has manifested an all-out attack on working, impoverished, and marginalized classes across the globe. The result has been ubiquitous structural unemployment and the deliberate creation of redundant and expendable working-class populations—*hyperproletarianized* wage laborers whom the Marxist theorist Robert Kurz labels "monetary subjects without money": "Human beings . . . cut off from the capitalist conditions placed on the satisfaction of their needs."[19] *Hyperproletarianization*[20] thus names the social and political processes under neoliberalism by which entire segments of the world's population find themselves divorced from the means of production and proletarianized as "free" labor, while at the same time perpetually denied access to formal labor markets or to gainful opportunities for the selling of labor power, or both. As Harvey explains, "For those left or cast outside the market system—a vast reservoir of apparently disposable people bereft of social protections and supportive social structures—there is little to be expected from neoliberalization except poverty, hunger, disease, and despair."[21] Hence, in every instance, Klein concludes, neoliberalism "has created a permanent underclass. . . . It is always a form of war."[22]

Véa's "definition of war" in *Gods Go Begging* speaks precisely to this neoliberal "form of war"—a war against the poor and exploited, rather than against poverty and exploitation, that King presciently criticized as mired in "political and social bankruptcy." King's "decaying cities," already ravished by the early effects of a creeping deindustrialization and racist politics of criminalization and hyperpolicing, prefigure the more flagrant social crises and immiseration of neoliberalism captured in Véa's narrative. Citing Sidney Wilhelm's *Who Needs the Negro?* (1970), Barbara Ransby notes that the 1960s witnessed "the growing marginalisation of Black workers to the American economy, foreshadowing the even more pronounced developments two decades later" under the neoliberal policies of the Reagan, Bush, and Clinton administrations.[23] Neoliberalism arguably compounded and codified social, political, and economic tendencies already taking shape in communities of color toward the end of the 1960s, as the failures and expanding crises of Fordist-Keynesian capital accumulation became increasingly visible. Ultimately, as the neoliberal state dismantled the social wage and Keynesian embedded liberalism to lay the groundwork for the restoration of unrestricted capitalist class power, it cast aside any pretense to a "War on Poverty" and instead waged all-out war against the working poor.[24] It is in this sense that, for Véa's *Gods Go Begging*, the "bombs in Vietnam explode at home," leaving in their wake decimated and impoverished urban spaces judged superfluous by the racism and economic violence of the neoliberal counterrevolution.

On the southeastern slope of Potrero Hill rests what Jesse Pasadoble calls the "free fire zone" of the Potrero Terrace and Annex public housing projects,[25] a set of barrack-style buildings constructed in the early 1940s to provide temporary quarters for the swelling ranks of new industrial workers in the city's shipyards and factories during World War II.[26] Initially, due to racist segregation policies, almost all public housing in San Francisco was exclusively reserved for white workers, with African Americans primarily settling in the Fillmore District and the Westside Courts housing development.[27] In the present-day of the novel, however, Potrero Terrace and Annex public housing serves as barracks for the African American "armies" of "street gangs" on Potrero Hill: "the Up the Hill Gang, the Down the Hill Gang, the Wisconsin Street Posse, and the Prisoners of the Projects," all responsible for the "[r]andom killings and drive-by shootings over in the housing projects."[28] As with other U.S. urban neighborhoods marked by a history of racist segregation, concentrated poverty, and high rates of joblessness, violence saturates the Potrero housing projects. When the psychiatrist Dr. Wooden remarks, "This is not Vietnam. . . . Life is not a war," Jesse's response expresses the novel's investment in marshaling tropes of warfare not only for figurative effect but also, and more importantly, to remind one of the all-too literal realities and grave consequences of inner-city violence in communities of color: "'It's not?' answered Jesse, a look of surprise on his face. 'Don't we live in a free-fire zone? There are seventy-five wars going on in this world right now, and only one of them matches the homicide rate in this country.'"[29] While visiting Mrs. Thibault, Calvin's mother, who already has lost two sons to Potrero Hill, Jesse again comments on the bloodshed pervading socially marginalized urban spaces: "Now Jesse knew why she [Mrs. Thibault] stayed indoors, a prisoner of her apartment. She was surrounded by a world on fire and she had resigned herself to the fact that she was nothing more than kindling."[30] The ghettoized neighborhoods on Potrero Hill hold residents captive, "prisoner[s]" to the mounting casualties from criminal turf wars and drug addiction, as well as from the economic and social violence of unemployment, racism, and poverty that gives rise to the latter in the first place.

Véa's representation of the Potrero Terrace and Annex housing projects stresses the importance of understanding the ghetto *not* as a place primarily defined by penury, high crime rates, social anomie, illicit activities, and deviant behaviors, as is popularly the case. According to Loïc Wacquant, "To say that [areas of extreme poverty] are ghettos because they are poor is to reverse social and historical causation: it is *because they were and are ghettos* that joblessness and misery are unusually acute and persistent in them—not the other way around."[31] The former approach applies "ghetto" merely as a descriptive term, which conceals more than it reveals about the politico-economic foundations of ghettoized urban areas in the United States. Ghettos denote not simply circumstances of economic scarcity and isolation. More crucially, the concept points toward the social relations, historical processes, and institutional mechanisms for the politically deliberate production of poverty and exclusion as a means to render vulnerable populations readily exploitable. The ghetto historically operates as a "sociospatial device" that facilitates the extraction of labor power and the enactment of racialized political control and social discipline.[32] It has always been an ideological and material formation in the service of exploitation and racist oppression. Organized around four elements of "ethnoracial control and closure"—stigma, constraint, territorial confinement, and institutional encasement—the ghetto functions "as an *ethnoracial prison*," Wacquant concludes.[33] No wonder Véa's characters feel trapped and imprisoned within the confines of Potrero Hill's ghettoized spaces.

Gods Go Begging maps the social topography of the ghetto as ethnoracial prison, what Martin Luther King Jr. once characterized as "the slow, stifling death of a kind of concentration camp life."[34] Mrs. Thibault is not the only "prisoner of her apartment" in the Potrero housing projects, whose "dreary rows of buildings" remain "affronted by neglect and veiled by the muddled human haze of five hundred marginal lives."[35] The ghettoized public housing on Potrero Hill is a place defined by "the death of hope," where "[e]very child born on this hill . . . entered this world without the slightest chance to succeed. That chance had been ritually excised at birth."[36] Neoliberal neglect, failure, and hopelessness permeate the bleak, prison-like atmosphere of the Potrero Hill ghetto. In fact, during closing arguments at Calvin's trial, Jesse comes close to invoking a prison camp in his description of the Potrero housing projects: "You live on a hill where the fences are topped with concertina wire, the shopkeepers are armed, and the earth is mined with failure."[37] This "slow, stifling death" enveloping the Potrero Terrace and Annex projects draws attention to the new social role of the ghetto after the neoliberal turn.

Under the Fordist-Keynesian regime of accumulation, the ghetto afforded a vehicle by which "to extract black labor while keeping black bodies at a safe distance."[38] Ghettos thus fulfilled a dual task—exploitation and social control—but neoliberalism reduces entire populations to the status of *unexploitable*: hyperproletarianized wage labor whose labor power is no longer profitable for capital to exploit (i.e., to put to work) in the valorization process. With an emphasis on flexible accumulation and deregulated capital mobility, neoliberalization has consigned millions of workers, particularly workers of color, to the ranks of the permanently unemployed and underemployed, an army of "monetary subjects without money" who find themselves adrift after postwar U.S. industrial capitalism reneged on the professed promises of the modern American Dream. Alongside neoliberal mass incarceration, the post-Keynesian "hyperghetto," as Wacquant calls it, now "serves above all to regulate, if not perpetuate, poverty and to warehouse the human rejects of the market."[39] Hyperproletarianized Black and Latino/a workers fall victim to the technics of social control and discipline embodied in the neoliberal hyperghetto. For Wacquant, then, the ghetto as "social prison" and the prison as "judicial ghetto" emerge in unison as a ruling-class solution for the generalized insecurity of state-sanctioned poverty and structural unemployment—the "production of nonproduction," Joshua Clover labels it—inherent to neoliberal profit-making.[40] Hence, Véa's acerbic naming of one of the Potrero street gangs, "Prisoners of the Projects," underscores the carceral dynamics of the neoliberal hyperghetto.

While neoliberalism marks a sharp decline in the standard of living for American workers, it is important to note that the idealized suburban leisure and affluence of the Fordist-Keynesian economy were systematically denied to entire segments of the U.S. working class, most especially families of color. Harvey stresses that "[n]ot everyone was included in the benefits of Fordism, and there were, to be sure, abundant signs of discontent even at the system's apogee."[41] Persistent inequalities triggered "serious social tensions," which "were compounded by the way in which race, gender, and ethnicity determined who had access" to the promised rewards of the postwar American Dream.[42] Already in the late 1960s, after over two decades of Keynesianism and the New Deal welfare state, "[m]ore than 60 percent of Black working people lived in urban industrial slums where their conditions were defined by poverty, exploitation, unemployment, inadequate education, and negligent medical care—conditions also experienced by at least fifty million poor and working people of all colors."[43] Due to racist and business-friendly allocation, the substantial government subsidies for and expenditures in post–World War II programs backing suburbanization, home mortgages, freeway construction, education, and public housing established stark racial and class hierarchies, upon which the rapacious excesses of neoliberalization would later prey. Commenting on federal housing policy, William Julius Wilson argues: "In short, public housing represents a federally funded institution that has isolated families by race and class for decades, and has therefore contributed to the growing concentration of jobless families in the inner-city ghettos in recent years."[44] San Francisco's public housing programs and urban redevelopment projects were equally marred by land speculation, overt segregation, and racist displacement and dispossession. Albert S. Broussard shows that the liberalism commonly ascribed to the city has remained "largely a facade" for its residents of color, adding that "San Francisco's image as a racially progressive city bore little relationship to the status of most blacks by the 1960s."[45] In fact, San Francisco "had become less open by 1960 as ghettoization accelerated," and by the close of the decade, "the same kind of institutional and physical ghetto that had emerged in Chicago and Cleveland during the First World War" was patently present.[46] Such racist trends persisted in the latter half of the twentieth century, as urban renewal and redevelopment proposals, hand in hand with neoliberal economic restructuring, forced poor and working-class African American families out of the city or into derelict and ghettoized low-income housing like the Potrero Terrace and Annex projects.[47]

Véa alludes to this past in *Gods Go Begging*, as atop Potrero Hill Jesse glimpses the ongoing ramifications of white flight and racial segregation across the San Francisco Bay Area: "Jesse turned his gaze to the east, toward the bay and the distant hills of Piedmont and Montclair. Beyond those towns were Concord, Vallejo, and Walnut Creek, all the bedroom communities of the East Bay. The blight of identical tract homes was still spreading, as whites fled toward the flatlands of Brentwood and the Delta."[48] Véa reverses the official discourses of urban "blight" widely employed after World War II to justify so-called slum clearance and higher-use redevelopment for freeway construction or of potentially lucrative urban locales—discourses that, more often than not, rested on the racist pathologizing of impoverished residents of color.[49] Conversely, it is postwar white flight that Véa figures as the "blight of identical tract homes" in the passage, no doubt a shot at the sterility and bland homogeneity now frequently associated with late-capitalist suburbia. But, these East Bay "bedroom communities" also prove "identical" with respect to race, not just architecture and cultural life, and thus evoke the long history of restrictive housing covenants and state-sanctioned redlining that facilitated the creation of racialized ghettos and barrios throughout the twentieth century. Jesse's dual reference to "blight" and white flight while visiting Potrero Hill signals Véa's explicit critique of the racism and class politics behind postwar ghetto formation, middle-class suburbanization, and the segregationist governmental actions that laid the groundwork for both. The American leisured ideal of suburban (white) neighborhoods resides far beyond the "litter-blighted" hilltop on which sits the Potrero Terrace and Annex housing units.[50] As Jesse thinks to himself after the buried bodies of several murdered young men are discovered, "On this hill the American Dream was there beyond the yellow tape" of the police cordon, which permanently encases poor Black families in the "free fire zone" of the Potrero Hill ghetto.[51]

Such long-standing negative effects of capitalist uneven development and state-sponsored racism make any facile attempt to challenge neoliberalism by calling for a renewed Keynesianism, or a return to the politics and economic policies of the halcyon age of post–World War II U.S. capitalism, an empty and self-defeating gesture. While Duménil and Lévy admit that neoliberalism represents "a form of 'aggressive' capitalism," they are quick to remind readers that the "world of the Keynesian compromise coexisted with colonialism and the Vietnam War."[52] Véa's novel, which juxtaposes the economic violence of contemporary neoliberal capitalism and the history of the American welfare state's war in Vietnam, likewise underscores Duménil and Lévy's contention that the "internationalization of capitalism has always been marked by exploitation and direct violence," since "*imperialism* has been, to various degrees and under various forms, a permanent feature of capitalism."[53] In the telling rationale of Colonel Kelvin Urban Junior, who ironically is attempting to bring the distraught and self-doubting army chaplain, Lieutenant William Calvert, back into the ideological fold, Véa sums up the political economy of U.S. imperialism:

> "Your poor Okie fruit-picking parents up in Oregon or your minimum-wage colored parents down in Watts don't want a reason for their dear son's death, they want a rationale. . . . Now, there is a huge difference between a reason and a rationale, young lieutenant. . . . A rationale is something that can be included in a prayer; it's something you can put into a sermon. It's a benediction! . . .
>
> "Think about it, what are you gonna say to those people? . . . There's millions of barrels of oil beneath the soil here? We need to keep Red China under control? Do we tell them we need to demonstrate all of these newfangled weapons for all of those buyers in the Persian Gulf, Iran, and Central America? Hell, there's a billion pristine lungs sucking oxygen in China. Do we tell them that we're fighting here so that our tobacco companies can open up these markets? Hell, no!"
>
> "You give them democracy and God! Now, that's the stuff of prayers. That's the stuff they can repeat on Veterans' Day and Memorial Day."[54]

Geopolitical power and imperialist rivalry, ruling-class financial interests, profitable extraction of natural resources, access to international consumer and labor markets—such are the veritable "reasons" why the sons of working-class families must sacrifice their lives in Indochina. The passage pierces the ideological "rationale" of "democracy and God" promoted under the jingoistic banner of American exceptionalism and unmasks what Véa earlier describes as a materialistic and sexist Cold War "mythology" subtending hegemonic images of the so-called American way of life: "Americans are sent here to fight against an evil and undefinable thing called Communism; to fight for blue jeans and convertibles and full-color foldouts of big-breasted blondes."[55] The account of the U.S. war in Vietnam that Véa advances in *Gods Go Begging* largely echoes Duménil and Lévy's critique of an overly romanticized and nostalgic longing for the lost Eden of midcentury America. Although neoliberalism embodies a particularly pernicious "power configuration"[56] for the stabilizing and guaranteeing of capital accumulation, the Fordist-Keynesian regime offered a social and political order no less committed to the prioritizing and securing of profit-making and the resolution of capitalism's perpetual crises on the backs of workers, both at home and abroad. Hence, for Duménil and Lévy, as for Véa, demands to imagine and create "other possible worlds" in the face of neoliberal economic violence must "not express a nostalgia for the past."[57]

If the Fordist-Keynesian compromise signaled "a *truce* after a long period of bitter class warfare," as José E. Limón describes it—a *truce*, nevertheless, that represented a "measured victory" for U.S. capital[58]—then the neoliberal counterrevolution marks the resumption of open hostilities, chiefly on the part of the capitalist class. It is difficult to deny that the neoliberal turn in the 1970s had an acutely devastating impact on U.S. cities and on working-class families of color relegated to rapidly deteriorating urban slums. Wilson specifically highlights neoliberalism's supplanting of "an institutional ghetto—whose structures and activities parallel those of the larger society"—by "a jobless ghetto, which features a severe lack of basic opportunities and resources, and inadequate social controls."[59] Pervasive structural unemployment and the transforming of organized labor into precarious poor are foundational to neoliberal capital accumulation, and the jobless hyperghetto now operates as one of the key sociospatial mechanisms by which the neoliberal austerity state produces, regulates, and contains the ever-growing hyperproletarianized surplus population in the United States. Moreover, racism is a constitutive element of neoliberalism, which relies heavily on what Ransby terms "the politics of expendability" to justify and rationalize its systemic production of vulnerable and cast-off subjects.[60] Throughout the 1980s and 1990s, the U.S. neoliberal state carried out "a campaign of terror against poor and working-class people, especially poor Black and brown people—a campaign consistent with the shifting needs of American capitalism."[61] This neoliberal "campaign of terror"—involving attacks on welfare programs and social services; deindustrialization, union-busting, and the move to flexible accumulation and deregulated labor markets; and the criminalization of poverty and ever higher incarceration rates—has left "a certain section of the population permanently unemployed and wholly superfluous to the economy."[62] The result has been a hyperproletarianized assemblage of wage workers who exist in a state of perpetual precarity and expendability—whose lives are fundamentally defined by the social relations of capitalism and, at the same time, are systematically denied access, as Kurz so aptly puts it, to "the capitalist conditions placed on the satisfaction of their needs." Jobless hyperghettos stand as both a response to and an outcome of this neoliberal counterrevolutionary war on the poor. As unemployed, underemployed, and debt-ridden working families of color are forced into ever deeper states of precarity and societal disenfranchisement, the ghetto as "social prison" enables the racist policing, regulating, and disciplining of populations the neoliberal austerity state deems superfluous and redundant.

These societal transformations are not random or arbitrary, nor the product of a self-correcting market's "invisible hand," but rather part and parcel of a concerted political project for class power. Ruth Wilson Gilmore and Craig Gilmore explain that "in the long aftermath of the so-called golden age of U.S. capitalism (c. 1938–1970), the increased vulnerability of workers and their communities, broadly defined across society and space, has resulted from purposeful abandonment organized by elites, as racial capitalism makes and consolidates the neoliberal turn."[63] In cities throughout America, neoliberalization manifests in the "intertwined imperatives of organized abandonment and organized violence" that animate the present-day class war on workers, especially workers of color.[64] Ruling-class social and economic warfare against impoverished working-class communities is the signature act of neoliberalism's counterrevolution, and according to Michelle Alexander, modern-day American hyperghettos are a direct product of neoliberal political economy:

> Almost overnight, black men found themselves unnecessary to the American economy and demonized by mainstream society. . . . The new system does not seek primarily to benefit unfairly from black labor, as earlier caste systems have, but instead views African Americans as largely irrelevant and unnecessary to the newly structured economy. . . . The intuition of those residing in ghetto communities that they had suddenly become disposable was rooted in real changes in the economy—changes that have been devastating to poor black communities as factories have closed, low-skill jobs have disappeared, and all those who had the means to flee the ghetto did.[65]

Economic restructuring, deindustrialization, and deregulated capital mobility—all of which have led to the proliferation of "monetary subjects without money"—are the main culprits behind what Wilson terms "the new urban poverty" of the jobless ghetto.[66]

In describing Calvin's upbringing in the Potrero Terrace and Annex housing projects, Jesse underlines the baleful state of precarity, alienation, and social futility occasioned by the wholesale disappearance of gainful employment: "His universe had been the Potrero Hill dwellings. His was a world without clocks, without books, without schedules, without a reason to wake up or a good reason to go home at night."[67] The children on the hill experience a moribund social world devoid of work, purpose, meaning, and future possibility. The capitalist discipline of "clocks" and work or school "schedules" vanishes for the residents of Potrero Hill, and while Véa does not romanticize the ostensible "security" of wage labor under capitalism, *Gods Go Begging* does draw attention to the material, psychological, and emotional violence inflicted by the politics of neoliberal neglect. Véa makes the point more explicitly when Jesse again comments on Calvin's day-to-day life on Potrero Hill: "In his past life there were no reasons to wake up in the morning and no particular reasons to go to sleep. There were no clocks in his home, no alarms to set, no calendars to mark. No one went to work in the morning and no one came home exhausted at night."[68] The persistent joblessness, systemic violence, and institutional abandonment that mar the Potrero housing projects belie the rosy triumphalism of neoliberal rhetoric. There is "no alternative" to neoliberal capitalism, Margaret Thatcher infamously proclaimed.[69] For working families of color on Potrero Hill, "no alternative" ultimately means an enduring state of *social death* under conditions of permanent class war. The hyperghetto as "social prison" acts as a race-making institution that enforces neoliberal forms of civic and social death on individuals buried alive within it.[70] Neoliberal logic actuates the ghetto and prison, in the words of Angela Y. Davis, as "a way of disappearing people in the false hope of disappearing the underlying social problems they represent."[71] Superfluous to the needs of capital and, in fact, possible agents of protest and thus of disruption to accumulation, hyperproletarianized workers of color are blamed for their own misfortunes and left with no legal or civil standing in the institutions and minds of the broader society. The social contradictions to which their day-to-day existence attests are rendered obscure and invisible, enclosed behind societal walls held up by the racist neoliberal mantras of "personal responsibility" and pathological criminal behavior—ideological formations repurposed from longstanding "racial scripts" adopted time and time again by U.S capitalism.[72]

Not surprisingly, then, the suffering and bloodshed on Potrero Hill remain concealed to the outside world: "For all intents and purposes these housing projects were completely invisible to the uncaring eye."[73] The "politics of expendability," primarily in the form of a racist law and order regime, works to justify the social and political indifference that neoliberalism holds toward unemployed and underemployed workers of color. As Ransby points out, "the current political climate in the U.S. is one in which repression and criminalisation of the poor are quite compatible with economic shifts that have created a superfluous class of workers."[74] Racist discourses of criminality and "personal responsibility" allow the victims of neoliberal violence to be (un)seen as the perpetrators, rather than the targets, and thus as culpable for the conditions of their own oppression. For the neoliberal austerity state, "it is poor people who are defective, and not the economy."[75] Ultimately, poverty is its own crime for neoliberals, as even Jesse confesses to the Biscuit Boy:

> "When I first met you in the jail upstairs, Calvin, I felt the way that each of the jurors felt when they first laid eyes on you: I felt that you were guilty. If not guilty of the crimes charged, you must certainly have been guilty of something. How could it be otherwise? How could it possibly be otherwise? You were a young black man from the Potrero Hill projects, one of the poorest places in the city."[76]

Born and raised in "one of the poorest places in the city," Calvin is found guilty at birth. The racism and extreme inequality endemic to neoliberalism stigmatize entire social spaces as deficient, inadequate, dangerous, and thus dispensable. With deft sleight of hand, neoliberals promote an ideology that places the blame squarely on the shoulders of the very communities that contemporary political economy already has abandoned and discarded in advance. Harvey notes that, at the same time neoliberalization "leaves larger and larger segments of the population exposed to impoverishment," the neoliberal state aggressively moves "to transfer all responsibility for well-being back to the individual." "Personal failure is generally attributed to personal failings," Harvey concludes, "and the victim is all too often blamed."[77] For this reason, the casualties of neoliberalism's war on the poor in the Potrero housing projects bear the guilt of their own deaths, both physical and social. With the exception of Mai and Persephone, violent deaths on Potrero Hill "usually involved stupefied drug addicts and rough squads of remorseless, fatherless children—tiny mercenaries who had accepted the risk. They were acceptable losses."[78] So long as the killings and shootings around the Potrero Terrace and Annex units claim the lives of "stupefied drug addicts" and "tiny mercenaries who had accepted the risk," the collective reaction is always the same: "They were acceptable losses."

As the narrator's sardonic tone indicates, Véa aims to problematize the underlying racism behind neoliberal discourses of "personal responsibility" and social expendability that so effortlessly chalk up the mounting deaths of Black and Latino/a children to "acceptable losses." Ruth Wilson Gilmore defines racism as "the state-sanctioned or extralegal production and exploitation of group-differentiated vulnerability to premature death," and the "acceptable losses" on Potrero Hill—the state-sanctioned "premature death" of countless youth of color—are meant to be read as one more painful reminder of its heinous cruelty and consequences.[79] Despite his unvarnished rendering of inner-city violence, Véa takes great pains to stress that the carnage wreaking havoc on Potrero Hill and on "the young vatos in the Mission" ultimately involves "kids"—"[d]ozens of kids" who prove more victim than perpetrator in *Gods Go Begging*.[80] "*C'est un ballet bleu infame!* . . . a French phrase that means lewd acts with underage boys," Amos Flyer exclaims while in Vietnam, "[t]hat's all this fucking war adds up to, lieutenant: lewd acts with boys."[81] A key trope conveying the multiple traumas of state violence,[82] Amos's "infamous blue ballet" by the end of the novel extends to every "combat zone" and "killing zone" across the globe, including the Potrero Terrace and Annex housing projects.[83] When Jesse hears that Calvin has been shot in the head, he sobs "a long, belated deluge for the children on the hill, *pour les enfants dans l'enfanterie*, for the infants who had always made up the infantry."[84] *Gods Go Begging* implies that the Biscuit Boy and all of the working-class children on Potrero Hill and other hills like it, from Vietnam to the United States, are drafted into wars not of their own choosing or making.

"It was always the sons of the poor who ended up on hills like this," Jesse thinks to himself in Vietnam.[85] For Véa, this ritual sacrifice of working-class youth in the name of profit and power reveals what Jesse calls "the ancient secret": "Human life is only worth what we agree it's worth. There's no intrinsic value."[86] Amos Flyer reasons that the mounting deaths of imperialist war are calculated, rationalized, and defended by the use of dehumanizing "euphemisms" that indifferently objectify and cast individuals as dispensable: "The sergeant hated euphemisms. In a place where battles were seldom won by anyone, the number crunchers and accountants in Saigon had gone crazy with them. Casualties had evolved into 'acceptable losses' and from there to 'limited breakage' or projected 'spillage.'"[87] Amos's reiterating of the phrase "acceptable losses" links the "sons of the poor" soldiering in Vietnam to "the stupefied drug addicts" and "tiny mercenaries" waging their own wars on Potrero Hill. Similarly, while standing before the "impoverished crypt" of numerous young men murdered and buried in the Potrero housing projects, Jesse draws a direct connection between the Vietnam War and neoliberal urban neglect in the United States: "There must be a million such shoddy graves in Vietnam and Cambodia."[88] By labeling the graves in Indochina and San Francisco "shoddy" and "impoverished," Véa reminds readers of the ways in which certain lives and localities are judged inferior, unworthy of empathy and grief, and thus easily discarded and disappeared. Such are the "devastating spaces of social death" produced by neoliberalism and its austerity state to enclose, discipline, and regulate "populations 'dead-to-others,'" individuals rendered "not just racialized but rightless, living nonbeings" who remain "ineligible for personhood" under neoliberal capital's regimes of value.[89] *Gods Go Begging* suggests that the Potrero Terrace and Annex housing projects as a whole embody an "impoverished crypt"—a racist, prison-like space of social death that entombs immiserated and criminalized workers of color now seen as surplus "living nonbeings," wholly superfluous to the profit-making of U.S. capital.

While visiting the Potrero Hill housing projects, Jesse's investigator Eddy Oasa remarks: "When the union movement was murdered in America, the bodies were thrown here and a thousand places like this."[90] Eddy's reference to the "murder" of the labor movement affords an apt synecdoche for the broader neoliberal turn, given the fact that, as Harvey indicates, a vital prerequisite to neoliberalization has been "the violent assault on all forms of labour organization and labour rights and heavy reliance upon massive but largely disorganized labour reserves."[91] Restoring unfettered ruling-class power in the United States necessitated the production of a hyperproletarianized assemblage of surplus workers, an outcome that has proven particularly devastating for working-class families of color, many of whose expendable "bodies were thrown" away in the new jobless hyperghettos and barrios of the neoliberalized city. Indeed, the "ruin" of Potrero Hill, with its "mounds of discards and heaps of trash," lies atop the "industrial rubble" of a once thriving shipping and manufacturing workforce in San Francisco.[92]

In 1943, as thousands of African Americans were moving to the city, the San Francisco Chamber of Commerce proclaimed the Bay Area to be the "largest shipbuilding center in the world."[93] Yet, by the end of the century, the postwar unionized jobs in the booming defense industry, manufacturing sector, and shipyards disappeared at the hands of neoliberal restructuring and deindustrialization.[94] On Potrero Hill, all that remains today of this organized industrial workforce is "the refuse and . . . the residue of squandered, half-lived lives."[95] Neoliberalization has generated a wasteland of hyperproletarianized redundant labor— superfluous and expendable wage laborers who now fall prey to the vagaries of deregulated markets and informal, often criminalized precarious work.

In *The Silver Cloud Café* (1996), the second novel in what Roberto Cantú classifies as Véa's "narrative trilogy,"[96] alongside his first novel *La Maravilla* (1993) and *Gods Go Begging*, readers are given an extended description of the history and effects of neoliberalism's "violent assault" in San Francisco. The passage is worth quoting at length:

> The city had grown hard since the days when Hunter's Point was a shipyard bustling with workers and the long docks were dotted with lunch boxes. A mortal rigor had set in slowly, imperceptibly, as the number of office workers doubled and redoubled on the myth of a service economy. Workers had been replaced by investors, insurers, and market prognosticators. Men and women without calluses had come to town and sealed themselves into towering glass closets. Their disciples had followed closely behind doing lunch and monotonously chanting the bottom line. New royalty had arrived, bringing their own priests with them.
>
> They hid up there, wagering on work as if somewhere steel would still be smelt. . . .
>
> The city ossified as the corporations exported their jobs under the new rationalization of a "global economy," the old "free-trade" characterization having run its expedient course.[97]

Véa keenly captures the restructuring and major shifts involved in the neoliberalization of the American economy: deregulated capital mobility and intensified globalization, financialization and expanded market speculation, deindustrialization and the proliferation of managerial and low-paying service jobs, mass unemployment and social dislocation, and lastly, the arrival of "new royalty" in the figure of superrich bankers, hedge fund managers, and chief executive officers. Reading the passage above, Patrick L. Hamilton points to the ways in which San Francisco "stiffens, corpse-like, as jobs are exported in the name of the 'global economy,'" adding that Véa "implicates capitalism in the state of affairs."[98] In fact, the passage homes in on the principal features of neoliberalization and capitalist uneven development that have remade U.S. cities in the interests of profit-making. Gregory D. Squires explains: "During the postwar years cities have been dramatically affected by the focus on downtown development which has generally taken the form of office towers, luxury hotels, convention centers, recreational facilities, and other paeans to postindustrial society."[99] Moreover, he adds that "the rise of service industry jobs has fueled downtown and suburban development, while the loss of manufacturing jobs has devastated blue-collar urban communities. . . . Consequently, serious social costs have been paid."[100] Working families, particularly in communities of color, have shouldered the heavy losses of neoliberalism's "creative destruction" in the service of capital accumulation: increasing inequality and extreme poverty, the curtailment of social welfare programs, and the material violence of neoliberal neglect and urban decay.

Véa associates this new pervasive poverty and joblessness in U.S. urban centers with neoliberalism's prioritizing of financial and fictitious capital, land speculation, and commercial development over now outsourced and offshored manufacturing and industrial production. What remains in neoliberalism's wake are the "industrial rubble" and "ruin" of a precarious social existence for those confined to America's jobless hyperghettos. However, for the "new royalty" of neoliberal finance capital, hidden away in glass towers, the toll exacted by their class war on the poor recedes into the long, dark shadows cast by the towering downtown skyline of the neoliberalized city. "Even in broad daylight," Jesse admits, places like the Potrero housing projects are "difficult to see."[101] "When viewed from the thirty-first floor" of a downtown high-rise, Véa affirms in *The Silver Cloud Café*, "the graffiti hastily scrawled on the tallest building's cornerstone was all but invisible. . . . the only thing that was clear was the price of things . . . not the cost."[102] The "price of things" accumulated in the name of valorization and profit, "not the cost" borne by those sacrificed to its logic, is the "only thing" that matters to the disciples of neoliberalism. For Véa, the needs and interests of corporate wealth thus eclipse "all but invisible" populations dead-to-others, whose hastily scrawled graffiti serves as the nettlesome vestiges of their criminalized "marginal lives."

Moreover, the "myth of a service economy" provides no real solace for the countless "unskilled" blue-collar workers rendered redundant and expendable by neoliberalization. Alexander observes that, while some college-educated and so-called high-skill workers benefitted from technological innovations and changes in the production process, "blue-collar workers often found themselves displaced in the sudden transition from an industrial to a service economy."[103] Writing about 1990s America, the setting for both of Véa's novels, Ransby puts it more bluntly: "Downsizing and the introduction of labour-replacing technology (i.e., computer technology, automation and biotechnology) have created a situation in which millions of jobs and prospective jobs in manufacturing and service industries are being rapidly erased. The impact of this retrenchment, which began at the low-skill job levels, has hit Black and Latino workers hardest. . . . there now exists a class of permanently unemployed men and women who are essentially surplus labourers in an increasingly 'streamlined' economy."[104] Deindustrialization, union-busting, and the transition to a service economy since the 1970s have left a now surplus and disposable precariat of color adrift in a treacherous sea of low-wage poverty jobs and persistent underemployment and unemployment.

The "marauding bands of tiny mercenaries" on Potrero Hill thus navigate an economic landscape bereft of opportunities and future prospects for the legions of hyperproletarianized workers in the United States. Survival and resistance, not avarice, define the mercenary squads of children on the hill, whose single mothers endure on the meager "C-rations" of the new austerity workfare programs and whose fathers have fallen victim to the bloodletting of jobless hyperghettos and mass incarceration, the neoliberal state's twofold apparatus of racist social control.[105] In *Gods Go Begging*, Potrero Hill's "tiny mercenaries" find themselves in the middle of a neoliberalized "killing zone" with few, if any, options at their disposal beyond the unlawful drug trade. "Redistribution through criminal violence," Harvey writes, stands as "one of the few serious options for the poor" under neoliberalism.[106] And Alexander reminds us that "for ghetto youths, drug sales—though rarely lucrative—are often a means of survival, a means of helping to feed and clothe themselves and their families."[107] Echoing Harvey and Alexander, Jesse admits to his partner Carolina that the "roaming squads" in the Potrero housing projects "were only boys doing battle for dominion of a squalid hillside . . . only children foraging for money and food."[108] For Potrero Hill's hyperproletarianized labor force, the illegal street economy becomes a last recourse for resistance and survival.

The situation is not much better for those employed in low-wage service sector jobs. Between 1973 and 1987, young African American men employed in the retail trade and service sectors received average annual incomes 25 to 30 percent lower than the wages once paid for manufacturing jobs.[108] Overall, when looking at the years between 1970 and 1989, the two initial decades of neoliberalization, one sees a more than 30 percent drop in real wages for the lowest quintile of income earners.[109] Under neoliberalism, as Wacquant notes, state-sanctioned poverty and precarious wage labor are the "new norm of citizenship for those trapped at the bottom of the polarizing class structure."[110] Rather than protecting the poor, the neoliberal austerity state utilizes the apparatuses of workfare, mass incarceration, and the hyperghetto to produce "*compliant workers fit or forced to fill the peripheral slots* of the deregulated labor market."[111] Yet, either for survival or as a form of resistance, many workers abandon the indignities and poverty wages of the service sector for the ostensible autonomy of informal and illegal economies. As Jesse enters the Potrero housing projects, he meets a young man standing guard in "a tattered Domino's pizza uniform, a paper hat with matching jacket," as his troop of fellow "mercenaries" carries out its drug trade on the hill.[112] Finding Jesse familiar, he says, "I think I remember something about a pizza parlor. Maybe I worked there. Was you my boss?"[113] The scene ironically underscores the limited economic choices and opportunities available to the new army of expendable, hyperproletarianized workers, signaling the social violence of neoliberal political economy in the figure of a street soldier clad in a Domino's Pizza uniform. Like many servicemen of color who deserted the military during the Vietnam War, this soldier conscripted into the army of precarious wage laborers also defected from his poverty-wage service-sector job. And, as his last act of defiance against an exploitative economic system that daily strips workers of their humanity and dignity, he steals a Domino's Pizza delivery van, which is now "parked halfway up the hill . . . put up on blocks and stripped clean"[114]—a fitting image both for the lack of socioeconomic mobility fostered by neoliberalism's nonunionized, low-wage service sector jobs and for the class violence of neoliberalization and its economic precarity that routinely leaves workers themselves "stripped clean."

In the end, the "mortal rigor" and social ossification of neoliberalized San Francisco reveals the "murder" not only of the "union movement" but also of the American social contract and its promise of security and leisure held forth by the postwar Fordist-Keynesian compromise. Organized labor's once-vibrant hopes and dreams in American exceptionalism, however misplaced and ideologically motivated, have been painfully betrayed, as Ransby maintains: "Historically, the notion of American exceptionalism has meant that most U.S. workers embraced an illusory 'middle-class' identity and felt privileged and distinct from workers in other parts of the world. The [neoliberal] economic and technological changes we are experiencing threaten to redefine that self-concept."[115] For Véa, the redeveloped San Francisco skyline stands as a cruel memorial to the cast-off working-class families whose daily sacrifices and suffering underwrite the "serious social costs" accrued by the "new royalty" of neoliberal affluence and power:

> The steel workers who built the skyline never knew that they were busy erecting their own memorial monoliths. They never knew that they would all vanish interstate leaving behind powerless jobless heirs who would someday divide up the Mission District and the Fillmore District into meaningless quadrants and then defend them to the death; penniless heirs who would fracture Double Rock and the Army Street projects into small warring nations. The steelworkers couldn't know that their children, retired in infancy, would live out their lives with live ammunition, hunting possessions in the unstable firmament.[116]

In *The Silver Cloud Café*, Véa prefigures the representation in *Gods Go Begging* of the Potrero Terrace and Annex housing projects, with its "armies" of "street gangs" waging war "on a squalid hill . . . for money and food." The "powerless jobless heirs" of the Fordist-Keynesian American Dream—"retired in infancy" and who therefore must resort to "live ammunition" as a means to survive under the "unstable firmament" of a Darwinian neoliberal order—are close kin to the "powerless" on Potrero Hill, likewise "obsessed with power" as a means to survive and for whom also "the slightest chance to succeed . . . had been ritually excised at birth." Both novels expose the reified social relations and material histories behind contemporary neoliberal political economy, which in Véa's estimation is the true perpetrator of war, violence, and bloodshed from the Mission and Fillmore Districts to the Double Rock, Army Street, and Potrero housing projects.

As Véa insists in *Gods Go Begging*: "The American Dream—the two-bedroom house with a white picket fence—had always been built on a graveyard. It had always been built at the expense of the Huron Nation, at the expense of the bison, and at the expense of the Vietnamese."[117] U.S.

neoliberalism proves no exception: its version of the American Dream materializes only for the select few and at the great expense of poor and working-class families. The U.S.'s imperialist legacies of dispossession, plunder, and death in the name of white supremacy, private property, and profit converge today in the neoliberalized city, where Véa bears witness to the ongoing class war and violence of capitalist political economy.

Notes

1. Martin Luther King Jr. "The Crisis in America's Cities: An Analysis of Social Disorder and a Plan of Action against Poverty, Discrimination and Racism in Urban America," speech, Southern Christian Leadership Conference, Atlanta, GA, August 15, 1967, 2, accessed August 29, 2016, http://www.thekingcenter.org/archive/document/crisis-americas-cities

2. King, "Crisis," 2.

3. King, "Crisis," 2.

4. See Ira Katznelson, *When Affirmative Action Was White: An Untold History of Racial Inequality in Twentieth-Century America* (New York: W. W. Norton, 2005).

5. King, "Crisis," 3.

6. King, "Crisis," 3.

7. Alfredo Véa, *Gods Go Begging* (New York: Plume, 2000), 2.

8. Véa, *Gods*, 2.

9. Véa, *Gods*, 279–80, 287–88.

10. Brian J. Williams, "'In This Same Shamble of Strewn Bone': *Gods Go Begging* and the Community of Loss," *Critique: Studies in Contemporary Fiction* 54.3 (2013): 318.

11. For an important exception, see Patrick L. Hamilton, *Of Space and Mind: Cognitive Mappings of Contemporary Chicano/a Fiction* (Austin: University of Texas Press, 2011), 147–85. For studies that deal with war, trauma, and masculinity in *Gods Go Begging*, see John Alba Cutler, "Disappeared Men: Chicana/o Authenticity and the American War in Viet Nam," *American Literature* 81.3 (2009): 583–611; William Arce, "Landscapes of Trauma: The Transnational Dislocation of Vietnam's War Trauma in Alfredo Véa's *Gods Go Begging*," in *Re-Framing the Transnational Turn in American Studies*, ed. Winfried Fluck, Donald E. Pease, and John Carlos Rowe (Hanover, NH: Dartmouth College Press, 2011), 97–118; and Williams, "In This Same Shamble of Strewn Bone."

12. Jeff Biggers, "More Than Measuring Up: An Interview with Alfredo Véa," *Bloomsbury Review* 20.1 (January–February 2000): 5.

13. Stuart Hall, "The Neoliberal Revolution," *Soundings: A Journal of Politics and Culture* 48 (Summer 2011): 10–11. See also David Harvey, *A Brief History of Neoliberalism* (Oxford: Oxford University Press, 2005), 2–3.

14. Naomi Klein, *The Shock Doctrine: The Rise of Disaster Capitalism* (New York: Metropolitan Books, 2007), 444.

15. See Gerard Duménil and Dominique Lévy, "The Neoliberal (Counter-)Revolution," in *Neoliberalism: A Critical Reader*, ed. Alfredo Saad-Filho and Deborah Johnston (London: Pluto, 2005), 9–10; and Michael Dowdy, *Broken Souths: Latina/o Poetic Responses to Neoliberalism and Globalization* (Tucson: University of Arizona Press, 2013), 6–7.

16. Harvey, *Neoliberalism*, 19.

17. Duménil and Lévy, "Neoliberal," 9.

18. The list is not meant to be comprehensive, but instead aims to highlight key features and tendencies of neoliberalism in the United States. In identifying and defining these principal characteristics, I draw from Harvey, *Neoliberalism*; Klein, *Shock Doctrine*; Dowdy, *Broken Souths*; Hall, "Neoliberal Revolution"; Duménil and Lévy, "Neoliberal"; Duménil and Lévy, "The Nature and Contradictions of Neoliberalism," in *Socialist Register 2002: A World of Contradictions*, ed. Leo Panitch and Colin Leys (London: Merlin Press, 2001), 43–71; Duménil and Lévy, "Costs and Benefits of Neoliberalism: A Class Analysis," *Review of International Political Economy* 8.4 (Winter 2001): 578–607; Wendy Brown, "Neoliberalism and the End of Liberal Democracy," in *Edgework: Critical Essays on Knowledge and Politics* (Princeton: Princeton University Press, 2005), 37–59; Jordan T. Camp, *Incarcerating the Crisis: Freedom Struggles and the Rise of the Neoliberal State* (Berkeley: University of California Press, 2016); and Loïc Wacquant, *Punishing the Poor: The Neoliberal Government of Social Insecurity* (Durham: Duke University Press, 2009).

19. Robert Kurz, quoted in Neil Larsen, *Determinations: Essays on Theory, Narrative and Nation in the Americas* (London: Verso, 2001), 55–56.

20. Thank you to Carlos Gallego for suggesting this term and for his nuanced comments on the (uneven) transition from labor as a "class-for-itself" at midcentury—to varying degrees, a politically conscious and organized proletariat—to a fragmented and politically divided *hyperproletariat* under neoliberal flexible accumulation.

21. Harvey, *Neoliberalism*, 185.

22. Klein, *Shock Doctrine*, 405.

23. Barbara Ransby, "U.S.: The Black Poor and the Politics of Expendability," *Race & Class* 38.2 (October 1996): 3.

24. Wacquant, *Punishing*, 77.

25. Véa, *Gods*, 169.

26. See BAYCAT, "Public Housing on Potrero Hill: A Timeline," *Potrero Hill Archives Project*, accessed August 31, 2016, http://www.potreroarchives.com/Archives/Public_Housing_video.html; Peter Linenthal et al., *Images of America: San Francisco's Potrero Hill* (Charleston, SC: Arcadia Publishing, 2005); Albert S. Broussard, *Black San Francisco: The Struggle for Racial Equality in the West, 1900–1954* (Lawrence: University Press of Kansas, 1993); and Josh Alperin, "Public Housing: Historical Essay," *Shaping San Francisco's Digital Archive @ Found SF*, accessed August 31, 2016, http://www.foundsf.org/index.php?title=PUBLIC_HOUSING

27. Broussard, *Black San Francisco,* 176–77.

28. Véa, *Gods,* 6, 24.

29. Véa, *Gods,* 63.

30. Véa, *Gods,* 174.

31. Loïc Wacquant, "Three Pernicious Premises in the Study of the American Ghetto," *International Journal of Urban and Regional Research* 21.2 (1997): 343.

32. Loïc Wacquant, "From Slavery to Mass Incarceration: Rethinking the 'Race Question' in the U.S.," *New Left Review* 13 (2002): 50.

33. Wacquant, "Slavery," 50–51.

34. Martin Luther King Jr., quoted in Wacquant, *Punishing,* 203.

35. Véa, *Gods,* 160.

36. Véa, *Gods,* 25, 163.

37. Véa, *Gods,* 272.

38. Wacquant, *Punishing,* 202.

39. Wacquant, *Punishing,* 70, 208.

40. Loïc Wacquant, "The New 'Peculiar Institution': On the Prison as Surrogate Ghetto," *Theoretical Criminology* 4.3 (2000): 378; Joshua Clover, *Riot. Strike. Riot: The New Era of Uprisings* (London: Verso, 2016), 26.

41. David Harvey, *The Condition of Postmodernity* (Cambridge: Blackwell, 1990), 137.

42. Harvey, *Condition of Postmodernity,* 138.

43. Camp, *Incarcerating,* 39–40.

44. William Julius Wilson, *When Work Disappears: The World of the New Urban Poor* (New York: Alfred A. Knopf, 1996), 48.

45. Broussard, *Black San Francisco,* 239–40, 242.

46. Broussard, *Black San Francisco,* 242.

47. See Broussard, *Black San Francisco,* 39–245; Alperin, "Public Housing"; BAYCAT, "Public Housing"; Amy Alexander, "Whither Black San Francisco: A Story in Pictures," *San Francisco Weekly,* February 25, 2015, http://archives.sfweekly.com/sanfrancisco/african-american-san-francisco-diversity-black-san-francisco/Content?oid=3434520; and Don Santina, "Ethnic Cleansing in San Francisco," *Counterpunch,* September 29, 2007, http://www.counterpunch.org/2007/09/29/ethnic-cleansing-in-san-francisco/

48. Véa, *Gods,* 169.

49. See Raúl Homero Villa, *Barrio-Logos: Space and Place in Urban Chicano Literature and Culture* (Austin: University of Texas Press, 2000), 66–110.

50. Véa, *Gods,* 163.

51. Véa, *Gods,* 164–65.

52. Duménil and Lévy, "Nature," 53; Duménil and Lévy, "Neoliberal," 10.

53. Duménil and Lévy, "Neoliberal," 10; Duménil and Lévy, "Nature," 51.

54. Véa, *Gods,* 126–27.

55. Véa, *Gods,* 79.

56. Duménil and Lévy, "Nature," 45.

57. Duménil and Lévy, "Neoliberal," 10.

58. José E. Limón, *Dancing with the Devil: Society and Cultural Poetics in Mexican-American South Texas* (Madison: University of Wisconsin Press, 1994), 102.

59. Wilson, *When Work Disappears*, 23.

60. Ransby, "Politics of Expendability," 1.

61. Ransby, "Politics of Expendability," 1.

62 Ransby, "Politics of Expendability," 4.

63. Ruth Wilson Gilmore and Craig Gilmore, "Beyond Bratton," in *Policing the Planet: Why the Policing Crisis Led to Black Lives Matter*, ed. Jordan T. Camp and Christina Heatherton (London: Verso, 2016), 187.

64. Gilmore and Gilmore, "Beyond Bratton," 190.

65. Michelle Alexander, *The New Jim Crow: Mass Incarceration in the Age of Colorblindness*, rev. ed. (New York: New Press, 2012), 219–20.

66. Wilson, *When Work Disappears*, 19.

67. Véa, *Gods*, 70.

68. Véa, *Gods*, 274.

69. Margaret Thatcher, quoted in Harvey, *Neoliberalism*, 40.

70. Wacquant, "Slavery," 57.

71. Angela Y. Davis, *Abolition Democracy: Beyond Empire, Prisons, and Torture* (New York: Seven Stories, 2005), 41.

72. See Natalia Molina, *How Race Is Made in America: Immigration, Citizenship, and the Historical Power of Racial Scripts* (Berkeley: University of California Press, 2014), and Khalil Gibran Muhammad, *The Condemnation of Blackness: Race, Crime, and the Making of Modern Urban America* (Cambridge, MA: Harvard University Press, 2010).

73. Véa, *Gods*, 160.

74. Ransby, "Politics of Expendability," 9.

75. Ransby, "Politics of Expendability," 3.

76. Véa, *Gods*, 272.

77. Harvey, *Neoliberalism*, 76.

78. Véa, *Gods*, 24.

79. Ruth Wilson Gilmore, *Golden Gulag: Prisons, Surplus, Crisis, and Opposition in Globalizing California* (Berkeley: University of California Press, 2007), 28.

80. Véa, *Gods*, 170, 168.

81. Véa, *Gods*, 96.

82. Véa repeatedly figures state-sanctioned violence as familial sexual abuse and trauma. See Arce, "Landscapes of Trauma," 110.

83. Véa, *Gods*, 272, 300.

84. Véa, *Gods*, 308.

85. Véa, *Gods*, 102.

86. Véa, *Gods*, 106–7.

87. Véa, *Gods*, 91.

88. Véa, *Gods*, 162–63.

89. Lisa Marie Cacho, *Social Death: Racialized Rightlessness and the Criminalization of the Unprotected* (New York: New York University Press, 2012), 32, 7, 6.

90. Véa, *Gods*, 170.

91. Harvey, *Neoliberalism*, 76.

92. Véa, *Gods*, 160.

93. Quoted in Broussard, *Black San Francisco*, 133.

94. See Santina, "Ethnic Cleansing"; Alexander, "Black San Francisco"; Alexandra Berzon, "A Place in Town That Will Not Die: Shipbuilding's Heyday Gone with Two World Wars, but Dry Docks Survive at Pier 70," *SF Gate*, July 3, 2005, http://www.sfgate.com/opinion/article/A-place-in-town-that-will-not-die-2657857.php#photo-2135039

95. Véa, *Gods*, 160.

96. Roberto Cantú, "Alfredo Véa Jr.," in *Latino and Latina Writers*, vol. 2, ed. Alan West-Durán, María Herrera-Sobek, and César A. Salgado (New York: Scribner's, 2004), 511.

97. Alfredo Véa, *The Silver Cloud Café* (New York: Dutton, 1996), 24.

98. Hamilton, *Space and Mind*, 163.

99. Gregory D. Squires, *Capital and Communities in Black and White: The Intersections of Race, Class, and Uneven Development* (Albany: State University of New York Press, 1994), 95.

100. Squires, *Capital and Communities*, 104.

101. Véa, *Gods*, 159.

102. Véa, *Silver Cloud*, 24.

103. Alexander, *New Jim Crow*, 50.

104. Ransby, "Politics of Expendability," 1–2.

105. See Wacquant, *Punishing*, 69, 109.

106. Harvey, *Neoliberalism*, 48.

107. Alexander, *New Jim Crow*, 209.

108. Véa, *Gods*, 274.

109. Wilson, *When Work Disappears*, 31.

110. Wilson, *When Work Disappears*, 25.

111. Wacquant, *Punishing*, xv.

112. Wacquant, *Punishing*, 101.

113. Véa, *Gods*, 170.

114. Véa, *Gods*, 171.

115. Véa, *Gods*, 171.

116. Ransby, "Politics of Expendability," 5.

117. Véa, *Silver Cloud*, 27.

118. Véa, *Gods*, 197.

CHAPTER 3

Quarantine Citizen

Latinx Poetry and the Matter of Capital

Michael Dowdy

> Since money does not reveal what has been transformed into it, everything, commodity or not, is convertible into money. Everything becomes saleable and purchaseable. Circulation becomes the great social retort into which everything is thrown, to come out again as the money crystal. Nothing is immune from this alchemy.
>
> —KARL MARX, *CAPITAL*, VOL. 1

Public Domain, Mónica de la Torre's third collection of poems, was published on November 1, 2008, the Day of the Dead, during capitalism's unfolding global crisis.[1] When *Public Domain* entered the public domain, it began to circulate, a commodity "saleable and purchasable" like any other, wherein de la Torre's poetic labor had congealed into "the money crystal." Poetry may be the prototypical "underperforming commodity," as poet-critic Jeff Derksen writes in his seminal work on neoliberalism,[2] but it is not "immune from this alchemy" that converts cultural products into exchange values and the money form. An inventive poet and deft translator, the Mexico City-born and New York City-based de la Torre develops poetic forms for investigating these processes and for critiquing neoliberal ideology. In *Public Domain*, "$6.82" presents one such form. The poem's title calls attention to money, or the lack thereof. Not only does the amount seem random—why not $6.81?—figuratively speaking it's pocket change, insufficient for buying a book of poems.

The accretive poem builds through the logic of accumulation, its anaphoric structure resembling a declaration of assets, as in financial transactions or tax returns. It is, by turns, contradictory, ambiguous, whimsical. After beginning with a figure of compromised circulation—"My economy is circular: I earn money from an institution that owns most of the businesses where I tend to spend most of my money"—de la Torre offers statements such as "My economy is quasi-medieval, trade-centered, and guild-like,"[3] "My economy does not allow me to say no," "My economy has no exchange value," "There are no surpluses in my economy,"[4] and "My economy mistakes what it means to trade in futures."[5] We intuit midway the title's referent: the price of "an unremarkable tuna sandwich" and "a liter bottle of Poland Spring water coming not from Poland but from Maine and bought at a university cafeteria in Uptown Manhattan."[6] Near the poem's end, therefore, "My economy doesn't force me to put my money where my mouth is" registers its irony subtly: the clichéd truism, a corollary of the vaunted *skin in the game* loved by politicians and economists, distracts from the tuna sandwich and the poet's particular trade, each of which achieve their use value "where [the] mouth is."[7] As de la Torre admits, "My economy is language."[8] This early declaration must be kept in mind at the last: "My economy is not even mine."[9] Alienation, from the product of one's own labor, and from the means of production, defines the poetry world and the capitalist one in which it is embedded.

De la Torre's seeming allusions to her particular "guild"—the Po Biz, Poetry Business, or Literature, whatever one calls the institutions, such as universities and presses, which sustain its social currency—and to its exploitative gift economy (i.e., adjuncts, unpaid internships)—tempt us to read "$6.82" as primarily addressing the workings of cultural capital. Yet such a focus displaces the monetization the title foregrounds and to which de la Torre turns in the poem's unusual coda following the terse final statement of alienation: "Word count: 682."[10] We learn here that de la Torre's poem had been up to something we could not previously discern. The poem asks: What are the relations between literary practice and capital accumulation, the poetic imagination and the money form? The answer is that each word is worth one cent, and that there may not be more words than the price of lunch. By reducing the poem to its exchange value, using a 1:1 scale, de la Torre enacts Marx's formula of exchange, where C = commodity and M = money. Here, C-M-C can be represented as 682-word poem-$6.82-lunch. The commodity is converted into money, which is then converted into a commodity, in an endless chain of exchanges between tuna fish and stanzas.

De la Torre's "$6.82" dramatizes a lived experience of neoliberalism, in particular the relentless commodification and financialization of all forms of life. Everything can be quantified, and it's best measured via the capitalist marketplace. This omnipresent ideology and its mixed outcomes have been of particular concern to Latinx poets. This chapter examines how Daniel Borzutzky and Urayoán Noel, writing in the aftermath of the 2008 financial crisis, use two poetic techniques associated with vanguard and avant-garde poetries to offer critiques of neoliberal ideology and outcomes. De la Torre's poem offers an apt starting point, with its serial and procedural forms. Series employ intensified forms of repetition, while procedures place constraints on the writing process, as in de la Torre's 682-word "count" or "limit." "Poems written under constraint and composed of recombined, appropriated text," Rachel Galvin argues, can "thematize the activity of appropriation itself as endemic to capitalism."[11] More broadly, subjecting the literary imagination to systematic procedures and repetitions underscores the dialectical tensions between poetry and what poet-critic Christopher Nealon calls "the matter of capital."[12] In Latinx poetics, this tension is magnified through the lenses of ethnicity and class, as the epistemological and ontological uncertainties of Latinidad have undergone scrutiny in recent debates about diaspora, citizenship, and the crisis of the undocumented. As de la Torre orders her sandwich, her conversation across classes and national origins suggests the ways in which the market collapses ethnic-national distinctions into a bland Latinidad that can be indexed, paradoxically, by the ordering of jalapeños: "You Puerto Rican, she asked? Don't think so, / said another one in Spanish. Let me answer. / No, what made you think so? The peppers?"[13]

Although many Latinx poets, including de la Torre, Rodrigo Toscano, and Carmen Giménez Smith, frequently utilize series and procedures, I focus in this chapter on two poets, one of Chilean descent, the other Puerto Rican, whose singular aesthetic practices offer materialist critiques of neoliberal capitalism. Borzutzky's serial forms and Noel's digital procedures exemplify Latinx poetry's nimble dialectical tools in times of capitalist crisis. But theirs are distinctive iterations of dialectical imaginaries that do not offer clear teleologies, obvious solutions, or discernible syntheses. Rather, as de la Torre's "$6.82" ends with "my" economy that is simultaneously "not mine," so too Borzutzky and Noel explore the contradictions (and creative possibilities) that arise when "your" body isn't "yours" but rather the market's and the state's. In discussing a different (Chicano) poem, Maria Damon pinpoints the dialectic key to de la Torre's poem and to the materialist poetics I examine below:

> Any resolution to the extreme split articulated in the poem would have to be dialogic, a matter of continual process, rather than a static and teleological "melting pot" assimilationism in which thesis and antithesis fuse and metamorphose in a smooth historical inevitability. Perhaps, if one can speak of a postmodern dialectic, it is one in which there can be no synthesis; solutions have to be more ingenious, more tactical, more provisional and partial. Perhaps there will be no "at home."[14]

If "dialectic" is modified with "Latinx" rather than the ill-fitting "postmodern," this line of thinking encapsulates how, in the past decade, Latinx poetics has emphasized what Damon calls "poetic activity."[15] In poems such as "$6.82," and in Borzutzky's recursive series and Noel's dizzying procedures, such "activity" foregrounds creative processes of appropriation, recycling, rewriting, parody, and collage. The product—the poem—cedes prominence to the process of production, and the synthesis—the poem's meaning, polish, and finish—cede primacy to the provisional statelessness of Latinidad. "Poetic activity" of this sort allegorizes the encounters between the money form, with its range of figural economies (metonymy, metaphor), and poetic forms. The processes of circulation and exchange in which these antagonisms are embedded come to inflection in moments of crisis.

In *The Matter of Capital,* Nealon examines how North American poetry of the past century found forms, during times of crisis, to confront capitalism. Recent developments in Latinx/a/o subjectivity have been generated in and through such crises. The iteration of Latinx poetics explored here has emerged during three convergent crises in the twenty-first century: the terrorist attacks of September 11, 2001; the 2008 financial meltdown; and the plight of nearly eleven million undocumented persons. For Nealon, the relationship between the "kind of matter" that capital and money are and the "kind of matter" that poetry might be determines the sorts of interventions poets and critics can make. Such a dynamic turns on the question of the "substantiality," or lack thereof, of money and poetry. Nealon asks:

> the question of what poetry is, or would have to be, in order to be opposed to capital: equally substantial, or equally insubstantial? Fleet and circulatory, like money, or defiantly valueless, money's opposite? Imitative of the movements that produce crisis and rushing headlong into it, or built to survive crisis and live on into a postcapitalist future?[16]

Borzutzky's and Noel's poems investigate these very questions, toggling between "rushing headlong" into neoliberal crisis and seeking precarious routes into durable "postcapitalist future[s]." The title of my chapter, taken from Noel's aptly named collection *Hi-Density Politics*,[17] indicates that rather than being "fleet and circulatory, like money," this iteration of Latinx poetics ultimately opts for material density as a way to explore these conditions of possibility. This mode of "poetic activity" is in keeping with Derksen's observation of a "rise of semantically dense cultural production" in the wake of September 11, 2001,[18] and with Damon's sense that "exhaustive discursivity"—omnipresent in Borzutzky and Noel—has the potential to empower alternative ethical imperatives.[19] Capaciously understood, this Latinx poetics produces an "irreducible opacity," Édouard Glissant's concept of relationality insistent upon the ethical, aesthetic, and strategic worth of eluding comprehension, celebrating "errantry's imaginary vision," and resisting interpellation into hierarchical regimes of economic and political order.[20]

My borrowing from Noel derives from his especially canny "poetic activity." His poem, "a throw of the dice will never abolish south beach," is a "free-form self-translation," in French and English, of Stéphane Mallarmé's "A Throw of the Dice Will Never Abolish Chance."[21] From Miami, "where the plastic palms sway," the poem's "quarantine citizen" delineates two cornerstones of the post-9/11 polis—the state surveillance of citizens and the nativist nationalisms that seek to quarantine citizens from their alien invaders:

> QUARANTINE CITIZEN!
> *Qu'ran/ /Teen / / Yen / / Op cit / /*
> GARRISON CITIZEN!
> *Garnish/ /Garish / / Nation / /*
> . . .
> *quasi/ / almost/ / could be . . .*[22]

What does it mean to be a citizen in quarantine? In garrison? Who is quarantined from whom? Borzutzky's "data bodies" and Noel's "body poetics" circulate within these "diasporous" enclosures, Noel's term in his study of Nuyorican poetry, *In Visible Movement*, which stresses the receptive, leaky, and radically open dimensions of diasporic subjectivity.[23] These bodies likewise navigate what William Anthony Nericcio identifies as the media economy of Latino representations, where such bodies carry the infectious diseases of stereotypes. "[T]he hierarchy of meaning that sustains the term 'stereotype,'" Nericcio argues in untangling the term's genealogy, "includes *physical* and *figural* violence: blows on metal (*typtein*), blows on paper (typewriting), *blows on flesh* (stereotyping)."[24] Borzutzky's and Noel's poems navigate the embodied, corporeal (non)incorporation of Latinos into the polis, the body politic. In Borzutzky's grotesque serialized fables and Noel's whimsical "free-form self-translations," (non)citizen bodies are circumscribed by quarantine (fences, limits, contagions), garrison (empire's fortified walls), and the "jokes" and mistranslations of stereotypes that characterize relations between the United States and Latin America.[25]

The poetic techniques examined in this chapter are common in, and commonly associated with, North American Language poetry and its offshoots. It is crucial, then, to account for the ways in which Latinx poets adapt, often via parody, the techniques of the white avant-garde. Such appropriations magnify the problematic claims of this coterie, whether it is the Language or conceptual poets, to a radical politics that nonetheless bars entry to writers of color, including but not limited to Latinos. Language poetry, Timothy Yu writes in *Race and the Avant-Garde*, "arrogate[d] to itself the ability to provide a total view of society and culture, while limiting the work of 'oppressed peoples' to communication within the codes of a circumscribed community."[26] A corollary critique of this exclusion focuses on the object of critique in this vein of experimental poetics: that literary practices, rather than capitalism, imperialism, and ethnocentrism, are the true target.[27] In contrast, the work of poets like Toscano, Derksen argues, "does not direct its primary challenge toward literary conventions, national canon formation, or positions within a cultural field, but rather toward the culture-ideology of neoliberalism and the transformations that globalization has materialized at a number of spatial scales (the nation, the city, and the citizen in particular)."[28] The same is true of Borzutzky and Noel.

The "quarantine citizen" in Borzutzky's and Noel's books navigates the hemisphere, from Chile to the United States, traveling the historical geographies of north-south relations, their treacherous migratory routes and attendant discourses of citizenship, statelessness, diaspora, and exile. Their explicit and oblique critiques of the Po Biz reveal its complicity with neoliberal ideals and outcomes. In "Poetry is Theft," Rachel Galvin theorizes how poetic procedures such as allusion, quotation, parody, and pastiche look different in Latin America and the Caribbean than they do in Anglo-European contexts.[29] These techniques of "radical re-authoring" emphasize "how poets appropriate literary capital through constrained recombination, recycling, and playful appropriations of language."[30] Galvin contextualizes such procedures within models of relation in the Americas, like Glissant's. Together, they "challenge the metaphysics of origin," providing traction against the alienation depicted in "$6.82," with its meditations on the illusory ownership of literary property. Broadly conceived, they challenge the origin tropes that refuse the undocumented ontological status as human beings, even as they are valued for their labor. For Borzutzky, this "radical re-authoring" takes the form of obsessively rewriting his own books. For Noel, his rewriting of Mallarmé, among other borrowings, utilizes what Galvin calls "a cannibalistic logic" that radically "re-authors its 'source' texts" by mixing and disordering genres, registers, and sociolects.[31]

To sketch this materialist Latinx poetics, the chapter unfolds in three sections. First, I offer a reading of Juan Felipe Herrera's *Lotería Cards and Fortune Poems*.[32] This collaborative, multimedia project uses serial and procedural techniques, works within substantial constraints, and creates a dialectical imaginary between tradition and innovation. Second, I discuss how Borzutzky's serial forms allegorize the body under duress, battered by the market and the surveillance state. Next, I show how Noel's poetic procedures introduce a repertoire of embodied gestures, postures, and sonic landscapes that gleefully critique the most troubling and absurd manifestations of global capital. In these sections, I aim to demonstrate how two of the most innovative, uncompromising, and politically astute Latinx poets pose challenges to neoliberal capitalism. In particular, I am interested in Borzutzky's and Noel's aesthetic critiques of both the ideology and the outcomes of neoliberalism's reduction of all human activities to market functions and values. To stage encounters with capital, their poems bend and pervert the language (terms, tropes, forms) of economics. Their figural and formal economies sometimes mimic the logic of capital and sometimes enact dialectical negations of it. To conclude, I offer some thoughts on the political questions, especially concerning Latinx citizenship, raised by these techniques, while also considering their "success" in confronting capitalist hegemony.

JUAN FELIPE HERRERA'S COPIA

Published in 1999, *Lotería Cards* presents a compelling precursor of the dialectical imaginary in Latinx poetics. Using procedures and constraints, and creating from received material forms, the book offers at once a singular vision and a derivative one. In the aftermath of NAFTA, with the rise of the Zapatistas and the antiglobalization movement, and the attendant anti-immigrant forces that took the form of surveillance and deportation regimes such as Operation Gatekeeper, Herrera and Mexican artist Artemio Rodríguez turned to an old, widely reproduced, and well-known piece of popular culture, the Mexican *lotería,* to understand material conditions at the turn of the millennium. I do not have space to discuss this project in all its complexity. Instead, I want to address the ways in which *Lotería Cards* affords a view of how the techniques of procedure, appropriation, and satire can be deployed to critique the stultifying omnipresence of capital and to model creative resistance to it.

Lotería Cards is a "radical re-authoring" of the traditional Mexican game of chance. The book combines two interrelated artistic processes, one collaborative and synchronic, the other historical, diachronic. In the first case, Herrera plays second fiddle (more on this figure of speech shortly) to Rodríguez's scintillating black-and-white linocuts of lottery cards. Rodríguez made the linocuts and then Herrera composed his poems while looking at them. In his introduction, Chicano artist and art historian Rupert García explains that Herrera followed the tradition of the *lotería* announcer, who, like a bingo announcer, "spontaneously composed" a poem in response to the selected card.[33] The resulting, unrevised "fortune poems," limited to a page apiece, foreground contingency, chance, and trust in the soundness of the centuries-old procedure. In reviewing the book, Catherine E. Wall calls the poems "transcriptions [of images] into verse," a description accounting for their procedural method but minimizing their radical contingency and relationality.[34] Together, the poems animate a multifarious dialectic—between tradition and innovation, popular and vanguard, Mexico and the United States (and Mexican and Chicano), Spanish and English (poems are in English with Spanish titles), and verbal and visual art (as in ekphrasis). Appearing on the eve of the twenty-first century, the book's eschatological orientation advances an apocalyptic vision, but this vision emerges from a turn toward the deep Mexican past that is sedimented in *lotería.*

As Wall and García emphasize, Herrera and Rodríguez's version of *lotería* is one of many interpretations of the game.[35] In this sense, theirs is a preeminent example of "copia," as theorized in *In Praise of Copying,* where Marcus Boon argues that copying, rather than the individualistic originality so prized, fetishized, and institutionalized in juridical forms such as copyright law, constitutes a guiding, if disavowed, artistic practice in world cultures.[36] One type of copying, which Boon calls "copia as abundance," emphasizes the "infinite number of ways of presenting, perceiving, disassembling, and reassembling objects and selves."[37] This "collective activity"[38] takes shape between Rodríguez and Herrera and between their interpretations and other versions. The game itself is syncretic, comprising the Aztec version, called *patolli* in Nahuatl, and the colonial one, *lotería*, which was introduced in the late eighteenth century. The Don Clemente version, dating from 1887, is most common; its colorful board of 54 cards can be seen all over, from taquerías to galleries. Rodríguez reinvents 25 of these 34, comprising a quarter of the book's 104 cards. These additions are often topical, provocative, and satirical, as with "El Mojado," "La Migra," "El Mal Gobierno," and "El Zapatista." They suggest that not only are specific cards reproducible, so too is the template for a card.

Lottery cards, it should be noted, can be appropriated for various ideological ends. This palimpsestic thickness, which enfolds a dialectical process of mutual antagonisms, takes numerous shapes, as indicated above. Armed conflict is especially fertile ground. Elena Albarrán, in examining Latin American "relics of material culture" such as dolls, games, and toys, including *lotería* cards, shows how their images of war do the ideological work of interpellating children into nationalist causes and Foucauldian regimes of discipline and punishment.[39] In her brief reading, Albarrán argues that Rodríguez and Herrera "have broken the institutionalizing power of the game by abandoning its rules and regulations."[40] Yet it is equally legitimate, following García, who sees the book operating "within" and "*beyond*" the *lotería* tradition,[41] to argue that by *following* "its rules and regulations" during the process of production, the authors transformed a tool of control into one of subversive critique.

The poem "El Ermitaño" (The Hermit) enacts this dialectical imaginary.[42] Wall rightly sees Herrera's poems in *Lotería Cards* as "intricately constructed," "surrealistic," "strange and nightmarish," "hallucinatory," and "enigmatic," with "antipoetic irreverence" and "hermeticism."[43] These key elements of Herrera's distinctive style are magnified via the procedural constraints. The last feature above directly undergirds the lottery card "El Ermitaño," depicting a fiddle player bent beneath a stone arch:

> Under the arch of Capitalism, or rather
> this bone of eons smoothed in brine & flesh fodder—

here I swing my axe, the blackish river
of delights and solitude. The solitude, well
it is a mountain, a lover now. It is an octagon
of slender naked renunciations. My eyes are accustomed.
My heart is accustomed. The song is different,
the song is rebellious.[44]

Herrera assumes the hermit's voice and viewpoint in a mixture of plainspoken speech and surreal meditation. The first line is a paradigmatic instance of Nealon's notion that poets use "topics, topoi, and techniques that produce a *textual imaginary* . . . to stage confrontations between poetry and capital."[45] Consider the process of making the poem. The poet views the linocut, sees traces of the archetypes in the Don Clemente version, though it has no "hermit," and *becomes* the hermit. In doing so, what comes to him, as the phrase goes, is the totalizing presence of Capitalism. The constraint "under" which this atomized individual, this hermit without recourse to community or collectivity, lives, creates, and works, is Capitalism, with a capital "C." This hermit is a figure of *homo economicus* (economic man), the fundamental form of the human in neoliberal ideology—a "solitude" that is a feature of the landscape ("a mountain") and the core of interpersonal relations ("a lover").

In this reading, the dialectic between "accustomed" and "rebellious" indicates that the current mode of artistic production doesn't brink distinctions between base and superstructure. The vertical topography is disoriented by the "arch"—Capitalism is the imaginary and the conditions of production alike. Culture emerges from below, where it is materialized in "bone," "brine," "flesh." Art and music are produced under constraint, within the brick-and-mortar of capital. Consequently, the fiddle is an "axe"—a tool of labor and resistance. In Borzutzky's books, the creating body is likewise under severe constraint. His serial poems, like Herrera's, are often surreal, but the younger poet creates narrative fables of the neoliberal state's violence.

DANIEL BORZUTZKY'S REPLICATING "DATA BODIES"

In "The Privatized Waters of Dawn," from *The Performance of Becoming Human* (hereafter, *Performance*), Borzutzky's National Book Award–winning fourth collection, the narrator interjects a modest assertion from the bathtub, where he is being tortured, with lit cigarettes, by "appraisers" from the

Chicago Police Department: "I have a faint idea of what it means to be alive."[46] Borzutzky's fables and satires do not often turn to understatement, except, as in this case, when the narrator's asymmetric response magnifies how state violence enters the bloodstream and transforms the body into something less recognizably human and, on occasion, more. We might find initial footing for understanding such monstrous settings in Borzutzky's biography. A Chicagoan of Chilean descent, Borzutzky's poetry emerges from, respectively, the North American and Latin American incubators of neoliberal ideas and policies, where forms of surveillance, discipline, and punishment essential to implementing and enforcing them have been tested. His relentless aesthetic critiques of neoliberalism are undoubtedly facilitated by his residence in the city of the Chicago Boys and Rahm Emanuel and by his knowledge of the Pinochet dictatorship. Yet as a fabulist, reading Borzutzky through a biographical lens detracts from his singular capacity to seek the edges of human experience, to explore via allegory the forms of infra- and supra-humanity produced by neoliberal globalization. Nor has he been tortured, like Raúl Zurita, the Chilean poet who Borzutzky translates and, to an extent, emulates, who *was* tortured following the coup of September 11, 1973, *because* he was a poet.

Instead, a guide to Borzutzky's poetics is found in the epigraph to his second collection, *The Book of Interfering Bodies* (hereafter, *Book*).[47] This quote from *The 9/11 Commission Report*—"It is therefore crucial to find a way of routinizing, even bureaucratizing, the exercise of imagination"—grounds the poet's allegories of the logic and apparatus of the surveillance state, its bureaucratic authoritarianism.[48] In short, the "state" that the neoliberal project was theoretically designed to eliminate or diminish.

According to the Oxford English Dictionary, to *routinize* is "to impose routine on" something, where *routine* is "a regularly followed procedure" and "a more or less mechanical or unvarying way of performing certain actions or duties." Imposing order on variable and unpredictable processes, routinization subjects the imagination, and thus the creative dimensions of human agency, to systematic protocols, controls, and procedures. Similarly, poetic procedures place constraints on the artistic process; ideally, when such constraints are elective, rather than imposed, paradoxically they can facilitate innovation. In satirizing the epigraph's logic, Borzutzky's books have developed a singular aesthetic that underscores the stakes of this routinization—the human body's survival under types of duress, from imprisonment and torture to the stymieing effects of the privatization and digitization of daily life. For Borzutzky, an assault on the body is an attack on imagination and vice versa: to routinize the imagination requires control over the body. His poems thus index the twofold experience of Latinx bodies in the aftermaths of September 11s: 1973 and 2001.

Unlike de la Torre's monetary procedure, Herrera's ekphrastic procedure, and Noel's digital procedures, Borzutzky's serial narratives build from looping, recursive, and accretive sentences. His fables frequently use objects of material culture. In *Book*, eighteen of thirty-eight poems are "books," beginning with "The Book of Flesh" and ending with "The Book of Interfering Bodies." These single-paragraph blocks of prose allegorize writing and reading, often in horrifying fashion. Addressing official negations of Chilean history, "The Book of Forgotten Bodies" begins:

> The reader who opens the Book of Forgotten Bodies finds nothing. There are no horses galloping through deserted villages in search of the men who used to ride them. There are no children crying for their parents who were thrown out of airplanes and into the sea. There are no soldiers who had their arms sliced off for refusing to obliterate innocent bodies. There are no rich men leaning against paradise trees as the drunk bodies of poor men stumble up to their houses to kill them. There are no bodies of hopeless virgins smashed on city streets by Mercedes-Benzes cruising through the gentle drizzle of a foggy day. There are no bodies abandoned on beaches. There are no corpses floating down rivers. There are no bodies hanging in the military barracks on island XYZ off the coast of nation ABC.[49]

In his third collection, *In the Murmurs of the Rotten Carcass Economy* (hereafter, *Murmurs*), "books" diminish to "memos," that form of bureaucrats, executives, and middle managers.[50] "Memos" appropriate capitalists' language, expanding that of *Book*, where a narrator declares: "I prefer the jargon of capitalists to the jargon of poets. / I love the word: 'liquidity.' / I love the world: 'asset.'"[51] Borzutzky reminds us that capitalists also have a poetics, which is to say a code for figuring the world via abstraction, euphemism, metaphor, metonymy, and so on. Borzutzky borrows and displaces, thereby making strange, the language of hedge funds, banks, MBAs, and CEOs. These word banks (pun intended) converge in his fabulist (anti-)romantic mode: "The night sky is enjambed with rotten assets."[52] In Borzutzky's books, the languages of poets and bankers are equally "rotten," their "assets" eating away at human bodies and their habitats.

In this materialist poetics bodies accumulate, like sentences and like capital, the desire to increase yields driving both literary and economic activity. The "bodies" that proliferate in Borzutzky's books are qualified by a dizzying number of adjectives. The two adjectives from which the others issue are "data bodies" and "authoritative bodies." The latter allegorizes Michel Foucault's functionaries and enforcers of the surveillance state.

After all, what are books, in the eyes of technocrats and venture capitalists, but bodies of data? And what are human beings, to economists, CEOs, and private equity models, but bodies of data? Devaluing the body enfolds a corollary process—the sacralization of data. In *Murmurs*, Borzutzky writes, "In the beginning there was data" and "I speak of data as if it is a form of prayer."[53] The poet's sense of writing, then, is correspondingly "a form of prayer and code-breaking at the same time."[54] Not counting scores of metonyms of the body (skin, teeth, mouth, bone, belly, bowel, intestines) and of synonyms for or states of the body (corpse, carcass), "body" or "bodies" appear hundreds, if not thousands of times, across Borzutzky's three recent collections, including fifteen times in the first poem of *Performance*. Together, they explore reproducible forms of infra-humanity, from which the distancing technique indicates both alienation from lived experience and the traces of the mutable self in every other "body." Here, imprisoned and colonized persons, refugees, and (im)migrants suffer "blows," in Nericcio's dual sense, from being deemed subhuman. In Borzutzky, these states of alien(ated) (non)personhood are defined by inhabiting a body that belongs to omnipresent "authoritative bodies." This goes for "illegals" as well as public workers. "Because you're a decrepit, public body," an "authoritative body" tells his torture victim, "you do not own yourself anymore."[55] In such contexts, poetry becomes, in Nealon's words, "the medium for registering obliterable life."[56]

Borzutzky's fables of "obliterable life" unnerve readers who prefer decorum and measured detachment. In his poems, such life is life "reduced," austere, "decomposed" to bare materials: decay, rot, death, contagion, disease, severed limbs, drool, piss, shit, vomit, internal organs forcibly removed, orifices forcibly penetrated, the body as a porous landscape for mining data, for extracting value, for the sadist state: in short, raw material and finished commodity. These bodies don't seem to work very much; rather, they are worked on, operated on, disassembled: "I do not know how to say that I have been shocked my legs have been privatized my fingers removed for austerity."[57] Taken together, the debased earth, sky, and bodies circulate in "the rotten carcass economy," the economic system, cultural logic, and cosmos of Borzutzky. This necrotic economy, of dead bodies revivified and commodified, is an extended topoi of what Joyelle McSweeney calls the "necropastoral."[58] "The term 'necropastoral,'" she writes, "re-marks the pastoral as a zone of exchange." This zone rejects the "hygienic borders of the classical pastoral," which conceals the possibility that "the anthropocene epoch is in fact synonymous with ecological endtimes."[59] Unlike the pastoral's tranquility, order, and verdancy, the necropastoral is characterized by a grotesque reproductive "activity" similar to the abundant "activity" of copia: "self-digestion," "eructations," "hunger," "hole making," "infectiousness," "anxiety," "contagion," "decomposition," "black fecundity," "spasming," and "declivities," all of which the pastoral represses.[60] These activities define Borzutzky's "rotten carcass economy." They convert "data," which is popularly figured as clean, crisp, sanitary (and sanitizing), neutral, objective—a Silicon Valley pastoral for the Digital Age—into carcasses to fertilize the cities of the superrich. Per McSweeney, Borzutzky's fables take the shape of "rat-bod[ies]" burrowing into the "edifices of hegemony."[61]

These fables gain momentum as rotting "data bodies" consume, and are consumed by, other bodies. Data, in essence, devours. The "data bodies" that haunt *Murmurs* become the signal human forms of an epoch in *Performance*. When the narrator of "Archive" declares, "I am writing a story of love in the time of data fascism,"[62] he sends up Gabriel García Márquez's *Love in the Time of Cholera* and the earlier "Love in the Time of Poetry" in *Book*. In this case, "data bodies" morph into "ash-bodies": "And the bodies are little stains in the sky of ash / And these bodies belong to the terrorist group that's called: humanity."[63] This precipitous conclusion has a double movement, figuring both humanity's capacity for destruction (of ecosystems, nonhuman life forms, and ourselves) and the possibility of a more generous, durable conception of personhood that would pose an existential threat to the neoliberal order, wherein *homo economicus* arbitrates all values through the prism of individual profit.

The manifold violence endured by these bodies is characterized by what Borzutzky calls, after the Peruvian César Vallejo, "blows." These "blows" produce a collective metaphysical state, spiritual condition, and structure of feeling, at once ecological and cosmological, structuring "the rotten carcass economy." Infra-humanity is defined by "blows," suprahumanity ("authoritative bodies," the superrich) by the lack thereof. Commerce between them is mediated by stereotypes, which Nericcio defines as "blows," "grotesque caricatures" that do "violence to the possibility of dialogue."[64] The narrator of "Archive" wonders, "How can it be that there are people who know nothing of the blows of life."[65] Alluding to Vallejo's "The Black Heralds," Borzutzky revises Vallejo's elliptical refrain, replacing the incomprehensibility of suffering with the insulation from suffering:

> There are blows in life, so powerful . . . I don't know!
> Blows as from the hatred of God; as if, facing them,
> the undertow of everything suffered
> welled up in the soul . . . I don't know![66]

As the title, *The Performance of Becoming Human*, implies, Borzutzky explores the performative dimensions of suffering, of receiving blows from above, "as from the hatred of God." This "God," as in Herrera's "El Hermitaño," is authoritarian Capitalism. Yet his performativity isn't a repertoire of embodied gestures, poses, and codes for enacting identity. Rather, this performance is that of an imprisoned or undocumented person trying to stay alive, to maintain dignity, to elude, to dissimulate, to give up, to die. This performance, moreover, is militantly private, and privatized, in dark, clandestine sites at the command of "authoritative bodies" who own the body's data, DNA, soul. Foucault quotes former inmates of a penal colony, who, "singing the praises of the new punitive policies of the body," said, "'We preferred the blows, but the cell suits us better.'"[67] Always a "becoming"—immanent, replete with fear, adrenaline, pain—this performance, heard in the inmates' "praises," is paradoxically relational. In their atomization, as economic data points, as individuals without recourse to forms of collectivity outside the marketplace, bodies nonetheless interact with, merge with, and are swallowed and consumed by other bodies, mutilated, torn apart, and consolidated in economic codes.

From these abject bodies, the possibility of resistance emerges in combinations of economic and romantic language. Archetypal words such as "love" and "light" that approach taboo in North American poetics (unless used ironically) structure Borzutzky's poetics, the crumbling infrastructure of another, more beneficent humanity buried within the structure of "the rotten carcass economy." He follows the Chilean poets Nicanor Parra, Roberto Bolaño, and Zurita, who use such words although—or, *because*—they have been used up. The first poem of *Performance*, "Let Light Shine Out of Darkness," displays this luminous, oneiric, fleshy, and pungent language. It begins with what it feels like to inhabit a devalued body: "I live in a body that does not have enough light in it / For years, I did not know that I needed to have more light / Once, I walked around my city on a dying morning and a decomposing body approached me and asked why I had no light."[68] Surely thinking of similar passages, in his blurb for *Performance*, Noel calls Borzutzky's sinuous sentences "sentences for a new sentience." This sentence is the primary unit of his poems, not the syllable or line, modeling unfolding forms of radical relationality. Contained by the twinned violence of the bank and the state, his pliable sentence always pushes back against it, making "holes" (McSweeney) in the sanitized borders. Ultimately, his sentence is defined by a double logic: to compose a sentence, and to endure one.

Borzutzky's books form an obsessive, continuous project of such sentencing, wherein he appropriates, serializes, and radically reauthors his previous "bodies." Near the outset of "The Mountain at the End of this Book," the final poem in *Performance*, he admits as much: "This mountain appears in every book I have ever written. Sorry if you were expecting something new."[69] "One should not be afraid to spend their entire life writing the same book," he says in *Murmurs*.[70] By this measure, Borzutzky's book is growing leaner and more powerful—*Performance* is half the length as, and much less word dense than, his previous two collections.[71] Even so, Damon's observations about Jewish diasporic poetics apply doubly to Borzutzky, who is a product of Eastern European and Chilean diasporas. Her explanation of how Jewish poets inherit a unique tradition of addressing God pinpoints Borzutzky's obsessive verse:

> This exclusive and awed address, with its exaggeratedly asymmetric power relation, can account for the "autism-in-public" aura that accrues around such monologistic outpourings; they are witnessed but not shared by readers or hearers; they are intended to be overheard, but the poet is not responsible to any audience but Absence. The writing/exegesis is a life pulse, a *sine qua non*, of diasporic subjectivity, and a fulfillment of the mandate (an eleventh commandment?) to leave not a scrap of history unattended to, uncollected, unremembered, unaccounted for, or, if loss is inevitable, unmourned.[72]

For Borzutzky, as for Herrera's hermit, the "exclusive and awed address" now addresses Capitalism. "[B]odies," a narrator in *Performance* deadpans, "are shared between the earth, the state and the bank."[73] In other words, Capitalism has become the Christian God, the conquering trinity. In this frame, Damon's reference to Walter Benjamin's imperative to collect every "scrap of history" makes sense of Borzutzky's obsessive circling, his urgency in documenting the lives of infra-humanity, Chilean disappeared, and Chicagoans tortured and incarcerated. In short, Borzutzky is "writing the same book" in a quixotic attempt to keep pace with the repeating violence of History and Capitalism.

For a poet working the vein of what Roberto Tejada calls a "failed practice," failure can be a productive state, an illuminating condition of possibility.[74] Yet in Borzutzky even this qualified optimism born in defeat is undercut by sudden shifts to stand-up modes. Throughout *Murmurs* and *Performance*, Borzutzky's narrators deploy constructions such as "Have you heard the one about," often about the butt of jokes, such as undocumented persons. Such comic tropes echo Nicanor Parra's and Pedro Pietri's antipoetry, yet in Borzutzky these invitations to be alert for the punchline meander, refusing resolution and closure:

> Have you heard the one about the knife that went deeper and deeper into the body without actually penetrating the skin? Certain bodies were asked to keep light sweet crude in their mouths to prepare for the next time the assets go rotten. The feasibility impact studies have shown that if the bodies are reduced there will be more liquidity in certain sectors of the rotten carcass economy. Cage production will increase as the housing market plummets. Frame manufacturers are exuberant. How many children can be held in empty swimming pools? How many children can be put in display cases at the zoo? Reductions, say the economists, inevitably lead to innovations.[75]

Without punchlines, there is no comic relief. Rather, like understatement, such "jokes" dramatize "blows." As Nericcio argues, these "blows" aren't *just* "emotional violence" experienced by "the butt of a stereotype's *joke*" but the physical violence explicit in the term's genealogy.[76] Finally, this violence is perpetrated by economists, who are the comedians and high priests of "the rotten carcass economy."

If Borzutzky's fables are "overdeveloped," his term satirizing economic development discourse, they manage to avoid insularity and self-regard. To this end, his privatization fables often merge with satires of the Po Biz, which does not. In "The Mountain at the End of this Book," as in other poems, the poetry "sector" and economic "sector" merge. "On the mountain," the narrator observes, "the free-market poems absorb themselves and regenerate into billions of the blankest verses there ever were."[77] From the pinnacle, "I look down into this mountain of gyrating bodies and sing a peaceful song about austerity and the privatization of our form and content."[78] Ultimately, however, privatization, austerity, and other tools of capitalist discipline and punishment greet the body upon waking. In "The Privatized Waters of Dawn," the narrator is haunted by his pending "deposit," like a paycheck, into a bank account: "I could not sleep the night before my appointment to be deposited into the private sector."[79] It ends:

> And as usual I watch from the bathtub of dawn until someone comes
> to conduct the daily appraisal of my body
>
> I cost much less than my historical value and the bank has no choice
> but to deny the loan I need in order to buy myself back
>
> My deflationary wounds
>
> My privatized blood
>
> My rotten carcass sinking into the privatized waters of dawn[80]

This convergence of romantic and economic terms in apartment bathrooms and in sewer-fields of shit, rot, and death constitutes, for Borzutzky, what is collectively handed down to children.

Borzutzky's fables are ultimately haunted by children, as fables are, and thus by the most vulnerable and by the future as much as the past. "The Mountain at the End of this Book" demonstrates this unnerving resemblance to children's books which the title distills. "This mountain," the narrator reports calmly, "is the last breath of this bedtime story for the end of the world."[81] Throughout his work, Borzutzky depicts love as a condition, process, and property of decomposition, making it more urgent, elusive, and, when it comes, fleeting. In the serial "Dream Song #17," which borrows John Berryman's favored form, the narrator offers "*a lullaby / for the end of the world*" before changing course to say that it's really "*about the beginning / what happens when we start to rot.*" The poem ends:

To avoid the hole
the children must sing sweetly, softly

To avoid the hole
they must fill their songs with love[82]

Thinking of children in Brazil abandoned to microcephaly, children in Flint with lead poisoning, children in Cleveland and other U.S. cities murdered by "authoritative bodies," is it so difficult to imagine them singing full-throated, in a round, oblivious to their fate, enacting what Tejada calls "the sore repetition of a song"?[83] Finally, like the double meaning of "sentence," "the hole" is a figure of the existential void and slang for solitary confinement. In each, "the hole" is where the privatized self resides. In Borzutzky, the scant light there reveals the monstrous bodies we are becoming under capital's totalizing poetics.

URAYOÁN NOEL, THE NEOLIBERAL CITY'S DIGITAL TRANSCRIBE

Noel shares with Herrera and Borzutzky the imperative to articulate the lived experience of neoliberal globalization from within the violent hemispheric historical geographies in which individual bodies must make their lives. But Noel's poetry foregrounds consumer identities and the prominence of "the neoliberal city"[84] as the decentered center of his diasporic digital poetics. Like Borzutzky, Noel's poetry sets radiating north-south coordinates from which his expansive poetic geographies spin. Rather than Borzutzky's fabulist renderings of Chile and Chicago, Noel's San Juan and New York City proceed from various literary formations: Latin American vanguard, Nuyorican wordplay, hip-hop and punk performance, and digital procedures. Each poet's dialectical imaginary converges on the privatized body, the consuming body, the body consumed by data, and ultimately the body consuming itself. In *Hi-Density Politics*, Noel asks: "Can there be a body politics in the digital era?"[85] Then, later, he poses this urgent, though ludic, necessity: "What we need here / is a body / a poetics / a bo-po / found, gestated, or prosthetic."[86] Crucially, the origin of this embodied poetics cedes primacy to its necessity—it may be appropriated, birthed, or artificial, and it will be damaged, just so long as it works. That is, as long as this body can live and move with a degree of freedom, agency, and creativity.

Noel's first books of poems invent manic forms of public address for the privatized consumer body, who is simultaneously rapt and revolted by the capitalist marketplace. *Las Flores del Mall* riffs on Charles Baudelaire's *Fleurs du mal* from San Juan's gargantuan Plaza Las Americas shopping mall.[87] *Kool Logic/La Lógica Kool* pays mock homage to Fredric Jameson's "Cultural Logic of Late Capitalism," blissfully cataloging the linguistic abundance produced, in part, by the globalizing forces of capital.[88] In facing Spanish and English title poems, this abundance unfolds as visceral sound play: "la utopia es un río / que vomita capital." The English "version" ends with a mash-up of exclamations:

> NAFTA, Mercosur, Hamas!
> DVDs and open mikes!
> Watercress and motocross!
> SUVs and mountain bikes!
>
> Trailer parks! Gated communities!
> Highrise ghettoes and favelas!
> Acquired diplomatic immunities!
> Self-help prophets! Braille novellas![89]

Whereas in these collections the density of allusions and polysyllabic rhymes is leavened by Noel's lyric-absurdist mode, the density takes on a typographic thickness in *Hi-Density Politics* and his most recent collection, *Buzzing Hemisphere/Rumor Hemisférico*.[90] Part of this shift can be explained by Noel's increasing use of digital, Internet-based techniques and procedures.

Based on visual appearance, Noel's digital procedures have little in common with the constraints imposed by traditional fixed forms, such as terza rima, which structures "Hi Then (salutation)," the first poem in *Hi-Density Politics*. For Noel, however, conventional and digital procedures share a logic. Emily A. Maguire argues that "Noel weds formal experimentation to an exploration of the conditions of poetry's production."[91] In this sense, the décima, Oulipo, and the BlackBerry exist on a formal continuum, in which conditions of production are mediated by changing technological and material forms, from ink to printing press to Internet. Technology accelerates the commodification of literary forms, even as it offers an opening for forming what Maguire calls "dissonant community." Noel's numerous smartphone poems mediate between the body and the world, the device serving as the era's episteme and affect generator. In *Hi-Density Politics*, for instance, "babel o city (el gran concurso)" and "guánica" are composed of "minute-long voice notes on a BlackBerry."[92] No poet is so tethered to a device—notwithstanding the laptop—nor has a poet wrung so much creativity from what might be seen otherwise as a crutch, barrier, or limit to poetic activity.

Digital poetries, according to Damon, have much in common with diasporic poetries. In Noel, they converge with propulsive creative energies. The tendencies to "discursive thickness," "exhaustiveness," and "excess" are shared by Borzutzky and Noel, as is the "depressive mania we associate with the Internet [that also] inhabits a diasporic aesthetic: polyglot, haunted, rapid-fire, wrecked."[93] What Damon identifies as the paradoxically paired qualities of this digital-diasporic aesthetic—on one side "surfeit," on the other "insufficiency"[94]—are particularly useful for understanding the hemispheric dimensions of Latinx poetics. The dual hemispheres of *Buzzing Hemisphere* are multivalent: north/south, English/Spanish, right/left, acoustic/phonological (which the book's epigraph from Mutlu Konuk Blasing's study of the lyric outlines),[95] each of which is disoriented (or crossed) by the poet's epileptic seizures. The apparatus uniting these hemispheres, tentatively and antagonistically, is capitalism, the neoliberal city's muse. In this latter sense, Noel's praxis fulfills a promise of Damon's theory, incorporating "an ethical commitment to debris (spam), recursion (looping), and anonymous/mass/vernacular cultural ephemera."[96] Yet whereas Damon's model disavows "culturally or historically acknowledged grand moments, or the monuments and reified great poems that codify such moments" in deference to mass cultural forms,[97] Noel juxtaposes high and low, from "watercress and motocross" to radically reauthored versions of Mallarmé, Aimé Césaire, and Baudelaire, among other ludic monuments to capital P Poetry.

In contrast to Borzutzky, who eschews notes, Noel's thorough notes suggest his preference for borrowing, appropriation, and homage. Galvin identifies in contemporary North American poetry "the fashion of footnotes": "Endnotes are common currency in back margins of poetry books published today in North America. They archive and index their sources in a quasi-scholarly fashion, assiduously referencing their source documents."[98] For some poets, however, notes are less fashion than function; Martín Espada's notes are pedagogical, teaching the erased Latino, Latin American, and working-class histories that his poems dramatize. For the innovative poets Galvin addresses, "[l]iterary strategies such as footnoting and citation create relationality," with notes "mak[ing] visible the constraints that structure their poems, in a mode reminiscent of the Oulipian penchant for texts that thematize or otherwise lay bare their constraints."[99] In *Hi-Density Politics*, Noel places the notes prior to the poems, highlighting their constructedness, their materials, edges, and seams. These *forenotes* present the poems as collaborative scores for performance, little language plays to be reenacted by readers.

Whereas the notes in *Buzzing Hemisphere* are restored to their "proper" place, after the "text," in each collection notes employ the passive voice. Following convention, this usage underscores constraints. Yet it reminds us here that unlike most poets Noel is a first-rate scholar. Notes are essential, not marginal, to his texts. The passive voice also belies the energy of his "poetic activity," with its emphasis on active agency. *Hi-Density Politics*'s "trill set" highlights the dynamism of performative procedure. The poem, Noel explains,

> was composed by reciting the first 13 poems from César Vallejo's *Trilce* (1922) into Dragon Naturally Speaking™ speech recognition software. The program's English (mis)interpretations of the Spanish words were then arranged on the page in keeping with the layout of Vallejo's original. As a performance piece, it is scored for two voices, along with either Vallejo's original or Clayton Eshleman's translations.[100]

Part two of Vallejo's original begins:

> Tiempo Tiempo.
>
> Mediodía estancado entre relentes.
> Bomba aburrida del cuartel achica
> tiempo tiempo tiempo tiempo.
>
> Era Era.
>
> Gallos cancionan escarbando en vano.

Boca del claro día que conjuga
era era era era.[101]

Noel's (mis)translates as such:

Dimple Dimple

Mint UBS bank island to entice
bone bubble lead on what they let chic
dimple D. and both he and opium will

Data Data

Dido scans the owner is co-bundle in buying
oh and I will be ethical to
a data in data and data[102]

Borzutzky and Noel are terrific "straight" translators, but something else entirely is happening here. Unlike Borzutzky's borrowing of Vallejo's "blows," moreover, Noel's unruly, crude, and cacophonous mistranslations of Vallejo foreground misunderstandings. Both projects aim at the violent heart of north-south relations, which can be seen as a historical series of mistranslations and plunders. In this rewriting of Vallejo, the default language of "translation" between north and south, Spanish and English, *is* capital—the automatic (though programmed) language of banks (UBS), buying and selling, bubbles, owners, bundles, and data that the online translator "hears" in the source poem.

Whereas *Hi-Density Politics* focuses on these multilayered performances, *Buzzing Hemisphere* emphasizes the procedural. Notes explain how poems were "composed with the aid of an online N+7 generator"; "almost entirely composed with an anagram generator app for smartphone"; "collage[d] [from] Internet search engine results (as in Flarf poetry)"; "performed by reading the Spanish original into a smartphone with voice recognition set to English"; "generated with a random-word generator app for smartphone and then (mis)translated using Google Translate"; and "produced by online buzzword and job-title generators."[103] These notes might map for some readers an uninviting terrain. On the contrary, Noel's poems reward patience (and bilingualism) with playful, incisive moments and an overarching virtuosity that disavows art for art's sake aloofness.

For example, "Deshoraciones"/"Sentiences" recalls *Hi-Density Politics*'s "try city®," with its "terse sets"/tercets of 333 three-word poems. The dateline informs us that they were composed at 2:22 a.m., "between cities," of 222 numbered utterances. (Both recall de la Torre's 1:1 scale.) Some utterances are "complete" sentences, others fragments, though each ends with a period, comprising a self-contained unit of language. A resonant block in the English version meditates on the solitary nature of writing:

> **21.** Today the voice has been bled dry. **22.** You write a poem. **23.** Mostly indented. **24.** Unintended elisions. **25.** Dented sentences. **26.** You think you're the poet unprecedented. **27.** Sincere in your promised city of morrow. **28.** You catalog sorrows of hemispheres. **29.** The bloggers of your ancient captivity. **30.** Surviving unconnected. **31.** In solitary refinement. **32.** Convertible and seeking capital. **33.** In other words sponsorship. **34.** In other words home. **35.** The precipice runs its course. **36.** The fever remains.[104]

This visually dense typography parodies the stylings of Language poets such as Ron Silliman. Its linear quantification of language, moreover, lays bare the poem's construction, perhaps providing an accounting (pun intended) of neoliberalism's financialization of life, the technocratic objectification, classification, and economization of experience. Noel's poem is a site for numbers as much as letters, begging the question: Has the basic unit of literary production been transformed by neoliberalism? Rather than sentences, "sentiences" are approximate affective syntaxes that orient the self in the world of streaming sense data. Just as the unit of society has changed—it is not the individual, but the numeral, the data point, that takes precedence for capital—so too the corresponding form of literary inquiry. It is remarkable that Noel finds some space to maneuver within these constraints, showing the way forward if not the way out of the neoliberal bind, where each (non-) citizen inhabits her own portable quarantine.

This chapter has shown how Latinx poets use series and procedures. Mónica de la Torre, Juan Felipe Herrera, Daniel Borzutzky, and Urayoán Noel offer materialist critiques of neoliberalism, with representations of the body creating under constraints, pressures, "blows." To conclude, I pose some questions about the stakes in, and the success of, the "quarantine citizen" who inhabits the constricted spaces of this materialist poetics. A short reading of "Signs of the Hemisphere"/"Letreros del hemisferio," in *Buzzing Hemisphere*, shows Noel generating another mode by which the "quarantine citizen" moves through increasingly corporatized enclosures, as in his "solitary refinement" and Borzutzky's "holes" of solitary confinement. "Signs of the Hemisphere" records the signs that saturate our necropastoral landscapes, transcribing them from two bus trips—from New York City to Albany in 2011, and from Rio de Janeiro to São Paulo in 2009. A common figure in Latinx poetics, in Noel the bus serves as a mobile enclosure for critiquing the constrictions of neoliberal freedom. The poem toggles between signs in English and Portuguese and unpunctuated verse in Spanish and English. The visual effect is painterly (or *coderly*), a canvas of textual signs coded for quick scanning, despite their density:

> *MANOR HOUSE CITIBANK BERGEN JAGUAR APPLEBEE'S NAIL AND SPA ESTHETICS ETOPIA DESKS BACKPACKING EASTERN MOUNTAIN SPORTS LA CUTINA HILLSDALE U-TURN SADDLE RIVER SPEED LIMIT 55 RACETRACK ROAD PUMPKINS FOR SALE SPLIT FIREWOOD COTTAGE GARDENS NO STOPPAGE OR STANDING AIRPORT SHUTTLE CURVE HOLLYWOOD AVENUE ALL TURNS HO-HO-KUS LITTER REMOVAL DECORATIONS FABRIC OUTLET LIGHTING BY GREGORY BOTTLE KING*[105]

When spread across an unfolding *interstatescape* such signs may assume a comfortable because intermittent place in one's visual field. But when clustered in this manner, they take on a perverse abundance, an absurdity, a senselessness, and, most of all, an incommensurability—between Jaguars and firewood, Citibank and pumpkins, a radical asymmetry echoes. For some, the bus; for others, the luxury car. For some, all turns are permitted, for others, a roadside produce stand will have to do.

Another poet might, on the bus trip from New York to Albany, write of the Hudson Valley, the wide river, rolling hills, apple orchards, or even gentrifying towns, but that poet would miss how nature is perceived by the "data body" *as* data. These signs now point nowhere but to themselves *as* data. In a verse section of the poem, Noel writes, "I'm missing the tongues of the tribe so I transcribe," and "meaning is notation."[106] What end does transcription serve? Does the labor in such seemingly indiscriminate observation replace the collective "tongues of the tribe"? Does the poet, who cannot speak for "the tribe," speak for and through capital, *the* tongue of the world's tribes?

Damon might view Noel's process as "encyclopedic salvaging."[107] Boon might deem it "an art of permutation and combination that plays at arranging the same in multiple ways."[108] Maguire argues that Noel "advocates poetry as 'scrawl'—rough, instinctive, in movement—rather than as static or choreographed production."[109] Here his poem mimics instead a *crawl*, slowing the bus to the news "crawl" at the bottom of a television screen or the "crawl" of ads and news on the Times Square ticker. Each has validity as aesthetic description, emphasizing how Latinx poetic activity salvages and recombines received material forms.

Yet Noel's transcriptions raise comprehensive questions about citizenship discourses, in the United States and across the hemisphere. His poem models a form of cultural citizenship valuing close attention, a way of reading the passing world, in at least three languages, finding across languages and north-south geographies what is shared and incommensurate. In such semantically dense and confusing spaces, what constitutes citizenship, beyond juridical forms? At their core, literary techniques such as procedures bring to the fore the relationships among origin, function, and form. The Latinx poetics analyzed here may refuse conclusive statements, avoiding easily consumable clarity in an age of geopolitical ambiguity. But this materialist poetics successfully lays bare the unforgiving logic of capital, even as the use of serial and procedural forms showcase how this very logic—of accumulation and abundance, in particular—serves as a fertile resource for a poetic activity that confronts neoliberal logic and outcomes. For these poets, origin (hence originality, purity) give way to the messier entanglements of trajectory and relation, which are both humble and ambitious, copied and copious. When citizenship forms are quarantined, shunted off from the things, ideas, places, and persons that could enter and change them, what and who are allowed into poems and nations will be dramatically narrowed. In contrast, the "body poetics" that Noel names and that Borzutzky implicitly seeks is multiscale, from the individual to the globe, and thus shot through with proliferating apertures, entry points, and crumbling walls. Where one comes from cedes primacy to the poetic activity of becoming, of inhabiting a body that resists the "blows" of capital's henchmen. This Latinx poetics carries a "diasporous" body politic, a polis, from which citizens of the hemisphere might emerge from their private quarantines.

Notes

1. Mónica de la Torre, *Public Domain* (New York: Roof Books, 2008).

2. Jeff Derksen, *Annihilated Time: Poetry and Other Politics* (Vancouver: Talonbooks, 2009).

3. de la Torre, *Public Domain*, 77.
4. de la Torre, *Public Domain*, 79.
5. de la Torre, *Public Domain*, 80.
6. de la Torre, *Public Domain*, 78.
7. de la Torre, *Public Domain*, 80.
8. de la Torre, *Public Domain*, 77.
9. de la Torre, *Public Domain*, 80.
10. de la Torre, *Public Domain*, 80.
11. Rachel Galvin, "Poetry Is Theft," *Comparative Literature Studies* 51.1 (2014): 41.
12. Christopher Nealon, *The Matter of Capital: Poetry and Crisis in the American Century* (Cambridge: Harvard University Press, 2011).
13. de la Torre, *Public Domain*, 78.
14. Maria Damon, *Postliterary America: From Bagel Shop Jazz to Micropoetries* (Iowa City: University of Iowa Press, 2011), 155.
15. Damon, *Postliterary America*, 206.
16. Nealon, *Matter of Capital*, 30.
17. Urayoán Noel, *Hi-Density Politics* (Buffalo: BlazeVOX, 2010), 46.
18. Derksen, *Annihilated Time*, 99.
19. Damon, *Postliterary America*, 214–16.
20. Édouard Glissant, *Poetics of Relation*, trans. Betsy Wing (Ann Arbor: University of Michigan Press, 1997), 115, 21.
21. Noel, *Hi-Density Politics*, 45–46.
22. Noel, *Hi-Density Politics*, 46.
23. Noel, *Hi-Density Politics*, 63; Urayoán Noel, *In Visible Movement: Nuyorican Poetry from the Sixties to Slam* (Iowa City: University of Iowa Press, 2014), 154–55. "Data bodies" appear across Borzutzky's collections.
24. William Anthony Nericcio, *Tex{t}-Mex: Seductive Hallucinations of the "Mexican" in America* (Austin: University of Texas Press, 2007), 123.
25. Not coincidentally, the "antidialecticism" Nealon traces in U.S. poetry has origins in Jacques Derrida's reading of Stéphane Mallarmé's poem (*Matter of Capital*, 14–15). Nealon relates this antidialecticism to the prohibition against totalizing critiques and thus to literary critiques of capitalism (*Matter of Capital*, 10).
26. Timothy Yu, *Race and the Avant-Garde: Experimental and Asian American Poetry since 1965* (Stanford: Stanford University Press, 2010), 50.
27. In *The Transformation* (Berkeley: Atelos, 2007), the poet-critic Juliana Spahr summarizes this dynamic (78).
28. Derksen, *Annihilated Time*, 97.
29. Galvin, "Poetry Is Theft," 26–27.
30. Galvin, "Poetry Is Theft," 20.
31. Galvin, "Poetry Is Theft," 22.
32. Juan Felipe Herrera, *Lotería Cards and Fortune Poems: A Book of Lives*, linocuts by Artemio Rodríguez (San Francisco: City Lights, 1999).

33. Rupert García, "The New within Tradition," introduction to *Lotería Cards*, by Juan Felipe Herrera (San Francisco: City Lights, 1999), x, xvii.

34. Catherine E. Wall, "Review of *Lotería Cards*, by Juan Felipe Herrera," *World Literature Today* 75.1 (2001): 120.

35. Rodrigo Toscano's absurdist fables, *Deck of Deeds* (Denver: Counterpath, 2012), loosely uses *lotería*. See Gallego, chapter 6, this volume.

36. Marcus Boon, *In Praise of Copying* (Cambridge: Harvard University Press, 2010).

37. Boon, *In Praise*, 72–73.

38. Boon, *In Praise*, 73.

39. Elena Jackson Albarrán, "Guerrilla Warplay: The Infantilization of War in Latin American Popular Culture," *Studies in Latin American Popular Culture* 24 (2005): 70.

40. Albarrán, "Guerrilla Warplay," 76.

41. García, "The New within Tradition," xix.

42. Herrera, *Lotería Cards*, 34.

43. Wall, "Review of *Lotería Cards*," 120.

44. Herrera, *Lotería Cards*, 34.

45. Nealon, *Matter of Capital*, 3.

46. Daniel Borzutzky, *The Performance of Becoming Human* (Brooklyn: Brooklyn Arts Press, 2016), 51, 52.

47. Daniel Borzutzky, *The Book of Interfering Bodies* (Callicoon, NY: Nightboat Books, 2011).

48. Authorized by President George W. Bush and the U.S. Congress, *The 9/11 Commission Report: Final Report of the National Commission on Terrorist Attacks Upon the United States* was published in 2004.

49. Borzutzky, *Book*, 49.

50. Daniel Borzutzky, *In the Murmurs of the Rotten Carcass Economy* (Callicoon, NY: Nightboat Books, 2015).

51. Borzutzky, *Book*, 28–29.

52. Borzutzky, *Performance*, 88.

53. Borzutzky, *Murmurs*, 32, 79.

54. Borzutzky, *Murmurs*, 16.

55. Borzutzky, *Performance*, 53.

56. Nealon, *Matter of Capital*, 31.

57. Borzutzky, *Murmurs*, 125.

58. Joyelle McSweeney, *The Necropastoral: Poetry, Media, Occults* (Ann Arbor: University of Michigan Press, 2015).

59. McSweeney, *Necropastoral*, 3.

60. McSweeney, *Necropastoral*, 19.

61. McSweeney, *Necropastoral*, 3.

62. Borzutzky, *Performance*, 58.

63. Borzutzky, *Performance*, 59.

64. Nericcio, *Tex{t}-Mex*, 123.

65. Borzutzky, *Performance*, 60.

66. César Vallejo, *The Complete Poetry: A Bilingual Edition*, trans. Clayton Eshleman (Berkeley: University of California Press, 2007), 25.

67. Michel Foucault, *Discipline and Punish: The Birth of the Prison*, trans. Alan Sheridan (New York: Vintage, 1995), 293.

68. Borzutzky, *Performance*, 11.

69. Borzutzky, *Performance*, 84.

70. Borzutzky, *Murmurs*, 15.

71. Published as this volume went to press, Borzutzky's *Lake Michigan* (Pittsburgh: University of Pittsburgh Press, 2018) extends this distillation of his singular "book."

72. Damon, *Postliterary America*, 219.

73. Borzutzky, *Performance*, 16.

74. Roberto Tejada, *Full Foreground* (Tucson: University of Arizona Press, 2012), 1.

75. Borzutzky, *Murmurs*, 40–41.

76. Nericcio, *Tex{t}-Mex*, 123.

77. Borzutzky, *Performance*, 88.

78. Borzutzky, *Performance*, 88.

79. Borzutzky, *Performance*, 52.

80. Borzutzky, *Performance*, 56.

81. Borzutzky, *Performance*, 85.

82. Borzutzky, *Performance*, 31, italics in original.

83 Tejada, *Full Foreground*, 59.

84. Taken from Arlene Dávila's *Barrio Dreams: Puerto Ricans, Latinos, and the Neoliberal City* (Berkeley: University of California Press, 2004), "the neoliberal city" structures Noel's poetry and criticism.

85. Noel, *Hi-Density Politics*, 29.

86. Noel, *Hi-Density Politics*, 63.

87. Urayoán Noel, *Las Flores del Mall* (Brooklyn: Ediciones Alamala, 2000).

88. Urayoán Noel, *Kool Logic/La Lógica Kool* (Tempe, AZ: Bilingual Press, 2005).

89. Noel, *Kool Logic*, 56.

90. Urayoán Noel, *Buzzing Hemisphere/Rumor Hemisférico* (Tucson: University of Arizona Press, 2015).

91. Emily A. Maguire, "'The Shuffle of the City Finally Becomes Us': The Corporality of Place in the Poetry of Urayoán Noel," *ASAP/Journal* 2.1 (2017): 172.

92. Noel, *Hi-Density Politics*, 6.

93. Damon, *Postliterary America*, 206–8.

94. Damon, *Postliterary America*, 207.

95. Mutlu Konuk Blasing, *Lyric Poetry: The Pain and the Pleasure of Words* (Princeton: Princeton University Press, 2007).

96. Damon, *Postliterary America*, 209.

97. Damon, *Postliterary America,* 209.
98. Galvin, "Poetry Is Theft," 33.
99. Galvin, "Poetry Is Theft," 32, 34.
100. Noel, *Hi-Density Politics,* 6.
101. Vallejo, *Complete Poetry,* 168.
102. Noel, *Hi-Density Politics,* 70.
103. Noel, *Buzzing Hemisphere,* 105–6.
104. Noel, *Buzzing Hemisphere,* 51.
105. Noel, *Buzzing Hemisphere,* 97.
106. Noel, *Buzzing Hemisphere,* 95.
107. Damon, *Postliterary America,* 207.
108. Boon, *In Praise of Copying,* 66.
109. Maguire, "'Shuffle of the City Finally Becomes Us,'" 166.

CHAPTER 4

Historical Materialism, The Decolonial Imaginary, *and Chicana Feminist Theories in the Flesh*

Marcelle Maese

In this chapter, I shall provide a long-overdue overview of the engagement between Chicana feminism and historical materialism, focusing particularly on the relation between historiography and literary criticism. The foundational feminist work, *This Bridge Called My Back: Writings by Radical Women of Color,* stands somewhat outside of, but in absolute relation to, these disciplines. In the 1981 preface to *This Bridge,* Cherríe Moraga coins the term "theory in the flesh" as a way of referencing the troubled but undeniable relation between radical women of color politics and a materialist analysis for revolution—and a way of bridging the two.

> Literally, for two years now, I have dreamed of a bridge. In writing this conclusion, I fight the myriad voices that live inside me. The voices that stop my pen at every turn of the page. They are the voices that tell me here I should be talking more "materialistically" about the oppression of women of color, that I should be plotting out a "strategy" for Third World Revolution. But what I really want to write about is faith. That without faith, I'd dare not expose myself to the potential betrayal, rejection, and failure that lives throughout the first and last gesture of connection.[1]

The problematic that Moraga names—the desire to write about faith while hearing the call for a materialist strategy—is the contradiction that I see at the heart of Chicana theories in the flesh. While foundational works of Chicana/o historiography and literary criticism engage in Marxism through different avenues, with the former debating internal colonialism and the latter engaging with dialectical criticism, *theories in flesh* contend with how each of these disciplines and different Marxist priorities relate with the sacred or nonsecular.[2] Various Chicana theorists of the flesh have articulated this problematic and have strategized (non)resolutions in different ways. While a full survey of their work is beyond the scope of this chapter, I want to emphasize the importance of writing an intellectual history that can articulate the interrelated (sometimes antagonistic, other times parallel, often times complementary) relationship between the frameworks of internal colonialism, dialectical criticism, historical materialism, and nonsecular forms of knowledge. In particular, I center indigeneity as I consider the relation between historical materialism and the nonsecular within Chicana/o studies, and I examine the unresolved tension between internal colonialism and the reclamation of indigeneity as a means for decolonization. Further, I hope to show how these interrelated frameworks reveal differences *within* Chicana feminist praxis.

While "theory in the flesh" was coined by Moraga in *This Bridge*, I emphasize the pluralistic "s" in *theories* of the flesh in order to emphasize the significant differences and productive tensions within Chicana feminisms. Because Cherríe Moraga and Gloria Anzaldúa were coeditors of *This Bridge*, their work is often conflated. I therefore use the metahistorical methodology outlined by Emma Pérez's *The Decolonial Imaginary: Writing Chicanas into History* (1999) to highlight important differences between Moraga and Anzaldúa, and to write *The Decolonial Imaginary* into a history of Chicana feminist materialisms. By revisiting *This Bridge* through the optics of *The Decolonial Imaginary*, I articulate the difference between Anzaldúa as "alchemist" and Moraga as "welder," motifs that narrate a very different yet shared investment in nonsecular forms of praxis in relation to socialist feminist class analysis. My goal is not only to recover the unresolved engagement with indigeneity and class struggle that characterizes Chicana/o studies, but also to rehear some of the different ways Chicanas have *spoken to each other* about economic and corporeal materialisms.

"ENTERING THE LIVES OF OTHERS": *THIS BRIDGE'S* TOTAL VISION OR SOUL WORK

In her 1981 preface to *This Bridge* (entitled "La Jornada" in the 2015 edition of the book), Moraga stresses the importance of documenting the various material contexts that make the publication of *This Bridge* not only possible but in high demand.

Remarking on the speed with which the project came together, she explains that the current analytics of revolution available to her—leftism, lesbianism, and feminism—need a sustained study of women of color thought as much as she does. She explains that neither the left, "with its shaky and shabby record of commitment to women," or lesbian separatism can offer her a revolutionary praxis that addresses the material and epistemic violence she witnesses on a daily basis.[3] Moraga locates what is missing by comparing what it's like to be in her body—a light-skinned Chicana that can pass for white while visiting Harvard—and in the body of a "14-year old Black boy [who] was shot in the head by a white cop." She writes, "I board a bus and ride it quietly in my light flesh to Harvard Square, protected by the gold highlights my hair dares take on, like an insult, in this miserable heat."[4] In contrast to the quiet ride to Harvard, the T-Line train abruptly stops on the ride to Black Roxbury, long enough for a "white man in jeans" to "throw a Black kid up against the door" and carry him away. Using the lived body as a conduit for analyzing the connection between different forms of violence, Moraga writes,

> I hear there are some women in this town plotting a *lesbian* revolution. What does this mean about the boy shot in the head is what I want to know. I am a lesbian. I want a movement that helps me make some sense of the trip from Watertown to Roxbury, from white to black. I love women the entire way, beyond a doubt.[5]

From the perspective of *lesbiana* desire, Moraga rewrites the civil rights scene of Black-white violence set in the context of public transportation. Like the "lesbian separatist utopia" that she refuses, this public scene of protest is not enough for her either. Her desire to travel between Black and white reaches beyond the academic politics of publishing and the geography of segregation. Instead, her desire for revolutionary praxis rooted in a radical "love of women" is consummated when she reaches the home of her dear friend and *colega* Barbara Smith. We learn that at the end of this particular *jornada* (or work shift), her real destination is not Roxbury but Barbara's kiss.

> By the end of the evening of our first evening together Barbara comes into the front room where she has made a bed for me. She kisses me. Then grabbing my shoulders, she says, very solid-like, "We're sisters." I nod, put myself into bed, and roll around with this word—"sisters"—for two hours before sleep takes on. I earned this with Barbara. It is not a given between us—Chicana and Black—to come to see each other as sisters.[6]

And so commences a love affair in *This Bridge* between radical women of color, a sisterhood that is not given but forged within struggle and reestablished in the intimacy of a solid embrace. In contrast to the shame and silent anger on the T-Line where the protection of light hair and skin feels like an insult, Moraga is no longer alienated from her body or alone in the work of antiracism. Instead, she has Barbara "in the flesh" who gives her a bed to sleep in, and the word "sisters" as an agitating lullaby and bedtime companion.

For many of us, Barbara Smith needs no introduction. However, it is worth noting the method that Moraga uses for introducing the sustained engagement of *This Bridge* with socialist feminists of color—she personalizes the exchange of ideas through the various relationships she has with the writers she studies. Moraga's *jornada* implicitly connects the socialist feminisms of the Combahee Collective in Boston to Rosario Morales's Boricua experiences with the Communist Party and the Chicago Women's Liberation Union.[7] Moraga writes in her preface that she would lose hope if she "believed, as Rosario Morales refutes, [that] we were unilaterally defined by class and color." Thus, we are forced to turn to the printed word in the anthology to better comprehend the layered dialogues these women enact as they speak to each other and to the particular movements for liberation of which they are a part. But when we turn to read Morales's analysis of class and capitalist patriarchy in "We're All in the Same Boat" or Combahee's "A Black Feminist Statement," we understand the ways these words on the page embody lived relations between women. A close reading of *This Bridge* reveals the care with which each contributor has read one another's work, and how the same care is taken when articulating disagreements. If the analytics of class is lost to the casual reader, it might be because these women do not prioritize being recognized as Marxists, or as legitimizing the sources of their knowledge through bibliographies. That work is also important, but to be done elsewhere. For example, one of the earliest versions of chapter 3 of *The Decolonial Imaginary* appears in *Between Borders: Essays on Mexicana/Chicana History* (1990), a collection of essays that includes a debate on the relationship between Marxism and a transnational Chicana/o studies methodology. While I will provide an analysis of this debate in a later section of this chapter, for now it is important to note how Pérez's theory in the flesh is contemporaneous with *This Bridge* and operates through an explicit revision of Marxist categories. By contrast, the authors of *This Bridge* claim complete autonomy as wordsmiths in search of vocabularies that can better articulate their lived strategies of community-making and resistance, a strategy that provides an equally viable expansion of our understanding of the relation between class, social totality, *and* emotional labor.

Of course, within the various traditions of socialist feminism that contextualize the particular historical moment of *This Bridge*, the analysis of the coproduced rather than causal relation between material and ideal is explored from a Marxist conception of ideology. More specifically, *This Bridge* and *Between Borders* are written at a time when socialist feminisms are debating the relevant of Louis Althusser's highly influential theory of ideology in relation to Michel Foucault's nondialectical study of power. Unlike *Between Borders*, however, the politics of citation in *This Bridge* for the most part engage with this debate by way of conversation between the authors in ways that address the specific needs of feminisms of color. This is the *radical* nature of their collection, or as Moraga and Anzaldúa clarify, "We use this term in its original form—stemming from the word 'root'—for our feminist politic emerges from the roots of our cultural oppression and heritage."[8] Moraga and Anzaldúa define *radical* differently than their white counterparts. Moreover, because cultural specificity is part of the way *This Bridge* expands a U.S.-based socialist feminism, I claim that in contrast to contemporaneous debates at the time of their writing, for the women of *This Bridge*, the nature of the relation between the material and nonmaterial, between dialectical and nondialectical, must include the roles of emotional labor and the nonsecular.

As preface to *This Bridge*, "La Jornada" operates by way of collective wisdom, a mining of conversations—public and private—that inform Moraga's method for systemic analysis and communal action. In contrast to her analysis of the social totality of racism, heterosexism, and class exploitation, Moraga cannot easily place faith within a materialist tradition. "La Jornada" concludes with an elucidation of this contradiction as stated in the passage quoted at the start of this chapter in which it problematizes the need to address matters "materialistically" while really wanting to write about "faith." Having already enlisted an incredible cohort of women—Barbara Smith, Rosario Morales, Adrienne Rich, Gloria Anzaldúa, and Audre Lorde—when Moraga reaches her most difficult theoretical threshold—how to link the nonsecular with materialist strategy—she makes an unexpected turn away from published authors and toward the personal writings of her mother, a figure with whom she has literally shared a body. That experience of sharing a body in the flesh with her mother "cannot be shaken from the ground she walks on."[9] Far away from home, her mother sends her a holy card and a note: "I am sending you this prayer of St. Anthony. Pray to God to help you with this book." In response, Moraga states, "a cry came up from inside me that I had been sitting on for months, cleaning me out—a faith healer."[10] Prayers to San Antonio, the saint of lost things, and *el santo del amor* address the search for a boyfriend or husband, and the problems of a difficult romance. And if he is not answering your prayer, popular Mexican Catholicism advises to *ponlo de cabeza*, turn him upside down. Faith healing, the release of a deep-seated cry, a mother's note—but how can these intimate sources of knowledge expand a materialist strategy for revolution?

In the "Afterword to the Second German Edition" of *Capital*, Marx distinguished his materialistic dialectics from Hegel's idealism by stating that, for Hegel, the world is the formal expression of ideas, but for Marx the exact opposite is true insofar as the "ideal is nothing else than the material world reflected by the human mind, and translated into forms of thought."[11] With Hegel, the dialectic is standing on its head, incapable of understanding the world as it really is and therefore unable to change it. But for us to change the world, to revolutionize it rather than simply philosophize it, we must locate the site of historical transformation within the struggle between classes, not strictly in the realm of ideas. In other words, we must turn the dialectic right side up again, so as to "discover the rational kernel within the mystical shell."[12]

For Moraga, a radical women of color politics must make room for nonantagonistic ways of knowing and changing the world. Hence, to change the world one must be loving, and political love, like desire, exacerbates the antithetical relation between idealism and materialism. In a way, what her mother advises regarding materialist strategy is *ponlo de cabeza*, and to really invert Marx's materialist dialectics would not be simply to return the dialectic to Hegel's position. It would be to move out of the antagonism between the rational and the mystical, or the material and nonmaterial. For Moraga, this means the faith of activists, or a materialist nonsecularity that complicates the mind-body split enacted by the opposition between idealism and materialism. Her mother confirms this point when, through an act of writing, she teaches Moraga that prayer can help her finish the book and hence find the love between radical queer women of color she seeks. For Moraga, the movement from mother's prayer to theory is but one example of the mutually empowering relation between nonsecular, emotional labor and materialist praxis.

While a study of the trajectory of Moraga's work shows a revision of her spiritual practices—practices that begin as we see with her mother's Saint Anthony and subsequently shift to indigenous forms of praxis—she doesn't prescribe the same avenue for those who claim a radical women of color politics. Instead, she opens up a materialist strategy to include the practices of woman's survival and the intimacy that accompanies them—Barbara's kiss, a mother's prayer—as different forms of faith that "believe that we have the power to actually transform our experiences, change our lives, save our lives." In this way, Moraga begins to define what she means by a theory in the flesh as a "total vision" that will not settle "for less than freedom even in the most private aspects of our lives."[13]

> The materialism in this book lives in the flesh of these women's lives. . . . Our strategy is how we cope. . . .[14] We are a family who first only knew each other in our dreams, who have come together on these pages to make faith a reality and to bring all of our selves to bear down on that reality.[15]

Again, given the insistence on the *radical* nature of writing that requires being rooted in cultural specificity, it is easy to miss the direct links that *This Bridge* makes to non-women-of-color Marxist feminisms.

Consider the fact that the title Moraga gives to part 2 of *This Bridge*, "Entering the Lives of Others: Theory in the Flesh," is in part taken from the work of Emma Goldman. This is significant because it is in part 2, both in the introduction and the essay that follows, "La Güera," that Moraga most directly defines theory in the flesh. In the introduction to this section, she states that

> [a] theory in the flesh means one where the physical realities of our lives—our skin color, the land or concrete we grew up on, our sexual longings—all fuse to create a politic born of necessity. Here, we attempt to bridge the contradictions in our experience. . . . We do this bridging by naming ourselves and by telling ourselves in our own words.[16]

Following the introduction, Moraga specifies in "La Guëra" how theory in the flesh provides both a coherent community of radical women of color politics—one that demands material transformation in terms of racial politics (skin color), sovereignty (land), and desire (sexual longing)—*and* maintains important historical and cultural distinctions across and within communities. The difference between Moraga's "La Güera" and Anzaldúa's "La Prieta" is a case in point that I will return to in the next section.

Whereas in "La Jornada" Moraga turns to her mother when she reaches a theoretical impasse produced by a perceived incompatibility between faith and materialism, in "La Güera" Moraga makes a similarly unexpected move by stepping outside a contemporary context of socialist feminisms of color and reaching toward the anarchism of Emma Goldman. What might seem like a detour is instead evidence of Moraga's deep commitment to studying various traditions of materialist feminisms—nonsecular, anarchist, academic, popular, and canonical. I find it significant that for an anthology uninterested in composing a Marxist bibliography, Moraga carefully cites "Was My Life Worth Living?," which appeared in *Red Emma Speaks: An Emma Goldman Reader*, published in 1972. Goldman is neither a typical feminist nor a typical Marxist, as her anarchist philosophy of free love and free motherhood was as critical of the Russian Revolution as it was of the U.S. women's suffrage movement. Deported from the United States under the 1918 Alien Exclusion Act for her outspoken lectures on communism and sexuality, Goldman soon left Russia because she could not support what she described as "Bolshevik Tyranny" and wrote that "the triumph of the State means the defeat of the Revolution."[17] It is easy to see how Goldman's lifelong critique of the nation-state as the government apparatus par excellence appeals to Chicana feminism considering that our critique of the borderlands moves beyond the politics of U.S.-Mexican history and indicts the global logic of border epistemology as inherently violent and colonizing. But perhaps not as obvious for those who are familiar with Goldman's relentless critique of all forms of what Althusser would later name the ideological state apparatuses—church, family, police, marriage—is her insistence on the relation between a humanizing freedom and the soul. In "The Tragedy of Woman's Emancipation," Goldman states, "the right to vote, or equal civil rights, may be good demands, but true emancipation begins neither at the polls nor in courts. It begins in the soul." In addition to her critique of the bourgeois and moralist nature of the suffragist movement, Goldman insists that "the most vital right is the right to love and be loved."[18]

Turning to the essay that Moraga directly quotes in her title for part 2 of *This Bridge* as well as in her essay "La Güera," we see that Goldman specifies how soul and faith are related to a praxis of love or "entering the lives of others." Similar to the way that Moraga is alienated from a lesbian separatist movement that ignores police violence against men of color, Goldman describes how the Haymarket Massacre and the hanging of anarchists that followed "left an indelible mark on my mind and heart and set me forth to acquaint myself with the ideal for which these men had died."[19] In response to both the police repression of the labor union activism at Haymarket Square and the Red Scare that followed, Goldman's essay "Was My Life Worth Living?" theorizes the roles of personal experience and witnessing for an anarchist philosophy of freedom. She explains:

> It requires something more than personal experience to gain a philosophy or point of view from any specific event. It is the quality of our response to the event and our capacity to enter the lives of others that helps us to make their lives and experiences our own. In my own case my convictions have derived from events in the lives of others as well as from my own experience. What I have seen meted out to others by authority and repression, economic and political, transcends anything I myself have endured.[20]

"The quality of response" that enables coalitional politics no doubt includes studying the philosophies of liberation that others practice. For this reason, Goldman does not only feel sorry for the Haymarket activists that were executed but, more importantly, she studies the ideals for which they were murdered. She clarifies that an anarchist philosophy is based on the belief in freedom, and that the "belief in freedom assumes that human beings can co-operate."[21] By way of conclusion, Goldman names the unrealized potential of human freedom via the "soul" in a manner that resonates with what Moraga names "the faith of activists."

> As in the past so I do now insist that freedom is the soul of progress and essential to every phase of life. . . . My faith is in the individual and in the capacity of free individuals for united endeavor.[22]

To me, *This Bridge*'s insistence on a "total vision" or a "theory in the flesh" that reclaims "intimacy" and "a desire for freedom for life between all of us, not settling for less than freedom in the most private aspects of our lives"[23] very clearly echoes Goldman's anarchist freedom whereby the "right to love and be loved" ensures a critical self-reflection that moves beyond state-sanctioned concepts of liberation. Following the publication of *This Bridge*, however, while Anzaldúa and Moraga continued to pursue a politics of soul work, they parted ways in terms of organizing a "united endeavor." While Moraga's indigenizing materialist feminism attempted to theorize an unresolved antagonism between class, race, and nation, Anzaldúa's conception of the new tribalism envisioned a resolution.

LA PRIETA Y LA GÜERA: EL MUNDO ZURDO AND THE SALT THAT CURES

In the first four sections of *This Bridge*, Moraga edits the chapters so as to bridge the earlier work of Emma Goldman with contemporaneous forms of socialist feminisms of color. By contrast, the last two sections of *This Bridge*, edited by Anzaldúa, interface a different engagement with materialist feminisms. While Moraga is preoccupied with how to write about a materialist faith, Anzaldúa's class anxiety reveals itself through a questioning of the ability to write altogether. "*Who am I, a poor Chicanita from the sticks to think I could write?* How dare I even consider becoming a writer as I stooped over the tomato fields."[24] While Moraga turns to her faith in activism in order to complete the writing of "La Jornada," Anzaldúa, in "A Letter to Third World Women," locates faith in the writing itself: "The act of writing is the act of making soul, alchemy."[25] While Moraga only implicitly writes of soul work by way of Goldman's praxis of "entering into the lives of others," Anzaldúa directly claims a women of color *spirituality* and aligns *This Bridge*'s racial and spiritual politics.

> We, the women here, take a trip back into the self, travel to the deep core of our roots to discover and reclaim our colored souls, our rituals, our religion. We reach a spirituality that has been hidden in the hearts of oppressed people under layers of centuries of traditional god-worship.[26]

Whereas Moraga's "theory in the flesh" highlights the difficult relation between faith and materialist critique, Anzaldúa theorizes the ways in which the writing by women of color empowers forms of soul making that cohere around a queer mode of relationality that she calls "El Mundo Zurdo," or The Left-handed World. "From our blood and spirit connection with" the "*colored, the queer, the poor, the female, and the physically challenged*," we "women on the bottom throughout the world can form an international feminism."[27] Because El Mundo Zurdo operates as home to an international feminism that empowers difference, Anzaldúa anticipates that not everyone will view the relation between soul making, race, politics, and writing in the same way because change "requires both the alchemist and the welder, the magician and the laborer. . . . Hand in Hand, we brew and forge a revolution."[28] She resignifies Moraga's "faith" in terms of the magic of alchemy and refers to "materialist strategy" in terms of the welder who labors.

While in "La Güera" Moraga implicitly recalls the anarchistic free love of Goldman, Anzaldúa's "La Prieta" further specifies how El Mundo Zurdo houses a leftist mode of relationality that encompasses the various forms of material and (non)material critique. Like Moraga's "theory in the flesh," Anzaldúa's analytics of structural oppression is expressed through "entering the lives of others" that prioritizes the body as a medium for historicizing colorism within communities of color and as an indexical site for the exploitation of emotional and physical labor. Thus, while Moraga is anxious about being light skinned, Anzaldúa resents being told to be weary of the sun because she will be mistaken for an *india*. Moreover, Anzaldúa recounts her work in the cotton fields alongside the "life-blood" being sucked out of her through her "role as woman nurturer—the last form of cannibalism."[29] Finally, while Moraga unearths an archive of socialists of color and anarchism, Anzaldúa's engagement with a tradition of Marxist feminisms operates through a different citation practice that is largely self-referential. She refers to herself as a "*third world lesbian feminist with Marxist and mystic leanings*."[30]

While tasked with the project of planetary change, Anzaldúa's alternative community or "network of kindred spirits"[31] makes room for difference because "some of us are leftists, some of us practitioners of magic. Some of us are both." Moreover, Moraga concretely identifies her position within

El Mundo Zurdo as someone who is not both. In the poem "The Welder" Moraga writes,

> I am a welder.
> Not an alchemist.
> I am interested in the blend
> of common elements to make
> a common thing.
>
> No magic here.
> Only the heat of my desire to fuse
> what I already know
> exists. Is possible.[32]

Hence, it would seem that the editors of *This Bridge* consciously mark a difference in their approach to theories in the flesh that prioritizes and politicizes the desiring body as a medium for "entering the lives of others." Moreover, the difference between Anzaldúa's alchemy and Moraga's welding reveals a distinct revision of the Marxist conception of class. While Anzaldúa's "Mundo Zurdo" welcomes those located outside the privileged position of heterosexual white male owner of modes of production—the "colored, the queer, the poor, the female, and the physically challenged"—Moraga's fusing of "common elements to make a common thing" does not include all forms of difference or marginalization. She carves out a particular place of analysis and community for working-class (queer) women of color feminism. While Anzaldúa expands a Marxist conception of class, Moraga specifies a particular grouping—feminists of color—within those who are denied ownership of their labor and the surplus value they produce. This different conception of class points to two distinct though not necessarily antagonistic critiques of the nation-state: a critique of all borders, or Anzaldúa's theory of borderlands and mestiza consciousness, and the right to sovereignty and self-determination, or what Moraga terms "autonomous dialogue entrenos."[33]

While the casual reader might gloss over these distinctions in *This Bridge*, Moraga's subsequent writings highlight how a manageable difference in 1981 was exasperated by 1984, contributing to the coeditors having a fall out. In "The Salt That Cures: Remembering Gloria Anzaldúa," Moraga describes the sad irony that while *This Bridge* had reinvigorated "women-of-color taking seed throughout the country, the gap of strained silence between Gloria" and Moraga "was already widening."[34] Three years after the publication of *This Bridge*, according to Moraga, Anzaldúa claimed that the anthology did not "reflect her vision," and that "had she been in better health, she would have done it differently."[35] Because she was ill with uterine cancer "resulting in a hysterectomy," Anzaldúa regretted entrusting Moraga with "loose rein over how to structure and articulate the politic of the book."[36] Moraga further explains why she did not contribute to *This Bridge We Call Home: Radical Visions for Transformation* (2013): "When I learned that the new collection was to include men and white women, I decided not to contribute, not out of a politic that can be dismissed as 'exclusion,' but due to what I perceived as *strategic*."[37] For Moraga, women-of-color feminisms are still at a preliminary stage insofar as we have yet either to "move beyond the racial categories and strategies" "formulated in response to the 1960s and 1970s people-of-color movements, as well as to white feminism and gay liberation" movements, or to coalesce as a "national network."[38] Reflecting on what *This Bridge* meant to her, and what she sees as the unfinished project of women-of-color feminisms, Moraga confirms Anzaldúa's claim that they in fact do not share the same vision. For Moraga, a "'new *Bridge*" would incorporate a contemporary "generation of Indigenous peoples and immigrants from the southern hemisphere, as well as from West and East Asia and the Pacific Islands" because to include "queer men and white women, at this stage of a U.S. feminism of color, would be to suggest that our movement had developed beyond the need for an autonomous dialogue entrenos."[39]

Moraga explicitly links her understanding of materialism to political strategy when she writes that while she does not disagree with the "*spirit* of her ideas," she is concerned with the dangers of Anzaldúa's conflation of a "beautiful idea" with a "*strategy* for resolving disparities between economic classes, ethnic communities, and women and men within a capitalist patriarchy."[40] Her distinction between idealism and materialism is grounded in a critique of Anzaldúa's "new tribalism." In many ways, Anzaldúa's "new tribalism" reworks her initial conception of "El Mundo Zurdo," or what I earlier described as an expanded reconceptualization of class insofar as she clarifies the relation between indigeneity and class as the basis for a leftist global unity. In contrast to what Anzaldúa considers her new class category, or "new tribalism," that includes all allies of the oppressed independent of their social location, Moraga troubles the openness of Anzalduá's vision by raising the question of tribal sovereignty and self-determination. For Moraga, the road to decolonization is "different for Indian and Xicano peoples than for non-Native because our oppression is distinct" and cannot be "cross-culturally applied" by non-Native people.[41] Moreover, from "the perspective of living tribal communities, the idea of a new, ethnically inclusive tribalism may resonate as yet another neocolonial attempt to dehistoricize"[42] and eliminate indigenous sovereignty from "national discourse on both sides of the border."[43]

Again, while this might seem like a teasing out of perhaps insignificant or pedantic distinctions, it is important to note that what Anzaldúa and Moraga share is a conscious effort to create social change at the level of theory, art, literature, political practice, and academia. Though they ultimately disagreed on whether or not to include white and male authors in anthologies, or if they saw the bridging work of women of color as operating *within* an imagined world of new tribalism or *across* autonomous spaces of difference, each has always conceived of liberation in terms of planetary rather than global horizons. For Moraga, an indigenous planetary horizon enlists "leftist and feminist communities" in creating a "common ground of *shared labor*" that supports "the reparation of extant Indigenous tribal communities."[44] Anzaldúa's "new tribalism" willfully discarded traditional Marxist terms such as class and materialism, terms she had initially made her own through her naming of "El Mundo Zurdo." By contrast, the trajectory of Moraga's writings led her back to these terms through a revised sense of the interaction between class, feminism, and indigeneity as categorically intertwined. In the fourth edition of *This Bridge*, published in 2015, Moraga links a planetary social justice movement to a U.S. women of color praxis, a reinvestment in the category of class, and indigenous sovereignty. While she acknowledges the importance of the Occupy movement because it reintroduced the "dirtiest five-letter word in 'America': C-L-A-S-S,"[45] she still poses the question, "What would it mean for progressive struggles to truly integrate a feminist of color politic in everything from climate change to the dissolution of the World Bank?"[46] In this vein, Moraga reinstates and realigns *This Bridge* with "the body—that site which houses the intuitive, the unspoken, the viscera of our being—this is the revolutionary promise of 'theory in the flesh.'"[47]

PÉREZ'S (UN)DISCIPLINED LOCATIONS WITHIN CHICANO HISTORIOGRAPHY, LITERARY CRITICISM, AND SOCIALIST FEMINISMS

Like the various *theories* in the flesh proposed by *This Bridge*, Emma Pérez's *The Decolonial Imaginary* also foregrounds a desire for revolution. Consider the following questions *The Decolonial Imaginary* poses. To what extent did the socialist-oriented politics of the Partido Liberal Mexicano (PLM) transform race, class, gender, and sexual relations in Mexico? To what extent did the Chicano Movement have an impact on these relations in the United States? Given the transnational scope of both the PLM and Chicano Third Worldism, what is the relationship between Mexican and Chicana feminism? For Pérez, part of the answer to these questions resides in analyzing the way we historicize these various liberation movements. Hence, the *Decolonial Imaginary* provides a metahistorical methodology that requires us to scrutinize the kinds of questions historians ask and the categories that inform how historical change is made legible and legitimate. Moreover, Pérez pairs metahistory with decolonial praxis by challenging the boundaries of traditional historiography and disidentifying with the mandate for performing the role of the objective historian.

In addition to citing the ways objectivity often operates as an alibi for the *his* in *his*tory "that often becomes the universalist narrative in which women's experiences are negated,"[48] Pérez also questions the subjective-objective binary whereby "literature is reduced or expanded by the 'imaginary' while history can only be 'real.'"[49] In particular, when "writing the history of the Southwest, the historian who accepts the notion of objectivity can often ignore the colonial relations that are already in place" and continue to be produced.[50] Thus, she places her own disidentification with the objective historian by naming the *colonial imaginary* as a structure that dictates "the very form of their/our objectivity by compelling authors to situate themselves in the making of the 'frontier' or 'the United States of America.'"[51] The term *colonial imaginary*, therefore, names how the logic of the frontier persists and coheres around the link between objective historiography and a border epistemology. Also, the periodization of American history completely disavows or truncates Chicana/o history specifically, and a planetary knowledge of the Southwest more broadly. For example, Spanish colonization and Native America is placed outside the properly historical insofar as scholars "must cross boundaries from the United States to Latin America and then to Europe to pursue the Spanish colonial Southwest."[52] Pérez further explains how the logic of the nation-state limits the study of American coloniality preceding 1776, and how a border epistemology is implicated in the historical erasure of Mexicanas, Tejanas, and Chicanas living in the twentieth century despite participation in multiple feminist movements, the Mexican Revolution, the U.S. and Mexican court system, public letters, and community organizing, all of which left a paper trail. More than simply recovering an archive that was lost, Pérez traces the ways in which each of these movements for social change fails to challenge the colonial imaginary despite their attempts to include previously ignored categories of analysis, such as woman, Chicano, or immigrant.

Perhaps most provocatively, *The Decolonial Imaginary* traces how the mechanisms of erasure that preclude writing Mexicanas into history in the early part of the twentieth century are reproduced in the 1970s by Chican*o* historians who, through a heterosexist link between nationalism and gender, appropriate *his*tory and thereby reproduce "the very colonial imaginary against which they rebel."[53] On the one hand, Pérez clearly asks us to engage with Chican*o* historians' significant revision of historical materialism, a revision that opens up an analysis of class exploitation to include the relationship between racialization and immigrant labor. Moreover, she explicitly historicizes this early Chican*o* engagement with coloniality as an overlooked precursor to the then emerging canon of postcolonial scholarship. However, Pérez is also weary of an overinvestment in labor as the singular prism through which to understand racialization because this type of critique, insofar as it naturalizes the relation between Chicana/o and immigrant, cannot adequately attend to the unique diasporic and indigenous configuration of Chicana/o history. A decolonizing break with the logic of the nation-state therefore requires challenging the parameters of the category of immigrant and complicating the modern ethos that produces a binary (and sometimes hierarchal relation) between Mexican immigrant and indigenous Mexican. This transborder framework is further complicated when we consider that the political sovereignty and nonsecular practices of tribal nations do not neatly fit into modern categories or narratives of race and class.

In addition to helping us better understand the unresolved relationship between historical materialism and Chicana/o indigeneity, Pérez interrogates how privileging the racialization of immigrant labor while ignoring exploitation in terms of sexuality contributes to the tenacious hold of the nation-state operating within the *colonial imaginary*. In explicit terms, Pérez's comparison of Mexican revolutionary and Chicano *movimiento* politics is couched within a critique of the various ways in which these explicitly Marxist platforms claimed to include the woman question in theory while enacting heterosexist and frankly homophobic lived practices. In other words, Pérez's metahistory works to advance the claim that *sin la lesbiana no hay revolución*. Pérez employs this refrain to make the point that historiographical practices exemplify the lived experiences of social organizing and create the grounds for Chicana/o communality. The nature of this linked relationship, however, is hardly mimetic or simple.

Pérez's writing on revolution historicizes the unresolved terrains of Chicana/o communality as expressed in this highly debated relationship between how we came to be and who we need to become. Her writing displays a consistent pattern of metacritical commentary that describes the academic and political circumstances that condition her scholarship. As a historian who studies the way women have been silenced and decontextualized, it makes sense that Pérez practices a type of self-archival performance that records her engagement with various and often conflicting intellectual traditions.

Moreover, time and again, she calls herself a historical materialist and a social feminist in an effort to distance herself from what some describe as the abandonment of Marxism that has characterized mainstream feminism since the late 1980s. What I find interesting is that she labels herself in this way even though her writing at times contradicts a historical materialist framework. That she can write about the PLM from an explicit Marxist understanding of ideology in 1991 and then write about the same movement from an explicitly antidialectical framework in 1999 (drawing on Homi Bhabha's concept of "third-space") is my case in point, a contradiction that Pérez specifically asks her readers to wrestle with rather than ignore.

Consider the metacommentary in two of Pérez's essays: her 1991 "Sexuality and Discourse: Notes from a Chicana Survivor," and her 1990 "'A La Mujer': A Critique of the Partido Liberal Mexicano's Gender Ideology on Women." The first essay, "Sexuality and Discourse," begins with the following statement: "My socialist feminist bias has spurred me in this direction. When I was a budding a graduate student in Chicana/o history and Women's history, I tried stubbornly to show that class-based movements subsumed gender."[54] These sentences are then followed by a footnote that is worth quoting at length.

> In an essay that I wrote in 1982 on the Mexican anarchist group *Partido Liberal Mexicano,* I argued that the nation-nationalist class-based movements placed women-workers' exploitation in the forefront, but dismissed their oppression in the home and in their social-sexual relationships with the male leaders of the organization. The essay should have been published years ago, but "political" circumstances delayed it. In light of current debates spawned by deconstructionists, this essay is dated but perhaps useful because it analyzes the gender ideology within nationalist class-based movements. . . . Again, I point out that in a region where socialism was attempted, women's issues were only brought to the forefront to benefit a male political arena.[55]

At first glance, "Sexuality and Discourse" and "A La Mujer" are contemporaneous works published a year apart from one another. However, as Pérez explains, almost a decade lapsed between the writing of the essay and its publication in an anthology entitled *Between Borders: Essays on Mexicana/ Chicana History.*[56] While Pérez does not specify the "'political' circumstances" that delayed her earliest writings on the PLM, a look at the anthology edited by Adelaida Del Castillo does provide the specifically *Chicana* socialist feminism that "spurred" Pérez into a different "psychoanalytic" direction.[57]

In her introduction, Del Castillo explains that several of the essays collected in *Between Borders* were initially presented at a 1982 conference, "Mexicana/ Chicana Women's History International Symposium," which featured "scholars and activists from Mexico and the United states who share research interests and teaching expertise on the history of Mexican women and organizational experiences."[58] Del Castillo further explains that given the combination of the conference papers and more recent essays published in the collection, *Between Borders* reflects "the maturation of the field in the 80s."[59] Indeed, the collection includes essays by Juan Gómez-Quiñones, Rosaura Sánchez, Antonia I. Castañeda, Vicki L. Ruiz, José E. Limón, and, of course, Emma Pérez, authors who have written foundational works for Chicana/o studies. It is important to note that literary critics like Sánchez and Limón and historians such as Castañeda, Gómez-Quiñones, and Ruiz are invited to speak on the question of transnational feminism, and in turn *The Decolonial Imaginary* echoes this methodology when Pérez undoes the binary relationship between subjectivity and objectivity that is often mapped onto the differences between literature and history.[60]

In addition to emphasizing the fundamentally interdisciplinary and transnational nature of Chicana/o Studies, Del Castillo explains that the "theoretical positions and conceptual frameworks" of *Between Borders* clearly represent a "polarization between those who argue that women's history (ethnic or otherwise) is best conceptualized from a historical materialist perspective and those who answer [that] Marxism has little or nothing to contribute to a critique of racism, sexism or patriarchy."[61] While Del Castillo doesn't identify where each of the authors falls within this polarization, I would add that there is also a significant difference *within* those who find Marxism useful. A reading of Pérez, Sánchez, and Limón, for example, reveals important differences within conceptualizations of Marxist Chicana feminisms.

While Limón draws on Frederic Jameson's concept of the political unconscious to render La Llorona as a "critical contestative performance in the everyday lives of the ordinary women of Greater Mexico,"[62] Sánchez states that "Chicana historians need fewer myths and more historical analysis."[63] Moreover, for Sánchez, a materialist Chicana historiography decenters gender because Chicanas are "interpellated by a series of different, competing and overlapping ideologies."[64] Hence, "positing 'gender' as the essential difference explaining the oppression of Chicanas is out of the question since Chicana scholars must consider class as well as ethnicity in their analyses."[65] For this reason, feminists "who see an oppression which is specific to women" cannot understand why "Chicana scholars, like their Black counterparts, have found it is not possible to understand the oppression of Chicano women without also taking that of Chicano men into consideration."[66] Limón agrees with Sánchez insofar as he claims that "the most powerful kind of feminism, speaks not only of women but through the power of women for *all* of the socially weak."[67] He further explains that in contrast to the official narratives of *La Virgen de Guadalupe* and *La Malinche* produced and circulated by "men-in-authority,"[68] "La Llorona remains largely *in the hands of women*."[69] Limón suggest that this narrative act "demonstrates that women control their expressive resource,"[70] and he links this symbolic resistance to "the first weak ones in Mexican history, the subjugated indigenous people."[71] Moreover, Limón clarifies that the emergence of La Llorona "in the colonial period and her persistence today" "speaks only to the political unconscious and compelling contradiction posed for women," or the first horizon of Jameson's hermeneutic model where social contradictions "are relatively manifest to those who experience them."[72] How, then, "is it possible for this decidedly female legend to also articulate"[73] the class interest that coheres around the folk masses of Greater Mexico? This only becomes possible when we move to Jameson's second horizon of interpretation where "'the organizing categories of analysis become those of social class,' more particularly the antagonistic and active relationship between 'a dominant and a laboring class.'"[74] For Limón, dialectical criticism offers a concept of totality that guides interpretations of La Llorona beyond the limited terrain of gender analysis toward a broader and more inclusive class consciousness.

Pérez's study of the PLM offers yet a different point of departure within Marxist critique. Pérez explains that while the "PLM strove to overthrow capitalism believing that only then would women and men achieve equality," they "failed to grasp that women's issues went beyond class exploitation"[75] because "gender has been subsumed by class precisely because of the social relations that create and are created by gender ideology."[76] While socialist feminism had established the relationship between the division of labor in the work force and in the family—for example, within heteronormative forms of marriage, the "housewife" reproduces "men's labor power"[77]—Pérez expands the dynamics of heterosexism to include the space of revolutionary social movements like the PLM. Pérez writes, "While women actively participated in all arenas of the revolution, they gained little from their contributions. Women's revolutionary activities were understood as extensions of the home."[78] Moreover, Pérez expands a historical materialist analysis of gender to include sexuality and analyzes the oppression of men from a different perspective than that of Sánchez and Limón by comparing the essays "A La Mujer" and "Que Hable el Maricón," linking antiwomanist behavior with homophobia. Pérez explains, "Just as Guerrero impugned unwomanly women, Flores Magón assailed unmanly men."[79]

By placing the different variants of Marxism in *Between Borders* in conversation, we gain better insight into the contradictory terrain that informs Chicana theories in the flesh. For example, we see that Limón echoes the PLM's failure to question heterosexism within a social formation organized around class or what Limón names "folk consciousness." Unlike Limón, Sánchez's Marxism advances a *feminist of color conception of totality* and attends to the different positionality of negatively racialized men within capitalism. And, like Sánchez, Pérez offers a *specific* critique of the U.S. engagement with British and French social feminisms: "But even as we learn from such thinkers, Chicana scholars must retain a sense of the grass-root movements that make up our community. These grass-roots movements, like the Partido Liberal Mexicano, most clearly confront issues of culture, class, gender, and sexuality in our community."[80] In this early essay, as in *The Decolonial Imaginary*, Pérez looks to Latin America for forms of socialism and historical materialism that can adequately account for the U.S. and transborder experience of (internal) colonialism and coloniality.

To close my comparative reading of Pérez, Sánchez, and Limón, I want also to address a range of responses to indigeneity, and how socialist feminism from a decolonial perspective can provide a nuanced and historicized analysis of nonsecular forms of knowledge. As Pérez writes in *The Decolonial Imaginary*, early Chicana/o historians reconfigured historical materialism for the purposes of studying the United States within an internal colonial paradigm. What feminism has added to the Chicana/o historical materialist paradigm is the call to further historicize the relations between capitalism, colonialism, *and* patriarchy. For example, Sánchez writes that

> [t]he experiences and struggles since 1848 offer ample opportunities for research without the need to resort to the idealization of a glorious past. Thus, tracing Chicana roots in Mexican history need not postulate direct links between us and La Malinche or Sor Juana Ines de la Cruz. References to Aztec goddesses similarly prove absolutely nothing and in fact have been used to idealize the status of Aztec women in pre-hispanic society, both in creative and historical projects, despite documentation which points to the subordinate status of women in pre-Columbian society.[81]

Sánchez's critique seems to place the well-known Chicana commitment to the nonsecular (in its Catholic and indigenous variants) outside the scope of material feminisms,[82] troubling a potential alliance that Sánchez opens up when she provides a brief overview of the socialist feminism debate regarding the relationship between patriarchy and capitalism. Citing the work of Zillah R. Eisenstein, Sánchez introduces a strand of socialist feminism that claims that patriarchy precedes capitalism. This line of thinking places in question the abstract categorical claim that the destruction of capitalism necessarily destroys patriarchy. Whereas Limón saw capitalism and patriarchy as analogous (if not homologous) phenomena, socialist feminism opens up the temporal relation between capitalism and patriarchy for debate. In different ways, Limón and Sánchez represent two bookends to a spectrum of a Marxism that excludes indigeneity. Contrary to Sánchez, Limón suggests that folk tales are useful for a Marxist hermeneutics not because they offer links to a glorious past, but because La Llorona offers a symbolic view into a utopian future. For Sánchez's historical materialism, patriarchy precedes capitalism insofar as women were subordinate in pre-Columbian societies. For Limón's Marxist cultural dialectical critique, the temporal relation between capitalism and patriarchy is untroubled, and indigenous social formations are feminized and reduced to mythic pasts and utopian futures. Nowhere to be found is an engagement with, for example, contemporary or historical forms of indigeneity that practice feminist and anticapitalist modes of production. In *Between Borders*, Pérez remains silent on the question of indigeneity and nonsecular forms of knowledge. Her investment in socialism from the south, however, points to an early attempt to engage with what would become one of the central points of decolonial feminisms in our current moment: the call to historicize the complex rather than seamless relation between colonization of the Americas and multiple, uneven forms of heteropatriarchy.

Like *The Decolonial Imaginary*, I see Chicana *theories* in the flesh as part of current modes of decolonial feminist thought that offer important revisions of the internal colonial paradigm. While class might appear as singular in the refrain "race, class, and gender," my close reading of the differences within Chicana feminisms reveals how Pérez, Anzaldúa, and Moraga expand socialist feminisms in ways that begin to address the material needs of indigenous and queer women of color.

THE "SITIO Y LENGUA" OF CHICANA HISTORICAL MATERIALISMS

In this chapter, I have shown how *The Decolonial Imaginary* asks us to revisit the lively debates within Chicana materialist feminisms archived in *Between Borders* and in *This Bridge*. In particular, I suggest that theories in the flesh expand a Marxist conception of social totality by providing a feminist of color articulation of previously rejected or undertheorized spheres of exploitation and liberation—the nonsecular, *lesbiana* desire, and indigenizing praxis. Theories in the flesh therefore enliven the *decolonial imaginary* by pointing to how a border epistemology places transborder materialisms of color outside the purview of "objective" U.S. historiography. As Norma Chinchilla explains, too often "the content of socialism and the meaning of Marxism" are understood in terms of "the developments in the Soviet Union and Eastern Europe."[83] By contrast, "As early as the 1950s, Latin American Marxists critical of traditional communist parties' intellectual and strategic dependence on the Soviet Union embarked on a search of an indigenous version of Marxism."[84]

More importantly, I want to suggest that Pérez's metahistory provides a way to contextualize the perpetual scholarly and political pull between addressing ways of thinking that exclude U.S. women of color and creating opportunities that cultivate difference and solidarity within Chicana feminism. I have already explored this conundrum in terms of the different ways Moraga and Anzaldúa revise a Marxist conception of class, and I now want to map a similar problematic onto the shift between Pérez's "sitio y lengua" and "third space feminism." While "sitio y lengua" emphasizes the ways in which Chicanas create autonomous spaces from which to develop our own language of analysis and ways of being, "third space feminism" attempts to recover the spoken but unheard words that have been lost to and preserved within what Homi Bhabha describes as the "time lag between the colonial and the postcolonial."[85] According to Bhabha, however, these interstitial, aural spaces fall outside a dialectical or Marxist understanding of change. Pérez therefore explains that "[w]hile I would not abandon historical materialisms, I would build upon a model with [Chela] Sandoval's differential consciousness, with the interstitial space where Bhabha locates culture."[86] I would, however, argue that Pérez does not provide a completed version of this model, and that this unresolved project reveals not so much her personal limits but the larger contradictions of Chicana theories in the flesh.

The trajectory of Pérez's work as historian, novelist, and advocate for queer women of color politics in academia provides a generous and rigorous overview of the state of Chicana feminisms for the last thirty years. My ongoing study of her writing as a whole gives me the sense that she is asking her readers to share this labor of love and is doing this work herself in what I call her "academic metacommentary." Simply put, it matters how we treat each other in academia, and I see Chicana theories in the flesh as a tenacious attempt to document the living body's engagement with theoretical, historical, and contemporary forms of revolutionary praxis and "heteropatriarchal institutional violence."[87]

Sadly, Anzaldúa did not live to see the fourth edition of *This Bridge*, published a decade after her death. For those of us who are mindful of the profound personal and scholarly impact that Anzaldúa's writing continues to evoke, it is difficult not to resent that she was awarded her doctorate posthumously or that she suffered through and eventually died from complications due to diabetes while not having the benefits of health insurance. I am left to wonder what Anzaldúa's "*third world lesbian feminist with Marxist and mystic leanings*" would make of the events that inform Moraga's introduction to the latest edition of *This Bridge*. How would Anzaldúa complicate Moraga's analysis of the Occupy movement or the Tunisian Revolution? How would Anzaldúa's evolving theorization of El Mundo Zurdo respond to Moraga's assertion that "Black women are Indigenous women, once forcibly removed from their ancestral homeland. If not in the specifics, the major ideological tenets of the 1977 Combahee River Collective statement can serve today as a treatise for Indigenous women's rights movements globally"?[88] In order to begin to answer these questions for ourselves, and perhaps even to hear the questions in the first place, we must first recognize *difference* within Chicana feminisms and historicize our various engagements with transborder and historical materialist feminisms of color.

Notes

1. Gloria Anzaldúa and Cherríe Moraga, eds. *This Bridge Called My Back: Writings by Radical Women of Color*, orig. 1981, 4th ed. (New York: SUNY Press, 2015), xl.

2. I use the provisional term nonsecular as a way to historicize the *longue durée* of the evolving and constitutive relation between *colonialism*, as an explicit form of theological violence and genocide for the purposes of capitalist accumulation, and *coloniality*, as a disavowed expression of this violence that links the secular status of the human with contemporary forms of legal redress. Founded on and constituted by the legal and theological separation between the human and nonhuman, the secular forecloses contemporary forms of protest by misrecognizing the politics of the nonsecular as either a call for religious tolerance or recognition within localized or multicultural expressions of late capitalism. Instead, the nonsecular I refer to contests the ontological and epistemological premises that enable the planetary organization of capitalist modes of production and accompanying social formations, such as the nation-state and the colonial/modern gender system. I am also building on the distinction between colonialism and coloniality that Nelson Maldonado-Torres outlines in "On the Coloniality of Being: Contributions to the Development of a Concept," *Cultural Studies* 21.2–3 (March/May 2007), as well as María Lugones's essay "Heterosexualism and the Colonial/Modern Gender System," *Hypatia* 22.1 (2007).

3. Anzaldúa and Moraga, *Bridge*, xxxv.
4. Anzaldúa and Moraga, *Bridge*, xxxvi.
5. Anzaldúa and Moraga, *Bridge*, xxxvi.
6. Anzaldúa and Moraga, *Bridge*, xxxvi.
7. Compare the Chicago Women's Liberation Union 1972 pamphlet "Socialist Feminism: A Strategy for the Women's Movement" (http://www.historyisaweapon.com/defcon1/chisocfem.html) and the Combahee River Collective's "A Black Feminist Statement," first published in Zillah R. Eisenstein's *Capitalism, Patriarchy, and the Case for Socialist Feminism* (New York: Monthly Review, 1978), republished in *This Bridge*.
8. Anzaldúa and Moraga, *Bridge*, xliv.
9. Anzaldúa and Moraga, *Bridge*, xl.
10. Anzaldúa and Moraga, *Bridge*, xl.
11. Karl Marx, *Capital, vol. I*, ed. Frederick Engels (New York: International Publishers, 1974), 19.
12. Marx, *Capital*, 20.
13. Anzaldúa and Moraga, *Bridge*, xli.
14. Anzandúa and Moraga, *Bridge*, xl.
15. Anzaldúa and Moraga, *Bridge*, xli.
16. Anzaldúa and Moraga, *Bridge*, 19.
17. Emma Goldman, *Red Emma Speaks: An Emma Goldman Reader*, orig. 1972, 3rd ed., ed. Alix Kates Shulman (New York: Humanity Books, 1998), 33.
18. Goldman, *Red Emma*, 167.
19. Goldman, *Red Emma*, 434.
20. Goldman, *Red Emma*, 434.
21. Goldman, *Red Emma*, 442.
22. Goldman, *Red Emma*, 443.
23. Anzaldúa and Moraga, *Bridge*, xl.
24. Anzaldúa and Moraga, *Bridge*, 164.
25. Anzaldúa and Moraga, *Bridge*, 167.
26. Anzaldúa and Moraga, *Bridge*, 195.
27. Anzaldúa and Moraga, *Bridge*, 196, emphasis mine.
28. Anzaldúa and Moraga, *Bridge*, 196.
29. Anzaldúa and Moraga, *Bridge*, 208.
30. Anzaldúa and Moraga, *Bridge*, 205.
31. Anzaldúa and Moraga, *Bridge*, 209.
32. Anzaldúa and Moraga, *Bridge*, 219.
33. Cherríe Moraga, *A Xicana Codex of Changing Consciousness Writings, 2000–2010* (Durham: Duke University Press, 2011), 123.
34. Moraga, *Xicana*, 117.
35. Moraga, *Xicana*, 122.
36. Moraga, *Xicana*, 122.

37. Moraga, *Xicana*, 122–23, emphasis mine.

38. Moraga, *Xicana*, 123.

39. Moraga, *Xicana*, 123.

40. Moraga, *Xicana*, 124.

41. Moraga, *Xicana*, 124.

42. Moraga, *Xicana*, 124.

43. Moraga, *Xicana*, 125.

44. Moraga, *Xicana*, 126.

45. Anzaldúa and Moraga, *Bridge*, xviii.

46. Anzaldúa and Moraga, *Bridge*, xix.

47. Anzaldúa and Moraga, *Bridge*, xxiv.

48. Emma Pérez, *The Decolonial Imaginary: Writing Chicanas into History* (Bloomington: Indiana University Press, 1999), xiv.

49. Pérez, *Decolonial Imaginary*, xv.

50. Pérez, *Decolonial Imaginary*, 5–6.

51. Pérez, *Decolonial Imaginary*, 6.

52. Pérez, *Decolonial Imaginary*, 8.

53. Pérez explains her choice to write Chican*o* with the "o" in italics: "I use 'Chicano' and not 'Chicano/a' or 'Chicana/o,' because I think that during the early years of conceptualizing Chicano history, the 'a' was still so peripheral that I would prefer to accentuate the 'o' of Chicano." Pérez, *Decolonial Imaginary*, 132n25.

54. Pérez, *Decolonial Imaginary*, 5.

55. Emma Pérez, "Sexuality and Discourse: Notes from a Chicana Survivor," in *Chicana Lesbians: The Girls Our Mothers Warned Us About*, ed. Carla Trujillo (Berkeley: Third Women Press, 1991), 179.

56. Adelaida R. Del Castillo, ed., *Between Borders: Essays on Mexicana/Chicana History* (Moorpark, CA: Floricanto Press, 1990).

57. An abridged version of "Sexuality and Discourse" appears as "Speaking from the Margin: Uninvited Discourse on Sexuality and Power" in *Building with Our Hands: New Directions in Chicana Studies*, ed. Adela de la Torre and Beatríz M Pesquera (Berkeley: University of California Press, 1993), 57–71. Here, the first lines of the essay read "[m]y socialist-feminist position has pushed me toward a psychoanalytic end, if only momentarily."

58. Del Castillo, *Between Borders*, iii.

59. Del Castillo, *Between Borders*, iii.

60. Like Pérez, the affinity between history and literature within this cohort is also evinced in the creative works by Gómez-Quiñones and Rosaura Sánchez. In terms of intellectual histories, it is worth noting the early date of the symposium that provides a genealogy of transnational feminisms that is often erased when we privilege a postcolonial framework, a privileging that, as Pérez states in *The Decolonial Imaginary*, often

ignores the important work of Chicana feminism specifically, and the Americas more broadly. For a detailed discussion on this topic, see Maylei Blackwell's periodization of "Indigenous Transnationalisms" and the Marxism of "Third World Women's Alliance" in Maylei Blackwell, Laura Biggs, and Mignonette Chiu, "Transnational Feminisms Roundtable," special issue of *Frontiers: A Journal of Women Studies* 36.3 (2015): 1–24.

61. Del Castillo, *Between Borders*, vii.

62. Del Castillo, *Between Borders*, 419.

63. Del Castillo, *Between Borders*, 13.

64. Del Castillo, *Between Borders*, 5.

65. Del Castillo, *Between Borders*, 17.

66. Del Castillo, *Between Borders*, 17.

67. Del Castillo, *Between Borders*, 427.

68. Del Castillo, *Between Borders*, 406.

69. Del Castillo, *Between Borders*, 416.

70. Del Castillo, *Between Borders*, 417.

71. Del Castillo, *Between Borders*, 426.

72. Del Castillo, *Between Borders*, 420.

73. Del Castillo, *Between Borders*, 421.

74. Del Castillo, *Between Borders*, 421.

75. Del Castillo, *Between Borders*, 459.

76. Del Castillo, *Between Borders*, 461.

77. Del Castillo, *Between Borders*, 462.

78. Del Castillo, *Between Borders*, 461

79. Del Castillo, *Between Borders*,467.

80. Del Castillo, *Between Borders*, 463.

81. Del Castillo, *Between Borders*, 13.

82. For a critique of how early writing by Anzaldúa and Moraga unwittingly reproduce the colonial perspective embedded in anthropological discourse, see Jennie Luna and Martha Galeana's "Remembering Coyolxauhqui as a Birthing Text" *Regeneración Tlacuilolli: UCLA Raza Studies Journal* 2.1 (June 2016): 7–32. While Luna and Galeana do not address historical materialism, this essay attends to Sánchez's important intervention into the historical inaccuracies that accompany early Chicana feminist engagements with indigenous ceremony. Moreover, Luna and Galeana critique the colonial imaginary operating within Chicana feminisms in an effort to advance a contemporary engagement with the nonsecular.

83. Norma Chinchilla, "Marxism, Feminism, and the Struggle for Democracy in Latin America," in *Materialist Feminism: A Reader in Class, Difference, and Women's Lives*, ed. Rosemary Hennessy and Chrys Ingraham (New York: Routledge, 1997), 218.

84. Chinchilla, "Marxism, Feminism," 219.

85. Pérez, *Decolonial Imaginary*, 6.

86. Pérez, *Decolonial Imaginary*, 11.

87. See the special edition of *Chicana/Latina Studies* 13.2 (Spring 2014) for a collection of essays on heterosexism within Chicano Studies and institutional violence. Marie "Keta" Miranda offers an insightful essay on Emma Pérez's relation to theories in the flesh in "Re-Membering Emotion: Bigotes and the Unblocking of Memories," and Norma Alarcon's *testimonio* "Conjugations: The Insurrection of Subjugated Knowledges and Exclusionary Practices" theorizes the heterosexist claim that feminism cannot objectively provide a materialist critique.

88. Anzaldúa and Moraga *Bridge*, xxv; this is note 6. In addition to noting Moraga's addendum to the Combahee Statement, Sandy Soto's 2015 post on *Bully Bloggers*, "A Lover's Discourse on a Bridge," outlines significant changes made across the four different publications of *This Bridge*. https://bullybloggers.wordpress.com/2015/03/22/a-lovers-discourse-on-a-bridge-by-sandy-soto/. For a historical and contemporary understanding of intersectionality as explicitly anti-capitalist, see Keeanga-Yamahtta Taylor, *How We Get Free: Black Feminism and the Combahee River Collective* (Chicago: Haymarket Books, 2017).

CHAPTER 5

A World Out of Whack

Criminal (In)justice and Financial Capitalism in Sergio de la Pava's *A Naked Singularity*

R. Andrés Guzmán

Sergio de la Pava is among the most promising of a new generation of Latina/o writers. Winner of the PEN Robert W. Bingham prize in 2013 for his debut novel, *A Naked Singularity*,[1] his path to literary success, however, has been somewhat unusual. Writing by hand on the train or in a courtroom waiting for a case to be called, de la Pava managed to write *A Naked Singularity*, a nearly 700-page book that some have referred to as a "messy masterpiece," during the spare moments he could find in his day job as a public defender in Manhattan.[2] Though he finished the novel around 2004, he decided to self-publish it in 2008 after receiving close to ninety rejections from prospective publishers. Even then it remained in relative obscurity until Scott Bryan Wilson, a critic for the online literary journal *The Quarterly Conversation*, gave it a glowing review that helped readers take notice.[3] Shortly thereafter it was picked up by the University of Chicago Press, which published the novel in 2012.

The novel is narrated in the first person by Casi, the main protagonist and a public defender in Manhattan, much like de la Pava. Employing a fast-paced and loquacious narrative style full of wandering and often hilarious digressions, it tells the story of Casi's frustrating experiences with the legal system, even though when we first meet him he has yet to lose a case. After losing a case for the first time, however, Casi is persuaded by his colleague Dane to attempt to attain perfection in another form by pulling off the perfect crime. Casi and Dane thus embark on a plan to rob a local Dominican drug boss of millions of dollars. Through it all, the sprawling narrative puts forth a merciless critique of the criminal justice system and the current model of broken windows policing, and figures a late modern city on the verge of collapse.

As with its publication history, *A Naked Singularity* is also unusual as a "Latino" novel. Besides the fact that both de la Pava and Casi are Latinos of Colombian descent, the novel is not centrally about "Latino" experience. While insights into such experience are certainly not absent, references to Casi's heritage and to notions of Latinidad are mostly restricted to the domestic space of his mother's home. It is here that, among other things, we learn about the family's immigration history,[4] are provided with a comical description of his female cousins' style,[5] hear code-switching and Spanish-inflected English, and are even provided with a recipe for both making *and* eating *empanadas*.[6] These episodes, however, make up only a small fraction of the novel, and Casi's ethnic background, along with the ethnic background of others, is rarely remarked upon otherwise, even while the narrative includes a range of other Latino characters. In reducing the representation of Latinidad to the domestic realm, de la Pava can be reproached for making it do the token work of adding a little bit of *sabor* and warmth to an otherwise bleak and bitterly cold outside world. By underplaying Casi's ethnic identity outside of his mother's home, the novel can be accused of an implicit assimilationist vision that tends to erase Casi's ethnic markers as he crosses the threshold into the public realm. And yet, throughout the novel, Casi continues to be out of place; he neither fits in well, nor tries to fit in well with his professional and social surroundings. In light of this, I would argue that the novel should be read, rather, as resisting what Rey Chow refers to as "coercive mimeticism," which is to say

> a process (identitarian, existential, cultural, or textual) in which those who are marginal to mainstream Western culture are expected . . . to resemble and replicate the very banal preconceptions that have been appended to them, a process in which they are expected to objectify themselves in accordance with the already seen and thus to authenticate the familiar imaginings of them as ethnics.[7]

Read in this way, de la Pava's almost stereotypical depictions of Latinidad seem included specifically to satisfy expectations for the representation of

Latina/o cultural difference, which he does before moving on, as I will argue below, to a more general reflection on racialization as a structural process, the impacts of which affect Latinas/os without being limited to them. Along these lines, I would argue that it is not only de la Pava's status as a Latino that shapes the novel's social vision but also, and perhaps in more significant ways, it is his vocation as a public defender that does so insofar as it has given him a perspective that has enabled him to diagnose the wider contemporary convergence of criminal justice, race, and class.

As of this writing, *A Naked Singularity* has yet to attract much, if any, academic attention, even as online reviews have continued to flourish. A reason for this lack of academic engagement may be the sheer range of topics upon which it touches, something that places high demands upon a critic continually forced by the narrative to venture beyond the bounds usually demarcated by academic fields of expertise. Such demands are obviously also placed on the general reader, which may be one of the reasons that the novel could be said to have resisted easy commodification, as evinced by the initial reluctance on the part of publishers to take a risk on it. Asked in an interview to name some of the main "ingredients" that went into the making of the novel, de la Pava cites *Moby-Dick*, *Crime and Punishment*, Beethoven's Ninth, René Descartes's *Meditations*, and theoretical physics.[8] Stuart Kelly has suggested that it may be considered part of a trend in contemporary literature that critic James Wood has described as "hysterical realism," a label that Wood uses to refer to novels that substitute facile wonders for narrative depth and character development.[9]

In some ways, *A Naked Singularity* does partake in creating the kinds of outlandish characters and plot twists that Wood mentions as characteristic of hysterical realism. Indeed, within its narrative world we find a defendant that speaks only in verse, a young girl who refuses to speak during the majority of the novel because, we come to find out, she was heeding her mother's advice not to say anything at all if she had nothing nice to say, and a neighbor that brings Ralph Kramden into existence after continuously playing reruns of *The Honeymooners*, just to name a few examples that resonate with those identified by Wood. "Appropriately, then," Wood specifies, "objections are not made at the level of verisimilitude, but at the level of morality: this style of writing is not to be faulted because it lacks reality—the usual charge against botched realism—but because it seems evasive of reality while borrowing from reality itself."[10] It is with regard to this last point that, in my reading, *A Naked Singularity* parts ways with Wood's characterization.

Far from being evasive of reality, it is in its very form that the novel both reproduces and contests the neoliberal ideology of financial capitalism that shapes our contemporary crisis-prone reality. My reading is informed by a Marxist approach, which holds that we can find in a text a dialectical relationship between ideology and form.[11] I concur, moreover, with Marcial González when he writes that one of the payoffs "in the critique of form . . . lies in the broadening of historical consciousness beyond the immediacy of the local realities represented in the literature. The critique of form in this sense seeks to deepen our understanding of the historical processes that inform the literary work and to which the work is a response."[12] Yet by "form," I refer not only to the literary techniques employed to tell the story, but more so to the form of the logical structures that inhere within the narrative world. And it is with regard to these logical structures that I address the issue of materialism. In line with these critical approaches, my reading begins by highlighting the overlapping of race and class within the imbrications of criminal justice and financial capitalism.

THE SYSTEM OF CRIMINAL (IN)JUSTICE

One of the novel's main narrative threads provides a critical perspective on the criminal justice system. At only twenty-four years of age, Casi is a talented lawyer (during the first part of the novel, he has yet to lose a case in his two years as an attorney), yet he is already becoming frustrated and disillusioned with the criminal justice system's inability to produce results resembling anything that could accurately be described as "justice." The first chapter opens with an epigraph taken from above the entrance to Criminal Court that rhetorically asks: "Why should there not be a patient confidence in the ultimate justice of the people?"[13] If we take "the people" to mean those charged with upholding the law and prosecuting those that violate it (as the term is usually taken to mean within such a context), then the narrator proceeds to demonstrate exactly why it is that we should, in fact, have no confidence in the ultimate justice of the people as carried out within our contemporary criminal justice system.

Indeed, the novel opens with a kind of crash course on this system, even going as far as including direct references to statutes from the criminal code. It interpellates the reader into the role of potential defendant by tracing the process by which "You" (the reader) can be transformed into a mere "body"—the "[i]narguably odious term used by N.Y.C. Department of Corrections and other court personnel to denote incarcerated criminal defendants."[14] "[I]f you learn only one thing from the ensuing maybe let it be this," Casi continues, recalling a time when he still devoted energy to trying to figure out how the system worked:

> [T]he police were not merely interested observers who occasionally witnessed criminality and were then basically compelled to make an arrest, rather the police had the special ability to in effect create Crime by making an arrest almost whenever they wished, so widespread was wrongdoing. Consequently, the decision on who would become a body was often affected by overlooked factors like the candidate's degree of humility, the neighborhood it lived in, and most often the relevant officers' need for overtime.[15]

In this way, we learn that arrests are frequently determined by auxiliary factors like socioeconomic status, place of residence, and officers' need to supplement their wages. Though factors like race and ethnicity are certainly correlated to place of residence, that they too are central is soon made explicit by the roster of Casi's clients, most of whom are African American, Latino, or immigrants.[16] Significant is the way in which Casi challenges the supposed self-evidence of crime by asserting that the police have a role in producing it. Though one can expect the objection that police practices, like "stop and frisk," for example, only uncover crime that was already taking place, the concentrated deployment of these practices in poor and racialized communities has had the effect of elevating the crime rates among its target population, as police stop individuals in an attempt to find any violations with which they can be charged. In 2011, 87 percent of individuals stopped by the New York Police Department were Black or Latina/o.[17] Similarly, Michelle Alexander notes that, while multiple studies have shown that "people of all colors *use and sell* illegal drugs at remarkably similar rates," nonwhites have borne the brunt of punishment for these crimes, in some states putting drug-related incarceration rates of Black men at around twenty to fifty times that of white men.[18] If one of the objectives of the novel's first chapter is indeed to teach You, the reader, how easily you can become entangled in the criminal justice system, then it follows that such a lesson would be most pertinent to a nonwhite readership.

In a way that resonates strongly with current concerns with the excessive use of force by police officers and the impunity that often shields them from prosecution, the reader is subsequently warned:

> Another way you have to be careful not to pick up more charges is by resisting capture, even if only verbally, because such conduct can incite some of your lesser blue pacifists into a bit of retributory violence, with said violence then necessitating that you be charged with Resisting Arrest (PL §205.30) if only by way of explaining your injuries; which injuries better be minor lest they result in the added felony charge of Assault in the Second Degree (PL §120.05[3]).[19]

This strategy by which police retroactively justify their violence is another way in which they are able to create crime. According to this perverse logic, the more severe the violence inflicted by the police, the more severe the charge against the victim; thus retroactively transforming the victim into the cause of his/her victimization.

In the case that an officer *is* charged with misconduct, he or she cannot be questioned for forty-eight hours, giving the officer time to retain an attorney and receive legal advice well before putting anything on record. Unlike the police, however, "you are currently operating under a different forty-eight hour rule," Casi tells the reader:

> This one says the police can harass, intimidate, lie, cheat, steal, cajole, make false promises, and delay your arraignment (where you would be assigned an attorney who would most assuredly *not* allow you to speak to the police) for forty-eight hours if that's what it takes to extract your statement. And it is following all that, not at the very instant you're arrested as mass entertainment would have you believe, that they will advise you of your Miranda rights so your ensuing statement will be admissible.[20]

Given all these factors that place a potential defendant at a structural disadvantage, the criminal justice system comes off as organized more to ensure the continuous production of "bodies" (thus feeding the machine of mass incarceration) than to work in the interest of justice. In interviews, de la Pava attests to experiencing a similar disillusionment with the criminal justice system as does Casi. "Doing the work, even though I find it gratifying, breeds in me a certain dissatisfaction, a certain anger," maintains de la Pava, "what is happening is mass injustice. Indigent people and racial minorities are being rounded up in huge numbers."[21] Despite the degree of absurdity that surrounds much of what happens in the courtroom and in the Public Defender's Office in the novel, de la Pava insists that the details concerning the criminal justice system are a hundred percent accurate.[22]

The way in which the novel begins thus firmly situates the story that follows within our late modern historical context. The contradictions evident in the criminal justice system are extended to other areas and abstracted to the level of form. As such, the diegetic world starts to be plagued by absurd inconsistencies that emulate the contradictions of contemporary society. One of the earliest clues that the narrative is headed toward the breakdown of consistent reason comes at the beginning of the explanation of the criminal justice system, the account of which Casi situates in a time "before anything even remotely insane had happened."[23]

NEOLIBERAL REPRESSION, FINANCIAL SPECULATION, AND THE END OF THE UNIVERSE

Mass incarceration and broken windows policing are products of the neoliberal era, with the first two serving as mechanisms through which to control and preempt social disturbances stemming from the dismantling of the welfare state and a swelling surplus population. Prison construction and the security industry in general have themselves become sites for the investment of surplus finance capital.[24] "Tough on crime" political rhetoric gained widespread support, moreover, as part of the reaction against both the radical movements of the 1960s and '70s and the economic insecurity felt by many as the post–World War II boom came to an end. One of the first places to implement the neoliberal combination of public austerity, regressive redistribution of income, and the usurpation of government functions by financial interests was precisely New York City in the mid-1970s.[25] Faced with a severe fiscal crisis, the city was forced to accept a bailout that not only put the interests of the creditors above the social well-being of New York City residents but allowed for a more structural restoration of class power that set the terms for the policies of the following decades. The political advantages of being perceived as tough on crime had by 1973 already led New York governor Nelson Rockefeller to pass the first of a series of drug laws imposing mandatory minimum sentences; a move that took sentencing discretion away from judges and gave it to the prosecutors that determined the charges.[26]

Writing at the end of the 1990s, around the same time that de la Pava began writing *A Naked Singularity*, Neil Smith notes the escalation in the use of legal and extralegal repression under the Giuliani mayoral administration to "clean up" New York City of the poor and the homeless in order to better create the image of the city as a place for tourism and business. This is consistent with the ways in which cities have transformed themselves in the wake of deindustrialization. In the case of New York City this has entailed the consolidation of the city as a financial command center and the reconfiguration of Manhattan as a heavily securitized space organized to facilitate undisrupted consumption.[27] Broken windows policing, which targets lower level violations, is central to this "cleaning" effort. Police Commissioner William J. Bratton and Giuliani, himself a former federal prosecutor, drafted a policy document titled *Police Strategy No. 5*, which set the basis for an aggressive strategy to "reclaim" New York's public spaces.[28] Taking the victims of neoliberal restructuring as the cause of urban insecurity, the mayor admitted to a group of newspaper editors during a supposedly confidential meeting that the removal and social exclusion of the poor, and especially the homeless population, was indeed "our strategy."[29] It is thus no surprise that a recurrent question first asked by Casi's nephew[30] and repeated by Casi himself several times is "what happens to the homeless when they die."[31]

The intersection between neoliberal governmentality and the pervasiveness of urban surveillance is also parodied in the novel. Toward the end, during the "world premiere" of a surveillance video capturing the abduction of an infant by two seven-year-old boys—an FBI intern had come up "with the *inspired and unprecedented* idea of hiring a hot young Bollywood director to cut the footage into a PG-13 feature length film to be released in New York only, with children and senior citizens charged double"[32]—Toad,[33] the mayor of New York City, declares what he considers to be the two biggest problems facing the city: "homeless people and unemployed actors."[34] That being so, he announces the creation of a taskforce, also named T.O.A.D., "the Team to heap assistance On Actors and other Destitutes."[35] "Seems that the *inhumanly frigid nature* of the past few weeks was causing the homeless to drop like flies or *attrit at record numbers*," we are told: "The crowd didn't seem to know how to respond to that information but then Toad began to describe the difficulties of *making it* as an actor in the city and his audience voiced audible support."[36] The mayor's ingenious plan to address these issues is for the city to hire unemployed actors to attend the funerals of the homeless and play the role of "bereaved friends and relatives."[37] This will help both create "the illusion of concern" for the homeless and provide jobs for the unemployed actors.[38] Similar to the way in which mass incarceration helps offset rural unemployment by paying (mostly white) workers to guard other unemployed workers (mostly of color), Toad's plan entails paying one part of the surplus population to pretend to mourn for the other.

On their own, the homeless are unable to attract any popular sympathy. Sympathy is reserved for the actors who are still trying to "make it," implicitly casting the homeless as a lost cause even though they too are trying to make it in the most basic sense of trying to stay alive. This fits quite well with the tendency of mainstream political discourse in the United States to focus primarily on the "middle class," rather than on the poor. Supporting this focus is the naturalization of poverty—the conviction that the poor will always exist no matter what, and thus that the elimination of poverty is no longer a realistic goal. Accordingly, not only are they undeserving of real concern (merely the illusion of concern will do) but are there only to be managed through removal or incarceration.

That the homeless have been naturalized, and thus dehumanized, is also evident in the way in which they too have essentially been reduced to "bodies" in the logic that guides Mayor Toad's plan. It is not with the living conditions of the homeless that he is concerned; he is concerned rather with what to do with their bodies after they die. Even then, the concern is simply to create the *illusion* that someone cared when they were alive. The logic behind Mayor Toad's plan is thus similar to governmental logic under neoliberalism, where government action is directed not at the root causes of social and economic problems, but rather seeks superficial remedies at the level of their effects. Though unemployed actors are provided with jobs under Toad's plan, the nature of their work and the value they produce is, like contemporary financial speculation, primarily symbolic.

Journalist Matt Taibbi has written a critical analysis of the contradictions of financial capital and the centrality of speculative bubbles to capitalist accumulation in recent decades. Of particular interest is Taibbi's description of the disconnection between the instruments of financial capital and the determination of value based on actual production. This disconnect is paradigmatic of the contemporary neoliberal economy wherein, by the end of the first decade of the twenty-first century, trading in "fictitious capital" in the form of derivatives reached six hundred trillion dollars compared to the fifty-six trillion dollars' worth of actual goods and services produced.[39] Dedicating an entire chapter to Alan Greenspan's role in facilitating bubble-creating deregulation, while giving speculators the confidence that they would be bailed out in the case of crisis, Taibbi notes how the speculative boom of the late 1990s required a reconceptualization of the very source of value. "Greenspan's eventual explanation for the growing gap between stock prices and actual productivity was that, fortuitously, the laws of nature had changed," exclaims Taibbi, "humanity had reached a happy stage of history where bullshit could be used as rocket fuel . . . the economy had entered a new era, one in which the rules were being rewritten," and where speculation on its own could act as a source of value.[40] Without dismissing the possibility that historical transformations in capitalism can require us to rethink some of Marx's basic concepts, with Taibbi we can nevertheless find at the root of contemporary financial speculation and subsequent busts an effective disavowal of the continuing necessity of a production-based theory of value—a disavowal carried out in order to force coherence upon the mounting evidence of disproportionate valorization driven by speculative activity. Yet we must also keep in mind that the scale of trade in fictitious capital is itself a response to the falling rate of profit in commodity production.[41] It is this systemic crisis of profitability that speculative activity attempts to overcome by symbolic means.

The belief that speculation or mere symbolic activity on its own can create value can be characterized as an idealist position.[42] A striking example is found in Taibbi's account of the market for collateral debt obligations (CDOs). In the midst of the housing bubble, banks found a way to trade the long-term income streams they expected to receive from home loans into short-term cash through a technique called securitization—that is, by putting mortgages into pools where they would be divided into smaller units and sold to investors as securities.[43] The investors' ability to make money depended on homeowners' continued ability to make payments on their loans, thus exposing investors to the risk that homeowners would default. Accordingly, the banks came up with an instrument called a collateral debt obligation and devised a multitiered system of payment based on the assessment of relative risk attached to batches of CDOs. This multitiered structure consisted of three levels (also known as "tranches"): a "senior" level of AAA-rated CDOs, a "mezzanine" level of BBB-rated CDOs, and a third "equity" level "whose tranche was commonly known as toxic waste."[44] The payment structure was organized such that all mortgage payments up to a certain limit went directly to the top level, thus ensuring that they would be paid first. Payments beyond that limit and up to the next limit would go to the second level. The lowest level would only get paid if everyone paid their mortgage.

Traders were able to sell both senior and toxic CDOs with relative ease because the former were perceived to be minimally risky (with *perception* being an important caveat[45]) while still paying a higher rate of return than other AAA investments like Treasury bills, and the latter, though much riskier, promised a far greater rate of return for the limited time the buyer expected to hold on to the CDO.[46] For the mezzanine level BBB-rated CDOs, however, the traders had a harder time finding investors because they were considered either too risky by the AAA buyers or not profitable enough by the others. "So what did they do with the BBB part?" asks Taibbi: "That's easy: they re-rated it as AAA paper!"[47] More specifically, they simply combined the mezzanine CDOs that would not sell with other such CDOs from other deals to create a new batch that was itself retiered, essentially creating AAA CDOs out of BBBs; a purely symbolic redesignation that actually made a given CDO more valuable in the context of subsequent deals. The idealist universe in which this took place was thus one that completely disavowed the material reality at the limits of its field of operation. Acting "as if" BBB CDOs were AAA effectively made them so in the universe of speculative trading. It is thus that an idealist speculative bubble was created that blew up when reality caught up to it, "nearly destroy[ing] the universe in 2008."[48]

While Taibbi indulges in hyperbole when he characterizes the 2008 financial crash as nearly destroying the universe—even if the real estate market collapse did indeed obliterate about 40 percent of the world's wealth[49]—we can note that at the end of *A Naked Singularity* something very similar happens, perhaps allegorically prefiguring the financial collapse that would culminate out of the historical moment de la Pava diagnoses, versions of which were already evident in the financial crises of the late 1990s and early 2000s. Indeed, as Giovanni Arrighi points out, the dominance of finance signals the end of systemic cycles of accumulation, with recent crises suggesting the waning of U.S. global power.[50] The naked singularity to which the title refers—a kind of black hole that is not black due to the fact that light is still able to escape its gravitational pull—causes the symbolic universe of the novel to implode upon itself.[51] Shortly before the actual implosion, Casi notes that the laws of nature are out of whack when he points out that it is raining outside in six-degree weather.[52] Casi's neighbor, Angus, a good "customer" of Columbia University, suggests that a naked singularity has begun to form. As a consequence, he warns: "Predictability, Space, Time, the physical laws, they mean less with every passing second and soon enough they'll mean absolutely nothing. Why now? Why the collapse? Too much matter dude, causing too great a pull."[53] The excess of matter, evoking the efficacy of material conditions, breeds inconsistency into the "laws of nature" that make up the novel's symbolic universe.[54] Yet here we should also heed Slavoj Žižek's insistence that "reality is not simply external to thought/speech, to the symbolic space, reality thwarts this space from within, making it incomplete and inconsistent—the limit that separates the Real from the symbolic is simultaneously external and internal to the symbolic."[55]

Far from simply being external to the symbolic, "reality" inheres as the symbolic's immanent real. "Reality" punches a hole in the symbolic and wreaks havoc in the form of inconsistency. The real finds a degree of positive support in the novel in the figure of Ballena, an enforcer for a local drug lord that Casi and his partner-in-crime Dane are forced to confront after they rob a group of drug dealers. Ballena cannot be adequately described as entirely human, and indeed appears to embody the site of amassing density as he concentrates in himself the malevolence and evil of the entire world.[56] Dane describes Ballena as "the sort of entity that has no regard for life or limb, its own or others, and respects no laws, natural or otherwise."[57] Similarly, after a run-in with Ballena, Angus tells Casi that "it was as if it was in shadows the whole time, only shadows it was itself creating."[58] It is thus hard to determine what Ballena actually *is* in that he functions as a formal entity that resists symbolic capture, one that jams the symbolic order at the same time that he distorts the world around him. Though I will demonstrate below that there are other figures of the real as well, for now I would like to underscore the way in which, at a formal level, the disruption of the symbolic by the real mirrors a materialist critique of the ideology of financial capitalism. As with the idealist speculative bubble above, the novel's symbolic universe implodes when it is punctured by the efficacy of its own real.

It is thus that the novel can itself be read as carrying out a materialist critique of contemporary ideology. The point, however, is not merely to return to the "real world," but to gauge the way in which historically specific modes of accumulation and class domination exert an influence over the imaginary world created by the author, and how the formal aspects of this imaginary world can themselves be read as a partial response to the former. The novel cues us to this type of reading in an instructive episode. Casi and Dane are walking to lunch when they pass by a construction site with a plywood wall built around it to block people's view. "Only this [wall] was blood red with a small black-velvet curtain in the vertical and horizontal center," Casi narrates: "The curtain covered a port/peephole and above it in gold letters: UNDER NO CIRCUMSTANCES SHOULD YOU LOOK INSIDE TO SEE MAN'S GREATEST INVENTION SINCE THE WHEEL. AGAIN, WE URGE YOU NOT TO LOOK INSIDE FOR ANY REASON!!!!"[59] As they walk by they see a man first read the injunction and then throw the curtain over his head to see what is behind it. Neither Casi nor Dane dwell on the meaning of this, though at one level it is clear that it is both the promise of seeing something special and the very prohibition against looking that stimulates the desire of passersby to peek behind the curtain. One of the lessons is that prohibition itself stimulates transgression. Yet we can also draw another lesson from this, which is that whatever the object that we expect to be behind the curtain, the one in relation to which our desire is stimulated, is beside the point; there need not be anything at all behind the curtain. This lesson can hence be read as residing at the level of interpretation, as a lesson on what we must focus on when we read. It is a lesson on how the structure of the content guides our desire (the stimulation of the latter by the promise of a pleasurable object placed out of reach, or by the thrill of a heist that we await), and as such it also suggests that what we must analyze lies not behind the curtain, but in the form itself—a form that constitutes itself in relation to its own real, its own hole.[60] As we will see, the novel also includes two approaches to the real through the figures of Casi and Dane.

A SPLIT SUBJECT AND A WORLD OUT OF WHACK

While at work one night, Casi meets Dane, a recent transfer from Florida who shares his preoccupation with mediocrity. Dane, it turns out, is nearly obsessed with the quest for perfection. This leads him early in the novel to bring up the question of whether one can achieve perfection by committing the perfect crime.[61] During a subsequent encounter, Dane recounts a previous attempt by him to attain perfection by providing a client with perfect representation. After detailing the extraordinary lengths to which he went to achieve this, he informs Casi that his ultimate failure led him first to despair and then paradoxically prompted him to set his sights on an even more difficult goal: "I think that the commission of a perfect crime *is* possible," he declares.[62] The quest for perfection thus becomes the ideal that guides Dane's actions, and he commits himself to convincing Casi to join him in this endeavor by stealing millions of dollars from a group of drug dealers during an upcoming high-level deal that they become privy to when one of Casi's clients turns state's evidence.[63]

Despite his initial objections and hesitations, Casi decides to take on the challenge as a way of overcoming the crisis he experiences upon losing a case for the first time. "Excellent. I love witnessing . . . moments like these," Dane explains, "when you make this kind of decision, when you decide you will not simply accept what the world is trying to force down your throat."[64] For Dane, ordinary existence in the world constitutes a kind of being-toward-death, a form of existence he fervently rejects. "[W]hen we execute our perfect plan perfectly," he tells Casi during an earlier meeting, "the very notion of *alive* will mean something different to you."[65] More than just the adrenaline rush that would surely come with pulling off the robbery, Dane suggests the advent of a new subjectivity, one that begins with a decision, like Casi's, to strive for something beyond the given. The punctual nature of the decision and its function as a turning point is underscored both by the epigraph that begins the chapter in which the decision is made—the epigraph is of two verses from James Russell Lowell's (another author and lawyer) nineteenth-century antislavery poem "The Present Crisis": "Once to every man and nation comes the moment to decide. / In the strife of Truth with Falsehood, for the good or evil side"—and by the one-page length of this chapter that closes part one of the novel.[66]

The function of "perfection" for Dane resonates with Alain Badiou's notion of an Idea, one that supports the production of an exceptional truth through the very break with the mundaneness of quotidian existence.[67] Again resonating with Dane's assurance to Casi, to "live," according to Badiou, is to live for an Idea.[68] Yet it is not difficult to notice that Dane's search for perfection is ultimately unable to break with the given, and in fact remains firmly trapped within the coordinates of neoliberal capitalist reason. Reaching perfection for him is a purely egotistical matter.[69] Further, he evinces a social Darwinist vision, one that could correspond as much to a hedge fund manager as to a gangster, when speaking earlier about the existence of poverty: "This is a fucking competition where your misery constitutes my triumph. . . . The only responsibility anybody has towards anyone else is to crush them like a bug should they get the chance. . . . Man is only being operated correctly when oriented exclusively toward his benefit and survival."[70] "Money is the fucking star of the show we're in. . . . They failed to acquire it even though they knew it would insulate them from all sorts of pains," he continues: "You tell me that nobody should die from a lack of money? I tell you it happens all the time, that this fact shows that money is a matter of life and death, and that it is therefore all the more inexcusable when someone chooses to ignore this fact and fails to get his hands on some."[71] Accordingly, he has no patience for people who suffer from poverty, and, much like the kind of neoliberal logic outlined above, he ultimately blames the victims of poverty for their own station by reducing the latter to individual choice. Dane, moreover, indirectly admits that his course of action is far from a break with the logic that structures our contemporary everyday life. This occurs when Casi brings up a Kantian ethical objection to the heist: "What shape would we be in if everyone took that approach and acted accordingly?" Casi asks. "Are you kidding? Where would we be?" Dane responds: "You're seeing it! That is what would happen. How much worse can it get?"[72] Consequently, if "perfection" for Dane functions similarly to Badiou's Idea in sustaining an exceptional process, it can nevertheless only ever be a simulacrum of the latter insofar as it remains firmly anchored within the bounds of existing politico-economic reason.

At bottom, Dane's notion of perfection is closer to a theological conception of the exception. We can see this in the status of infinity that Dane presupposes in his discussion of perfect numbers—that is, a number (like the number 6) whose multiplicative factors (1 x 2 x 3) can also be added together to produce it (1 + 2 + 3 = 6). He mentions that although he has only been able to ascertain "about thirty-nine of these numbers," he believes that "there are in fact an infinite amount of them with infinity itself being a form of perfection," that, as such, "inspires an awe that is religious in nature."[73] The coupling of infinity with perfection evinces a pre-Cantorian, romantic conception of infinity—one that situates it on a distant horizon, leaving it as mere potential and denying its actuality.[74] Such is a *finite* conception of infinity. Thus, though his quest for perfection pushes against the limits of finitude, his conception of infinity remains firmly anchored within a finite matrix. Infinity appears as nothing more than the unreachable beyond of a finitude we can't escape, essentially functioning as a figure through which finitude attains its own closure. If idealism performs a closure that enables it to deny its inherent inconsistency or immanent split, to disavow its real by covering its gap with an object, then we can see that Dane's attempt to break out of the bounds of mundane experience ultimately results in a renewed idealism, with "perfection" taking the place of the inaccessible object.[75]

With all this said, however, I would like to begin to close by engaging in some speculation myself and wager a final interpretation that has yet to be suggested by anyone who has written on de la Pava's book, as far as I have been able to find. There are a number of things that make one wonder whether, in fact, Dane is but a figment of Casi's imagination and Casi is perhaps either insane or dreaming. During one of their earlier meetings, Casi notes that Dane "seemed almost inhuman, not really subhuman or superhuman though; more like metahuman," and that his face "seemed to disappear the longer you looked at it."[76] Described in terms that resemble the description of Ballena, Dane appears as another limit figure, but one that wavers on the edge of existence. They part ways after their meeting. Casi runs into a colleague, but after the colleague leaves Dane reappears: "He didn't explain or anything but instead just resumed as if there had been no interruption."[77] Dane, as a matter of fact, always seems simply to appear and disappear. "And just like that, poof, he was gone,"[78] Casi states at the end of an earlier encounter. After a meeting with another colleague in his apartment, Casi recounts, "Toomberg left and moments later it wasn't so much that Dane knocked on the door as it seemed to open on its own with him in the doorway."[79] Later, it is Dane who has just left Casi's apartment when Toomberg arrives. Casi asks Toomberg if he saw anyone on his way up and he says that he did not.[80] During the meeting that had just ended, Dane even responds directly to Casi's thoughts.[81] Finally, in the novel's closing pages, Casi sees Dane again after a long absence. At the end of their brief conversation, Casi turns away for a second and, when he looks back, "Dane was gone. I moved my head quickly looking everywhere for him but it was as if he'd never appeared at all."[82] Taken together, the ways in which Dane is described, the fact that Toomberg does not see him, and his ability to respond to Casi's thoughts point to the possibility that Dane is a product of Casi's mind.

Besides the additional consideration that the interactions between Casi and Dane rarely include a third party, the epigraphs at the beginning of several chapters also suggest the interpretation I propose by repeating the theme of doubt. Chapter 14, for example, begins with an excerpt by William Occam that states: "No more things should be presumed to exist than are absolutely necessary."[83] If this is so, perhaps Dane need not exist at all. He could be a figment of Casi's imagination, a figure akin to Tyler Durden in *Fight Club* (1999), albeit with the opposite politics.[84]

As Casi himself states at the beginning of this same chapter, this time developing the theme of doubt with reference to Descartes, if we begin to place everything in doubt we have to acknowledge "that *right now* could be nothing more than a mere dream."[85] The inconsistencies of the world that Casi narrates, then, may suggest that more than just Dane is a figment of Casi's imagination.[86] Before he wakes on the morning of his twenty-fourth birthday, Casi has a peculiar dream. He dreams that his skull is being pried open and that his brain is being studied by a group of medical students led by a female doctor with a ptosic eyelid:

> Here's the cerebral cortex which we purposely dim so that only day to day affairs are of concern and it is within this very banality that we thrive See his amygdala? What he most fears threaten him with, dangle it, not as mere possibility but as overwhelming probability, a proven technique with this sort of specimen . . . Always remember that we are here not to cure but to sicken So while normally at this point we begin to suggest the toxic, break down the healthy, and foster disorder, here an entropic chaos is already spreading virtually unchecked seeking its own heat death . . .[87]

The dream is of a pseudo-medical scene with criminological and colonialist undertones, where the personnel manipulate the patient's brain to ensure the patient's subjugation and docility. As we have already noted, Casi, much like Dane, is also concerned with being exceptional. He precisely fears that he will remain stuck at the banal level of day-to-day affairs. On this morning, one of the first feelings he experiences upon waking is disappointment when he compares himself to people like guitarist Eddie Van Halen, author Mary Shelley, and boxer Wilfred Benitez, all of whom had accomplished great things before the age of twenty-four—"they and so many others mocked me,"[88] Casi confesses. Significantly, however, the doctor in the dream points out that, while this would usually be the point where they would begin to make the brain malfunction, Casi's brain is already plagued by entropic chaos that is quickly spreading.

This entropic chaos evokes a situation similar to the one in which the naked singularity is at work, but it occurs at the level of Casi's own brain and psyche. It functions as another figure of the real that is introducing inconsistency. Insofar as the world of the novel is mediated through Casi's subjectivity in his function as narrator, the naked singularity itself may be nothing more than the outward projection of the entropy taking over his own mind.[89] Accordingly, the narrative world is plagued with absurd episodes. At one point, for example, Casi confesses to a priest about the heist—even mentioning that someone had died—before it actually takes place, which suggests a glitch in logical time.[90] We are led to reject the possibility that this episode may simply be a flash forward in the story after a later, postheist, exchange with Dane:

> "The sacrament of confession. I participated in it, sort of." [Casi tells Dane]
> "When?"
> "I don't know, a couple of weeks ago maybe."
> . . .
> "But if it was a couple of weeks ago." [i.e., before the heist had taken place]
> "It's hard to explain but—"[91]

This temporal inconsistency is left hanging, unresolved. The confession itself, however, is far from routine when Casi inadvertently breaks the confessional booth in the process. Rushing to get out of there, he is flagged by the priest who tries to get Casi to sign a release. It turns out the entire confession has been recorded as part of a new TV show called *Clerical Confessions*. "You want me to agree to put what I just said on Television," Casi exclaims. "No it's not TV, it's HBO," insists the priest.[92]

Similarly, when Casi appears for a hearing regarding a contempt of court charge against him, he finds that he is to be represented by Devin Quackmire, a teenager who is not even a lawyer. "The testimony itself was not that damaging although Quackmire's crosses often bore little relation to any conceivable issue and seemed to betray an unhealthy fascination with things like favorite foods and turn-ons," notes Casi.[93] The presiding judge, who is herself a complainant in the hearing, puts on a white-curl wig and carries a tricycle-sized gavel.

This hearing is followed by a second one, where Casi again sits as the defendant. This one is a disciplinary hearing internal to the Public Defender's Office and is run by a committee named "C.O.C.K. . . . the **C**ommittee to **O**ust **C**asi **K**wickly."[94] It too is presided over by individuals that are also counted among the aggrieved. That this hearing, like the previous one, has lost all semblance of reasonable protocol and is structured to the disadvantage of the defendant (like the criminal justice system as explained by Casi earlier, but exacerbated) is made plain when he is notified: "In all instances the reading of the charge will constitute full, complete, and irrefutable evidentiary proof of that charge in and of itself, meaning no further corroboration will be required."[95] After the hearings, Casi is in the lobby when he sees evidence of Ballena. He manages to escape out of the building and hurries home. "By the time I got to my building I was well-disguised having purchased a Yosemite Sam hat and giant novelty sunglasses at the subway station," he tells the reader.[96]

Clearly, the world has become inconsistent. The very rules of reason and the parameters of reality are collapsing, similar to the way the laws of nature are breaking down due to the naked singularity. If indeed Casi's mind is breaking down from the entropy spreading throughout his brain, the occurrence of everything after the initial explanation of the criminal justice system, including the heist, is put in doubt. Like the idealist bubble of financial capital, which was popped by its own real, the narrative world, as Casi's imaginary creation, descends into chaos due to its own ineradicable real. Casi's mental state, moreover, is conditioned by the "insanity" of late modernity, intimating that what we take to be the cause of narrative chaos is rather the symptom of our times. After all, as Mark Fisher notes: "The 'mental health plague' in capitalist societies would suggest that, instead of being the only social system that works, capitalism is inherently dysfunctional."[97]

CONCLUSION

As I have demonstrated in this chapter, a Marxist and materialist approach opens up the text to its politico-economic context in a way that allows for its interpretation as an object that, in its dialectical relationship with the context of its creation, is both conditioned by *and* a response to the latter. Latina/o and ethnic minority literatures, on the other hand, do not so much demand the addition of categories of race and ethnicity to class, but rather highlight that class formations are always already imbricated with the production of ethnic and racial difference. Accordingly, de la Pava's novel begins by highlighting the structural injustices of a criminal justice system increasingly made to deal with the social consequences of neoliberalism. It depicts a setting where official politics blend into entertainment, where the poor and homeless become mere "bodies" to be managed, and where image is everything. The novel, which takes place in one of the world's main financial centers and was written during a time rife with speculative activity, reproduces the formal logic of the ideology of neoliberal financial capitalism, with its idealist disavowal of its own real, in the mind-set that characterizes Dane. By means of the (real) entropy that plagues Casi's mind and the naked singularity that destroys the universe, however, the novel also formally prefigures the impending collapse that would manifest itself in 2008, the year of its first publication—the prior iterations of which can be found in the series of financial crises of the late 1990s and early 2000s. What the figures of entropy and the naked singularity show is that the real always comes back to disrupt any idealist fantasies.

The recklessness and destructive power of financial speculation, moreover, sits uneasily with the phenomenon of mass incarceration and the near-ubiquitous calls for "fiscal responsibility" that most often serve to gut government services that overwhelmingly affect the racialized poor. The contradiction lies in the fact that the racialized poor are made to bear the brunt of the state's legal and extralegal repression precisely in the name of securing a social order designed to create a good "business climate"—that is, one that is made to better attract financial investment, speculation, and consumption—when it is financial speculation that proves to be much more dangerous than, for example, any of the violations for which Casi's clients are tried. The real danger, we should learn, lies not in the petty crimes of which most of Casi's clients are accused, but in the predominant neoliberal politico-economic ideology that threatens our existence in much more profound ways.

Notes

1. Sergio de la Pava, *A Naked Singularity* (Chicago: University of Chicago Press, 2012).

2. "An Interview with Sergio de la Pava," *Believer*, October 3, 2012, accessed May 2, 2016, http://logger.believermag.com/post/32817533978/an-interview-with-sergio-de-la-pava; Susanna Rustin, "Sergio De La Pava: 'My Book's Not Perfect, but It's What I Set Out to Do. I Wanted It to Have a Propulsive, Angry Core,'" *Guardian*, June 27, 2014, accessed May 2, 2016, http://www.theguardian.com/books/2014/jun/27/sergio-de-la-pava-naked-singularity-interview

3. Scott Bryan Wilson, "A Naked Singularity by Sergio de la Pava," *Quarterly Con-*

versation, October 4, 2010, accessed May 2, 2016, http://quarterlyconversation.com/a-naked-singularity-by-sergio-de-la-pava

4. Casi's mother was the first to leave Colombia for the United States in an act of rebellion against her own mother, who prohibited her from marrying Casi's father. Eventually, "there followed a genuine exodus of Colombian *tourists* who overstayed their INS welcome" (De la Pava, *Naked*, 117; emphasis in the original).

5. "The heavily-made-up women all wore indecent-exposure-short skirts and heels in the smack of winter and looked like they should be elegantly twirling their hands in the vicinity of A New Car" (De la Pava, *Naked*, 120).

6. De la Pava, *Naked*, 118–20.

7. Rey Chow, *The Protestant Ethnic and The Spirit of Capitalism* (New York: Columbia University Press, 2002), 107. For a reading of the concept of coercive mimeticism in Latina/o studies, see Antonio Viego, *Dead Subjects: Toward a Politics of Loss in Latino Studies* (Durham, NC: Duke University Press, 2007). For a similar analysis of the politics of authenticity in the making of the ethnic canon, see Carlos Gallego, *Chicana/o Subjectivity and the Politics of Identity: Between Recognition and Revolution* (New York: Palgrave Macmillan, 2011), 180.

8. "Interview," *Believer*.

9. Stuart Kelly, "A Naked Singularity by Sergio De La Pava—Review," *Guardian*, August 29, 2013, accessed May 2, 2016, http://www.theguardian.com/books/2013/aug/29/naked-singularity-sergio-pava-review; James Wood, "James Woods' Classic Takedown of Faux-Dickensian 'Hysterical Realism,'" *New Republic*, July 24, 2000, accessed May 5, 2016, https://newrepublic.com/article/61361/human-all-too-inhuman

10. Wood, "Hysterical Realism."

11. See Fredric Jameson, *The Political Unconscious: Narrative as a Socially Symbolic Act* (Ithaca, NY: Cornell University Press, 1981).

12. Marcial González, *Chicano Novels and the Politics of Form: Race, Class, and Reification* (Ann Arbor: University of Michigan Press, 2009), 14.

13. De la Pava, *Naked*, 2. This quotation is itself taken from Abraham Lincoln's inaugural address a month before the start of the Civil War in 1861.

14. De la Pava, *Naked*, 3.

15. De la Pava, *Naked*, 3.

16. The issue of race and the criminal justice system is also addressed more directly later in the novel when an attorney declares: "This [court]room and the criminal justice system as a whole is the frontline. This is where modern-day segregation lives on" (De la Pava, *Naked*, 79). Responding to the charge by another colleague that his statement is an exaggeration, this attorney proceeds to provide statistics on the rates at which Black men are subject to various forms of correctional control (De la Pava, *Naked*, 79–80).

17. Christopher Mathias, "NYPD Stop and Frisk: 15 Shocking Facts about a Controversial Program," *Huffington Post*, May 15, 2012, accessed May 23, 2016, http://www.huffingtonpost.com/2012/05/13/nypd-stop-and-frisks-15-shocking-facts_n_1513362.html

18. Michelle Alexander, *The New Jim Crow: Mass Incarceration in the Age of Colorblindness*, 2nd ed. (New York: New Press, 2012), 7; emphasis in the original.

19. De la Pava, *Naked*, 4.

20. De la Pava, *Naked*, 5; emphasis in the original.

21. Rustin, "Sergio de la Pava." The black rat that is caged and tortured by Casi's neighbors later in the novel to teach it that life is beyond its control also suggests a parallel with race and the correctional system in the United States (De la Pava, *Naked*, 339).

22. Annasue McCleave Wilson, "Fighting for Justice," *Publishers Weekly*, April 13, 2012, accessed May 2, 2016, http://www.publishersweekly.com/pw/by-topic/authors/interviews/article/51486-fighting-for-justice-pw-talks-with-sergio-de-la-pava.html

23. De la Pava, *Naked*, 3.

24. Ruth Wilson Gilmore, *Golden Gulag: Prisons, Surplus, Crisis, and Opposition in Globalizing California* (Berkeley: University of California Press, 2007), 58. Todd Miller, *Border Patrol Nation: Dispatches from the Front Lines of Homeland Security* (San Francisco: City Lights Books, 2014), 35–55.

25. David Harvey, *A Brief History of Neoliberalism* (New York: Oxford University Press, 2005), 45–46.

26. A judge in the novel, Judge Preskill, also details the problems with the Rockefeller drug laws and the restrictions they place on the ability of judges to determine different kinds of sentences (De la Pava, *Naked*, 158).

27. David Harvey, *The Urban Experience* (Baltimore: Johns Hopkins, 1989), 45–53. Cf. Mike Davis, *City of Quartz: Excavating the Future in Los Angeles* (New York: Vintage Books, 1992).

28. Neil Smith, "Giuliani Time: The Revanchist 1990s," *Social Text* 57 (Winter 1998): 2.

29. Quoted in Smith, "Giuliani Time," 9.

30. De la Pava, *Naked*, 121, 123.

31. De la Pava, *Naked*, 130, 141.

32. De la Pava, *Naked*, 659; emphasis in the original.

33. Mayor Toad seems to blend elements of both Giuliani and his successor, Michael Bloomberg. Combining a background in criminal law (Giuliani) and in finance (Bloomberg), together they represent the link between the criminal justice system and neoliberal financial capitalism that I emphasize in this chapter.

34. De la Pava, *Naked*, 659.

35. De la Pava, *Naked*, 659.

36. De la Pava, *Naked*, 659; emphasis in the original.

37. De la Pava, *Naked*, 660.

38. De la Pava, *Naked*, 660.

39. David Harvey, "*Commonwealth*: An Exchange," *Artforum* 48.3 (November 2009): 214.

40. Matt Taibbi, *Griftopia: Bubble Machines, Vampire Squids, and the Long Con That Is Breaking America* (New York: Spiegel and Grau, 2010), 60.

41. Fredric Jameson, "Culture and Finance Capital," in *The Jameson Reader*, ed. Michael Hardt and Kathi Weeks (Malden, MA: Blackwell, 2000), 259; Giovanni Arrighi, *The Long Twentieth Century: Money, Power and the Origins of Our Times* (New York: Verso, 2010), 237.

42. By "idealism" I refer to a tendency that can be said to privilege imaginary constructions over their material conditions to the extent that such constructions are given precedence without regard for the determinations or constraints that puncture and "split" them.

43. Taibbi, *Griftopia*, 84.

44. Taibbi, *Griftopia*, 85.

45. Even AAA-rated CDOs were mostly junk since the rating agencies' own financial dependence on the investment banks incentivized them to hand out high ratings and essentially keep the bubble going (Taibbi, *Griftopia*, 85–86).

46. Taibbi, *Griftopia*, 89–90. That is, before they would themselves "unload their loans on someone else before [the homeowners] start[ed] defaulting" (90).

47. Taibbi, *Griftopia*, 93.

48. Taibbi, *Griftopia*, 48.

49. Taibbi, *Griftopia*, 74.

50. Arrighi, *Long Twentieth Century*, 129.

51. Roger Penrose, *The Road to Reality: A Complete Guide to the Laws of the Universe* (New York: A.A. Knopf, 2005), 767–68.

52. De la Pava, *Naked*, 658.

53. De la Pava, *Naked*, 661.

54. The naked singularity could also be interpreted as alluding to the attacks of 9/11. The attacks and the implosion of the World Trade Center are indeed often talked about as marking the end of an epoch and the beginning of a new one. The focus of the current reading, rather than being in strict opposition to this alternative reading, can perhaps bring out some of the structural factors that the latter would also need to account for.

55. Slavoj Žižek, *Absolute Recoil: Towards a New Foundation of Dialectical Materialism* (New York: Verso, 2014), 223.

56. De la Pava, *Naked*, 512, 613.

57. De la Pava, *Naked*, 568.

58. De la Pava, *Naked*, 656.

59. De la Pava, *Naked*, 160.

60. Cf. with the connection that Žižek establishes between Marxist and Freudian readings: "In both cases the point is to avoid the properly fetishistic fascination of the 'content' supposedly hidden behind the form: the 'secret' to be unveiled through analysis is not the content hidden by the form . . . but, on the contrary, *the 'secret' of this form itself*." Slavoj Žižek, *The Sublime Object of Ideology*, 2nd ed. (New York: Verso, 2008), 3; emphasis in the original.

61. De la Pava, *Naked*, 93.

62. De la Pava, *Naked*, 191; emphasis in the original.

63. De la Pava, *Naked,* 276.

64. De la Pava, *Naked,* 313.

65. De la Pava, *Naked,* 306; emphasis in the original.

66. De la Pava, *Naked,* 313.

67. See Alain Badiou, *Logics of Worlds: Being and Event II,* trans. Alberto Toscano (London: Continuum, 2009).

68. Badiou, *Logics of Worlds,* 510.

69. De la Pava, *Naked,* 306.

70. De la Pava, *Naked,* 173.

71. De la Pava, *Naked,* 175.

72. De la Pava, *Naked,* 308.

73. De la Pava, *Naked,* 179.

74. Georg Cantor was the first to posit the actuality of infinity, and, indeed, to posit the actuality of infinities of different sizes. On the difference between pre- and post-Cantorian conceptions of infinity, see Badiou, "The Subject and Infinity," in *Conditions,* trans. Steven Corcoran (New York: Continuum, 2008), 211–27.

75. While Dane and Casi are able to steal the money, the heist falls short of perfection.

76. De la Pava, *Naked,* 92.

77. De la Pava, *Naked,* 92.

78. De la Pava, *Naked,* 71. The use of this line from *The Usual Suspects* (1995) also foreshadows Dane's status as a kind of criminal mastermind.

79. De la Pava, *Naked,* 402.

80. De la Pava, *Naked,* 439.

81. De la Pava, *Naked,* 439.

82. De la Pava, *Naked,* 673.

83. De la Pava, *Naked,* 343.

84. Even here, however, doubt remains since another version of the quote, also known as "Occam's Razor," states that given two hypotheses, one should choose the one with fewer assumptions. And we certainly assume much more if we posit that Dane does not exist than we do if we posit the opposite. We thus seem to have an undecidable proposition. Given the praise of doubt with which the chapter begins, and despite (or perhaps because of) my own doubt as to the certainty of my interpretation here, I choose the side of doubt.

85. De la Pava, *Naked,* 343; emphasis in original.

86. After all, at one point Judge Cymbeline also responds to Casi's thoughts (383).

87. De la Pava, *Naked,* 60; emphasis in the original.

88. De la Pava, *Naked,* 61.

89. The fact that toward the end of the novel Casi has trouble recognizing the face of his sister, Dane, and Angus suggests that, at the very minimum, he may be beginning to suffer from prosopagnosia (492–93, 655, 671–72).

90. De la Pava, *Naked,* 419.

91. De la Pava, *Naked*, 606.
92. De la Pava, *Naked*, 420.
93. De la Pava, *Naked*, 649.
94. De la Pava, *Naked*, 650; emphasis in the original.
95. De la Pava, *Naked*, 651.
96. De la Pava, *Naked*, 655.
97. Mark Fisher, *Capitalist Realism: Is There No Alternative?* (Washington, DC: Zero Books, 2009), 19.

CHAPTER 6

Pornocapitalism and the Translucent Borders of Social Identity in Deck of Deeds

Carlos Gallego

Studying the intersection of market relations and sexuality is certainly not a new project in the history of critical theory. In her book *The Triumph of Venus: The Erotics of the Market*, for example, legal scholar Jeanne Lorraine Schroeder—utilizing psychoanalysis and Continental philosophy as her primary interpretive methodologies—explains how eroticism, dating back to ancient Greece, constitutes the most fundamental form of market relations.[1] Calling upon the work of Jacques Lacan and G. W. F. Hegel to counter the "law-and-economics" paradigm that currently frames our understanding of market relations, Schroeder argues that the "rational-irrational" dichotomy that currently dominates our discourse about the market obfuscates their interdependency—the fact that they are "mirror images of each other"—thereby limiting the erotic possibilities that remain latent in market interactions.[2] Rather than favor either passion (the irrational) or reason (the rational) as the appropriate mind-set for market relations, Schroeder argues for a balance between the two: "Through reason, the abstract person comes to understand that she can only actualize herself through recognition by other subjects. . . . Therefore, she rationally desires others: logic tells her to give way to passion. . . . [Yet] even at the ecstatic moment of *jouissance*, the subject must preserve a moment of the rationality that makes desire possible."[3] Stated differently, reason inspires us to desire, and passion—as an active form of desire—is what moves us to satisfy our desires within reason. This, in turn, allows reason to control our passions, which underscores the fundamental interdependency between reason and desire (or the rational and irrational), a thesis first made famous by Hegel and later developed by theorists like Lacan. Consequently, one can argue, as Schroeder does, that the false dichotomy of the rational-irrational model governing our law-and-economics understanding of the market reproduces an indefinite imbalance, which explains one of the many reasons underlying capitalism's past and current failures.

Published in 2004, Schroeder's book follows in the intellectual footsteps of Marxist-friendly critical theorists like Marcel Mauss, George Bataille, and Herbert Marcuse, who were equally interested in uncovering the hidden eroticism of market relations—or what could otherwise be understood as the anthropology and psychology underlying parliamentary capitalism as a political economy. Bataille and Marcuse were particularly drawn to the underlying eroticism of not only the market but society in general, very much in the tradition outlined by post-Enlightenment intellectuals like Friedrich Nietzsche and Sigmund Freud. Bataille's theory of human expenditure, for example, is grounded in his philosophical theory regarding the economics of waste and excess in human civilizations.[4] Being an institutionalized space where both consumer waste and excess are not only permitted but encouraged, market capitalism stands out as a good example of a system constantly negotiating the parameters of its *telos* (i.e., profit) as a means of avoiding an excessive waste of wealth, which can lead to "a financial crisis." Simply stated, consumers can partake in wasteful and excessive consumption, but when institutions do so—like the major risks banks such as Goldman Sachs took leading up to the 2008 financial crisis—it is at the peril of the entire economy, which is why the U.S. government is perpetually renegotiating its role regarding market regulation.[5]

In a somewhat similar line of inquiry, Marcuse—taking his cue from earlier Frankfurt School theorists like Max Horkheimer and Theodor Adorno, who criticized the underlying barbarism of capitalism as a continuation of the primitive and violent mindset that equates exchange value with sacrifice[6]—also argued for the liberation of human *eros* from the shackles of capitalism. He famously stated that the one-dimensionality of modern individuals is created by a technologically advanced society that represses human freedom (particularly the erotic and emotional) in favor of techno-capitalist interests.[7] So long as human *eros* is manipulated and controlled by state-sponsored capitalism, only the select few that constitute the nation's financial oligarchy—what is now commonly referred to as the 1 percent—

will enjoy the true benefits of human freedom, keeping any revolutionary fervor in ideological check.

While the long history of scholarship analyzing the interconnections between market capitalism and eroticism continue to be studied and developed by scholars like Schroeder, I do not find what I understand to be the pornographization of such market eroticism to be as widely examined. There are, however, contemporary writers, especially Latino/a poets, who allude to this new stage in capitalist development in their work, highlighting how certain practices and forms of behavior, though socially unhealthy, are culturally normalized and celebrated via a market-based ethics of desire. Rodrigo Toscano is one such poet, and his 2012 work, *Deck of Deeds*,[8] offers an exemplary series of portraits that demonstrate how pornocapitalism arrests individual desire by framing excess as an accessible entry point into publicly visible but nevertheless highly restrictive spaces of obscene pleasure and wealth—"new publics" that circulate in our culture as transparent and alluring yet prohibited spaces inhabited by transgressive subjects that are themselves defined by a decadent excess. Based on the popular Mexican "lotería" game—which is similar to American bingo except that, instead of numbers and letters, symbols and figures are used on the play cards—*Deck of Deeds* depicts the individuals that make up these new publics as postmodern "lotería" archetypes who exploit their financial or political agency, or both, to cross the traditional borders of class, nation, and culture, thereby embodying capitalism's ability to survive crises by circumventing sociopolitical and cultural barriers that might otherwise enact the formation of a collective class consciousness.

In the sections below, I argue that Toscano's work reveals how contemporary capitalism, like pornography, manipulates one's desire by preying on the intersubjective nature of human identity. In this manner, Toscano's "lotería" portraits exemplify how capitalism perverts the dialectic of desire that is supposed to facilitate mutual recognition and transforms it into a dialectic of desire based on dehumanization and socially sanctioned practices involving, but not limited to, the excessive circulation of the self as spectacle-commodity. Building on a dialectical materialist tradition that understands market economies as inherently functioning on the manipulation of psychic dynamics, particularly desire and the conflation of identity with wealth and excess, I utilize the term *pornocapitalism* as a means of showing how affluence in contemporary capitalist societies functions as an obscenely excessive-yet-appropriate form of existential agency. Using examples from

Deck of Deeds, I demonstrate how the logic of the spectacle-commodity economy that characterizes late capitalism succeeds by privileging lifestyles that are defined by decadent public practices, normalizing behavioral and personality traits traditionally defined as pornographic in their excessiveness. I conclude the chapter by giving examples of how pornocapitalism manifests itself in contemporary U.S. political culture, grounding the critique inherent in Toscano's portraits in actual historical figures and events.

PORNOCAPITALISM, IDEOLOGY, AND THE COMMODITY-SPECTACLE ECONOMY

Marxist theorists, dating back to Karl Marx himself, have often referred to eroticism and the politics of sexuality as a means of explaining the oppressive nature of capitalism. Thus, to fully appreciate the pornographization of the market eroticism studied by scholars like Schroeder, it is necessary to first clarify my use of the term "pornography." Originally, specifically in ancient Greece, the term was used as an adjective to describe one who writes about prostitution, a definition that was cemented by a French treatise on prostitution published in 1800 entitled *pornographie*. By the mid-nineteenth century, the term "pornography" had been expanded to include anything that could be considered obscene, especially in representational mediums like literature and the arts.

Twentieth-century theories of pornography advanced this mid-nineteenth-century definition, offering more inclusive uses of the term that focus mostly on explicit representations of the obscene—obscenity here referring to anything considered too erotic, graphic, or sexual. This emphasis on explicitness and representation is important in that the excessive (and therefore deemed unnecessary) details associated with pornography allow theorists to continually redefine its complexity in order to account for other social phenomenon, like Abraham Kaplan's thesis regarding "the pornography of violence," an idea he introduced in a 1955 essay entitled "Obscenity as an Esthetic Category."[9] In this essay, Kaplan defines pornography as "promotional: it is the obscene responded to with minimal psychic distance . . . [It] serves to elicit not the imaginative contemplation of an expressive substance, but rather the release in fantasy of a compelling impulse."[10] This more expansive understanding of pornography is actually better aligned with contemporary definitions that define the pornography of violence first introduced by Kaplan as the "explicit description or depiction of violence in a manner intended to stimulate or excite."[11] Still, I would add to these definitions the all-important notion of excess. As Bataille reminds us, pornography is obscene because it is excessive in its detailed representations of sexuality or some other practice, like violence, which is commonly referred to as gratuitous. Such overly detailed representations create an explicitness that is meant to elicit a specific effect, particularly excitation and pleasure, while satisfying "a compelling impulse." As a result, the less detailed or explicit a representation is, the less obscene it can be, thus the less pornographic.

Unpacking the relationship between the pairing of eroticism and the market with pornography and prostitution in Marx's work is important because it is the latter (i.e., prostitution) that Marx uses as an analogy to describe the relationship between worker and property owner under capitalism. As he writes in a footnote to the *Economic and Philosophic Manuscripts of 1844*, prostitution "is only a *specific* expression of the *general* prostitution of the *labourer*, and since it is a relationship in which falls not the prostitute alone, but also the one who prostitutes . . . the capitalist, etc., also comes under this head."[12] Here, Marx is basically comparing the selling of one's labor in a capitalist economy to a form of prostitution, with private property owners serving as pimps and workers as prostitutes.

Marx's analytical framing of prostitution as analogous to capitalism positions workers as unknowing victims of a mystifying political-economic ideology, which explains the working class's continual endurance of unjust living and working conditions (i.e., their seemingly willful prostitution). As Marx famously explained, once workers become aware of their exploitation and false consciousness (i.e., ideological indoctrination), they will revolt against state-sanctioned capitalist exploitation in such a way as to radically transform their conditions of existence and fully actualize their humanity, mainly by de-alienating their relationship to labor and production.[13] This classic Marxist definition of ideology depends heavily on the power of class consciousness, which is the key to political revolution in that it transforms the alienated subject's ideological perception of reality (i.e., the status quo understanding of American democracy as guaranteeing equality for all, despite material evidence to the contrary) into the undeniable witnessing of one's own exploitation and the subtle ways we enable it (i.e., the irrefutable truth of material inequality in so-called democratic societies).

However, as the twentieth century demonstrated, the adaptive and transformative powers of capitalism and its accompanying ideologies cannot be underestimated, especially since the more desperate capitalism becomes in hiding the contradictions that make up its ideological core, the more creative it seems to be in mystifying the inequalities produced by said contradictions. This conundrum provides the backbone for the Marxist narrative regarding the absence of a global proletarian revolution in light of capitalism's oppressive global regime, a narrative developed by theorists like Fredric Jameson and David Harvey, both of whom have published extensively on the rise of postmodernity as being the manifestation of "late capitalism" (to use Ernest Mandel's term) and its neoliberal ethics of financial deregulation.[14] The importance of late capitalism as an interpretive model is not so much the historical periodicity implied by the term "late" but rather its compatibility with critiques of neoliberalism. Whether we understand our contemporary political economy as "the cultural logic of late capitalism" (Jameson), post-Fordist, neoliberal capitalism (Harvey), or cultural capitalism (Slavoj Žižek), the underlying constant in these analyses is that our contemporary political economy functions very much on an ethics of globalization, speculation, deregulation, transnationalism, and ideological fantasies centered on individual identity and lifestyle choices.[15]

Documenting similar transformations in capitalism from a somewhat different perspective, Guy Debord was one of the first critical theorists to study how ideological fantasies fuel the capitalist economy of spectacle and, one could argue, speculation. As a member of the Situationist International, Debord published an essay in 1966 entitled "The Decline and Fall of the Spectacle-Commodity Economy," which, interestingly, is a defense of the 1965 Watts riots in Los Angeles.[16] Debord's basic argument is that the riots encapsulate the contradictions and tensions between representations of democratic, multicultural inclusion (i.e., spectacle) and the realities of alienated material conditions of existence for African Americans in the United States. Debord explains how this spontaneous uprising exposed the economic truth of disenfranchisement under capitalism: systemic political and economic marginalization (in this case, racist disenfranchisement) is a necessary evil meant to sustain established structures of oppression and privilege, which continue to function unabatedly. The Watts riots were therefore legitimate reactions to the institutionalized fact that economic wealth and political empowerment will never be made available to the African American population, regardless of legislative changes like the 1964 Civil Rights Act: "American blacks are hated and treated as criminal, [and] monetary riches will never make them acceptable in America's alienated society . . . because blacks as a whole must *represent poverty* in a society of hierarchized wealth."[17] Debord's point is that the African American population within the United States can never achieve economic equality as it is their predetermined place to function as representatives of poverty, of the ever-present capitalist threat that keeps the rest of the population ideologically compliant and docile. To prove Debord's point, one need only invoke the recent examples of Ferguson, Missouri, or Baltimore, Maryland as but two illustrations of the systemic oppression—both economically and through state sanctioned violence—targeting the racialized poor in the United States.

The genius of Debord's analysis, however, is not his prophetic anticipation of the contradictions we are currently witnessing, like the ironic tensions of an urgent and much-needed Black Lives Matter movement emerging within the celebrated spectacle of the nation's first Black president—a contradiction that is hard to accept for many scholars, like Cornell West, who actually anticipated "Hope and Change" during Obama's tenure only to be eventually disappointed.[18] Instead, Debord's brilliance lies in what he found to be the central problem underlying the spectacle-commodity economy—the problem of abundance, which brings us back to the problem of obscenity-as-excess within what I'm calling pornocapitalism: "*Freedom now* is the password of all the revolutions of history, but now for the first time it is not poverty but material abundance which must be dominated . . . not just [by] changing the way it is shared out, but redefining its every orientation, superficial and profound alike. This is the first step of an immense struggle, infinite in its implications."[19] Debord's point here can be easily missed or misinterpreted—he is not arguing that poverty no longer exists or is not experienced by alienated individuals in a capitalist society; his defense of the Watts riots as an understandable reaction to the class warfare waged against racial minorities in the United States is evidence of this fact. Instead, I understand Debord's call to action against material abundance as a criticism of the manner in which the spectacle-commodity economy sidesteps the problem of sociopolitical inequality by reveling in the production of excess and promoting ideologies of enjoyment. According to Debord, Watts proved that poverty is not an economic inevitability but rather a manufactured necessity used to legitimate material abundance for a select few. *The problem is not lack but excess, an excess so widespread that it obscures the lived realities of economic oppression (of lack).* This is what made Watts such a problem for the United States in particular and Western nations in general, beyond the confines of Los Angeles to places like Paris and Mexico City: as a precursor to the more famous revolts grouped under the heading "May 1968," Watts broke through the spectacles of multicultural-democratic inclusion, individual freedom, and economic-social mobility that would come to define the ideological core of neoliberalism. Under the traditional Marxist model, the revolts of the 1960s—especially 1968—should have resulted in widespread revolution, but they did not. On the contrary, they seem to have ushered in an era of neoliberalism and late capitalism under the guise—one could even say spectacle—of "progressive change."

This historical fact constitutes a central point of contention among many critical and Marxist theorists, with a long list of brilliant studies addressing the why and how of this revolutionary failure, beginning with Louis Althusser's famous essay "Ideology and Ideological State Apparatuses" to more recent theories like Žižek's thesis concerning the sublime object of ideology and Alain Badiou's theory of being and the event. My own contribution builds upon such studies in that pornocapitalism—as an interpretive model—helps explain how the material abundance critiqued by Debord has come to define the central ethic of contemporary capitalism, curbing the potential for political and economic revolution. Such dampening of revolutionary fervor is in large part due to the expansion of the spectacle-commodity economy and the assimilation of traditionally disenfranchised communities into mainstream culture. Under this new model, the individual is no longer simply or only prostituted for his or her labor and, therefore, alienated from his or her humanity; in addition to the commodification of labor, the individual can also exist as a potential spectacle-commodity, which redefines the relationship between capitalist commodification and individual alienation. In contrast to the traditional capitalist model of working hard—or cleverly—to get ahead, pornocapitalism invites the excessive and uninhibited commodification of the self in a manner that elicits excitation and pleasure rather than alienation.

A concrete example of the individual as spectacle-commodity is the rise of the so-called selfie movement, a cultural phenomenon centered on an excessive narcissism that finds value in the rapidly growing social media economy. The alienation that a worker may experience in his or her job may be easily resolved through the self-actualization and existential value that he or she may receive through this alternative economy, which never ceases to be a subset of the larger capitalist economy as a whole. Consequently, the eroticism of the market, which contains the potential for radical human interaction, is co-opted for the purposes of profit, while the alienation that is supposed to lead workers to unite and revolt against socioeconomic injustices is medicated by the excessive—some would say obscene—public displays of self-fashioning found in the social media economy. Alienation therefore becomes a choice, not a systemically imposed condition of existence, especially when existential fulfillment (or dis-alienation) is only a tweet, Facebook post, or YouTube video away. Pornocapitalism is thus very much a form of Kardashian capitalism, an economic empire founded on nothing but the self as spectacle-commodity—which, in this case, originates with a "leaked" sex tape—that nonetheless generates profit in the millions, combined with a Donald Trump attitude toward politics and public health, which is equally invested in the spectacle-commodity economy of branding (I revisit this connection between Trump and pornocapitalism in the postscript to this chapter). And this is Debord's point—that abundance offers the ideological fantasies of inclusion-through-recognition and of freedom-through-luxury. As a result, the possibility of collective revolt is minimized, as the spectacle-commodity economy encourages individuals to pimp themselves out in a hopeful rather than alienating manner, rewarding isolationism and narcissism through social media while promoting sociopolitical fragmentation within the working class.

PORNOCAPITALISM IN *DECK OF DEEDS*

The Chicano poet and labor activist Rodrigo Toscano captures the tone and feeling of pornocapitalism—particularly the social effects of its accompanying ideologies, such as the self-as-spectacle-commodity—in his work, *Deck of Deeds* (2012). The opening poem to the collection, entitled "Los Exploradores"—which translates as "the explorers," a term I assume is meant to highlight the speculative nature of contemporary capitalism, specifically in the oil industry—encapsulates how dis-alienation functions under pornocapitalism:

> ### LOS EXPLORADORES
>
> Last summer, while on their first gulf-wide helicopter tour, they
> learned how to increase their inner-narrating capacities with a
> titanium-coated needle. They prefer to stoke it in small basements
> of large soccer stadiums south of the equator in case they encounter

> too much cerebrospinal spillage, or regulation. Their favorite fantasy is that they're successful motivational vocabularists for hire to a half dozen oil executives from Russia on a visit to New York who install an indecipherable ethicalism into their brains, one by one.
>
> Last week, while still twisted on dichlorobenzidine after a night of doctoring EPA reports, they licked the sweet crude slime from a 200-meter drill bit before going in for a final, deep plunge. Just as they were about to induce a frontal cranial orgasm for the stockholder's executive board, they looked into their faces in a reflective aluminum hotel bar counter-plating in Houston. When they saw how hot their mouths looked, smeared with oil, spit, and tar gas residue, they gazed into their own eyes and whispered, "We're such . . . sluts."[20]

Described as logging in "ten thousand miles of air travel each month working as a union trainer and coordinator throughout the U.S.," Toscano is in the unique position of interacting with many of the microcommunities that make up the cultural landscape of contemporary American society, ranging from explosive-smuggling college students to oil speculators.[21] Reading like a character study from a Thomas Pynchon novel, the first paragraph places us in the shadowy underworld of oil speculation in the age of late capitalism. The poem underscores the importance of ideological fantasy and identity ("they learned how to increase their inner-narrating capacities" and "Their favorite fantasy is that they're successful motivational vocabularists for hire"), as well as transnationalism ("half dozen oil executives from Russia on a visit to New York") and the neoliberal politics of modernization ("small basements of large soccer stadiums south of the equator").

While the role of ideological fantasy in identity construction seems fairly straightforward in the poem, as does the transnationalism of the various locations and nationalities mentioned throughout, the geopolitics of neoliberal modernization may seem less obvious. As one of the darker aspects of neoliberalism, "small basements of large soccer stadiums south of the equator" refers to the practice of incarcerating and torturing people in "developing countries" as a means of controlling popular dissent, a practice that not only exemplified the United States' aggressive and interventionist foreign policy during the Cold War era, but one that symbolically ushered in the new world order of neoliberal transnationalism. One famous example of U.S. interventionism in other nations, particularly those "south of the border," is the clandestine involvement of the United States in the Chilean military coup lead by General Augusto Pinochet, who rounded up and "detained" (most of these detainments eventually became "disappearances") approximately 10,000 students, workers, and political activists in Santiago's National Soccer Stadium in 1973.

Whereas the first paragraph of this poetic portrait establishes a setting that helps introduce the protagonists, the second paragraph provides an explicit picture of how their "favorite fantasy" plays out in the real world, where narcotics are used to fuel a night of EPA report doctoring for the purposes of creating orgasmic profit margins. The pornographic imagery in the poem is obvious, from licking "the sweet crude slime from a 200-meter drill bit" to "hot . . . mouths [that] looked, smeared with oil, spit, and tar gas residue." Despite these graphic details that some readers may find obscene, the pornographic quality of the poem does not arise from the confirmation that the protagonists—as employees—function as prostitutes to the oil industry ("We're such . . . sluts") but rather in the pleasure that they receive from their lifestyle. These are not alienated bureaucrats—contemporary versions of Gregor Samsa—trapped in a Kafkaesque world, slaves to the whims of globetrotting Russian oil moguls; instead, they are living a perverted fantasy as successful ideologues, most likely as lobbyists, consultants, or think-tank intellectuals.

The point of "Los Exploradores" is not to highlight the manner in which these individuals are alienated from their labor or that they are exploited for the benefit of someone else (they are, after all, staying up all night "working"); instead, the poem—by emphasizing the role of excess and pleasure—underscores the extreme self-absorption that is required to maintain the self-as-spectacle-commodity. The obscene nature of their lifestyle elicits an eroticism that is transparent in its extravagance. These are not workers who will protest the material conditions of their existence; these are employees—or better yet, team members—who advertise their supposed alienation on Facebook and Instagram, documenting their helicopter tours as evidence of a decadent and enviable lifestyle.

They're sluts because of their obscenely hyper-yet-superficial self-awareness (note the "reflective aluminum hotel bar counter-plating," which serves as a distorted and distorting mirror) and not because they lick slime off drill bits.

Toscano also addresses the excessively ironic—some might say offensively contradictory—nature of pornocapitalist public service and its discontents in "El Sirviente" ("The Servant"), where he outlines the ways in which this new form of capitalism encourages the avoidance of alienation by not only promoting the type of self-medicated, state-sponsored hypernarcissism seen in "Los Exploradores" but also the manner in which what is perceived to be "the social" is itself controlled and managed by those assigned the duty of serving "the public." More specifically, the decadence that Toscano underscores in this poem epitomizes the obscene neoliberalist erasure of the public/private divide, an erasure that pornocapitalism achieves by conflating economic freedom with market deregulation, thereby erasing policies meant to protect the public from excessive private interests while offering jingoisms regarding freedom and individualism, a practice that was made transparent with the Panama Papers, a "giant leak of more than 11.5 million financial and legal records [that] exposes a system that enables crime, corruption and wrongdoing, hidden by secretive offshore companies."[22] But as "Los Exploradores" makes evident, the privatization of the public—from the idea of "the self-as-spectacle-commodity" (i.e., selfie) to the excessive privatization of public services, including schools, prisons, medical clinics, and retirement centers—only leads to the endangerment of society in the name of private economic interests, underscored in "Los Exploradores" with the doctoring of Environmental Protection Agency (EPA) reports for the purposes of maximizing profits for the oil industry. In that poem, the negative environmental impact caused by the corporate propensity for maximum profit is obvious and not too surprising when taking into account the subjects of Toscano's portrait. But "El Sirviente" riffs off themes presented in "Los Exploradores" as a means of showing the totalizing effects of pornocapitalism run amok, particularly in individuals and institutions charged with protecting the health and prosperity of society as a whole.

The contradictions underlying the act of being a public servant in a pornocapitalist world are immediately introduced by Toscano's use of understatement and irony in the first line: "It's been a busy week for the public servant."[23] The two keywords are "busy"—which functions as an understatement—and "public," which will quickly be proven to be an ironic euphemism for private agendas and interests. The poem describes a seemingly typical workweek for the public servant, listing his daily activities from Monday through Saturday. Whoever the public servant is, he has obvious ties to power at the highest levels of government, as evident in the second and third sentences, which describe the public servant planning a "presidential tour in China" on Monday and allowing "Canada's visiting Tar Sands rep [to] take an impromptu whiz in the Oval Office" on Tuesday.[24] The cultural and political capital inferred by references to "presidential tours" and access to the Oval Office underscores the access to power that underlies the seemingly humble title of "public servant"; in this case, power is deliberately obscured by job titles alone, since "public servant" suggests more social and civil service than power brokering. The public servant's investment in private interests is equally displayed in the third sentence, which describes how "he lowered the black curtains on the International Labor Organization's 'Respiratory Diseases' yearly report." As opposed to the obscene obfuscation of truth seen in "Los Exploradores," who doctor EPA reports for the private oil investors they work for, here we have a "public servant" who similarly muddies—or worse yet, completely censors, as suggested by the finality of lowering "black curtains"—the truth of environmental health hazards commonly associated with multinational corporations. The excess associated with pornocapitalist politics is here framed in the figure of a "public servant" who uses his access to power in order to undermine the public he supposedly serves, instead favoring private profiteering, thereby ironizing his position and function as a "private enforcer" or lobbyist. Toscano's portrait thus recalls Jonathan Swift's "A Modest Proposal" in that the contradictions the poem underscores emerge as more than comical or satirical—they become obscene in their excess.

The poem continues highlighting the public servant's commitment to serving private corporate interests at the expense of public safety: he agrees to "lowering minimum standard requirements for Hazardous Waste cleanup while visiting Mexico," promises "to limit labor union 'influence' at the Commerce Club in Boston," and fights for "a Free Trade Zone late into the night" at the "Dominican Republic's embassy."[25] What emerges in Toscano's portrait is thus the picture of a corporate lobbyist disguised as a public servant enforcing an obscene hyperhegemony that serves private interests at a global scale. This is not too different from the accusations of corruption against Securities and Exchange Commission regulators who failed to intervene in the 2008 housing crash. The fact that many left their government positions for private sector employment only underscores the excessive erasure of private/public interests in government agencies. Moreover, the public servant's administration of a global hyperhegemony is cleverly disguised through diversification—note the various geographic locations and nationalities in play, making it difficult to pinpoint the exact beneficiaries of the public servant's actions while further ironizing his job title. This latter point is emphasized on "Saturday," when the public servant directs "his staff"—which suggests another moment of irony in the power implied by a servant having a staff, highlighting the contradictions of what serving actually means—"to wring out as much 'working language' as can be had from the word *freedom*."[26] As the poem suggests, language is peddled as propaganda, which is by definition immune to logical contradictions and the oxymoronic thinking that is captured in the poem's title. The poem makes it obvious that the public's health and safety, which the public servant is supposed to protect and ensure, is simply a rhetorical ruse to enforce power and control *over* the public in the name of private interests. Service here does not imply reasonable democratic governance but rather the unreasonable—even obscene—erasure of the "public" altogether.

This subtle but important theme in Toscano's poem—the obscene contradictions that underlie public service in an age of pornocapitalism—is shown through the lack of human community or relationality in the poem, which is revealed in the public servant's interactions with other individuals. Rather than being a man of the people, as his title may imply, the public servant is portrayed as the type of corporate figure who has no moral or ethical qualms about the human consequences of firing, hiring, and promoting people within an organization. For the public servant, service is about protecting private interests, not human relationships or healthy communities. For example, he is described as firing an "'over sensitive' staffer after a department meeting" on Tuesday, while hiring "a staffer he met at a Lithium Industries mixer" on Wednesday.[27] Readers familiar with the "Lithium Industry" will quickly pick up on Toscano's unrelenting critique of pornocapitalism's catastrophic impact on the environment, obscene in itself. However, the main point is to underscore the theme of the poem, which is here represented by the erasure of the private/public divide in the form of the public servant's presence at a private sector event. Not only is his presence suspect, but it is framed as another example of the excessive erasure of the private/public divide, as the public servant not only attends the "mixer" but hires a corporate staffer to further his private interests in "public service." The fact that the Lithium Industry staffer is more than likely a replacement for the "'over sensitive' staffer"—a person who was probably reacting to the blatant pursuit of private interests disguised as public service—proves the point that the public servant surrounds himself with people who will further his narrow agenda while dismissing individuals who question it or are concerned about it (I return to this issue in the postscript).

The public servant's power-brokering and agenda-promoting personality demands the kind of nonrelationality that typifies his treatment of staffers. After replacing the "'over sensitive' staffer" he fired on Wednesday with the "Lithium Industries staffer" he met on Thursday, we come to discover that the public servant also dismisses an "'over inquisitive' staffer" on Friday only to promote the "Lithium Industries staffer" that same "evening . . . by e-mail."[28] The fact that the public servant promotes the "Lithium Industries staffer" within twenty-four hours of meeting him showcases his attitude toward staffers in general and his agenda in particular: staffers are not human individuals whom he relies on for advice and support but rather tools employed in his pursuit of securing and advancing private interests under the guise of public service. Who the individual staffer is as a person is irrelevant to whether or not the staffer will comply and contribute to the public servant's pornocapitalist philosophy of service. Even his interaction with staffers that may share his public service philosophy, such as the "Lithium Industries staffer," reflect the public servant's philosophy of treating people as tools or parts within an already established and functioning machine, as evidenced by the fact that this friendly staffer is promoted via e-mail, suggesting an impersonal and disconnected form of human interaction. Regardless of such dehumanization, the poem makes it a point to minimize the obviously negative—if not obscenely contradictory—impact of the public servant's philosophy and seemingly antisocial personality by returning to irony in the very last line: "Busy week for the public servant."[29] Toscano's use of irony as humor in the last line helps underscore the dark—if not pornocapitalist—nature of the portrait, as it emphasizes an efficient and seemingly unstoppable undermining of the public interests that the public servant supposedly represents.

The last poem I would like to offer for analysis combines many of the themes already present in the previous two poems from *Deck of Deeds*. The poem "Los Espias" ("The Spies") focuses on two individuals who seemingly engage in an e-mail exchange involving governmental secrets and political scandals, all implicating prominent public and private figures. In an age of social media and information technology, the importance of what information gets "leaked" and how it circulates speaks not only to the communicative realities of our contemporary moment but also to the excessive flow of private information in the public sphere, a reality that is at the heart of pornocapitalist thinking. The political consequences of living in an information-driven age powered by social media became evident with WikiLeaks and figures like Julian Assange and Edward Snowden, even if many consider the distinct motivations of each individual's "leak" to be very different. Nevertheless, what websites like WikiLeaks reveal is that, in an age of pornocapitalism, if the revolution is not televised (a point that is worth reconsidering in an age of reality television), then it will certainly be tweeted and commented about on Facebook, as was evident during the so-called Arab Spring. Similar to "El Sirviente" and people like Assange—who has been publicly accused of interfering with the 2016 presidential election—the figures in "Los Espias" apparently have access to power in the form of information, which they exchange via secondary, private e-mail accounts in an effort to manipulate public policy and government representatives with embarrassing—if not criminal—disclosures (or "leaks") of private information or activities.[30] Equally important is the "tech bro" jargon that permeates the poem, captured brilliantly by Toscano's use of the e-mail format as the poem's form.

The poem introduces the secretive nature of the email exchange by incorporating the e-mail addresses of the sender and receiver, along with a subject line that implies on ongoing exchange:

> From: Pixter1000@hotmail.com
> To: Suckerforsecrets@hotmail.com
> Re: re: you owe me one[31]

The usernames of the individuals in this exchange reveal that they are using personal e-mail accounts, illustrated by the "hotmail" extensions they utilize rather than what we assume are more institutionally assigned addresses and extensions (such as .gov or .edu). The propensity for scandal and secrecy is evident in the usernames themselves—"Suckerforsecrets" is transparent in its meaning, while "Pixter1000" more than likely refers to someone who takes pride in distributing "pix" or pictures. Moreover, it is evident from the subject line that this exchange has bounced back and forth at least twice (the original "send," plus the two subsequent "regarding" indicators, represented by the "Re: re:"). The "tech bro" thinking that will eventually characterize the pornocapitalist nature of the poem is evident in both the language of the subject line—"you owe me one"—and the opening sentence: "Dude, I hope this covers my 'outstanding balance.'"[32] One can reasonably assume from such language, and the masculine homoeroticism that defines the sexual undertone of the poem, that both figures are male even if their sexual identity as such remains ambiguous.

The poem goes on to explain that Pixter has sent Suckerforsecrets an "attachment" from a "text" he discovered in "Pyongyang's Chief Diplomat's cell log" sent from "Guzzler Guy 13."[33] The obvious pornographic nature of the picture is alluded to in the sender's reaction to the unexpected discovery:

> Fuck. If this wasn't enough of a
> mind-bender for me to be peering straight into my North Korean
> "strictly for public consumption" foreign policy glossary spread-
> sheet, to find out that the pic was snapped by my very own Chief
> of Communications—that—has me reeling. What the fuck! Are
> they in cahoots?[34]

The unique traits of pornocapitalism I have been describing are alluded to throughout this e-mail exchange: the transnational nature of contemporary capitalism is evident in the nations mentioned, which include North Korea, the United States, Norway, and Barbados, to name a few; the circulation of the self as a spectacle-commodity in the social media economy, here taking the form of a black market of information manipulated by anonymous insiders; the almost complete erasure of the public/private divide, which is painfully evident in the hacking of several public figures' personal accounts; and the overlapping of geopolitical interests with personal predilections of a sexual nature, which is alluded to in the answer to the question "Are / they in cahoots?"[35]

In response to seeing this graphic image, the writer continues speculating about this shocking revelation:

> I knew they both attended the same Home Brew-
> ing Seminar in Portland last summer, but I had no clue. Well, back
> then I didn't, but since then, a postcard from Taplands Jamboree
> 2011 came to the Oval Office, 'Thanks for the Bellyful Barrels of
> Fun!'[36]

Similar to "El Sirviente," the individuals in "Los Espias" use private information to undermine public policy, but the private interests that benefit from the conflation or erasure of the private/public divide remain unclear. Nevertheless, what is obvious is that these figures are not champions of freedom and democracy acting as whistleblowers to reveal the depth of corruption within the world of geopolitics: "Dude, we're sickos to the max, you and me, and it's good we'll never / come to any public accord over Global Internet Security."[37] What these details reveal is that these two individuals are likely hackers or Internet trolls, or both, who scavenge the depths of digital databases to find potentially compromising information that they can use to extort prominent political figures or to simply amuse themselves.

This theme of amusement or indulgence-as-obscenity is introduced by the pornocapitalist dissonance created around the concept of pleasure in the poem, expressed in Pixter's simultaneous disgust and attraction for his actions. Not only does he acknowledge that he and Suckerforsecrets are "sickos to the max," but he also confesses to being disturbed by the nature of the secrets they uncover and what they may reveal about an elite geopolitical class that enforces an effective yet invisible global hyperhegemony:

> Honestly, I wish I hadn't seen this, but I have to admit, that pic of
> your *Ministre de la Défense* handing the Ukrainian Minister of Trade
> Norway's "Getting around OPEC" petro-policy outline in The Strip
> Steakhouse men's b-room in lower Manhattan—gets me really going.[38]

The emotional dissonance created by the simultaneous feelings of regret ("I wish I hadn't seen this") and desire ("gets me really going") helps shape the obscenity that defines the poem both formally (it's a "dirty" e-mail that must be circulated in secret) and thematically (the protagonists and their world are represented as corrupt). This obscenity is why the protagonists are "sickos to the max"—they use their access to information in an excessive manner, profiting from their criminal activity in the form of pleasure-as-amusement.

Indeed, just as capitalism acts pornographically in its transgression of limits, creating a sociopolitical environment defined by obscenity-as-excess, so too do the protagonists in "Los Espias" transgress what they perceive to be the limits of their power by pushing the proverbial (digitized) envelope that contains the scandals of corruption within the geopolitical world, all seemingly for their personal amusement:

> Last night I took it *really* deep. I made go viral
> this vid of my Chief Diplomat to Barbados receiving from Barbados' Minister of Justice an envelope of Columbian Cartel protec-
> tion money—and had the guy arrested on the spot—live![39]

The enthusiasm represented by the exclamation mark highlights how pleasure overrides guilt within the pornocapitalist mindset. Even after confessing that he sometimes wishes he didn't have access to the information that he shares with Suckerforsecrets, Pixtar nonetheless dives deeper into the underground world of hacking/trolling and ups the ante by having a prominent corrupt public figure arrested for his involvement in a geopolitical network of corruption that involves everything from the United Nations to drug cartels. The key to understanding the significance of such escalation in activity is again found in the exclamation mark—a formal marker that highlights the theme of obscene pleasure in the poem. We are not informed of any profit resulting from making the video "go viral," but we are privy to the excitement and pleasure that the results elicit in Pixtar, which implies that profit in this case is equivalent to pleasure. Consequently, the excessive access to information that the poem's protagonists have is represented as obscene in both its content—most of the information involves corruption or implied sexual depravity—and form (the e-mail exchange is itself gratuitous in that it is unnecessary but nevertheless elicits pleasure in the form of power and amusement, similar to the practice of sexting). In "Los Espias," Toscano is showing how the philosophical claim that knowledge is power can be just as easily aligned with the thinking and actions of J. Edgar Hoover as Friedrich Nietzsche.

Toscano's varied portraits of late capitalist subjects in *Deck of Deeds* capture the pornographic nature of contemporary capitalism, and it's important to reiterate that this is not simply due to the presence of—or references to—sexuality in the poems; if that were the case, then one would have to concede to the pornocapitalism of the late nineteenth and early twentieth century, of Oscar Wilde and F. Scott Fitzgerald. Or, to use a different example, it would be like saying that the pornographic nature of a film like *The Wolf of Wall Street* (2013) lies in its explicit representation of sexuality and prostitution, captured in the famous airplane scene, and not in the uninhibited, aggressive, and violent ethos that is promoted as the key to economic (and sexual) success throughout the film, regardless of actual financial consequences to clients or the market economy. That is the true obscenity of such narratives and the protagonists behind them, whether it is Jordan Belfort, Bernie Madoff, or Toscano's "Exploradores." As pioneers of pornocapitalism, such individuals serve as role models of how to navigate—successfully and unsuccessfully—a new capitalist paradigm in which opulence is not necessarily tied to financial power nor functions as a reminder of a misguided idealism, the type captured in the exuberant but alienated lifestyles of famous American figures like Jay Gatsby or Howard Hughes. In the world of pornocapitalism, religion and the illusion of social mobility are no longer the only opiates of the masses—the self as spectacle-commodity and its currency in social media is but one example of our hypermediated material realities.

The problem for Marxist scholars and activists is that such currency simulates de-alienation while entrenching disenfranchised individuals even more in the spectacle-commodity economy. As Debord wrote decades ago, "the spectacle is a drug for slaves"; I would argue that spectacle has evolved to the point of obscenity, obfuscating the conditions of our existence and experiences on a daily basis. Yes, "the spectacle is a drug for slaves," and as such it continues to function as the latest ideological remedy for individual alienation in an alienated and alienating world. Such seemingly totalizing situations, with no apparent exit or liberating revolution on the horizon, make the work of writers like Toscano that much more relevant to understanding the contradictions and rapidly developing changes in both our geopolitical and personal lives. The genius of a poetic text like *Deck of Deeds* is that it offers psychological insight into the Pynchonesque personalities that make up the pornocapitalist paradigm that is overcoming traditional American politics as we know it. Toscano's work sheds light on the world vision such individuals ascribe to, one of uninhibited privatization, limitless profit, lust for power, and an excessive need for public adulation. It is the essence of capitalism in its most extreme, its most pornographic manifestation yet. As such, the poems in *Deck of Deeds,* as Roberto Tejada states on the jacket to the book, offer the "major and minor arcana in the divinatory art of our immediate future, they betray the dirty secret that our Republic of Letters is no sanctuary from the celebrity narcissism and predatory conduct of global finance capital." Dirty, secretive, narcissistic, predatory, and above all, immediate as a future—these are the qualities that I find make *Deck of Deeds* the book of Genesis for a pornocapitalist world order in the making.

POSTSCRIPT: PORNOCAPITALISM AND THE U.S. PRESIDENCY

It would be remiss of a Marxist analysis focusing on contemporary Chicano/a-Latino/a poetry to not address recent developments in national affairs, which have reinvigorated debates regarding the interpretive registers of class and race as methodologies for analyzing historical events and cultural artifacts. As events like the 2008 economic crash and social movements like Occupy and Black Lives Matter continue to demonstrate, the sustained, violent oppression of racialized and working-class peoples in the United States not only persists—it has intensified. Therefore, the similarities and overlap between Toscano's portraits of pornocapitalist subjects with the actual reality of contemporary U.S. politics is too uncanny to pass up, even if limited to a brief postscript analysis.

The current socioeconomic climate in the United States is in part defined by the increased visibility of "new publics" consisting of reactionary individuals committed to an ideological paradigm grounded in the sociopolitical fantasy of "making America great again."[40] For some, this paradigm shift entails a form of racial policing, "returning" to a 1950s model of white racial dominance in all areas of society—economic, political, cultural, and so forth—while for others it signals the rise of populism as a political force, a force that (perhaps unknowingly) may be manipulated by a financial-political oligarchy looking to maintain or even strengthen its socioeconomic dominance and global influence. The political and ideological dissonance that emerges from these different viewpoints is one of the many ways that pornocapitalism affects current U.S. affairs.[41] Moreover, though racist nationalism and working-class discontent (as strands of current U.S. populism) seem an odd couple—if not a contradiction—considering the diversity of peoples that populate the United States, such dissonance is not without historical precedent; and it is no accident that the scholars and intellectuals who first demystified such contradictions and dissonance as both intentional and agenda driven were all, to some degree, Marxist or materialist scholars.[42]

Donald Trump's presidency has been widely interpreted as a historical event marking a worldwide retreat from global capitalism and the neoliberal ideologies that have dominated the political-economic scene for almost half a century. While some scholars understand Trump's victory as a combination of populist anger toward the D.C. establishment and the rise of ethno-nationalist sentiments centered on culture wars that have been previously addressed but never truly resolved—specifically economic, racial, and gender inequalities (Debord's aforementioned critique of the Watts riots being one example)—others view his ascendency to the U.S. presidency as the natural culmination of a political-economic crisis (or agenda, depending on one's perspective) that has been evolving for decades. I find that

Trump's presidency is symptomatic of a neofascist capitalist paradigm that I'm calling pornocapitalist due to its aggressive emphasis on social recognition through self-promotion within a spectacle-commodity economy that conflates exuberant self-aggrandizement with existential worth, as well as the intertwining of excessive wealth with pornographic pleasure (violently obscene sexuality being one manifestation of this paradigm, as the infamous Billy Bush–"Access Hollywood" leaked tape demonstrates). In short, I argue that pornocapitalism has found its political champion—or lotería archetype—in Donald Trump.

In the spirit of concision, I focus specifically on Trump's excessive and often obscene use of social media and the spectacle-commodity economy, particularly his attempts to define his presidency via Twitter. He has already boasted that his electoral victory signals a paradigm shift toward a more aggressive, pornographic form of political (dis)engagement, as shown in his infamous tweet defending his maniacal use of social media: "My use of social media is not Presidential—it's MODERN DAY PRESIDENTIAL. Make America Great Again!"[43] Trump's use of Twitter as his main communication platform betrays an obsession with image control and public adoration, unsurprising character traits given his reality television celebrity persona. However, his narcissistic fixation on the self-as-spectacle has resulted in a flood of inappropriate comments across a range of issues, many of which lie outside the purview of what are considered presidential priorities. One such tweet concerned an ongoing feud with Mika Brzezinski, a popular morning television cohost who has been critical of Trump's presidency. Referring to a supposed request to meet at his Mar-a-Lago estate, Trump tweeted his reason for declining: "She was bleeding badly from a face-lift. I said no!"[44] The reply from lawmakers was swift and critical, denouncing Trump for what many considered "disgusting" (Rep. Katherine Clark) or "vile" (Rep. Lucille Roybal-Allard) comments that are "beneath the office and represents what is wrong with American politics" (Sen. Lindsey Graham).[45] Such bipartisan condemnations not only speak to the extreme lack of presidential decorum but also to Trump's excessive obsession with self-image and his aggressive narcissism, aggression that seems unhinged and petty when directed at specific media figures and journalists. Nevertheless, unable to control his pornocapitalist persona, Trump doubled down on his comments a couple of days later, tweeting the aforementioned declaration that he was "MODERN DAY PRESIDENTIAL" in an apparent rebuke of the criticism surrounding his "vile" and "disgusting" tweets.[46]

Trump's aggressive narcissism and fixation with the self-as-spectacle mirrors the personality traits of Toscano's portraits, particularly the prioritization of self-interest over public health practiced by "El Sirviente" and the glamourized self-absorption of "Los Exploradores." As president of the United States, it is understood that one will be criticized often, but Trump's personality—one that tends toward excess and spectacle—cannot abide social media "dislikes," thus he responds excessively and violently when his self-as-spectacle is threatened within the spectacle-commodity economy. Such personality traits—when politicized—betray a fascist psychology or mind-set, which theorists like Theodor Adorno studied diligently, analyzing everything from radio shows to films and music, always attentive to the authoritarian unconscious that permeates all of these culture industry tools. One can only imagine what such theorists would think of Trump's fixation with social media and the aggressive narcissism that drives it.

In regard to this chapter, the incontrovertible overlap between the portraits in *Deck of Deeds* with our contemporary political reality underscores the critical and highly educational dimension of Toscano's work: it pierces through the fog of spectacle to highlight the fact that such fog is actually smoke, and that the world has been burning for some time. *Deck of Deeds* allows us insight into the plotting and thinking of the arsonists behind the newest (yet long-standing) political model of social cleansing by economic fire that seems to be accelerating under this new pornocapitalist paradigm—in addition to portraying the figures that are sparking the flames.

Additionally, Toscano's poetry, following in the tradition of Latino/a experimental poetics, exemplifies the theoretical and cultural potential inherent in Chicano/a literature. His work transcends the industry model of reducing Latino/a authors to cultural ambassadors who represent the essential life experiences that define certain identities as marginal or "other," or both. Instead, Toscano's poetry highlights the systemic ways in which certain groups of people—from large populations to local worker unions—are framed as different and thus potentially threatening for the purposes of empowering those who benefit the most from such divisions. Building on a literary tradition founded on an ethic of *mestizaje*, Toscano underscores the various networks of interconnectivity that make up both our individual identities and our respective worlds.

What he accomplishes in *Deck of Deeds* is, in many ways, an updated version of what *mestizaje* looks like when viewed through the lens of power, wealth, and excess rather than culture and bloodlines. As with most of his work, Toscano's book—like much of Latino/a literature—challenges us to rethink the manner in which our identities are simultaneously an expression of our deepest existential understanding of agency (i.e., the "self") and socially promoted labels, which can be symbolically imposed in order to maintain sociopolitical networks that manipulate the vulnerabilities of identity-thinking (i.e., an individual's sense of "self" and the potential threats to it) in order to accumulate, centralize, and exercise power over others. In this manner, *Deck of Deeds* functions as a contemporary example of how the Latino/a literary cannon continues to be defined by a politics of resistance and an ethos of radical social justice.

Notes

1. Jeanne Lorraine Schroeder, *The Triumph of Venus: The Erotics of the Market* (Berkeley: University of California Press, 2004).

2. Schroeder, *Venus*, 2–3.

3. Schroeder, *Venus*, 3.

4. See Georges Bataille, *Visions of Excess: Selected Writings 1927–1939* (Minneapolis: University of Minnesota Press, 1985). Of particular interest is the essay entitled "The Notion of Expenditure."

5. This emphasis on excess—whether individual, institutional, or corporate—is not meant to imply that it is the sole source of capitalism's problems. As Marx famously demonstrated, capitalism as a political-economic philosophy is doomed to a fate of perpetual crises due to its inherent laws of accumulation, which cannot avoid the socioeconomic problems or crises that emerge with the polarization of wealth and power that capitalism invites and normalizes.

6. See Max Horkheimer and Theodor Adorno, *Dialectic of Enlightenment* (Stanford: Stanford University Press, 2007).

7. For examples, see Herbert Marcuse, *One-Dimensional Man: Studies in the Ideology of Advanced Industrial Society* (Boston: Beacon Press, 1991), *Eros and Civilization: A Philosophical Inquiry into Freud* (Boston: Beacon Press, 1974), and *An Essay on Liberation* (Boston: Beacon Press, 1971).

8. The publisher, Counterpath Press, describes the work as "comprised of seventy poetic prose image captions (sans images) whose titles are inspired by the popular Latin American loteria card game. Written by a poet who logs in an average of ten thousand miles of air travel each month working as a union trainer and coordinator throughout the U.S., the 'cards' reflect a dizzying array of cultural-geographic locations, each one acting as a scene-setter for highly dystopian portraits of 'people' caught in a tangle of industry-specific 'predicaments.'"

9. Abraham Kaplan, "Obscenity as an Esthetic Category," *Law and Contemporary*

Problems 20 (Fall 1955): 544–59. Available at http://scholarship.law.duke.edu/lcp/vol20/iss4/3

10. Kaplan, "Obscenity," 548.

11. Oxford English Dictionary, "Pornography," *OED Third Edition*, 2006, accessed February 4, 2017. http://www.oed.com

12. Karl Marx, *The Marx-Engels Reader*, ed. Robert C. Tucker, (New York: W. W. Norton, 1978), 82.

13. For Marx's classic theory of ideology, see *The German Ideology* in *The Marx-Engels Reader*, 146–200. For a more contemporary theory of ideology, see Louis Althusser's "Ideology and Ideological State Apparatuses" in *Lenin and Philosophy*, trans. Ben Brewster (New York: Monthly Review Press, 1971), 127–86.

14. See Ernest Mandel, *Late Capitalism* (New York: Verso Classics, 1999).

15. See Fredric Jameson, *Postmodernism or The Cultural Logic of Late Capitalism* (Durham: Duke University Press, 1992); David Harvey, *The Condition of Postmodernity* (Cambridge: Blackwell, 1990); and Slavoj Žižek, "First as Tragedy, Then as Farce (RSA ANIMATE: First as Tragedy, Then as Farce)," *YouTube*, July 28, 2010, accessed February 4, 2017. https://www.youtube.com/watch?v=hpAMbpQ8J7g

16. Guy Debord, "The Decline and Fall of the Spectacle-Commodity Economy," in *Situationist International Anthology*, ed. and trans. Ken Knabb (Berkeley: Bureau of Public Secrets, 1981), 153–59.

17. Debord, "Spectacle-Commodity," 156.

18. See Patrick Gavin, "Cornel West: Obama a 'War Criminal,'" *Politico*, February 15, 2013, accessed February 4, 2017. http://www.politico.com/story/2013/02/cornel-west-obama-a-war-criminal-087702

19. Debord, "Spectacle-Commodity," 156.

20. Rodrigo Toscano, *Deck of Deeds* (Denver: Counterpath, 2012), 1.

21. See http://counterpathpress.org/deck-of-deedsrodrigo-toscano. Importantly, Toscano's work for the Labor Institute—which focuses on worker health and safety, as well as workplace environmental concerns and economic justice—has allowed him to collaborate with major worker unions and governmental agencies, like the United Steelworkers and the National Institute for Environmental Health Science, respectively. Such work experience and knowledge are evident throughout Toscano's poetry, including *Deck of Deeds*.

22. "The Panama Papers: Politicians, Criminals, and the Rouge Industry That Hides Their Cash." *International Consortium of Investigative Journalists*, April 2016, accessed February 4, 2017. https://panamapapers.icij.org/

23. Toscano, *Deck of Deeds*, 6.

24. Toscano, *Deck of Deeds*, 6.

25. Toscano, *Deck of Deeds*, 6–7.

26. Toscano, *Deck of Deeds*, 7.

27. Toscano, *Deck of Deeds*, 6.

28. Toscano, *Deck of Deeds*, 6.

29. Toscano, *Deck of Deeds*, 7.

30. "U.S. officials conveyed their conclusion that Assange is a willing participant in a Russian intelligence operation to undermine the U.S. presidential election." See Ken Dilanian, William M Arkin, and Robert Windrem, "U.S. Urged Ecuador to Act against WikiLeaks Leader Assange," *Nbcnews.com*, October 20, 2016, accessed February 4, 2017. http://www.nbcnews.com/news/us-news/u-s-urged-ecuador-act-against-assange-n669271.

31. Toscano, *Deck of Deeds*, 37.

32. Toscano, *Deck of Deeds*, 37.

33. Toscano, *Deck of Deeds*, 37.

34. Toscano, *Deck of Deeds*, 37.

35. Toscano, *Deck of Deeds*, 37.

36. Toscano, *Deck of Deeds*, 37.

37. Toscano, *Deck of Deeds*, 38.

38. Toscano, *Deck of Deeds*, 37.

39. Toscano, *Deck of Deeds*, 38.

40. "Make American Great Again" was Donald Trump's campaign slogan.

41. Nick Land, the alt-right philosopher, explains this ideological dissonance in slightly different terms: "The new dominant ideological polarity . . . displays the culmination of an *ideological-class inversion*, decades in coming, which has aligned the masses—and in particular the native working class—with the right, and social elites with the left. In consequence, populism has been firmly locked into place as a phenomenon of the right." See Land's "Trump's Warsaw Uprising," *Jacobite*, July 12, 2017, accessed July 16, 2017. https://jacobitemag.com/2017/07/12/trumps-warsaw-uprising/

42. The precedent I am referring to is 1930s Germany, while the intellectuals I reference are those who addressed the rise and predicted the triumph of fascism, most of them being of Jewish descent. What these theorists taught us—many from the famous Frankfurt School or eventually associated with the founding of the "University in Exile" at the New School for Social Research in New York City, or both—is that the dangerous combination of racism and classism can be used to target specific populations while promoting a spectacle of social unification, historical progress, and economic prosperity. Though the Nazis did not advocate a redistribution of wealth in a Marxist sense, their appeal to nationalist socialism allowed them to circumvent any realistic economic model and simply subjugate the German economy to the needs and interests of the Nazi Party, which were considered synonymous to the needs and interests of the German nation and people. Thus, the promise of economic prosperity was strongly tied to nationalist allegiance, with the most faithful nationalists experiencing the most prosperity, while those who defied the Nazis were essentially viewed as inviting their own economic disenfranchisement, or worse. As Emil Lederer, the famous Jewish economist and sociologist, noted in 1937, the "National Socialist [. . .] economic system [is] based on a

totalitarian concept of the state to which everything—economics included—must conform, under coercion if necessary." See "The Economic Doctrine of National Socialism." *Annals of the American Academy of Political and Social Science*, 191 (May 1937): 219–25.

43. @realDonaldTrump (July 1, 2017). https://twitter.com/realDonaldTrump/status/881281755017355264. It should be noted that Trump usually tweets from his own personal account (@realDonaldTrump) and hardly ever uses the actual President of the United States account on Twitter (@POTUS) for communication, outside of retweeting his own tweets.

44. @realDonaldTrump (June 29, 2017). https://twitter.com/realDonaldTrump/status/880410114456465411

45. See J. Freedom du Lac and Peter Holley, "'Mr. President, Please Grow Up': Lawmakers Slam Trump's 'Vile' Mika Brzezinski Tweets," *Washington Post*, June 29, 2017, accesses August 22, 2017. https://www.washingtonpost.com/news/powerpost/wp/2017/06/29/mr-president-please-grow-up-lawmakers-slam-trumps-shocking-mika-brzezinski-tweets/?utm_term=.9f450aac9b9b

46. It is important to note that Trump has also used Twitter to communicate official policies, such as his ban on transgender American military personnel. He infamously tweeted: "After consultation with my Generals and military experts, please be advised that the United States Government will not accept or allow transgender individuals to serve in any capacity in the U.S. Military." One of his more vocal critics, Sen. John McCain (R-Ariz.), who is the chairman of the Senate Armed Services Committee, replied by stating that "[t]he president's tweet this morning regarding transgender Americans in the military is yet another example of why major policy announcements should not be made via Twitter." See Abby Phillip, Thomas Gibbons-Neff, and Mike DeBonis, "Trump Announces That He Will Ban Transgender People from Serving in the Military," *Washington Post*, July 26, 2107, accessed August 22, 2017. https://www.washingtonpost.com/world/national-security/trump-announces-that-he-will-ban-transgender-people-from-serving-in-the-military/2017/07/26/6415371e-723a-11e7-803f-a6c989606ac7_story.html?utm_term=.0765eddb86c6

CHAPTER 7

Bodega Sold Dreams

Middle-Class Panic and the Crossover Aesthetics of *In the Heights*

Elena Machado Sáez

Puerto Ricans Quiara Alegría Hudes and Lin-Manuel Miranda brought Dominican York to Broadway with *In the Heights,* which won a Tony for Best Musical in 2008. The reception of *In the Heights* hailed it as a welcome change from prior Broadway musicals about Latinxs, namely *West Side Story* and *The Capeman*—in other words, as a musical that challenges the racial borders of the Great White Way. I instead read *In the Heights* as representative of a middle-class politics that is haunted by the inability to speak for a working-class experience of Latinidad and threatened by the stereotypes of chaos and poverty associated with U.S. Latinx working-class subjectivities. The musical is also preoccupied with the crowding out of the middle class from urban centers like New York City via the gentrification of ethnic enclaves and the concurrent disappearance of small, local businesses. The tension over what constitutes an authentic depiction of Latinidad informs what I call the crossover aesthetics of the musical. *In the Heights* seeks to translate for a predominantly white mainstream audience a set of cultural referents that are specific to a unique ethnic, racial, classed U.S. Latinx literary tradition. The musical acknowledges how decontextualization facilitates the move between U.S. Latinx and mainstream public spheres and, in turn, its vision of a pan-Latinx community. *In the Heights* is troubled by the work of crossing over and by the history of how U.S. Latinxs have been depicted on the Broadway stage. While it focuses on the concerns of a U.S. Latinx business class, the musical also references the ways that the artistic and activist legacy of the Nuyorican community challenges the priorities of crossover consumption. The nuances of the play's crossover aesthetics are flattened out by a reception that is fixated on delimited notions of cultural authenticity. I aim to complicate the expectation of authenticity attached to this play, peeling away the hyperpositive guise of pan-Latinidad celebrated by the reception and even at times the musical itself. In turn, I perform a reading of *In the Heights* that acknowledges, first, how the musical is in dialogue with a U.S. Latinx civil rights generation, and second, how the musical embodies a crisis of imagination and authority on the part of U.S. Latinx middle-class cultural creatives. By adopting the conceptual frameworks from Alberto Sandoval-Sánchez's essay, "An Octopus with Many Legs: U.S. Latino Theater and Its Diversity" (1999) and Elda María Román's *Race and Upward Mobility: Seeking, Gatekeeping, and Other Class Strategies in Postwar America* (2017), I argue that supplementing an analysis of *In the Heights* with an appraisal of the identity politics of its authors and their discursive inheritances can help us critically examine the musical's crossover aesthetics.

The question of how is it that two Puerto Ricans end up writing a musical about a Dominican neighborhood leads us to an interesting set of historical contexts. On the one hand, the representation of a pan-Latinidad is a contemporary phenomenon that represents a shift away from the theatrical traditions of the civil rights generation. Sandoval-Sánchez describes how "a new kind of transculturation, one that results from the interaction and transaction with other Latino/as," has transformed "[w]hat was once a unique ethnic theater (i.e. Chicano, Nuyorican)" into "a conglomerate and fusion of Latin American ethnonationalist roots and experiences."[1] The representation of pan-Latinidad stems from the diversification of the U.S. Latinx population within the United States—for instance, the shift from a Latinx population in New York City that was dominated by Puerto Ricans (and to a lesser extent Cubans) to one that includes other immigrant diasporas, like that of Dominicans as well as Mexicans and Central Americans. The *In the Heights* character of Carla perfectly encapsulates this pan-Latinidad when she explains that "[m]y mom is Dominican-Cuban, my dad is from Chile and PR, which means I'm Chile-Domini-Curican, but I always say I'm from Queens!"[2] Within the world of theater, a homogeneous representation of class in relation to Latinidad has curiously accompanied the cultural diversification of the New York Latinx population. Sandoval-Sánchez notes that the most recent generation of cultural creatives produce a "sanitized" depiction of pan-Latinidad by excluding working-poor experiences:

> Since the 1980s, the move for many professional U.S. Latinos/as has been to make it in the mainstream and, in order to do so, the barrio experience and political/social agenda must be displaced and erased. Some playwrights, on their yellow brick road to success, promote hegemonic middle class values and silence the dramatic plots of "ghetto" realities. There are no roles for losers, delinquents, drug addicts, and "uneducated" Spanish-speaking Latinos/as, primarily because these plays are not written for barrio audiences, migrant workers, illegal aliens, and their concerns. In mainstream productions, the act must be cleaned up when the curtain rises. Middle-class Anglo-American audiences expect to be mesmerized with the exoticism of magical realism and to be entertained with rags-to-riches stories or sagas of assimilation and success.[3]

I would argue that this transcultural Latinidad with its privileging of cultural translation and upward mobility also functions as a writerly strategy, a crossover aesthetics that is responsive to the historical exclusion of Latinidad from Broadway and the burden of representation that is placed on the isolated cases of Latinx-authored productions that make it onto the mainstream stage. *In the Heights* is therefore in dialogue with the literary tradition of U.S. Latinx writing preceding it, especially a 1960s Nuyorican imaginary.

The gaps in Broadway's representation of Latinidad on the basis of class is referenced in two ways: with the characters' deployment of civil rights vocabulary that historically gave voice to the concerns of the downwardly mobile, and with the blackout scene, which reproduces the invisibility of the working poor as a concrete threat (we see the material damage wrought by this population, the destruction of the bodega, but the people who perform this violence never emerge onstage). Via the characterization of Graffiti Pete and Usnavi, the musical acknowledges how capitalism relies on competition between the working and middle classes, and that an alliance between them is necessary to prevent the neighborhood's gentrification by implicitly white upper-class elites. At the same time, the musical inherits the ambivalent relationship to the marketplace of Nuyorican artists, who envisioned the market as a place that could productively broaden access to cultural production while also negatively decontextualizing Latinx-produced art.

I begin my analysis by addressing how the identity politics of the librettist and lyricist have been deployed in order to authorize *In the Heights* as a more affirmative, upbeat, and therefore more authentic representation of Latinidad. Following the lead of Sandoval-Sánchez who argues that "it is vital to locate playwrights in given relations of power and discursive formations in order to determine their identity politics,"[4] I trouble the multiculturalist label of authenticity attached to Hudes and Miranda by highlighting the authors' autobiographical descriptions of their educational and class backgrounds. The Puerto Rican heritage of Hudes and Miranda uniquely informs their conflicted class associations and migratory experiences, while also marking them as part of a contemporary generation that Elda María Román describes as wrestling with and producing narratives about "status panic" or the vulnerable positioning of middle-class ethnics.[5] With a more nuanced picture of the authors' identity politics, I resituate the upward mobility narrative of *In the Heights* within a history of Nuyorican performance poetry, focusing on how the musical repurposes the iconography of bodegas, coffee, and lottery tickets from Pedro Pietri's "Broken English Dream" and Miguel Piñero's "La Bodega Sold Dreams." In the final section of this chapter, I analyze three songs from *In the Heights*: "In the Heights," "96,000," and "Blackout." I explore how the musical populates the neighborhood of the barrio in these songs and how it defines community by articulating the shared concern of class struggle. The translation of a Nuyorican imaginary into a mainstream cultural product about an urban Dominican American community relies upon the depiction of a pan-Latinx solidarity that is in actuality quite class-specific, deploying the imagery of class disempowerment from the civil rights generation to describe the struggles of a contemporary business-owning middle-class population. At different moments, this appropriation is fractured by the violence that it requires in order to erase these symbols of their unique historical context (especially evident in the musical's citywide blackout scene), while at the same time, the ideology of the play cannot help but refer back to and be indebted to Nuyorican progressive, working-class movements.

WRITERLY AUTHORITY, AUTHENTICITY, AND IDENTITY POLITICS

In the introduction to the libretto of *In the Heights*, Jill Furman emphasizes the distance between *In the Heights* and the Broadway musicals about

Latinidad that came before it. *In the Heights* "helped usher in a new era on Broadway by being the first musical to successfully integrate hip-hop into the aural landscape" and depict "Latino culture in a positive and realistic light" as opposed to the "more stereotypical and negative" "previous theatrical examples."[6] The ghosts of *West Side Story* and *The Capeman* as well as the Broadway "firsts" of U.S. Latinx theater remain nameless but powerful counterpoints in Furman's narrative. As Sandoval-Sánchez notes, "general audiences" interpreted the first U.S. Latinx-authored plays that crossed over into Broadway—*Short Eyes* in 1973, *Zoot Suit* in 1979, and *Cuba and His Teddy Bear* in 1986—as "embodiment[s] of derogatory stereotypes of U.S. Latinos/as."[7] Due to the "burden of representation" placed on U.S. Latinx theater, the working-class aesthetics of such productions could "easily perpetuate the stereotyping of U.S. Latinos as delinquents, gang members, criminals, drug users, or as underdogs of the disenfranchised American working class."[8] By indirectly referencing the staging of a class-specific Latinidad associated with poverty and underemployment, Furman reassures readers that now is a "new era on Broadway" that can genuinely claim to integrate Other stories into the Great White Way.[9] *In the Heights* reaffirms its corrective vision of the U.S. Latinx community, with music "never heard before in a musical" accompanying a new perspective on Latinidad that Furman finds is "positive and realistic."[10] A peculiar equation emerges where affirming positive aspects of the Latinx experience is read as an authentic gesture, while representing oppression or adverse conditions is necessarily deemed stereotyping.

Furman's marshaling of cultural authenticity to authorize the symbolic significance and success of the musical also informs the way she positions the creative voices of Lin-Manuel Miranda and Quiara Alegría Hudes:

> [W]e began trying to find a writer who could make the book sing in the same way the music did. Enter Quiara Hudes, who had recently received an MFA from the playwrighting program at Brown University. She and Lin had similar backgrounds, and like the *In the Heights* character of Nina Rosario, Quiara was the first person in her family to go to college, having received her undergraduate degree in musical composition from Yale. She understood the world and the story completely, and also had a real feel for the rhythms of the neighborhood.[11]

With this origin story about the collaboration between Miranda and Hudes, Furman calls attention to the parallels between these creative minds in terms of shared "backgrounds" as well as an "understanding" and "feel" for the "rhythm" of Washington Heights.[12] But aside from Hudes's experience as a first-generation college student and the vague allusions to a common Latinidad, what exactly *are* the identity politics of the lyricist (Miranda) and librettist (Hudes)? Much of the advance press and reception for the musical takes up this mantle of cultural authenticity by affirming specific biographical elements to authorize the art of Miranda and Hudes. For example, Robert Hofler from *Variety Magazine* highlights the geographical proximity of Miranda's childhood home to the imagined locale of the musical: "Miranda actually grew up in Inwood, the neighborhood just north of Washington Heights in Manhattan."[13] Hofler's label of "legit" "groundbreakers" also places demands upon Miranda and Hudes to authenticate the musical via these autobiographical routes.[14] Such statements recall the burden of representation that Sandoval-Sánchez describes as part and parcel of U.S. Latinx crossover experiences on Broadway.

By contrast, critic Campbell Robertson of the *New York Times* follows the claim that Miranda has "musical bona fides" by deconstructing the lyricist's cultural authenticity.[15] Asking him to describe "the experience of growing up in Washington Heights," Robertson extracts a response that appears to call into question Miranda's access to authentic U.S. Latinx culture. Miranda states that during his childhood "[m]ost of [his] friends were white and Jewish" and that he "was pretty isolated from" local Latinxs.[16] Robertson describes Miranda as "profoundly affable" and "self-deprecating," with the implied lack of cultural authenticity as something that the playwright is apologetic but forthcoming about.[17] In turn, Robertson highlights the non-Latinx social sphere of Miranda's childhood friendships (as opposed to his family, for example) as a context that explains the aesthetics of the musical as well as its Broadway success: "The focus on outsiders, people who are in the neighborhood but are not exactly of the neighborhood, was no coincidence given Mr. Miranda's experience."[18] The characters' lack of belonging to the space of Washington Heights is attributed to Miranda's biography rather than the depiction of their racial or class backgrounds. This outsider-ness is also tied to the "neighborhood's rose-tinted-portrait" of Latinidad,[19] which Robertson equates with the whitewashing of this ethnic neighborhood's realities. The status of *In the Heights* as a musical, a "genre [that] tends to be filled with those kinds of characters anyway,"[20] excuses or necessitates an upbeat and optimistic portrayal, although the success of a musical like *West Side Story* appears to call into question the claim that joyful idealism is endemic to the genre. The review qualifies the Broadway success of a U.S.

Latinx production by emphasizing that its authenticity has been compromised by its appeal to a mainstream audience. Such critical popularity is deemed a sign of how effectively the musical caters to the desires of white Broadway audiences, with "rap that appeals to people who normally don't like rap."[21]

I find these responses to *In the Heights*, which either hail the musical as the arrival of a finally authentic U.S. Latinx voice that rectifies racial stereotypes or decry it as an assimilationist vehicle that sells out Latinidad, to be quite unsatisfying. The either/or assessment of the musical's authenticity misses out on the opportunity to examine the ways that the musical speaks to the conflicted artistic inheritance of contemporary U.S. Latinx writers—in other words, how the writers themselves explore the stakes of cultural belonging via their creative production. Román's important intervention into the analysis of "aspirational narratives"[22] and engagement with what "ethnicity means[s] in the context of middle- or upper-middle-class experiences" has interesting implications for my exploration of Hudes's and Miranda's identity politics.[23] Román discusses "the unprecedented growth rates" experienced by "African American and Mexican American middle classes" after World War II as an economic reality that transformed not only the representation of such populations within mainstream culture—such that "Black and Latina/o actors began to reflect a wider set of vocations by portraying white-collar professionals and people in high status positions"—but also produced a "middle class panic" among U.S. minority cultural creatives.[24] I expand upon Román's argument by positing that Miranda and Hudes belong to a Puerto Rican generation of middle-class artists who are "grappling with the simultaneous expansion and contraction of group boundaries" for Latinidad.[25] Just as a middle-class status is a shared personal and historical context for these cultural producers, the problem of ethnic and class allegiances is a central concern. World War II did indeed spur the growth of a Puerto Rican middle class, but it is important to note that Operation Bootstrap created a different experience of upward mobility for Puerto Ricans, since as Ramón Grosfoguel notes in *Colonial Subjects* (2003) that the project sought to "transform Puerto Rico into a symbolic showcase of the American capitalist model of development for the Third World."[26] Such a transformation required the elimination of extreme poverty on the island via the "emigration of the lower strata of the island [which] made possible the showcasing of Puerto Rico to the extent that it allowed the upward mobility of those who stayed."[27] Puerto Rican citizens on the island versus the mainland were valued differently and given diverging paths of class mobility: "Since the Puerto Rican showcase was directed at islanders and not migrants, U.S. state resources were channeled to the former, not the latter. Those who migrated did not receive the proper state support . . . end[ing] up in the metropoles' urban ghettos as unskilled low-wage workers with one of the highest poverty rates in the United States."[28] Immigration did not equal upward class mobility for Puerto Ricans. Quite the opposite, those who moved to the mainland experienced a horizontal journey from rural to urban poverty, while their counterparts on the island were buoyed by federal government investment and support. As Puerto Rican middle-class creatives, Miranda and Hudes inherit a contradictory association of mobility and class status, provoked by how the middle-class ascension of one Puerto Rican community required the expulsion of another.

In order to arrive at a more nuanced picture of the complex negotiations over cultural authenticity and appropriation that are central to the emplotment of *In the Heights*, I'd like to highlight a key set of continuities in the biographies of Lin-Manuel Miranda and Quiara Alegría Hudes: family politics and activism as well as an experiential education in border crossing. Miranda's parents are both middle-class professionals who emigrated to the United States, belonging to that island generation whose upward mobility was facilitated by Operation Bootstrap. His father, Luis Miranda, "was an adviser to late New York Mayor Ed Koch" and "continues to work as a campaign consultant."[29] The parental model of activism is an important parallel linking the biographies of the musical's lyricist and librettist. Hudes's parents are often described as working class, and her mother, Virginia Perez, "graduated high school" and had a successful career in the nonprofit sector.[30] Hudes explains that "[m]y mom worked at American Friends Service Committee doing activist work around the country for teenagers of color," ran the "CHOICE hotline in Philadelphia" which answered "question[s] about sexuality, about violence, about reproductive" rights, and also founded "Casa Comadre, which was based in the Latin community and offered resources" to underprivileged women.[31] Miranda and Hudes therefore come from families where political activism is valued, often with work geared toward transforming establishment institutions (like political campaigns) as well as addressing problems of social justice and equality in terms of race, class, and gender. In other words, they are both witnesses to the importance of activism within Latinx public life and how the work of social justice is key to improving a minority community's access to political power and change.

On the surface, the biographical trajectories of the creators of *In the Heights* can be read as a simple story of educational privilege and success. Both artists attended highly selective public high schools and went on to obtain degrees at elite private colleges. Nevertheless, their autobiographical accounts describe similar transformative experiences of geographic and cultural border crossings that belie the assumption of cultural assimilation. Román describes how a "minority culture of mobility" is in part produced by the tensions that middle-class cultural producers experience between their class and ethnic allegiances.[32] Such artists pay what Román calls an "identity tax" as a result of upward mobility, that there is in effect "a price to pay for one's nonwhite racial identity."[33] By extension, "ethnic cultural production serves both as a product of this tax and as a payment of the social and aesthetic dues given to both the mainstream and the ethnic community."[34] A culture of mobility arises as a survival strategy "to deal with marginality and inequality" as well as out of an obligation to prove one's worth or belonging to normative (white) society and to one's particular ethnic group.[35] In reviewing their autobiographical statements, Miranda and Hudes are shown to draw upon and contribute to this vocabulary of mobility, a discourse that processes the limits of class and ethnic affiliation.

Miranda "grew up commuting between a Hispanic neighborhood in northern Manhattan and a highly selective Upper East Side public school for gifted kids."[36] He describes the transition as resulting in the "bifurcation of my childhood" that taught him to "code-switch."[37] Miranda recalls that border-crossing as "super stark when there's another language involved" such that "they call me Lin at school and Lin-Manuel at home. I speak Spanish at home and English at school."[38] Robertson's emphasis on Miranda's outsider status in relation to Latinidad focuses on only one public—that of his formal education—but Miranda's commentary reveals that traveling between the space of home and school entailed a constant process of shifting identifications and community belonging. Miranda also frames his education at Wesleyan in terms of a rerooting via a pan-Latinx culture:

> I lived in a Latino program house my sophomore year at Wesleyan. It was called La Casa. . . . [Y]ou had to write an essay to get in about why you were a Latino community leader, and that was the first time. . . . [T]here were kids whose parents owned *bodegas*, and there are kids whose

> parents were both Wesleyan alums and they always knew they were going to Wesleyan and they're Latino, but they've got the code switch down easy like I do.[39]

Affinity housing connects Miranda to a population of middle-class U.S. Latinxs who similarly had to translate themselves as they moved between Latinx and white-dominant communities. Miranda also cites the "Latin Pop boom of '99/2000" as an important inspiration for *In the Heights*, with "Ricky Martin, Marc Anthony, Jennifer Lopez all of a sudden becoming mainstream."[40] Popular culture provided models of crossover aesthetics that were reinforced by the college community of Latinxs that Miranda found at Wesleyan. Miranda's autobiographical narrative valorizes his ability to navigate different publics, moving back and forth between U.S. Latinx and mainstream U.S. culture.

Hudes also describes her childhood as one that entailed constant transition: "Growing up in West Philly and having family in North Philly placed me in two very distinct neighborhoods, both with a strong sense of community and history, where interesting ethnicities and nationalities were always mingling."[41] In contrast to Miranda, she describes her home space as non-Latinx and middle class. Hudes explains that she was raised "in West Philly, which is not Puerto Rican but a much more diverse international immigrant community. We were the only Latinos I knew in that particular neighborhood."[42] She was hyperaware of the class differences between her home neighborhood and that of her mother's family in North Philly: "[Y]ou could see these nice houses, with paint on the window ledges and all that stuff. Then block by block you'd see it transform. . . . Then there'd be three vacant lots, and one house that's boarded up, and one that has burned down. I learned to be aware of that class dichotomy, even within my own family."[43] Traveling between these different class and ethnic communities, Hudes recalls "being frustrated that there were members of my family with whom I was very close, but who, in terms of the infrastructure of Philadelphia, were invisible and unknown."[44] While Miranda describes a shift of upward mobility, from his home barrio to the school neighborhood, Hudes narrates the transformative effect of downward mobility in visiting her extended Puerto Rican family. She emphasizes the same feeling of bifurcation as Miranda, crediting her ability to read the class shifts in different geographic spaces of Philadelphia to her self-identification as a biracial and bicultural child: "You cross one street and all of a sudden the whole landscape of the city changes. I was very aware of these things and I think of being of mixed background—being half Jewish and half Puerto Rican—and also being much lighter than the rest of my family, I was always shuffling between communities. I was inside and outside of those communities at the same time."[45] Routinely crossing over the borders of class, race, and culture was a defining aspect of Hudes's familial context.

Both the lyricist and librettist acknowledge this experiential education informed their conceptions of artistic obligation and contributions to *In the Heights*. One of the lessons that Miranda learned in high school from seeing the fallout on Broadway over *The Capeman* was to accept the logic equating positive depictions of U.S. minority populations with realism and authenticity, to value a "more realistic world" with "the small business owner and not the guy on the corner."[46] His desire to create "a show with Latino people where we aren't gang members and drug dealers" focused on creating an alternative to non-Latinx productions on Broadway, which was later reinforced by his encounter with a U.S. Latinx middle-class community in college. Miranda came to see the role of the U.S. Latinx playwright in terms of an ethical imperative: "I think writers of color . . . that's partly your responsibility," "you have to write the show that only you can write."[47] If the working-class realities of U.S. Latinxs had "been super well represented already," then the obligation was to depict another layer of the community that was invisible to the mainstream.[48] While *In the Heights* is Miranda's brainchild, Hudes played a significant role in the translation of the play for Broadway as well as the formalization into a published libretto of what had been up to that point a routinely amended script. Based on her knowledge of her extended family, Hudes saw the experiences of working-class Latinxs as equally excluded from mainstream depictions of Latinidad. She describes the collaboration between herself and Miranda as "a weird tango" because "there was already an extant script, with a full complement of songs" when she was brought into the creative process by Furman and her production team.[49] Furman notes that the primary plot of *In the Heights* prior to Hudes's involvement was "a small love story that happened to be set in the particular area of Washington Heights."[50] Hudes remarks that she was "able to get more conflict into the show for the Broadway draft" by involving the existing characters "in new plots, notably the ups-and-downs of three businesses on the musical's iconic block in Washington Heights."[51] The creative partnership of Miranda and Hudes generates the emplotment of a transcultural Latinidad and crossover aesthetics. Furman describes the outcome of this collaborative process in terms of the script "morph[ing] into a love letter to the entire neighborhood and its diverse Latino culture," with a new emphasis on "the immigrant experience and chasing the American Dream" within the context of gentrification.[52] With both artists shaped by and invested in a culture of mobility, the joint project of the musical articulates the middle-class panic of a Latinx population. The identity politics of Miranda and Hudes as well as the unique dynamics of their artistic exchange inform the Broadway production of *In the Heights* and its libretto, especially the ambivalence the musical expresses regarding the relationship between artistic production, the mainstream market, and social class allegiances.

NUYORICAN PRECURSORS AND THE WORKING-CLASS LATINIDADES OF THE CIVIL RIGHTS GENERATION

The profiles of Miranda and Hudes confirm Sandoval-Sánchez's description of the new generation of U.S. Latinx playwrights as "professionals who have received formal education, who are an integral part of the middle class, and whose home is here in the U.S."[53] The cultural specificity of their middle-class Puerto Rican backgrounds is vital to the way *In the Heights* imagines Dominican York. *In the Heights* revolves around a bodega as the crossroads for community building and conflict. As Sandoval-Sánchez notes, "These new playwrights revisit, re-vision, and reimagine the history of Latino diaspora, exile and nostalgia, as new hybrid identities are articulated and constructed on the stage."[54] *In the Heights* engages the signifiers of working-class Latinidad, and I analyze Pedro Pietri's "Broken English Dream" and Miguel Piñero's "La Bodega Sold Dreams" to identify the working-class aesthetics that the musical is revisiting and revising. Following this overview, I turn to the opening musical performance of *In the Heights* in order to reflect on how the symbols of the bodega, coffee, and the lottery are repurposed to imagine a transnational Latinidad with middle-class inflections. Here my argument departs from that of Román, who avoids "rags-to-riches tales" in favor of representations "of class mobility achieved through various types of labor."[55] Despite the musical's attention to small-business owners, the happy ending of the musical ultimately credits the lottery for their mobility and the salvation of the neighborhood bodega's future. In so doing, the musical appears to echo the civil rights critique voiced by the Nuyorican poets—that the American Dream formula of working hard to get ahead is a lie, that the tax levied by institutional racism means that labor cannot facilitate upward mobility.

From the biographies of Pedro Pietri and Miguel Piñero, one can ascertain the unique historical contexts that inform the creative production of these Puerto Ricans, who resided in New York City during the sixties: the Vietnam War, the economic recession, the prison industrial complex, and social justice movements. Juan Flores in *From Bomba to Hip-Hop* (2000) notes the "emergence of a new generation of New York Puerto Rican politics and culture in the 1960s, when community-based and nongovernmental organizations were formed to fill the representational void."[56] "Aware of this vacuum," Nuyorican cultural workers "responded by establishing makeshift, neighborhood spaces."[57] Pietri and Piñero were key collaborators in the formation of these grassroots cultural institutions. Pietri, the son of a dishwasher, returned from the Vietnam War and joined the Young Lords civil rights group. His most famous public performance, a reading of "Puerto Rican Obituary," took place in 1969 when the Young Lords occupied the First Spanish Methodist Church in order to institute a free breakfast program.[58] Miguel Piñero, a junior high school dropout, was released on parole from Sing Sing Prison in 1973 and his first play, *Short Eyes*, was performed that same year on the Broadway stage.[59] Together with Miguel Algarin and a number of other U.S. Latinx poets, Pietri and Piñero founded the Nuyorican Poets Café in 1973.[60] While they came to poetry by different routes, both creative writers were born in Puerto Rico in the 1940s and migrated to New York City when they were young children. The urban environment and their experiences growing up in working-class neighborhoods—Pietri in Spanish Harlem and Piñero on the Lower East Side—shape the depiction of Latinidad within their art. Pietri and Piñero's model of intertwining activism and art is an important legacy and context for interpreting *In the Heights*, especially the way the musical imagines the landscape of the U.S. Latinx barrio, the concerns of those who reside there, and the power dynamics of exploitation and competition between working-class and business communities.

In Pedro Pietri's "Broken English Dream" (1971), the "we" of Latinidad is bonded by a shared experience of poverty, which is defined by exploitation and debt. The poem opens with a revised narrative of Christmas Eve and its much-awaited arrival of a joyful gift: "It was the night / before the welfare check / and everybody sat around the table / hungry heartbroken cold confused."[61] The stark reality of hunger makes clear that the welfare check will do little to alleviate the systemic suffering of this family. The domestic space is not only claustrophobic—"hanging out in the kitchen / which was also the livingroom / the bedroom and the linen closet"[62]—but it provides no sense of belonging or security. The community of the poem teeters on the edge of subsistence and homelessness, with the "slumlord" demanding "the rent we were unable to pay six month ago" and threatening eviction.[63] The street is not an idyllic alternative, described as a "place where the night lives and the temperature is below zero three-hundred sixty-five days a year."[64] These U.S. Latinxs are the working poor, who "dream about jobs you will never get" and find they can "work full time and still be unemployed."[65] There is no escape from the cycle of poverty since one can "graduate from school without an education" in "the united states of installment plans / One nation under discrimination."[66] Genuine employment and intellectual growth are illusions, part and parcel of the deceptive advertising offered to the Latinx working-class. The immigrant Latinx community of the poem finds that racism and economic injustice prevent upward mobility: "We follow the sign / that says welcome to America / but keep your hands off the property."[67] There is no access to ownership, only marginality. The shared concern of this community is survival, but such a goal is depicted as perpetually out of reach. The poem suggests that class struggle informs ethnic identity and that sixties Latinidad in particular emerges as a response to the economic realities of capitalism.

In addition to the real estate market, the poem populates the Latinx barrio with various other businesses: grocery stores, pawn shops, funeral parlors, liquor stores, and prostitution. These industries are depicted as parasitical, exploiting the local population, deriving profit from their patronage: "The grocery stores were outnumbered by / funeral parlors with neon signs that said / Customers wanted No experience necessary / . . . a liquor store / everywhere you looked filled the polluted / air with on the job training prostitutes."[68] The business owners give nothing back to the community, or, worse, market a self-destructive narrative of freedom: "Vote for me! Said the undertaker: I am / the man with the solution to your problems."[69] The opposition between the interests of the businesses and the barrio is emphasized by the fact that these owners do not reside in the city but are "White business owners from clean-cut / plush push button neat neighborhoods," who enjoy the fruits of their financial success from the safety of their suburban homes.[70] The consumption and debt economy reinforces the systemic oppression in this "america / land of the free / for everybody / but our family."[71] The historical contexts of U.S. empire and Operation Bootstrap, the industrialization of Puerto Rico, are referenced as broader forces that define the Latinidad of the poem's community and its experience of discrimination on the U.S. mainland. The Bootstrap project promises that the immigrants will receive "the leading toothpaste" in exchange for the purchase of a "box of cornflakes on the lay-away plan."[72] Meager individual gains are rationalized by the government's economic policy in order to support the debt trade, with debt identified as a valuable commodity within the U.S. capitalist economy. Even U.S. Latinx cultural practices can be reoriented toward such exploitation, since "this is america / where they keep you / busy singing / en mi casa toman bustelo."[73] The poem concludes with a return to the domestic space, now framed by the commercial jingle of Bustelo coffee, a sinister soundtrack for a decontextualization that reinforces the cycle of poverty.[74] The icon of coffee and the themes of property ownership, class mobility, and the marketplace are revisited by *In the Heights*, but they take on a different signification because of the primacy of middle-class Latinidad in the musical.

Miguel Piñero's poem, "La Bodega Sold Dreams" (1980) opens with a first-person voice who aspires to become a cultural creative: "dreamt i was a poet / & / writin' silver sailin' songs."[75] The appeal of this dream lies in the imagined power of the poet to undo the condition of class oppression that Pietri describes in his poem: "words / strong and powerful crashing' thru / walls of steel & concrete / erected in minds weak / & / those asleep."[76] The ideal poet persona possesses an authoritative voice that transforms the consciousness of the Latinx population, awakening their minds with new knowledge about their social condition. The poem posits the urban locale of the bodega as an ambivalent space that can facilitate the poet's educational imperative, serving as a marketplace for circulating a liberating counterculture. The Spanglish-inflected words of the "poeta" will establish an alternate economy of ideas, "strikin' a new rush for gold / in las bodegas where our poets' words & songs are sung."[77] The poet's task is to create a new imaginary for the Latinx barrio and, by extension, a more intellectually sustaining mode of survival. This dream of embodying the poet persona is cut short by a "but" that enumerates the obstacles that stand in the way of the first-person narrator's vision. The "workin' of time / clock / sweatin' / & / swearing' / & / slavin' for the final dime" alludes to the precarious condition of the working poor.[78] The harsh reality of labor conditions inspires the poem *and* threatens writerly creativity: "perspiration insultin' poets / pride."[79] Without the possessive marking the subjects—which reads "poets" instead of "poet's" or "poets'"—this line references sweat as insulting the artistic community's work as well as the poets' ability to insult and critique the labor situation of U.S. Latinxs. Similarly to Pietri, Piñero's poem is marked by cynicism about the function of work, questioning labor's potential for facilitating class mobility. "La Bodega Sold Dreams" values the work of developing an aesthetic, a vocabulary about mobility that can depict the unique challenges of the Latinx working class, while alluding to how the profit-logic of "slavin' / for the final dime" can undermine the development of that barrio creativity and poetic sensibility.[80] By the poem's conclusion, the bodega is part of a larger structure of exploitation, one that results in the "poet's dreams / endin' in a factoria as one / in a million / unseen."[81] If the poet's work is circulated by the bodega, then the poem anxiously seems to ask, for what purpose? Nuyorican poetry of the civil rights generation depicts the barrio and its downward mobility as a challenge to U.S. Latinx imagination while also serving as a *source* of creative inspiration. The poetry of Pietri and Piñero reveals that status panic is not merely the providence of the middle class, that the "fear of falling" further down the social hierarchy is an anxiety of the working class as well.[82] The poetry also identifies the marketplace as an obstacle and vehicle for the progressive political projects of a Nuyorican working-class population. Depending on how the final line of Piñero's poem is read, even the opening dream of becoming a poet is potentially part of an economy of "paper candy" that deadens the imaginations of the Latinx working class.[83] Does the final line of "buyin' bodega sold dreams" refer to the narrator as consumer or, equally provocatively, to the reader? The ambivalent relationship of cultural production to the marketplace depends upon imagining the reader as part of the "we" who claim "our poets."[84] The poetry of Pietri and Piñero envisions a working-class Latinx audience, as opposed to the Broadway context of spectatorship that shapes *In the Heights*. Nevertheless, the icon of the bodega as a space of community, consumption, and economic exchange is revisited by the musical, imagining how the song of a bodega owner can give voice to the struggles and dreams of a U.S. Latinx middle class.

MIDDLE-CLASS MOBILITY DREAMS: THE SONGS OF "IN THE HEIGHTS" AND "96,000"

I turn to the opening song of *In the Heights* to analyze how the musical populates its barrio, constructs the relationship between the bodega and the community, and imagines a shared concern that connects the members of the barrio together. The song "In the Heights" introduces the bodega owner, Usnavi,[85] performing the first task of the workday, opening shop "at the break of" dawn and encountering "this little punk I gotta chase away."[86] The synopsis from the 2008 Broadway cast recording describes Usnavi's nemesis more generously as "a young man [who] sprays graffiti onto a bodega awning" and whose "artistic reverie" is interrupted by the business owner. While the libretto does not describe the confrontation using these terms, it confirms Graffiti Pete's identity as "an artist."[87] Graffiti Pete is "revealed painting various walls in the neighborhood" and responds, "Pshh," when Usnavi yells, "Yo, that's my wall."[88] The musical opens with two competing creative visions, with the graffiti from the working-class streets placed at odds with the "welcome to the neighborhood" song by the middle-class bodega owner. Graffiti Pete is successfully banished from the song's articulation of community, and along with it the alternative vision of the neighborhood that his art might embody and provide. The imaginary of Usnavi's song is born out of a need to distinguish the work of the bodega from the antiestablishment and supposedly delinquent labor of the graffiti artist, which challenges Usnavi's claim to property ownership. In Usnavi's signature song, we can hear some significant parallels between Nuyorican performance poetry and the anthem "In the Heights." The barrio remains a place of economic challenges, where there are "endless debts"[89] "bounce[d] checks,"[90] and "bills to pay."[91] However, the cast of characters who "struggle in the barrio"[92] are now described as the owners of the bodega, the cab company, the salon, and even the piragua cart. In this population, "everybody's got a job" and "got a dream,"[93] a dream that is informed by a middle-class context of privilege, such as the financial challenges of sending a daughter (Nina) to college (and to Stanford, no less!).[94] Usnavi articulates the history, shared struggles, and horizon of this middle-class community, explaining that "my parents came with nothing. / They got a little more. / And sure, we're poor, but yo, / at least we got the store."[95] While offering a chronology of immigrant upward mobility, Usnavi aligns this middle-class existence with poverty. This metaphorical poverty is an expression of status panic; Usnavi is referencing a contemporary narrative in the United States about the disappearance or stagnation of the middle class. Such narratives rarely acknowledges how communities of color might experience this phenomenon, or the tax of racial oppression that they still pay for upward mobility. The musical's chorus reaffirms Usnavi's crossover vision of pan-Latinx solidarity by repeating that they and their families also come "from miles away."[96]

After introducing himself as an immigrant from the Dominican Republic, Usnavi encounters a second set of challenges to the enterprise of the bodega: a broken fridge during a heat wave. Losing the ability to keep the milk cold for the coffee threatens the capitalist logic of the bodega business, "cuz I'm not makin' any profit / if the coffee isn't light and sweet."[97] The relationship of the bodega to the community of Washington Heights consists of providing coffee: when the chorus declares "in the heights / I can't survive without café," Usnavi responds, "I serve café."[98] Framed as essential to survival in the neighborhood, coffee symbolizes a rerooting via cultural consumption—Abuela Celia's solution to the broken fridge is her "mother's old recipe" of "one can of condensed milk."[99] At the same time, coffee also represents an addiction to decontextualization as a strategy for enduring the rat race of economic competition. The chorus asserts that "in the Heights / I buy my coffee and I go / set my sights / on only what I need to know."[100] The call and response between the chorus and Usnavi locates him as the authoritative voice that will articulate what knowledge is necessary for survival—a role that recalls Piñero's poet persona. Usnavi offers his customers a community identity that is working class in construct, despite the middle-class economics of business ownership: "we came to work and to live and we got a lot in common."[101] The pan-Latinx unity that Usnavi envisions is based in a present tense existence and ownership of Washington Heights, declaring that "today's all we got, so we cannot stop, / this is our block."[102] The motivation for middle-class struggle is a shared horizon of "the day that we go from / poverty to stock options."[103] The bodega is the center of a barrio ethos that glosses over the past and present of immigrant poverty in order to endorse a communal project of continued upward mobility. The logical conclusion to this American Dream of "In the Heights" is Usnavi as an absent owner like the businessmen in Pietri's poem: "one day I'll be on a beach / with Sonny writing checks / to me."[104] The tourist-exile fantasy is undercut during the course of the musical, with Usnavi deciding that he would rather assert his belonging in Washington Heights than enable the gentrification of the barrio by becoming one of "them." Usnavi becomes a "reformed character," analogous to Román's assessment of Evie Gomez in Michele Serros's novel *Honey Blond Chica*: a protagonist who turns away from idealizing "the leisure-class habits of immobility and waste" to adopting "a bourgeois ethic of personal drive and perseverance."[105] Ironically, it is the lottery winnings that facilitate this reformation, rather than the hard work of running the bodega itself.

The activist overtones of this happy ending, which redefines the privilege of upward mobility as standing ground rather than moving up and out, is complicated by the way the song "In the Heights" imagines the relationship to the theater community, underscoring some key contradictions of the middle-class anxiety about gentrification. Usnavi directly addresses his white listeners by sympathizing with their fears about entering diverse ethno-scapes like Washington Heights: "Now, you're probably thinkin', 'I'm up shit's creek! / I've never been north of Ninety-Sixth Street.' / Well, you must take the A train / even farther than Harlem to northern Manhattan and / maintain."[106] Usnavi acknowledges his theater audience's ignorance of the barrio locale, as opposed to the experiential knowledge of his customers. Referencing Duke Ellington's rendition of "You Must Take the A Train," Usnavi positions himself as a translator for the Broadway audience, instructing them on how to overcome their (racist and classist) prejudices to discover the forbidden and exotic spaces within New York City. Usnavi frames his work as narrator and bodega owner in terms of possessing the authority to speak for the concerns and dreams of both barrio and Broadway populations. Emphasizing the reeducation of the theater audience, Usnavi warns "I hope you're writing this down, I'm gonna test ya later. / I'm getting tested times are tough on this bodega."[107] By claiming that he will test their acquisition of knowledge, Usnavi asks the audience to see the musical as an opportunity for expanding their horizons. Encouraging them to venture into the barrio as tourists with himself as guide, Usnavi articulates another layer of shared community, an alliance based on the communal struggle of "the test:" challenges to the mainstream audience's socioeconomic and racial boundaries are equated with the economic testing of Latinx small businesses. However, with the audience positioned as ethnic outsiders, they also potentially feed into the gentrification that already threatens the "dime-a-dozen / mom-and-pop stop-and-shop."[108] The direct address to the audience is followed by an explanation of how the U.S. Latinx middle class is being pushed out of the barrio: "Two months ago somebody bought Ortega's / (*Points to the salon.*) Our neighbors started packin' up and pickin' up / and ever since the rents went up / it's gotten mad expensive."[109] The "somebody" who is able to afford the rising cost of living in northern Manhattan functions as the Broadway audience's double, hinting at another layer of power dynamics between Usnavi and the theater's spectators. The references to the audience also acknowledge the production context of the Broadway musical. Similarly to the ethnic sitcoms that Román examines, *In the Heights* is "constrained not just by genre conventions but also by the management of ethnic differences by white financers" and producers.[110]

The 1960s iconography of the lottery returns in the musical as a shared investment in the hope for upward mobility. In "Puerto Rican Obituary" (1969), Pedro Pietri depicts the Nuyorican community as the living dead, stuck in a liminal space because of the American Dream's empty promises. In the poem, the lottery industry is an institution that promotes the propaganda of economic uplift as within reach of the working class: "All died / dreaming about america / waking them up in the middle of the night / screaming: Mira Mira / your name is on the winning lottery ticket."[111] The characters suffer a purgatory defined by debt and underemployment all the while hoping for a means of upward mobility, for their "number to hit"[112] or to win the "irish sweepstakes"[113] so that they can access the privilege of ownership and mobility, for example, "a trip to Puerto Rico."[114] The desperation is such that even the dead are called to task, to "help those who you left behind / find financial peace of mind" by telling them "the correct number to play"[115] The song "96,000" from *In the Heights* maps out a U.S. Latinx community's lottery dreams with some parallels to Pietri's poem, namely, the hope for liberation from a cycle of pointless labor, a future that promises "no breakin' your neck for respect or a paycheck."[116] Additionally, the musical references a materialism that reinforces the debt trade, with a character fantasizing about starting "my life with a brand-new lease / Atlantic City with a Malibu Breeze."[117] Diverging from the Nuyorican poetry of the civil rights generation, "96,000" incorporates a set of perspectives that convey alternate avenues for spending the lottery winnings, from an individualist "Donald Trump" business school model[118] to a sixties activist community project that will "finally fix housin' / give the barrio computers," teach children "about gentrification,"[119] and "invest in protest."[120] These apparently contradictory values, of individualist capitalist success versus progressive social justice projects, are placed on a continuum via the lottery industry. In so doing, *In the Heights* acknowledges a civil-rights-era model of an activist poetics as well as the contemporary realities of a city that is quickly gentrifying and dominated by the Wall Street banking class. The different voices that articulate their lottery dreams eventually coalesce by the end of the song, with the group emphasizing that with the financial award "we could pay off the debts we owe."[121] The final declaration of a unified shared concern in terms of freedom from debt is representative of how the musical adapts the signifiers of Nuyorican poetry and its vision of U.S. Latinx working-class struggles. The musical articulates the ways in which the vision or horizon of U.S. Latinx cultural creatives has changed since the sixties, where the concerns centered on the inner city and white flight, to the contemporary historical moment of a rapidly gentrifying city that increasingly caters only to elites. The racial tax remains, functioning as "a reminder that no matter their class standing, they still have lower status" and the Latinx middle class is vulnerable to rising living costs.[122] I'll return to discussing this dynamic between the civil rights and millennial generations in the next section about the musical's song "Blackout."

FROM PUNKS TO PROPERTY POLICE: THE SONG "BLACKOUT"

The winning lottery ticket goes to Abuela Claudia in *In the Heights*, and upon her death, the money eventually is redistributed to all the besieged business owners in the barrio. The fantasy of "96,000" and its dream of upward mobility out of debt thus is depicted as an attainable reality. These business owners continue to face a threat from without, the implicitly white gentrification of the neighborhood, and a threat from within, for example, the graffiti "punk" that Usnavi has to chase away—an internal threat that becomes allegorized in the blackout scene that takes place at the climax of the musical.

The song "Blackout" interrupts the crossover aesthetics of the musical by acknowledging the menace that the working poor pose to the upward mobility dreams of the Latinx middle class. While this disadvantaged barrio population remains at a distance, the blackout scene alludes to the status panic that lies at the heart of the musical's model minority narrative. The fictional neighborhood's loss of power has two historical referents, the August 14, 2003 power surge that caused a blackout across the Northeast Corridor and the July 13, 1977 so-called night of terror where New York City lost power due to a lightning strike. The more contemporary blackout was, frankly, uneventful, since there was less crime reported during the 2003 power outage than during the same time frame the previous year. The 1977 blackout, however, occurred at night during a heat wave and in a city whose joblessness rate had reached 1930s Depression era levels. New York City was in a recession and declared bankruptcy in 1976, leading to steep cuts in social services, especially those serving poor communities. The loss of electricity led to looting, with images of people tearing the grates off of storefronts televised throughout the nation. Thousands of people were arrested during the blackout, so many that they had to be processed at Yankee Stadium. The blackout cemented the image of 1970s New York City as "dangerous" and "broke,"[123] a chaotic space produced by governmental and commercial disinvestment (for example, the spectacle of the Bronx burning during a Yankees game or of the famous *New York Post* headline of President Gerald Ford telling the city to drop dead) and whose deterioration was accelerated by white flight to the suburbs.

While *In the Heights* is set in the 2000s, the blackout scene evokes the violence, fear, and stereotyping associated with the 1977 incident. Similar to how the autobiographical context of Inwood is mapped onto the geographic and symbolic space of Washington Heights,[124] the song "Blackout" strategically distances the contemporary present from the past (in other words, it is not a flashback to that specific historical period) while also acknowledging the symbolic inheritances that continue to inform depictions of Latinidad for mainstream audiences. The ghost of urban poverty and unrest haunts the musical's imaginary of Latinidad, temporarily questioning and undermining the upward mobility narrative of lottery winnings. In so doing, the musical acknowledges the limitations of its vision of pan-Latinidad for crossover consumption, a Latinidad that is transcultural in its articulation but that remains uniquely raced and class-specific. The song "Blackout" acts as the most explicit depiction and expression of status panic in the show. The images of destroyed storefronts returns from the perspective of middle-class Latinxs, with Usnavi's bodega suffering a slashed awning and broken window[125] as well as "a stolen register."[126] The references to the crime wave, "with people lootin' and shootin',"[127] strategically resignify the blackout so that it speaks to the concerns of middle-class Latinxs and imagines an alliance with the street via the upward mobility and assimilation of Graffiti Pete. Usnavi, the Piragua Guy, Camila the co-owner of the Rosario Car Service, and Daniela, the owner of the salon, are all desperately trying to either protect their property or find somebody who will do so in their absence. The chorus of "Blackout" repeats "we are powerless," revisiting the civil rights language of economic disempowerment of working-class Latinxs. However, this phrase positions the business class as victims to the invisible hordes of the poor whose criminality threatens their livelihood. The blackout presents a crisis of vulnerability for the U.S. Latinx middle class, one that exposes their fear of the working-class communities they serve. Ironically, it is the 1977 blackout that is credited with providing the first generation of hip-hop artists with access to the technology necessary to produce the very genre that inspires *In the Heights*. Furman describes the musical as reflecting a "tapestry of music" that can be heard "walking from 181st to 191st in the neighborhood," including "the rap blaring from the boom boxes strapped to bicycles."[128] The crossover success of hip-hop musicality on Broadway originates in the rise of hip-hop during the 1970s, an emergence that early practitioners connect to the 1977 blackout providing extraordinary (albeit temporary) access to the means of production for this musical genre. In *Yes Yes Y'all: The Experience Music Project Oral History of Hip-Hop's First Decade*, Grandmaster Caz recalls obtaining a "new mixer and turntable"[129] during the blackout, while U.S. Latinx DJ Disco Wiz argues that "before the blackout, you had about maybe five legitimate crews of DJs. After the blackout, you had a DJ on every block. . . . That blackout made a big spark in the hip-hop revolution."[130] The blackout scene is therefore key to the crossover aesthetics of *In the Heights* in that it indirectly references the cultural heritage that shapes its creative imagination and was produced by working-class populations. The song "Blackout" depicts a present-day crisis of property ownership for the middle-class Latinxs in the neighborhood as much as it symbolically references a past where a similar crisis provided the working poor of New York City with access to the technology to create rap and hip-hop as well as find a new (mainstream) public.

The musical also depicts the blackout as a moment of opportunity, with the loss of power setting the stage for a new alliance between working- and middle-class Latinxs. Graffiti Pete chooses to help Sonny protect Usnavi's bodega, marshaling fireworks to "distract the vandals."[131] Sonny also linguistically aligns Graffiti Pete with the business class by declaring "I see some thugs comin'. Man, we gonna get jacked up!"[132] The transformation of this character from a street punk who disrespects personal property to a guardian of the bodega is accomplished via his incorporation into the capitalist economy. Sonny takes his winnings from the lottery and presents Graffiti Pete with "a business proposition."[133] Not only do they both fix the grate on the bodega, but Sonny pays Graffiti Pete to paint "a huge graffiti mural of Abuela Claudia that says paciencia y fe."[134] The rags-to-riches miracle of the lottery enables Sonny to pay Graffiti Pete for his artistic labor. Presented with this memorial as the artistic rehabilitation of the bodega's security system, Usnavi changes his mind about selling the store as well as his evaluation of the "punk."[135] Usnavi tells Graffiti Pete that he's "got a job," presenting him with "some money" to "finish up" the mural.[136] Street art, previously on the margins of the barrio's public in the musical and outside of its capitalist logic, is now on a legitimate and respectable career path. The antagonism that was evident at the start of the musical between Usnavi and Graffiti Pete vanishes. The street and the business classes are unified by the artistic project of securing the bodega, rebuilding it so that it withstands the threats of downward mobility and gentrification. The musical incorporation of hip-hop into the Broadway genre of the musical is therefore an expression of this crossover aesthetic, which aims to merge the different ethnic and class-specific strains of U.S. Latinx cultural production in order to imagine a pan-Latinx affiliation via the market. Just as the inspiration of Graffiti Pete's mural is working class, in the figure of Abuela Claudia, so is the hip-hop popular culture that gives voice to the musical. At the core of the middle-class aesthetic of *In the Heights* is a project of intraethnic solidarity that is ambivalent about the means by which such solidarity is achieved. The musical credits a lottery prize for the upward mobility of both Graffiti Pete and Usnavi, which is essentially Wall Street speculation sung in a minor key. Since the characters' hopes are invested in a game of chance, the musical offers an unlikely path for others to follow and find solidarity in the face of systemic oppression and racism. *In the Heights* instead emphasizes the provisionality of intraethnic collaboration via this once-in-a-million opportunity.

CONCLUSION

In his historiography of U.S. Latinx theater, Sandoval-Sánchez concisely remarks on the key shifts and distinguishing features of the post-sixties era. "[M]any professional U.S. Latinos/as" understand that for "mainstream productions the act must be cleaned up when the curtain rises."[137] The sanitized representation of Latinidad means that plays "are not written for barrio audiences . . . and their concerns" and their emplotment often "promote hegemonic middle class values and silence the dramatic plots of 'ghetto' realities."[138] Does *In the Heights* exemplify "hegemonic middle class values" in this sense? My answer is yes and no. Yes, inasmuch as the musical privileges the concerns of a U.S. Latinx middle class and therefore does not explicitly address a working-class or "ghetto" perspective. Yes, because it does imagine and invoke a non-Latinx audience, a mainstream Broadway spectatorship. And yes, the emplotment of the musical posits a trajectory of successful upward mobility. However, I temper this assessment by arguing that the categorization of "hegemonic middle-class values" doesn't tell the whole story about this musical's crossover aesthetics. Román's work, for example, suggests that contemporary minority artists in the United States are producing a culture of mobility, one that wrestles with the impossibility of meeting hegemonic expectations for middle-class subjectivities. The references to a Nuyorican civil rights imaginary reveal that the "barrio experience and political/social agenda" are central to how contemporary U.S. Latinx cultural creatives negotiate their positionality within the mainstream. Even as the pressures of crossing over onto Broadway may lead to the displacement of working-class subjectivities, the discursive inheritance from those cultural precursors cannot be erased. *In the Heights* is haunted by the voices it cannot integrate into its narrative of middle-class mobility while it is also indebted to the language of working class-struggle, which allows it to articulate the economic challenges that the U.S. Latinx middle class faces, such as the rising costs of living in terms of real estate (gentrification) and access to education. Usnavi imagines that "in five years, this whole city's rich folks and hipsters"[139] will become a dead-end horizon that threatens middle-class Latinidad. As the bodega migrates to the Broadway stage, the civil rights vocabulary and imaginary of Nuyorican experience is adapted to articulate the concerns and anxieties of contemporary U.S. Latinx middle-class cultural creatives. *In the Heights* speaks to the creative conflict that these artists encounter and engage as they produce new narratives of mobility—the inherent tension between the ethical imperative to avoid mainstream stereotypes of Latinidad while also seeking to depict the multifaceted diversity of this U.S. ethnic community.

Notes

1. Alberto Sandoval-Sánchez, *José, Can You See? Latinos on and off Broadway* (Madison: University of Wisconsin Press, 1999), 107.

2. Lin-Manuel Miranda and Quiara Alegría Hudes, *In the Heights* (Milwaukee: Applause Theatre & Cinema Books, 2013), 118.

3. Sandoval-Sánchez, *José*, 119.

4. Sandoval-Sánchez, *José*, 118.

5. Elda María Román, *Race and Upward Mobility: Seeking, Gatekeeping, and Other Class Strategies in Postwar America* (Stanford: Stanford University Press, 2017), 135.

6. Jill Furman, Introduction to *In the Heights* by Lin-Manuel Miranda and Quiara Alegría Hudes (Milwaukee: Applause Theatre and Cinema Books, 2013), xi.

7. Sandoval-Sánchez, *José*, 115.
8. Sandoval-Sánchez, *José*, 115.
9. Furman, "Introduction," xi.
10. Furman, "Introduction," xi.
11. Furman, "Introduction," ix.
12. Furman, "Introduction," ix.
13. Robert Hofler, "'The Groundbreakers: Legit," *Variety Magazine* 9 (October 2008): A23.
14. Hofler, "Groundbreakers," A23.
15. Campbell Robertson, "You're 27. Here are Millions to Stage Your Musical," *New York Times*, February 18, 2007, A9.
16. Robertson, "You're 27," A9.
17. Robertson, "You're 27," A9.
18. Robertson, "You're 27," A9.
19. Robertson, "You're 27," A9.
20. Robertson, "You're 27," A9.
21. Robertson, "You're 27," A9.
22. Román, *Race*, 1.
23. Román, *Race*, 3.
24. Román, *Race*, 3–4.
25. Román, *Race*, 17.
26. Ramón Grosfoguel, *Colonial Subjects: Puerto Ricans in a Global Perspective* (Berkeley: University of California Press, 2003), 108.
27. Grosfoguel, *Colonial*, 109.
28. Grosfoguel, *Colonial*, 110.
29. Brian Hiatt, "'Hamilton': Meet the Man behind Broadway's Hip-Hop Masterpiece," *Rolling Stone Magazine* 29 (September 2015), accessed January 7, 2016. http://www.rollingstone.com/culture/features/hamilton-meet-the-man-behind-broadways-hip-hop-masterpiece-20150929?page=2
30. Kathleen Potts, interview with Quiara Alegría Hudes, "Water by the Spoonful," *Guernica* 2 (July 2012), accessed January 4, 2016. https://www.guernicamag.com/interviews/water-by-the-spoonful/
31. Potts, Interview.
32. Román, *Race*, 18.
33. Román, *Race*, 11.
34. Román, *Race*, 18.
35. Román, *Race*, 18.
36. Hiatt, "Hamilton."
37. Hiatt, "Hamilton."
38. Rembert Brown, "Genius: A Conversation with *Hamilton* Maestro Lin-Manuel Miranda," *Skewed & Reviewed* 29 (September 2015), accessed January 7, 2016, http://

grantland.com/hollywood-prospectus/genius-a-conversation-with-hamilton-maestro-lin-manuel-miranda/

39. Brown, "Genius."

40. THNKR, "*Les Mis* Inspires Creator of *In the Heights*!" *YouTube*, January 17, 2013, accessed January 7, 2016. https://www.youtube.com/watch?v=aewv9UKEYkk

41. Alexis Greene, "No Place Like Home: Quiara Alegría Hudes Tells a Philadelphia Story All Her Own," *Theatre Communications Group* (October 2008). Accessed January 4, 2016, https://www.tcg.org/publications/at/oct08/hudes.cfm

42. Potts, interview.

43. Greene, "No Place Like Home." Hudes's children's book, *Welcome to My Neighborhood! A Barrio ABC* (2010), provides unique insight into her vision of a working-class U.S. Latinx barrio.

44. Greene, "No Place Like Home."

45. Potts, interview.

46. THNKR, "*Les Mis*."

47. THNKR, "*Les Mis*."

48. Brown, "Genius."

49. Greene, "No Place Like Home."

50. Furman, "Introduction," ix.

51. Greene, "No Place Like Home." Hudes describes her stepfather as "a total businessman" and reveals that "[t]he father who owns the taxi stand in *In the Heights* is kind of modeled after" her stepfather.

52. Furman, "Introduction," x.

53. Sandoval-Sánchez, *José*, 116.

54. Sandoval-Sánchez, *José*, 116.

55. Román, *Race*, 7.

56. Juan Flores, *From Bomba to Hi-Hop: Puerto Rican Culture and Latino Identity* (New York: Columbia University Press, 2000), 178.

57. Flores, *From Bomba*, 179.

58. For a discussion of Pietri's theatrical writing, see David Crespy, "A Nuyorican Absurdist: Pedro Pietri and His Plays of Happy Subversion," *Latin American Theatre Review* 45.2 (2012): 25–43.

59. For a comparative analysis of the Broadway reception of *Short Eyes* and *Zoot Suit*, see Ashley Lucas, "Prisoners on the Great White Way: *Short Eyes* and *Zoot Suit* as the First U.S. Latina/o Plays on Broadway," *Latin American Theatre Review* 43.1 (2009): 121–35.

60 The official website for the Nuyorican Poets Café provides an extensive list of its poet founders: http://www.nuyorican.org/history-and-awards/

61. Pedro Pietri, *Pedro Petri: Selected Poetry*, ed. Juan Flores and Pedro López Adorno (San Francisco: City Lights Books, 2015), 13.

62. Pietri, *Selected Poetry*, 13.

63. Pietri, *Selected Poetry*, 13.

64. Pietri, *Selected Poetry*, 13.

65. Pietri, *Selected Poetry*, 14.

66 Pietri, *Selected Poetry*, 15.

67. Pietri, *Selected Poetry*, 16.

68. Pietri, *Selected Poetry*, 14.

69. Pietri, *Selected Poetry*, 14.

70. Pietri, *Selected Poetry*, 14.

71. Pietri, *Selected Poetry*, 16.

72. Pietri, *Selected Poetry*, 16–17.

73 Pietri, *Selected Poetry*, 17.

74. The official website for Café Bustelo (http://www.cafebustelo.com/en/cafe-bustelo-history/) provides an intriguing history of the brand's origins, which includes the migration of the first owner from Spain to Cuba to Puerto Rico and finally to East Harlem, El Barrio, where the business officially got its first start.

75. Miguel Piñero, *La Bodega Sold Dreams* (Houston: Arte Público Press, 1985), 5.

76. Piñero, *La Bodega*, 5.

77. Piñero, *La Bodega*, 5.

78. Piñero, *La Bodega*, 5.

79. Piñero, *La Bodega*, 6.

80. Piñero, *La Bodega*, 5.

81. Piñero, *La Bodega*, 6.

82. Román, *Race*, 153.

83. Piñero, *La Bodega*, 5.

84. Piñero, *La Bodega*, 5.

85. The name of Usnavi evokes the title and main character of Pedro Juan Soto's *Usmaíl* (1959; English translation, Sombrero Publishing, 2007). Soto's novel is set on the island of Vieques during the controversial establishment of a U.S. Navy base. The name Usnavi places emphasis on the U.S. military control of Puerto Rico and its economy, and by extension the island nation's lack of self-determination in terms of its (in)ability to patrol its borders and facilitate trade.

86. Miranda and Hudes, *In the Heights*, 1.

87. Miranda and Hudes, *In the Heights*, xv.

88. Miranda and Hudes, *In the Heights*, 1.

89. Miranda and Hudes, *In the Heights*, 4.

90. Miranda and Hudes, *In the Heights*, 7.

91. Miranda and Hudes, *In the Heights*, 4.

92 Miranda and Hudes, *In the Heights*, 4.

93. Miranda and Hudes, *In the Heights*, 7.

94. Miranda and Hudes, *In the Heights*, 4.

95. Miranda and Hudes, *In the Heights*, 12.

96. Miranda and Hudes, *In the Heights*, 12, 13.
97. Miranda and Hudes, *In the Heights*, 2.
98. Miranda and Hudes, *In the Heights*, 4.
99. Miranda and Hudes, *In the Heights*, 3.
100. Miranda and Hudes, *In the Heights*, 7.
101. Miranda and Hudes, *In the Heights*, 12.
102. Miranda and Hudes, *In the Heights*, 13.
103. Miranda and Hudes, *In the Heights*, 12.
104. Miranda and Hudes, *In the Heights*, 12.
105. Román, *Race*, 153.
106. Miranda and Hudes, *In the Heights*, 3.
107. Miranda and Hudes, *In the Heights*, 3.
108. Miranda and Hudes, *In the Heights*, 6–7.
109. Miranda and Hudes, *In the Heights*, 3–4.
110. Román, *Race*, 148.
111. Pietri, *Selected Poetry*, 4.
112. Pietri, *Selected Poetry*, 5.
113. Pietri, *Selected Poetry*, 7.
114. Pietri, *Selected Poetry*, 7.
115. Pietri, *Selected Poetry*, 8.
116. Miranda and Hudes, *In the Heights*, 50.
117. Miranda and Hudes, *In the Heights*, 50.
118. Miranda and Hudes, *In the Heights*, 48.
119. Miranda and Hudes, *In the Heights*, 52.
120. Miranda and Hudes, *In the Heights*, 52.
121. Miranda and Hudes, *In the Heights*, 58.
122. Román, *Race*, 11.
123. Reporting on photojournalist Bolivar Arellano, Dana Farrington writes, "In the raging 1970s, New York City was dangerous, broke and at times on fire. Latinos in the city were taking to the streets, running for office and carving out artistic spaces. 'Latino' at the time in New York meant 'Puerto Rican.'" Farrington, "Photographing Puerto Rican New York, with a 'Sympathetic Eye,'" *National Public Radio* (October 26, 2013), accessed January 28, 2016, http://www.npr.org/sections/codeswitch/2013/10/26/231704827/photographing-puerto-rican-new-york-with-a-sympathetic-eye
124. Miranda rationalizes this distance by stating that "[i]t's a case where the song 'In the Heights' finds the musical. . . . I wasn't going to write, 'In Inwood'" (Hofler, "Groundbreakers," A23).
125. Miranda and Hudes, *In the Heights*, 101.
126. Miranda and Hudes, *In the Heights*, 102.
127. Miranda and Hudes, *In the Heights*, 89.
128. Furman, "Introduction," x.

129. Jim Fricke and Charlie Ahearn, *Yes Yes Y'all: The Experience Music Project Oral History of Hip-Hop's First Decade* (Cambridge, MA: Da Capo Press, 2002), 130.

130. Fricke and Ahearn, *Yes Yes Y'all*, 131.

131. Miranda and Hudes, *In the Heights*, 90.

132. Miranda and Hudes, *In the Heights*, 90.

133. Miranda and Hudes, *In the Heights*, 146.

134. Miranda and Hudes, *In the Heights*, 150.

135. Miranda and Hudes, *In the Heights*, 150.

136. Miranda and Hudes, *In the Heights*, 151.

137. Sandoval-Sánchez, *José*, 119.

138. Sandoval-Sánchez, *José*, 119.

139. Miranda and Hudes, *In the Heights*, 150.

CHAPTER 8

The Dialectics of Presence and Futurity in the Contemporary U.S. Latino/a Novel

Mathias Nilges

In his 2014 essay "The Future as Form," Marcial González draws our attention to an important and thus far underappreciated aspect of the contemporary U.S. ethnic novel: its formal mediation of "a migration not only toward or away from a geographical place or a geopolitical sense of community, but across the temporalities of history itself."[1] González reads these formal strategies in the novel and the histories (the importance of the plural should be noted here) that they attempt to render legible as a way to challenge a trend in the contemporary American novel that amounts to what Fredric Jameson calls "an immense privileging of the present."[2] González isolates this suggestion from a 2012 lecture by Jameson delivered at the University of California, Berkeley, in which Jameson suggested that we ought to understand this privileging of the present as connected to a larger crisis of futurity: "We seem to have forgotten the ability to conceptualize the future in our contemporary historical moment. We find it easier to imagine the end of the world than the end of capitalism."[3] And while Jameson's suggestion certainly strikes us as both timely and important, this argument has in fact been one of the underlying propositions that has for quite a few years now informed his work. Already in his 1994 book *The Seeds of Time*, Jameson argues that "it seems to be easier for us today to imagine the thoroughgoing deterioration of the earth and of nature than the breakdown of late capitalism; perhaps due to some weakness in our imagination."[4] What better proof of this weakness in our imagination, one may not altogether facetiously note, that critical discourse is still wrestling with the implications of this suggestion? After all, the notion of a pervasive crisis of futurity and universal contraction of temporality into an ever-broadening present not only extends into Jameson's more recent work[5] but also has informed a recent boom of sorts in critical and theoretical production.

In addition to Jameson, a wide range of critics and philosophers, including Franco Berardi, Maurizio Lazzarato, Paulo Virno, Paul Virilio, Bernard Stiegler, and Jacques Rancière have over the past few years foregrounded the phenomenon of a general broadening of the present and the disappearance of the future. Lauren Berlant's *Cruel Optimism* centrally revolves around the epistemological, literary, and political challenges that our "broad, stretched-out present" brings with it, and, as Hans Ulrich Gumbrecht argues,

> it is clear that, during the final decades of the twentieth century and within Western culture at least, the future progressively lost its quality of being an "open horizon of expectations," and turned into a zone that now appears both inaccessible for our predictions and tendentiously unappealing for our desires. Between a future that seems to be closed and a past open to inundate our present, the present has begun to expand from that "imperceptibly short moment of transition" into a broad dimension of simultaneities.[6]

We find similar logical propositions in much-discussed works, such as Mark Fisher's *Capitalist Realism: Is There No Alternative?* (2009), in which Fisher examines those forms of subjectivity and psychological conditions that are associated with what he terms our endless Eternal Now. In such a situation, the project that González isolates—the novel's ability to respond to the purported omnipresence of the end of time, of a crisis of futurity that massively privileges the present to which, we are told, we are unable to imagine an alternative—becomes all the more pressing. After all, to speak of the omnipresence of the contemporary, of an ever-expanding present that draws all elements of futurity into itself and that evacuates notions of change and of the new into the same omnipresent instant, may in one sense be aimed at a critique of contemporary capitalism and the universalizing impulses of neoliberalism that seeks to subsume all aspects of life under the logic of the market. However, there is a profoundly troubling side-effect here, which is the denial of competing temporalities in the present that are connected to a history of multiple temporalities—especially those bound up with race and ethnicity. Yes, it is clear that interventions that decry the loss of traditional forms of futurity and temporality in the context of capitalism's victory march across the globe may initially be aimed at a critique of capitalism. But this narrative and the critique of the temporality of contemporary capitalism may in fact do more damage than good. After all, it is centrally bound up with an erasure of alternative temporalities that this account of a crisis of futurity must obscure in order to maintain itself. One of the aims of this chapter, then, is to explore the ways in which novels such as *Lunar Braceros* restore our attention to those forms of temporality that are excluded not only from the structures of contemporary capitalism but also from critiques that take aim at the limiting temporal structures of contemporary capitalism yet fail to hit the target.

In what ways, then, then, might the contemporary Latino/a novel offer ways of thinking past the by now infamous limitations of a time that seems to absorb competing temporalities and all aspects of futurity into the same, repressive present? One answer, I shall argue in this chapter, lies precisely in the Latino/a novel's commitment to developing formal and generic strategies for laying bare those multiple temporalities of history to which González draws our attention, those temporalities of which contemporary critical and theoretical dialogue does not offer us any accounts. The purportedly uniform present of contemporary capitalism, I would argue, is a time for the political Latino/a novel.

What I mean here specifically is not simply that the Latino/a novel engages with problems of time and politics on a purely topical level or simply as a matter of content. Rather, I will argue that the Latino/a novel takes on an active political role in this context insofar as it insists upon its own importance and function in the process of developing new forms of thought that may allow us to historicize and explore that which may lead us beyond the present. This is an emphasis on the active, political function of literature that I will discuss from a Blochian perspective in the second half of the chapter. More recently, Cathy Caruth has insisted upon the importance of returning to such an understanding of literature in the context of formulating a literary critical project for the twenty-first century. In fact, from the standpoint of such an understanding of literature, any crisis of futurity appears not as an endpoint to literature but instead reveals itself as a common point of departure for the work of literature. For literature, Caruth argues, is always precarious and always struggles with the possibility of endings and foreclosures of the future insofar as literature is "a mode of language and an institution whose very being essentially touches on the possibility and fragility of its own future."[7] In fact, since literature itself always contains a reflection upon its own possibilities and ends, it assumes a crucial function in our ability to imagine the future, since it develops forms of futurity that lead us beyond the present. "The future," Caruth argues accordingly, "cannot be thought without literary forms of articulation that exceed the language in which we refer to what we know."[8] One central aim of my chapter, then, is to explore the ways in which the contemporary Latino/a novel addresses itself to the current crisis of futurity precisely by turning toward literature's inbuilt dialectical tension between futurity and literature's own future and presence that contains the seeds of both futurity and literature's own future possibility.

To be sure, it is not difficult to list a number of recent novels that would confirm the overall diagnosis of an end of time and futurity. What remains frequently unexamined, however, is a second point that calls into question the notion of a contemporary crisis of futurity and contraction into omnipresence: such an account of the conditions of contemporaneity only appears persuasive when one ignores that the cultural and literary examples that critics mobilize in order to make their points are virtually entirely lifted from a white canon of contemporary literature. Time appears to have exhausted itself, and the absence of change indeed strikes us as an important political problem if we only examine the work of William Gibson, Cormac McCarthy, Don DeLillo, and the ever-growing list of white postapocalyptic novels. If, however, we turn to contemporary Latino/a novelists, for instance, then we get a strikingly different narrative of the return to time. Novels such as Rosaura Sánchez and Beatrice Pita's *Lunar Braceros: 2125–2148* (2009) show quite clearly that what is elsewhere understood as a categorical crisis of futurity in politics and thought is not only a self-imposed limit (accepting the epistemic dead ends that neoliberalism brings about) but also an erasure of futurity and time that is directly inflected by a specific politics of race and migration/immigration. Novels such as *Lunar Braceros* illustrate that we are far from being confronted with the universal contraction of time into omnipresence. Instead, our present moment, while clearly determined by material structures that radically change our dominant temporal episteme, is at its heart defined by a plurality of temporal structures that are in turn connected to particular structures and histories of power and domination.

Sánchez and Pita's novel is certainly not the only novel that carries out this kind of work. The notable sense of bewilderment and amusement that pervades novels such as Junot Diaz's *The Brief Wondrous Life of Oscar Wao*

(2007), for instance, is poignantly connected to the novel's attempt to deploy speculative fiction to trace the history of noncontemporaneity and exclusion from the present as a key strategy in the history of colonialism and of racial domination and exclusion in a moment in which white authors and mainstream society lament the apparent inability to escape a universal, singular present. The political work of novels such as *Lunar Braceros* and *Oscar Wao*, therefore, is twofold: first, they return us to an account of the literary and of the novel that formulates futurity out of the novel's engagement with limits, endpoints, and with the conditions of the its own possibility; second, these novels lay bare the lack of attention to competing forms of temporality that are excluded from the dominant temporal episteme of the capitalist present, which shows further that the notion of an eternal present and omnipresent contemporaneity can only emerge by way of such an implicit exclusion of alternative forms of temporality. The reason for this chapter's attention to *Lunar Braceros* is that it is a rarely discussed text in the midst of the growing field of Latino/a speculative fiction, one that, I shall argue, fascinatingly lays bare some of the field's central characteristics, aims, and strategies. As such, it is of great heuristic value for an essay such as this one, which aims to map some of the broader contours of a Latino/a literary criticism that interrogates the productive contradictions between the Latino/a novel and currently energetic theoretical dialogue focusing on crises of time and temporality in our present.

In his 2014 article "Prospects for the Present," Jeffrey Insko describes the temporal turn in American studies as "by now flourishing in such fertile soil that it has developed a number of distinct, if intertwined, branches: queer studies, body/affect, print and material culture, aesthetics, transnationalism."[9] But in what relation does the temporal turn stand to Latino/a literature and Latino/a literary studies? The relative absence of work in this field may suggest that it has not yet arrived, but, I would suggest, it also is not at all clear what particular shape the temporal turn ought to take in Latino/a studies, whether or not it should be embraced in its current form, and what its implications are for the field. I shall return to these disciplinary and indeed methodological considerations later in this chapter. For now, I will suggest that while Latino/a studies may not yet have embraced the temporal turn or signed on to the pervasive narrative that places us squarely into the middle of a large-scale temporal crisis that is bound up with a crisis of thought proper (can we imagine an alternative beyond the present of contemporary capitalism?), time certainly is neither uniform nor exhausted if we look at the Latino/a novel. So, we have to ask, as González does, in what ways the engagement with the crisis of time and the resistance against neoliberalism's repressive temporality gives form to the contemporary Latino/a novel. But we must also ask the question that addresses the other aspect of this dialectical connection: In what ways are the forms that the Latino/a novel develops to address this crisis also a way for us to develop new forms of thought, new ways of conceiving of time and temporality that offer blueprints for thinking past the purported impasses of neoliberal thought? As we shall see, the contemporary Latino/a novel participates importantly in literature's efforts to give us those forms of thought that are missing from contemporary sociopolitical, critical, and theoretical dialogue. In other words, the Latino/a novel creates forms that allow us to read and think past the limitations of the neoliberal present. Sánchez and Pita's *Lunar Braceros* offers us one illustrative example of the contemporary Latino novel's commitment to this project.

Lunar Braceros is a novel that advertises the significance and stakes of recent Latino/a science fiction literature, a field that, while growing more rapidly in recent years, has not yet received the kind of attention that it deserves. While Afrofuturism is by now a staple on many syllabi for university courses on American ethnic fiction, and while the publication of the first collection of Indigenous science fiction, *Walking the Clouds* edited by Grace L. Dillon (2012), was greeted with much fanfare and praise, Latino/a science fiction (sf), in particular literary sf, has been struggling to create a comparable degree of critical interest. The publication of Diaz's *Oscar Wao* massively increased the attention to speculative fiction in Latino/a literature, but, with few exceptions, critical examinations of the novel remain preoccupied with analyzing topics and themes within the novel instead of developing a more sustained inquiry into the function of speculative genres and forms in the contemporary Latino/a novel. Indeed, the specificity of the novel itself is often lost in such work. Though well intentioned, examinations of Latino/a sf that study literature, film, as well as other art forms (I shall briefly discuss such an article later in this chapter), remain unable to speak to the important ways in which Latino/a sf novels not only engage with the crises of our present as sf texts but also as novels. After all, the novel has from its inception been bound up with matters of time and temporality, with the attempt to narrativize (material) history. When we ask how the Latino/a sf novel engages with today's crisis of temporality, therefore, we must ask not only how it does so on the level of content but also how it does so as a novel.

It is precisely on this level, then, that we must evaluate both the strengths and the limitations of *Lunar Braceros*. While the novel is inordinately and intelligently composed, it is also clearly aimed at a left academic audience; in part because it so often says and does the right things, it appears at times rather ham-fisted. But precisely because the novel's main strength lies in its commitment to exploring the specific imaginative and political possibilities of the novel form, *Lunar Braceros* is a novel that is possibly best regarded as a "do as I say, not as I do" kind of text.

Lunar Braceros may in this sense be read as a novel about method, as a novel that engages throughout in a self-reflexive interrogation of its own political possibilities as an sf novel. The same is true for a range of other important novels that a longer project would have to discuss. One example here is Ernest Hogan's *Cortez on Jupiter* (1990). If William Gibson, often billed as the godfather of cyberpunk whose work is instrumental for the historical development of recent sf, revolutionized the way we think about time and history in relation to the shelf life of genres, then we may say that Hogan's novel accomplishes the same for Latino/a literature. And while her essay focuses on a variety of media (film, installation, literature, and so on), Lysa Rivera importantly foregrounds the role of sf and speculative fiction for the development of contemporary political Latino/a literature, reading what she calls "Chicano borderlands science fiction" as attempts at offering "critical visions of globalization both today and in the near future" that "insist on reading late capitalism as a troubling and enduring extension of colonial relations of power."[10] Rivera also notes early on in her essay that there is, in particular since the early 1990s, a growing body of Chicano sf literature. Works such as Alejandro Morales's *Rag Doll Plagues* (1991) and Ernest Hogan's *High-Aztech* (1992), she suggests, point to the existence of an "under-examined history of Chicano/a cultural practice that employs science-fictional metaphors to render experiences of marginalization visible and to imagine alternative scenarios that are at once critically informed and imaginative."[11] Of particular importance in this context is the publication of Matthew David Goodwin's *Latin@ Rising* (2017), the first anthology of Latino/a sf and speculative fiction.[12]

What I attempt to add in this chapter to such important calls for increased critical attention to this aspect of Latino/a literature is a focus on the historical and temporal function of sf and speculative fiction in Latino/a literature. As is no doubt apparent by now, I am suggesting that it is of the utmost importance to historicize this field of Latino/a literature doubly, not only in the diachronic sense that traces the history of such genre fiction within Latino/a literature but, and this will be the focus of my inquiry for the remainder of this chapter, also in the synchronic sense as a way of highlighting the uses of genre fiction in the contemporary Latino/a novel as a way to speak to and to develop models for thinking beyond the temporal impasses of our neoliberal times. It is in this latter sense—by offering ways to challenge a pervasive narrative that understands the time of the neoliberal present as a uniform, repressive, and confining form of temporality, and by illustrating that this narrative of temporal uniformity dangerously obfuscates the history of strategies of colonial and racist power that continue to rely upon temporal exclusion and segregation as ways of naturalizing racial and national distinctions—that Latino/a sf makes an important political contribution. After all, these plural forms of temporality that are attached to the history of colonialism and racial segregation remain largely unchallenged in the present, though they assume, on the surface, a more "palatable" form in neoliberal multiculturalism. Racial segregation is often hidden in plain sight when it is displaced onto a temporal plane. The denial of presence must also be understood as a temporal matter, that is, since doing so draws our attention to the ways in which narratives of racial or ethnic difference are upheld in different forms, namely as narratives of temporal difference. This frequently takes the form of bestowing upon a racial or ethnic group a "quintessential pastness" or noncontemporaneity, one that denies presence at the same time that it can be celebrated as a positive, marketable identity attribute in the context of multicultural diversity management. Even after only considering the broad contours of this problem, we cannot help but wonder, with regard to the much-discussed notion of the end of time, the crisis of futurity, and the temporal uniformity of the omnipresent instant that purportedly marks our time and to which we are unable to imagine an alternative: Whose narrative is this, and what alternative narratives of time must it disregard in order for it to maintain any sense of stability or coherence? No doubt, all those whose background includes long and disparate histories of exclusion—which always also includes narratives of temporal exclusion that participate in a denial of presence from which such narratives often constitutively exclude subjects by naturalizing racial difference as temporal difference—and whose history is full of narratives of being denied presence through the combination of temporal and structural exclusion and segregation, must grimace at the bitter historical irony of this short-sighted aspect of contemporary critical debate.

But let me now turn to Sánchez and Pita's novel in order to isolate some of the details of the inquiry that drives this chapter. *Lunar Braceros* is an epistolary sf novel in which the narrator assembles pieces of communication from family members and friends in an attempt to reconstruct the events that make sense of the history of the narrator's family, community, and of the world-historical events that frame the novel's narrative.

The narrator, Lydia, assembles these fragments into a narrative that is aimed at the future, at helping her son, Pedro (who assumes narrative duties later in the novel), understand the reasons, consequences, and challenges of the fight against the latest manifestation of capitalism in which his family and friends are engaged:

> Tío, my mother left me these nanotexts with lunar posts, lessons, bits and pieces of conversations, and notations with friends who sent them to me after she and my Dad went up North eight years ago. I put them all together and I've been reading them over and over, and now I think it's time you read them.[13]

The narrativization of history and of historical struggles aimed at the next generation of activists via nanotexts, short messages and bits of communications that are arranged into a narrative that depends as much on their placement in the novel as on the reader's ability to parse this fragmented and at times nonlinear flow of messages, is from the beginning of the novel presented as a matter of assemblage and discontinuity that traces history as more than a matter of chronolinearity. As a result, the temporal lines that lead to the future are always both fractious and plural. From the beginning, too, the temporal setting of the narrative shifts back and forth between the future time that forms the constant of the narrative arch, events that are the past for the narrator or her son (but lie in the future for us), and proleptic anticipations of future change. What emerges is an account of historical time that is not simply a matter of a dominant, uniform temporal regime but rather of an always plural time that is defined by a plurality of frequently contradictory temporalities. This attempt to trace countertemporalities that are bound up with their own history of colonial violence, racial exclusion, and social stratification is one of the novel's constants, and its form—the discontinuity of nanotexts and multiple narrative perspectives—aims to give form to this logic.

In *Lunar Braceros*, the earth has been devastated by the ecological and social consequences of a new stage of capitalism in which the nation-state has largely given way to the rule of what the novel calls "corporate conglomerates" that, supported by military rule, violently and ruthlessly expand capitalism's interests and restructure the planet according to the demands of the market. This new, accelerated, and increasingly violent form of capitalism is described in the novel as the New Imperial Order, or the NIO, in clear allusion to George H. W. Bush's "new world order" that supported the rise to dominance of neoliberalism in the 1980s and 1990s. The majority of the novel's narrative shuttles back and forth between providing the reader with detailed context about this new historical moment and the events that led up to it and the story of a new form of proletariat that operates waste storage facilities on the moon. Earth has long run out of capacity for waste storage while the new wave of capitalist production has also devastated Earth's ecosystem more generally.[14] Much of the "incentive" for workers to apply for the dangerous work on the moon arises from the living conditions on Earth where the proletariat is forced to live in reservations. Whereas the reservations function as holding basins for a "controlled laboratory labor force" and constitute "a disciplinary society that [is] useful to the state," employment on the moon initially appears to offer an escape and a form of employment that appears less precarious than life in the reservations.[15] However, while, as Lydia remembers, the moon and space used to be places of imagination onto which people could project their hopes and dreams for the future, this past site of a potentially different future has been all but erased by capitalism's expansion. The moon, Lydia knows, has been reduced to merely another "spatial fix for global capital" that ensures the future solely as a matter of capitalist expansion and the exploitation of new resources.[16]

The sense of an increasing foreclosure of avenues for futurity and the seeming impossibility of imagining positive social change, the narrator notes quite quickly, creates a sense of captivity and lack of prospects that functions as a further incentive for workers to sign up for the immensely dangerous new jobs that space exploration has created. At the same time, in order to further this sense of temporal captivity in a present without alternatives, the support systems of capitalism engage in a secondary project of temporal erasure:

> The government was hard at work on two related memory projects. One involved purging memory on all digitized materials that were publicly accessible. This called for revising historical accounts not favorable to

> the Cali-Texas government. It was an enormous project that required outsourcing to various points in the south.[17]

The result of these joined temporal projects, the narrator notes, is the impression of being caught in the eternal present of capitalism to which there appears to be no alternative:

> I became more and more cynical and, in some way, began to give up on my hope for any kind of a better future. Perhaps social change wasn't even possible. Perhaps there really was no alternative and capitalism would rule forever and we would all live and die on our Reservations and in our prison cells. Gabriel's death cemented my depression. I didn't even want out anymore, just to be done and over with it all. Basta ya, I said to myself more than once.

Initially, therefore, it seems as though the novel replicates the well-known narrative of the crisis of futurity that results from the full subsumption of all aspects of life under capitalism to which we are unable to imagine an alternative. But *Lunar Braceros* undercuts this notion of a complete and utter exhaustion of history and temporality that traps the characters in a perpetual capitalist present by making it clear throughout that the characters' experience of the end of futurity is materially and historically specific—it is bound up with precise systemic and structural pressures and thus constitutes not a categorical end of time but rather a symptom of a particularly repressive and limiting stage of capitalism that must be opposed.

In *Pressed for Time*, Judy Wajcman argues that it is imperative for us to understand time as "the result of our collective entanglements with the material world."[18] This suggests, moreover, that time "is infused with power relations, such as those of gender, race, and class."[19] As a result of its connection precisely to these power relations, Jacques Rancière argues in "In What Time Do We Live?" that time is never singular but always rife with multiple temporalities, which means that we must "call into question the thesis of the homogeneity of time":

> There is no global process subjecting all the rhythms of individual and collective time to its rule. There are several times in one time. There is a dominant form of temporality, for sure, a "normal" time that is the time of domination. Domination gives it its divisions and its rhythms,

> its agendas and its schedules. . . . It tends to homogenize all forms of temporality under its control, defining thereby what the present of our world consists of, which futures are possible, and which definitely belong to the past—thereby indicating the impossible.[20]

From this perspective, the novel helps us understand contemporary capitalism's omnipresence not as a definitive endpoint of time nor as the actual erasure of competing temporalities from our present, but as the ongoing attempt at strategic temporal homogenization. The idea of the timelessness of the present emerges as a result of focusing solely on those instances in which the new capitalist dominant imposes its temporal logic upon our time.[21] But capitalism, the novel's narrator knows, is not able to define our present entirely. Capitalism has always aimed to standardize temporality. In fact, the rise of capitalism was bound up with and required the abstraction and standardization of time. Yet to assume that capitalism is able to fully erase all competing temporalities is to disregard the temporal contradictions of our present that either are a crucial part of the experience of the present for groups who have been and are today still subject to a variety of strategies that aim to deny presence. To simply decry the uniformity of time under capitalism is to disregard the violence and the contradictions that mark the struggle for participation in the contemporary.

From the beginning, therefore, the novel's discussion of the violent limitations that capitalism imposes even upon the imagination of the workers is dialectically bound up with a secondary narrative arc in which the narrator revisits past historical moments that stand in stark relief to the social organization of capitalism:

> The Incas in pre-Columbian times divided the land into three parts, one part for the temple and priests, one part for the Inca and his family, and the rest of the land for the people. The latter was divided in equal shares. Each man received enough land for himself and upon marriage was assigned land for the couple. For every child born into the family the man received an additional portion of land. The division of land was renewed every year and portions were increased or diminished according to the numbers in the family.[22]

Yet it is important to foreground that this return to past moments in history in the novel is not merely a matter of nostalgic backward-gazing. These passages certainly contain a degree of nostalgic longing, but the novel asks us to understand nostalgia not simply as an expression of longing for the good (or at least better) old times. As S. D. Chrostowska shows, there is a dialectical account of nostalgia that can help us appreciate the necessary distinction between two kinds of nostalgia, one backward oriented and the other connected to a utopian project. Adapting Svetlana Boym's distinction between "restorative" and "reflective" nostalgia, Chrostowska argues that, as opposed to restorative nostalgia that "spatializes time" and that "repristinates" a "transhistorical reconstruction of the lost 'home,'" reflective nostalgia, as we find it in the work of Theodor Adorno, "dwells in longing as such and does not seek restoration qua 'homecoming.'"[23] Reflective nostalgia in Adorno, Chrostowska claims, functions "as a means of critical-philosophical insight into, and so a mode of resistance to, the present."[24] As a consequence, this turn to the past functions in Adorno's work—and, I would propose, also in Sánchez and Pita's novel—as "a critical principle that brings thought to the point of awakening, at which time utopian desire takes over as the principle of social-political transformation."[25] It is in this way that we can understand the dialectics of time and space in Sánchez and Pita's novel, which mobilizes memory and past historical precedents not as a way to stabilize identity or history through fixing a point of origin or home but instead as the basis for a utopian project aimed at restoring a lost sense of hope, a hope that contains "a belief in indeterminacy, urgency, and potentiality."[26]

As exemplified by Rivera's essay, those few critics who have discussed *Lunar Braceros* tend to focus on matters of space and place. And this is no doubt justified. After all, the novel itself strongly insists on the important role of space and place:

> This is your home, the place that will define you in some crucial way, in the way that place makes us what we are, the source from which you gain particular insights and perspectives. Space is formative, and when you grow up and become an astronomer, Pedro, you will need to remember this alternative space in which you were born and recall always that space is a product of social relations.[27]

But, possibly due to the large emphasis that Latino/a studies tends to place on matters of space and place, a lacking focus on time runs the risk of missing the specificity of such passages. Precisely because space is understood as the product of a social relation, the novel insists on the need to temporalize and historicize space insofar as it is bound up with the history of social relations. Removing this analytical coordinate means missing half of the novel's logical structure. This dialectical structure is already put in place by the quote from Albert Einstein that Sánchez and Pita employ as the novel's epigraph: "*Space by itself, and time by itself, are doomed to fade away into mere shadows, and only a kind of union of the two will preserve an independent reality.*"[28] Throughout the novel, time and space remain inseparable and also irreducible to each other, and their dialectical connection acquires historical specificity by the novel's commitment to representing it always as bound up with the material structure within which the dialectic of space and time takes concrete historical form. Space as the product of social relations is always mediated through time in the novel, and it is the constant dialectical tension between both poles out of which precisely those possibilities for transcending the limiting present emerges, which are initially hard to see for the characters. Temporalization and historicization facilitate a utopian trajectory in the novel that is aimed at "the production of new spatial relations, maybe—hopefully—even in outer space, on another planet." "But," Lydia continues, as she impresses upon her son the importance of continued historicization of both the present and the past, "I want you never to forget this particular place, our commons, and that it represents a rejection of everything that is hegemonic and dominated by capital relations. Maybe it'll serve as a model for you and others like you to build a new beginning elsewhere."[29]

Sánchez and Pita's novel thus complements what González describes as "a growing number of American ethnic novels that can be characterized as futuristic, egalitarian-aspiring novels."[30] But while novels such as Ana Castillo's 1994 novel *Sapogonia* accomplish this, as González shows, by working through the limits of traditional literary forms from within,[31] Sánchez and Pita and other sf authors work outside of established literary tradition. This is not to say, however, that *Lunar Braceros* abandons tradition tout court or that it "bucks tradition," as one reviewer suggests.[32] Rather, Sánchez and Pita's novel encourages us to think about tradition differently and dissociates tradition from identity. Additionally, the novel carefully keeps separate the historicized version of tradition that can be activated for the present from notions of tradition as stasis or as historical repetition as experienced by the lunar braceros: "at a social organization level the Moon modules were turning out to be a recapitulation of Earth history."[33] In *Lunar Braceros* any instance that may appear to be a matter of repetition conceived as simple sameness ultimately points not toward identity and origin but instead to historically specific matters of structure, class, and social form.

Accordingly, whenever *Lunar Braceros* returns to the past and engages with problems of tradition or memory the novel does so in a way that conjures up Max Horkheimer and Adorno's famous line from *Dialectic of Enlightenment*: "what is at stake is not the conservation of the past but the redemption of past hopes."[34]

The importance of such dialectical historicization establishes the general coordinates of the novel's logic with regard to the relation between past, present, and future. In fact, Sánchez and Pita are so committed to this methodological approach that they compose a passage in which Jameson's work makes an appearance. As is the case for large portions of the novel, characters struggle to make sense of the seemingly discontinuous and fragmented nature of time. How, characters wonder throughout, is it possible to articulate the relationship between historical precedents and present situations that these precedents may resemble without collapsing the difference between past and present? As Lydia already notes in the beginning of the novel, writing appears to be of help here, though one particular character channels one of Jameson's most well-known *dicta* to lend further specificity to the matter: "HISTORICIZE, HISTORICIZE, FRANK SAYS, RECALLING THE WORDS OF AN ALMOST FORGOTTEN 20TH CENTURY LITERARY CRITIC."[35] While it may initially seem that this invocation of Jameson is about little more than the brief, fleeting pleasure of having understood a reference that carries little additional weight than offering the reader an increased sense of being included in the book's intended audience, passages such as these are not merely throwaway pieces of the novel designed to appease its academic readership. Rather, they are indices of the fact that Sánchez and Pita above all seek to compose a novel that contains its own methodological framework—for both novelistic writing and literary criticism. After all, much like the best sf, the best critical methods are developed and historically deployed in order to allow us to see things we have not yet seen and provide us with a vocabulary that helps us make meaning of and speak to problems for which we previously lacked the appropriate interpretive forms and language. Yet the political dimension of the novel is not confined to a level of epistemology or hermeneutics, though it is certainly no small feat to task oneself with composing a novel that allows us to read and historicize the contemporary otherwise. Still, the novel is also committed to maintaining a dialectic of theory and practice, a relation that emerges particularly strikingly in the novel's utopian dimension. As Raymond Williams argues, the least politically meaningful manifestations of both sf and utopian literature are versions of these genres that are speculative in a purely universal, timeless manner.[36] Examples of this include techno-optimistic narratives of future change and innovation or pure representations of a future paradise. Yet, the version of sf or utopia that is, according to Williams, properly political and historical is what he calls the "willed transformation," "in which a new life has been achieved by human effort,"[37] and which constitutes, he adds, "the characteristic utopian . . . mode in the strict sense."[38] Throughout *Lunar Braceros* it is clear that what is required and what Pedro will ultimately strive to bring about is such a willed transformation, a radical change to social and material life.

In this sense, the dialectical materialism of *Lunar Braceros* and its temporalization of the present by way of a reactivation of past historical movements that remained incomplete develops a utopian logic for contemporary Latino/a literature whose political logic parallels the historical development of a particular strand of utopian thought that leads from the work of Ernst Bloch to Jameson's writings on sf. In his essay "Traces of Hope," in which he engages with the question of the relation between memory, history, and the future in the context of utopian thought and anticapitalist social change, Jack Zipes foregrounds the significance of Ernst Bloch's distinction between *anamnesis* and *anagnorosis*. Zipes argues that for Bloch anagnorosis is a "shock of recognition" that "brings back a trace or fragment from the past in such a new way that it can be reactivated and transformed for future action,"[39] as opposed to the stasis and conservatism that he sees as connected to anamnesis. Sánchez and Pita's version of sf is aimed at precisely such a relation to the past through which the novel recovers futurity and is able to historicize the structures of the present. Bloch's notion of the *Novum*, Zipes adds, importantly depends on recollection, which "must be re-utilized as historicized memory that anticipates and guides political action."[40] What we find in *Lunar Braceros* is not merely an attempt to work out what Latino/a sf may look like in the present but to determine what forms hope and futurity may take—that is, how we may think the relation between past and present in order to wrest political and social change from the grip of capitalism's omnipresence. Zipes considers the work of Bloch of the utmost importance for our time, to no small degree because Bloch "militantly insists that we continue to look for utopian signs in our heritage and do not tolerate the abandonment of hope in overcoming the alienating conditions of capitalism."[41] We may understand the importance of *Lunar Braceros* in much the same way.

In "Remembering the Future," Vincent Geoghegan elaborates upon this aspect of Bloch's thought. "In *anagnorosis,*" he writes,

> memory traces are reactivated in the present, but there is never simple correspondence between past and present, because of all the intervening novelty. The power of the past resides in its complicated relationship of similarity/dissimilarity to the present. The tension thus created helps shape the new."[42]

This dialectic of past and present out of whose tensions the temporality emerges that we may subsequently understand as futurity lies at the heart of *Lunar Braceros*'s mobilization of the sf genre. Sf serves as the novel's generic framework that is able to bring together a historicization of the present and *anagnorosis*, the historicization of memory in utopian thought. It may consequently be possible to argue that, much like Bloch's thought, *Lunar Braceros* is about more than the retemporalization of the present and the recovery of futurity as hope. "Since present concerns and future hopes do have such a structuring role in memory," Geoghegan writes, "contestation at these levels will feed back into the memory. Thus, paradoxically, talking about the future may be one way to come to terms with the past."[43] And this, after all, is not only the action performed by the narrator of Sánchez and Pita's epistolary sf novel, whose attempt to imagine future political action is always dialectically bound up with the reconstruction of Pedro's understanding of the past, but it is also the form of historicizing and temporalizing the act of reading that the novel encourages or maybe even demands. It is to no small degree the insistence upon this form of reading and interpretation that constitutes the political force of *Lunar Braceros*. And while fostering a form of thought or reading that allows for a historicization of the present and the recovery of hope and futurity is certainly no small goal, in *Lunar Braceros,* as in Bloch's writings, accounts of the utopian potential of returning to memory and the past as a way of recovering the latent utopian possibility that resides in the unfinished parts of past desires or movements are frequently followed by the assertion that no part of this development can come to fruition without committed human agency, without a "willed transformation" of the kind at which the novel is ultimately aimed. For "the past is not an open treasure-trove," as David Kaufmann reminds us, stressing that "it has to be claimed," since "progress is not the self-actualization of the world—it is, at its best, a product of human choice and bravery in the face of terrible odds."[44] Therefore, what we do not get in *Lunar Braceros* is clumsy, naïve utopianism that simply aims to imagine a new, ideal world. Instead, the project of Sánchez and Pita throughout the novel resembles that of Bloch, who, Kaufmann notes, aims to "create a science of the future from the materials . . . at hand."[45] It is precisely such an engagement with the present at hand, utilizing its materials and examining the dialectical tensions when it is brought into contact with unfinished, reactivated past hopes and precedents, that is able to transcend the reifying uniformity of the temporal episteme of contemporary capitalism that elsewhere is critically examined and narrativized as nontranscendable.

The constant move back and forth between interrogating the past, critiquing the present, and thereby trying to open up a pathway to the future that structures *Lunar Braceros* contains a particular way of looking at the present. That the present out of which it emerges, and not the actual future setting of the plot, is the true focus of any sf novel worth its salt is well known.[46] But by juxtaposing the present, which makes it difficult for the novel's characters to imagine substantive social change, with a past that contains unfulfilled utopian potential, Sánchez and Pita develop a sf narrative that, instead of refusing the present entirely for an idealist future utopia, makes visible what Bloch calls the "latent potential" in the present, which, as Peter Thompson explains, can be better understood as "preilluminations, of a better world, messages of hope sent to us from a not yet possible future reality but already known to us from our own need for the fulfillment of past desires and memories as 'anticipatory consciousness.'"[47] And so, when Pedro ultimately sets off into the world committed to engaging in the fight that may bring about a better world, not yet knowing what that world may look like, *Lunar Braceros* sets itself apart from naïve projections of an ideal future by focusing its efforts instead on opening up the present. The core of the politics of utopia of *Lunar Braceros* lies in its aim of facilitating an anticipatory consciousness that emerges out of the contradictions of the present, contradictions that become visible by tracing the lineages of history's unfulfilled utopian desires through the history of their repression. The "historical surplus," as Bloch would have it, of these unfulfilled historical desires and precedents refuses to be silenced, and its demands on our present are a cornerstone of what Bloch calls the "not yet," the latent potential in the present that makes it the always multitemporal starting point for the next stage in the historical process.[48] This is, then, to return to González's article with which we began, a matter of opening "the opportunity to devise political strategies in the present that are based on the anticipation of what a future society might look like."[49] As González suggests as well, novels that pursue such projects are not interested in "utopia in the broad, idealist sense." Rather, he argues, what structures such novels "is a futuristic vision that is grounded in the political realities of the present, which are in constant tensions with the capitalistic and colonial legacies of the past."[50] In this sense, *Lunar Braceros* offers a blueprint for a kind of utopian project for the Latino/a novel that follows a dialectical notion of utopia.

The Blochian dimension of the novel also becomes apparent in its reconfiguration of time, not as a problem of subjective experience but of a collective relation to the world that is always materially determined and historically specific. Peter Thompson outlines the bases of Bloch's account of the difference between these two ways of understanding time as follows:

> Time as a subjective concept . . . only exists in our heads, meaning that we are not only at liberty but also condemned to treat it as we see fit. And in that sense, the present—that is . . . lived, and experienced time—exists only as incomprehensible chaos and confusion on which we try to impose order. In the face of this confusion, the Now, the moment of existence, is so full of everything that it can appear to us only as a void."[51]

The process of ordering time into a coherent narrative accordingly gives way to the anticipatory impulse that ultimately drives its plot. Time itself and the relation to the future is increasingly understood to be a matter not of identity or subjectivity but of collectivity, of class. Only in this way, by refusing the limit of the subjective and of a pure focus on being or identity (the latter, of course, being infamously activated and encouraged by contemporary capitalism in ways that may help identify one possible source of the "weakness of our imagination" that seemingly traps us in an inescapable present), does the novel construct spaces of hope and of future possibility. In Bloch, Thompson suggests, "the question of being and time posed by Heidegger . . . becomes . . . a question of social being within collective time. For Bloch, time is a class issue."[52] Similarly, in *Lunar Braceros* both the relation to the past and the engagement with the challenges of the present is for the narrator never a matter of identity but instead of class:

> COMPAÑEROS, IT IS WORK THAT UNITES US AND EVERYTHING AND ANYTHING THAT SERVES TO DIVIDE US IS TO THE BENEFIT OF THE CAPITALISTS. WHAT IS CLEAR IS THAT THERE CAN BE NO STRENGTH IN OUR MOVEMENT AS LONG AS THERE ARE WAGE-LESS WORKERS, THAT IS, SLAVES ON THE RESERVATIONS, BECAUSE WHAT ARE THOSE RESERVATIONS BUT PRISONS? THE PEOPLE WITHIN THE RESERVATIONS, OUR PARENTS, BROTHERS AND SISTERS, CANNOT LEAVE; THEY CONSTITUTE AN INDENTURED LABOR POOL, WITHOUT RIGHTS, WITHOUT FREEDOM. WHILE THE CORPORATIONS CAN USE THOSE WORKERS WITHOUT SHARING WITH THEM ANY PART OF THE SURPLUS VALUE THEY PRODUCE, OUR OWN SALARIES HAVE REMAINED LOW AND WE LIVE UNDER CONSTANT THREAT OF BEING LAID OFF AND HAVING OUR JOBS OUTSOURCED TO A RESERVATION.[53]

Class, not identity, becomes the precondition for a critical relation to the present and a formulation of future change in the novel. Accordingly, time and the future are regarded as matters of class, which is to say that time is not an aspect of subjective experience but part of the structural logic of a stage in material history. Time, in other words, ought not be experienced but instead must be historicized as form and consequently understood as historically specific insofar as different moments in history and different stages of capitalism are bound up with different forms of time that become an aspect of reproducing capitalist relations of production. "Ultimately," Lydia knows, a politics of class must replace a politics of identity, since "capital can undo any ties or links on the basis of race, ethnicity, language or color."[54]

In the concluding pages of the novel, this privileging of class as a way to historicize the temporality of past, present, and future is underscored by the lunar workers' departure from the lunar waste site. Having learned that corporations are saving costs by murdering the workers instead of allowing them to return to Earth after the end of their contract, the small group of workers that was able to subdue the station's security personnel finds a way to escape back to Earth. What is clear to all of them is that returning to Earth must mean engaging in resistance against the violence and exploitation of the present system. A better future, the workers know, can only emerge from a collective effort: "at the end of our Moon tour . . . we all woke up; it then became extremely important to live and that's when we developed solidarity and became like a family."[55] Toward the end of the novel, the narrator adds that "the thing is that only participation in collective action ever gave me a sense of freedom, a sense of being more than a caged animal, whether on the Reservation, in prison, or up on the Moon for almost two years."[56] This complete embrace of the collective and the futurity and hope it offers replaces the sense of being unable to escape the present of capitalism with which the novel begins, illustrating that the perception of a unified, repressive temporality that structures the present and erases the future did not arise from an actual structural critique of the present but instead from the inability to think time formally, structurally, and beyond the subject. "Depending on where someone stands physically," Bloch writes, "and above all in terms of class, he has his own times. . . . various years are always beating in the one which is just being counted and dominates. They contradict the Now."[57] What Sánchez and Pita give us is a novel about a way of seeing the present otherwise, of reading our time structurally and historically. In doing so, we are able to make legible the multiple temporalities that, even throughout the most repressive times, structure the present and carry the seeds of social change, of latent utopian potential. The multiple temporalities of the present are bound up with class position, with histories of repression, segregation, and colonial power, and these are the temporalities that refuse the narrative of an omnipresent, eternal Now. "We know that the universe has many histories," the novel's narrator observes, "that it undergoes many changes and faces many possible turns or possibilities, for example, the creation of galaxies."[58] One of the important aims of Sánchez and Pita's novel is to devise ways of making these many histories and the possibilities with which they are bound up legible. The novel's form and its use of the sf genre, therefore, is at every point motivated by the desire to determine what forms hope may take. And in doing so, Sánchez and Pita have composed a novel that makes a contribution to a vitally important project for our time: "we had to do something to maintain some kind of hope alive."[59]

Notes

1. Marcial González, "The Future as Form: Undoing the Categorical Separation of Class and Gender in Ana Castillo's *Sapogonia*," in *Class and the Making of American Literature: Created Unequal*, ed. Andrew Lawson (New York: Routledge, 2014), 215.

2. González, "Future as Form," 215.

3. González, "Future as Form," 216.

4. Fredric Jameson, *The Seeds of Time* (New York: Columbia University Press, 1994), xii.

5. See Fredric Jameson's "The End of Temporality," *Critical Inquiry* 29.4 (2003); "New Literary History after the End of the New," *New Literary History* 39 (2008); and the final section on time and history in *Valences of the Dialectic* (New York and London: Verso, 2008).

6. Hans Ulrich Gumbrecht, "Shall We Continue to Write Histories of Literature?," *New Literary History* 39 (2008): 528.

7. Cathy Caruth, "Afterword: Turning Back to Literature," *PMLA* 125.4 (2010): 1087.

8. Caruth, "Afterword," 1088.

9. Jeffrey Insko, "Prospects for the Present," *American Literary History* 26.4 (2014): 836.

10. Lysa Rivera, "Future Histories and Cyborg Labor: Reading Borderlands Science Fiction after NAFTA," *Science Fiction Studies* 39.3 (2012): 416.

11. Rivera, "Future Histories," 415.

12. For more information, see http://www.latinospeculativefiction.com/

13. Rosaura Sánchez and Beatrice Pita, *Lunar Braceros: 2125–2148* (New York: Book-Mobile, 2012). Kindle file. All quotations are expressed through location markers. Location 80 (hereafter abbreviated as "loc. page number").

14. Sánchez and Pita, *Lunar Braceros*, loc. 148.

15. Sánchez and Pita, *Lunar Braceros*, loc. 187.

16. Sánchez and Pita, *Lunar Braceros*, loc. 580.

17. Sánchez and Pita, *Lunar Braceros*, loc. 628.

18. Judy Wajcman, *Pressed for Time: The Acceleration of Life in Digital Capitalism* (Chicago: University of Chicago Press, 2014), 34.

19. Wajcman, *Pressed for Time*, 34.

20. Jacques Rancière, "In What Time Do We Live?," *Politica Comun* 4 (2013); http://dx.doi.org/10.3998/pc.12322227.0004.001

21. I outline the temporal logic of neoliberal capitalism, its origins, and its limitations along with the novel's formal strategies that refuse this temporal logic in some detail in these essays: Mathias Nilges, "Finance Capital and the Time of the Novel or, Money without Narrative Qualities," *TOPIA* 30–31 (spring 2014): 31–46; "Neoliberalism and the Time of the Novel," *Textual Practice* 29, no. 2 (2015): 357–77; "Fictions of Neoliberalism: Contemporary Realism and the Temporality of Postmodernism's Ends," in *Neoliberalism and Contemporary Literary Culture*, ed. Rachel Greenwald-Smith and Mitchum Huehls (Baltimore: Johns Hopkins University Press, 2017).

22. Sánchez and Pita, *Lunar Braceros*, loc. 257.

23. S. D. Chrostowska, "Thought Woken by Memory: Adorno's Circuitous Path to

Utopia," *New German Critique* 40.1 (2013): 94.

24. Chrostowska, "Thought Woken by Memory," 95.

25. Chrostowska, "Thought Woken by Memory," 95.

26. Chrostowska, "Thought Woken by Memory," 96.

27. Sánchez and Pita, *Lunar Braceros*, loc. 635.

28. Sánchez and Pita, *Lunar Braceros*, loc. 23. Emphasis in original.

29. Sánchez and Pita, *Lunar Braceros*, loc. 369.

30. González, "Future as Form," 226.

31. González, "Future as Form," 226.

32. Angie Chabram-Dernersesian, "Bucking Tradition: Sci Fi with a Chicana/o Latina/o Twist," *Confluencia* 26.1 (2010): 192.

33. Sánchez and Pita, *Lunar Braceros*, loc. 1032.

34. Quoted and translated modified by Chrostowska, "Thought Woken by Memory," 93.

35. Sánchez and Pita, *Lunar Braceros*, loc. 1005. Capitalization in original.

36. Raymond Williams, "Utopia and Science Fiction," in *Culture and Materialism: Selected Essays* (London: Verso, 2006), 198.

37. Williams, "Utopia," 196.

38. Williams, "Utopia," 199.

39. Jack Zipes, "Traces of Hope: The Non-synchronicity of Ernst Bloch," in *Not Yet: Reconsidering Ernst Bloch*, ed. Jamie Owen Daniel and Tom Moylan (London: Verso, 1997), 4.

40. Zipes, "Traces," 4.

41. Zipes, "Traces," 5.

42. Vincent Geoghegan, "Remembering the Future," in *Not Yet: Reconsidering Ernst Bloch*, ed. Jamie Owen Daniel and Tom Moylan (London: Verso, 1997), 22.

43. Geoghegan, "Remembering," 29.

44. David Kaufmann, "Thanks for the Memory: Bloch, Benjamin, and the Philosophy of History," in *Not Yet: Reconsidering Ernst Bloch*, ed. Jamie Owen Daniel and Tom Moylan (London: Verso, 1997), 41.

45. Kaufmann, "Thanks," 51.

46. In fact, Samuel Delany famously associates such sf writing that lacks a critical relation to the present with bad adventure fiction, calling it "our true anti-literature" and its protagonists our "true anti-heroes . . . who move through unreal worlds amid all sorts of noise and manage to perceive nothing meaningful or meaningfully." *The Jewel-Hinged Jaw: Notes on the Language of Science Fiction* (Middletown: Wesleyan University Press, 2009), 8.

47. Peter Thompson, "Ernst Bloch, *Ungleichzeitigkeit* and the Philosophy of Being and Time," *New German Critique* 42.2 (2015): 56.

48. Thompson, "Bloch," 56.

49. González, "Future as Form," 221.

50. González, "Future as Form," 221.
51. Thompson, "Bloch," 58.
52. Thompson, "Bloch," 58.
53. Sánchez and Pita, *Lunar Braceros*, loc. 448.
54. Sánchez and Pita, *Lunar Braceros*, loc. 1209.
55. Sánchez and Pita, *Lunar Braceros*, loc. 1210.
56. Sánchez and Pita, *Lunar Braceros*, loc. 1430.
57. Quoted in Thompson, "Bloch," 60.
58. Sánchez and Pita, *Lunar Braceros*, loc. 593.
59. Sánchez and Pita, *Lunar Braceros*, loc. 1181.

CHAPTER 9

Crisis and Migration in Posthegemonic Times

Primitive Accumulation and Labor in La Bestia

Abraham Acosta

Over the course of the last twenty years or so, and with considerable trepidation over the full—though as yet largely undetermined—political and intellectual implications, critics have begun asserting that regions such as Latin America, if not already the planet in its entirety, have entered a posthegemonic age.[1] This shift in the contemporary grounds of modern political organization does not necessarily suggest that the nation-state no longer exists or has become obsolete, because it hasn't; it appears still to serve a vital function to global capital. Nor should arguments critical of this shift convince us into thinking that the nation-state represented some kind of ideal form of social organization that was ultimately betrayed and corrupted by an evil global capitalism, for there was never a time in the history of the nation-state where it was not profusely and intricately entwined in conflicts with communities over land, labor, and wages. What critics are remarking through this idea of a posthegemonic historical era are the cumulative economic and juridical effects—beginning from a series of concerted U.S.-backed interventions in various Latin American countries such as Guatemala in 1954, Cuba in 1961 (unsuccessfully), and Chile in 1973—that resulted in successfully undermining the region's ability to curb U.S. imperialism in the hemisphere. Subsequently, and on a much larger scale, treaties like the North American Free Trade Agreement and the Central American Free Trade Agreement provoked a profound and far-reaching transformation in the nature and structure of state sovereignty in its relation to global capital.

In effect, the nation-state in Latin America currently obtains as a geopolitical form which we can no longer seem to recognize in Latin America and whose critical realities we can no longer ignore. Gareth Williams, for instance, opens *The Other Side of the Popular* referring to the "uneven and incomplete and ongoing passage from national to postnational cultural and political paradigms" resulting from their "profound and far-reaching redefinition and restructuration in the face of increasingly transnational realities."[2] He adds further that "the profound economic and sociocultural transformations of the last thirty years, together with the recent emergence of the so-called neoliberal order, denote a radical shift and a fundamental weakening in the foundations of the modern nation-state."[3] The term posthegemony, therefore, means not only the decentering of the nation-state model under conditions of contemporary neoliberalism, but consequently the urgency to fundamentally rethink current theories of state political power in order to offer a more adequate accounting of its contemporary social, political, and cultural effects. One predominant theoretical model in particular stands out as warranting a critical reassessment: the notion of hegemony itself. As developed in Antonio Gramsci's prison writings from the 1930s, the notion of hegemony refers to political power shared between elite and allied social classes and characterized principally as a system of rule over the subordinate classes through a combination of leadership, coercion, and consent.[4] As we also know, Gramsci's theory of hegemony has proven persuasive in formalizing an account of the internal political dynamics and contradictions inherent in the modern nation-state model, which in turn led it to serve as the principal theory of power and an interpretive framework within cultural studies. In Latin America, for instance, the notion of hegemony and a cultural studies framework enabled a much needed and nuanced understanding of the ways in which Latin American nation-states experienced not only their independence from Spain in the nineteenth century but also their revolutionary and national-popular period throughout much of the early twentieth century. However, beginning in the late twentieth and into the twenty-first century—from the military dictatorships in the Southern Cone and the counterrevolutionary subversion in Central America, to the currency crises, international bailouts, trade agreements, and the emergence of drug cartels and narco-violence throughout the hemisphere—the manifestation of state power in the region no longer reveals itself as hegemonic, as if the very dynamic and processes attributed to hegemonic articulation have undergone irrevocable transformation.

Undoubtedly, a fundamental characteristic of this new era is the increasing number of border crises that are no longer simply between or among nation-states but between larger networks of global economic forces and displaced, vulnerable pockets of surplus labor within national territories. So, while it is not surprising that we are seeing these crises in particular geopolitical border zones such as the U.S./Mexico border, their primary significance may not essentially nor necessarily be tied to simple geopoliticality but to larger and deeply entrenched networks of circulation and exchange between migrants, coyotes, and narco cartels. For instance, we have recently come upon the five-year anniversary of the first of the two known massacres at San Fernando in Tamaulipas, Mexico, the first discovered in August 2010 and the second in April 2011, where a total of 265 bodies, many of them Central American, were unearthed from numerous mass graves along Mexican Federal Highway 101 (just ninety miles outside Brownsville, Texas). The bodies showed signs of rape and torture, and as Salvadoran journalist Óscar Martínez himself reports, the migrants were ultimately killed by the drug cartel los Zetas as a message to rogue *polleros* (migrant smugglers, also known as coyotes) of the consequences of crossing migrants without permission and failing to pay the fee the Zetas place on every migrant crossing through their territory and using their routes.[5] For the present discussion, three things stand out from this incident that inscribes it fully within this posthegemonic register: (1) while these were not state-sanctioned killings, they were nevertheless an act of sovereign decision-making by los Zetas, who effectively rule and tax these smuggling routes; (2) the migrants, unfortunately, exemplify the collateral damage produced by disputes between coyotes and a narco-smuggling organization that has aggressively taken over logistical and economic control of migrant trafficking; and (3) los Zetas are by no means a homogenous group nor simply a gang of Mexicans exploiting and killing non-Mexicans. Rather, they are a multinational organization composed of men and women from virtually all parts of Latin America, including the very countries these 265 migrants were no doubt escaping from. There is a really strong possibility that the members of the Zetas who participated in these massacres were actually killing members of their own community, as is the possibility that these foot soldiers were probably migrants themselves before they were recruited to join these cartels. No doubt, many members of the cartels are themselves in Mexico unlawfully, like the migrants they seek to exploit, but their relation to these organizations immunizes them from biopolitical vulnerability. Consequently, if contemporary sociopolitical crises like these can no longer be defined as simple confrontations between national actors––that is, between citizens who belong and noncitizens who do not––but rather as contradictions that emerge between the production of surplus labor populations and the global forces regulating their circulation (and thus as part of an ongoing primitive accumulation––the production of itinerant populations for capitalist wage labor), the new problem to address is how to rearticulate and reconceive what notions like borders and migration mean in this posthegemonic era of blurred lines between sovereignty and global capital.

The recent and unprecedented surge of young, unaccompanied Central American children arriving at the U.S./Mexico border is the latest instance of posthegemonic crisis highlighting the violent and precarious living conditions in countries like Honduras, Guatemala, and El Salvador. Furthermore, caught not only between gang violence and the exploitative neoliberal economic policies at work in their home countries, migrants who flee are then subsequently forced to traverse and negotiate the even more violent drug and migrant trafficking networks that await them on their journey. The present chapter engages this posthegemonic relationship more directly through a reading of Óscar Martínez's journalistic account of recent Central American migration in Mexico, *Los Migrantes que no importan*. Recently translated as *The Beast*, this narrative documents with harrowing detail the perilous journey Central American migrants face when traversing Mexico.[6] I will suggest that Martínez's account obtains as a most incisive and urgent accounting of the posthegemonic conjuncture outlined above, one comprised by the interaction between global capital and migration. But before I develop my reading of *The Beast*, let us first turn to a key formulation in Marx's understanding of capitalism that will be of critical value in this discussion.

The intersection between global capital and migration is hardly accidental. In fact, and not unlike poverty, this social predicament doesn't exist naturally but must be produced, with manufactured conditions. Ironically, these conditions are usually produced through moments of upheaval from a previous social order. The conventional history of capitalist modernity grounds itself as the narrative of peasant liberation from feudal society. And yet, while Marx's account in *Capital* does not deny this fundamental characteristic of capitalism, his critique springs from those new beginnings. The name Marx gives to the violent and irruptive transition from feudal to capitalistic society is primitive accumulation:[7]

> The starting-point of the development that gave rise both to the wage-labourer and to the capitalist was the enslavement of the worker. The advance made consisted in a change in the form of this servitude, in the transformation of feudal exploitation into capitalist exploitation.[8]

The operative phrase in this passage is "a change in the form of this servitude." That is, for Marx, the transition from feudalism to capitalism, understood as a narrative of liberation, signals merely a shift in the form of the peasant's servitude and exploitation.

And yet Marx emphasizes that it would be a mistake to diminish or disallow the magnitude of this transition, which amounts to no less than a critical alteration in the terms and stakes of the modern political order. As such, while each order represents a servile and exploitative environment, this similarity does not therefore make them equal; rather, the difference between the two is precisely what is needed to understand both primitive accumulation and the freedom that conditions it.

As Marx observes, in "the history of primitive accumulation . . . the expropriation of the agricultural producer, of the peasant, from the soil is the basis of the whole process."[9] Primitive accumulation, therefore, serving as the name for the prehistory to capital, emerges with the peasant's "emancipation":

> Hence the historical movement which changes the producers into wage-labourers appears, on the one hand, as their emancipation from serfdom and from the fetters of the guilds, and it is this aspect of the movement which alone exists for our bourgeois historians. But, on the other hand, these newly freed men became sellers of themselves only after they had been robbed of all their own means of production, and all the guarantees of existence afforded by the old feudal arrangements.[10]

The words "emancipation" and "escape," in this passage, are enlisted as the themes through which to understand the condition of a peasantry that has been expropriated from the soil and hurled into urban factories.

But there is another figure that Marx employs in his work, one that more effectively demonstrates the contradictions at work in primitive accumulation. In chapter 28, vol. 1 of *Capital*, entitled "Bloody Legislation against the Expropriated since the End of the Fifteenth Century," Marx writes, "The proletariat created by the breaking-up of the bands of feudal retainers and by the forcible expropriation of the people from the soil, this free and rightless proletariat could not possibly be absorbed by the nascent manufacturers as fast as it thrown upon the world."[11] Translator Ben Fowkes appends the following note to his use of the word "rightless" in the passage, adding, "Here, as elsewhere in this context, Marx uses the word '*vogelfrei*', literally 'as free as a bird', i.e. free but outside the human community and therefore entirely unprotected and without legal rights."[12] In this context, and at the most decisive historico-political conjuncture signaling the emergence and the virtual prostration of the newly created wage-laborer, the very condition of rightlessness under primitive accumulation is figured through the word "vogelfrei" as a most radical form of freedom. Or rather, that radical freedom itself translates to a sheer rightlessness, to not belonging or pertaining. What this means for the present discussion is that, if primitive accumulation is the process wherein the peasant is violently divorced from their means of production, released from all the guarantees and protections provided by the previous social order, and left with only their own labor power to sell, then primitive accumulation represents not some bygone foundational historical event within capitalist development, but rather an ongoing and continuous process of capitalism's seemingly interminable subsumption of peoples and natural resources. Consequently, it is possible that what we are currently witnessing and naming posthegemony is actually another hemispheric-wide era of primitive accumulation.

The present posthegemonic context is therefore bearing witness to a crosshatching of primitive accumulation with the dynamics of the narco-cartel industry, that is, alongside the emerging ana-legal forces (that is, outside or beyond the sphere of Law) that in effect are competing with the state itself for the very means of control. Such a conjuncture, however, does not mean to suggest that the narco threat comes from "outside" the state or beyond capitalism, rather, the "War on Drugs" is itself an internally produced antagonism. Gareth Williams puts the problem between the state and cartels as follows:

> The War on Drugs is a conflict that is internal to capital, rather than being a conflict between external sovereign domains or distinct ideas of social organization. . . . The cartels are the bourgeois principle of private property and individual wealth monopolization manifested in its most naked form. The conflict arises because the cartel is capital actively desutured from the law, and therefore convened into a potentially par-

> allel sovereign imperium within national territory. There is, then, *open* enmity between the state and the cartels because these are a direct challenge to the suture of territory, population, and market within the juridical order. But there is no ideological conflict between sovereigns or real enemies, for the explicit ideology of the enemy is the explicit ideology of the friend and vice versa.[13]

In other words, what is at stake both in the Tamaulipas massacre as well as in the passage from Williams is the extent to which the state remains an indelible critical actor even if its role has shifted or weakened under posthegemonic conditions—that is, what Williams calls a "parallel sovereign imperium within national territory." As he argues, the state and cartels are not incommensurate with each other; it is not an ideological either/or since they are not mutually exclusive of each other, nor are any of the two outside of capital in any way. For instance, investigations have revealed that the seventy-two victims who constitute the first of the two massacres in Tamaulipas were kidnapped from charter buses running on federal highways that boasts numerous checkpoints. Given these circumstances and the evidence of collusion between the Zetas and local and federal state units, the massacres at San Fernando serve as a paradigmatic precursor to the Ayotzinapa mass kidnapping where forty-three students went missing after being arrested by local police in Iguala, Mexico on September 26, 2014.[14] The students are feared dead though their remains have yet to be found.

As such, the problem before us is how to rearticulate and reconceive what notions like borders and migration mean and how they function in this neoliberal era of unparalleled cultural and economic porosity and the increasingly indistinct nature of licit and illicit violence. If, for instance, we contend that the contemporary is fundamentally marked by radically different conditions generated by certain key political and economic reconfigurations on a global scale, might it then be the case that the migrational flows, practices, and border environments encountered today are marked by this same radical quality? Is it possible (or rather, are we prepared for the possibility) that the conditions of migration and social heterogeneity we are witnessing today are of such a profoundly and radically different sort that current theories of language, representation, and subjectivity might now be inadequate to account for it? In other words, given the precarious and exceedingly violent conditions of displacement, expropriation, and exploitation in the contemporary period, has the migrant subject's very relationship to language undergone irrevocable alteration? Have we entered what may also be called a "postmigrant" era under global capital?

I argue that Salvadoran journalist Óscar Martínez offers us such a glimpse into what I am calling the postmigrational in his work *The Beast*. In effect, *The Beast: Riding the Rails and Dodging Narcos on the Migrant Trail* provides the reader with a glimpse of the critical realities facing contemporary Central American migrants, not at this or that geopolitical border region, but rather at each and every stage of their journey as they navigate the other, countless, violent, and exploitative borders set up within Mexico, or perhaps more aptly put, the countless, violent, and exploitative borders that is Mexico itself. Much like other recent migration narratives, such as Luis Alberto's Urrea's *The Devil's Highway*,[15] Martinez's account moves away from attributing any essential significance to geopolitical borders as sites of analysis and offers a critical reflection on the question of negative, or non-Mexican, itinerancy within and through Mexico itself. In many ways, *The Beast* is a postmigrant narrative, as it is informed by and provides a narrative figuration of the very properties that characterize the contemporary neoliberal conjuncture, where unfettered global capital, in this case the cartels, has eclipsed the nation-state as the privileged and binding center of economic and social life.

However, we may question if cultural and critical thought is itself sufficiently attuned to these rapidly and radically moving market shifts and population flows to provide a glimpse of what precarity and borders should mean under postmigration.

Consider the very first lines of Martinez's text, which create a distinction between two different kinds of itinerancy: "There are those who migrate to El Norte because of poverty . . . and there are those who don't migrate. They flee."[16] In this brief passage, Martinez offers us an instance of internally divided and competing modes of entry into El Norte––between those who "migrate" and "the stream of escapees . . . those fleeing poverty, those fleeing death."[17] With this distinction, Martinez both invokes the notion of primitive accumulation and foregrounds the internal disjunction inhabiting the itinerant moving body: "Fleeing takes speed . . . migrating though, takes strategy."[18]

The notion of fleeing as an unqualified, unregisterable activity of itinerancy is itself not some throwaway notion, either, for one could argue that it conditions Martínez's entire narrative. The first section of the book details the harrowing journey that awaits migrants as soon as they cross the border into Chiapas, Mexico. Dubbed La Arrocera, this sparse 160-mile long stretch of ranches between the cities of Tapachula and Arriaga is riddled with local gangs, smuggling networks, and even poor ranch hands armed with guns and machetes, all lying in wait to ambush unsuspecting migrants. And this is before they even catch a glimpse of the Mexican train system, La Bestia, which most migrants take as a means to cross the rest of Mexico. La Arrocera, like Tamaulipas, and like La Bestia itself, are, according to Martínez, all "lawless territory," zones of exceptionality where the only rule of law is the freedom either to "give up, kill, or die."[19]

Let us consider, for instance, Martínez's recounting of a scene involving the killing and kidnapping of numerous migrants while riding the train itself in Tenosique, Tabasco. The account begins with a Honduran named El Puma and his men that go collect money from the migrants as they wait for the train to depart. "You have to pay him to get onto the train," Martínez emphasizes. "Those who don't pay don't go. Those who resist get to meet him, his crew, his machetes, and his *cuerno de chivo* [AK-47 assault rifle]."[20] "People who know him," Martínez relays, "say He works for los Zetas."[21] In the very next town, a group of eight men climb aboard the slow-moving train and within minutes put on ski masks, draw their weapons, and jumping from train car to train car, begin robbing the migrants and kidnapping the women. In this scene, too lengthy to cite here, Martínez recounts how the assailants were met with fierce resistance not once but twice. In each case, and despite the death of one migrant and the kidnapping of two women, the *polleros* managed to force the masked assailants off the train. By the third stop, however, the assailants caught up to the train yet again and this time, with heavily armed reinforcements, forced the *polleros* to give up their position. "It was Los Zetas," was the refrain among the remaining migrants.[22]

This scene is central to understanding both posthegemonic Mexico and Martínez's account of it. Masked or not, everyone involved in that scene knows who the assailants worked for. The trains, it becomes clear, operate and are synchronized with the needs of los Zetas. And not a word of this incident, which includes numerous deaths and at least two kidnapped women, Martínez later tells us, will ever appear in the press. It simply doesn't register. It doesn't read and it remains fundamentally inscrutable from within a conventional hegemonic political order. In other words, posthegemony, if it were to have any representational dimension at all, would be only expressible as an aesthetic framed by primitive accumulation: a postmigrational understanding of expropriation and itinerancy as a constitutive, ongoing dynamic of contemporary human life.

But of course, that is only half of it. According to Martínez, the second half of the journey––from the state of Tabasco to virtually all border crossing points into the United States––consists in the paradoxical and yet impossible demand to avoid any contact with the cartels before they reach the border itself. Of course, this is a paradoxical and impossible task because, as Martínez demonstrates, the cartels already control all established migrant routes and the coyotes have almost all already been conscripted into their service. That is, there are virtually no migrant routes that are not already populated, taxed, and policed by the cartels themselves; there are simply no migrants crossing the border who are unaccounted for and who have not already paid the fee for being allowed to pass. Even more insidious is the fact that coyotes are now not only limited to their traditional occupation of guiding migrants to the border but have also now been enlisted to secure migrants for kidnapping and extortion. Interviews with migrants, *polleros*, and government officials lead Martínez to the following interconnected assessments about drug trafficking, global capital, and political sovereignty: "When Los Zetas take over, they take over everything. They've monopolized crime . . . and whoever wants a job, any kind of job, has to somehow work for Los Zetas"[23] As Los Zetas explain:

> From now on you work for us, they announced. From now on, you won't have any problems with the migration authorities. From now on, any games worth just a few pesos are over. We're going to take over this route, charge any coyotes who pass through here, punish those who don't pay, and kidnap those who don't travel with someone hired by us. That was their offer.[24]

What such passages render abundantly clear is that there is virtually no route not controlled by, nor any one coyote who isn't already involved with, cartels like the Zetas.[25] Whether the coyote indeed works as a migrant's guide through Mexico and the border, or one who simply feigns such occupation to enact a group kidnapping, both are enterprises run and organized by cartels. They are an industry run entirely off of migrant bodies. As such, these conditions push Williams's notion of "parallel sovereign imperium" (i.e., capitalist entities competing for control of the state) to its utter limit. In effect, what we are seeing is primitive accumulation as an ongoing historical process, wherein people are forcibly divorced and extricated from the land and from a specific mode of production toward another. If the precarity that primitive accumulation generates—vogelfrei, "free and rightless and as a bird"—can be said to equally characterize the migrant's condition during itinerancy, it also means that the Maras (from the Mara Salvatrucha cartel) and Zetas have been able to fully absorb virtually all local labor forces (smaller gangs and local coyotes) in the interest of consolidating and structuring trafficking routes, not only for narcotics but for the already expropriated and incoming migration flows through Mexico toward the U.S. border. Trafficking itself then may have emerged as a mode of production unto itself, wherein the migrant, unlike narcotics, is interpellated as laborer and consumer simultaneously.

In this light, it may behoove us to consider if the primitive accumulation we are seeing presently under groups like Los Zetas operates in the same way as it does in Marx's account. In other words, if in Marx's account property is the thing being accumulated during the era of enclosure, what then are the Zetas and other narco groups accumulating in their exercise of parallel sovereignty? And how do their interests in acquiring capital coincide with the interests of U.S. firms in securing rightless laborers? This is indeed an urgent and most pressing question if we are to come any closer to comprehending the stakes at this present neoliberal conjuncture. Of course, there is no easy answer to this. As a way to broach this question, it is important to note that while most scholars remain solidly behind the proposition that primitive accumulation is an ongoing, integral component of capitalist development and not just its historical "prime mover," the scholarship is less decided on its more specific function under neoliberalism. Some are even beginning to suggest that primitive accumulation, while it was conceived even by Marx himself as the process by which the land obtains as the principal object of appropriation, is a process ultimately more about labor. Tom Brass, for instance, argues that if primitive accumulation functioned historically as a principal form of "de-peasantization" that generates the otherwise "free" labor force necessary for capitalism to function as conventionally understood (laborers who freely voluntarily sell their labor where there is a market for it), primitive accumulation currently operates as a form of "deproletarianization" that instead compels laborers to surrender their ability to sell their labor, thereby unconcealing a deeply ingrained regime of unfree labor that belies this most basic assumption about capitalism as such.[26]

If this is indeed the case, then it may stand to reason that global capitalism, turning in on itself ever more, has reconsolidated and repackaged migrant labor as a commodity in its own right that now demands a market. The cartels assume control over that market.

Given these conditions, it seems that contemporary migrants do not "migrate" anymore; that is, maybe it is no longer accurate to speak of this contemporary phenomena as migration, for migration—as documented in *Los migrantes que no importan*, Luis Alberto Urrea's *The Devil's Highway*, as well as Gloria Anzaldúa's *Borderlands/La Frontera*[27]—is no longer what happens in Mexico, even if the result of this new process continues to provide displaced, itinerant labor channeled toward the U.S./Mexico border.

As Marx says of the flax produced from large-scale industry after primitive accumulation, "The flax looks exactly as it did before. Not a fiber of it is changed, but a new social soul has entered into its body."[28] That is, while the migrant laborer's path to the United States through Mexico today may look very much like it did before, "a new social soul has entered its body," which is to say that this itinerant laborer now is imbued and marked with the traces of radically transformed, post-NAFTA conditions of production, including the unavoidable passage through La Arrocera toward the city of Arriaga (in lieu of taking the now abandoned railroad that once began in Tapachula, Mexico, first damaged during Hurricane Stan in 2005); the emergence of cartels like the Mara Salvatrucha, los Zetas, and other breakaway groups that have commercially expanded into human trafficking. Moreover, the Secure Fence Act of 2006[29] not only financed the extension of the border wall further through California into Arizona and through parts of Texas, making the final passage to the United States even more difficult and precarious than ever before, but the very erection of this wall also created the topographical conditions for cartels to assume effective control over key border-crossing territories (gaps within the wall itself) for exclusive use in their trafficking operations. As a result, "migration," as a concept simply appears incapable of accounting for these new, cross-hatched, and drastically intensified conditions of neoliberal labor production.

Additionally, in a passage that further opens up and displaces normative geopolitical assumptions about migrancy, Mexico, and the U.S. Southwest, Martinez cites a fellow rider on the train expounding on the ultimately biopolitical significance of La Bestia: "The Beast is the Rio Grande's first cousin because they share the same blood, Central American blood" ("Este es primo hermano del río Bravo, porque la misma sangre tienen, sangre centroamericana").[30] At stake in this brief pronouncement is a pivotal assertion of a formal equivalence between the U.S./Mexico border and the Mexican train system that comprises the Beast's route from South to North. The claim is rather straightforward: Central American blood shed along the railroad tracks throughout Mexico is the same blood that is shed all along the U.S./Mexico border. "La misma sangre tienen" is a remarkably polyvalent statement in that it tells us just as much as about La Bestia as it does about the U.S./Mexico border. The analogy in effect works both ways, emphasizing not only the extent to which La Bestia is considered a harrowingly violent yet still irrevocably Central American institution *within* Mexico, but also, and more acutely, acknowledging just how much the U.S./Mexico border is itself stained and sustained by the blood from otherwise non-Mexican itinerant labor flows. It tells us through the trace of sanguinity that the train and the border are of the same genus, of the same distinction, the same exceptional division. As such, if the U.S./Mexico border acts as a partition that both joins and separates two national territories, so too then does the Beast function as an intraterritorial border, being as it were the "first cousin" of the Río Grande, and one that so happens to run through the entirety of Mexico——straight down the middle——ultimately and irretrievably dividing Mexico itself. The implications of such a proposition are both profound and far-reaching. On the one hand, this pronouncement contends that La Bestia constitutes an internal border within Mexico itself, a zone of posthegemonic double-exclusion ("lawless territory") marked only by the non-Mexican blood that greases the train's tracks. On the other hand, it proposes that this Central American blood, through its double-exclusion from predominant historico-political imaginaries about the U.S. Southwest as constituted between Mexican and Anglo settlers, might thereby also condition the very distinction between Mexican and Chicano communities along both sides of the border.[31]

In many ways, therefore, this pronouncement reveals an irreducible figure of exception inhabiting both borders, and the analogy appealed to in this statement is drawn from this shared figure of exception. "Central American blood" names this exceptionality, and being neither a race, ethnicity, nor a specific country, the former also characterizes this exceptionality's sheer heterogeneity (non-Mexican blood) relative to the disputed geopolitical territoriality within which this blood is shed. If, as this claim goes, La Bestia and the U.S./Mexico border are comprised within a heterogeneous and immiscible compound of non-Mexican blood, then neither, it can be argued, can serve as a real source of cultural identification. Such a claim of formal consistency between two distinct entities, however, may provide some critical insight into how posthegemony results precisely from the compounding of this double-exclusion along La Bestia and the double-exclusion at the U.S./Mexico border, which perpetuates the contemporary reproduction of itinerant labor populations needed for global capitalism.

It is important to recognize that despite narratives such as Martínez's, which tell the stories of poor and frightened Central American migrants in southern Mexico running along moving trains, grasping for the ladder tracks, this juridico-economic mapping of itinerant, commodified labor at the U.S./Mexico border does not begin there; rather, it is more appropriate to understand that it extends to the border. In effect, it may be more accurate to suggest that this mapping extends outwards *from* the United States itself, rather than toward it. In other words, it may be that the non-Mexican labor force we are now seeing arrive at the U.S./Mexico border is not a sudden and unforeseen occurrence entirely independent of any U.S. involvement in the region. Nor is this labor force completely incompatible with the kinds of work needed from these otherwise undesirable, undocumented immigrants. The United States is getting the labor force it needs and with desired specifications. Not unlike poverty, these itinerant populations are not historical accidents; they must be produced, as must their conditions of possibility.

While this process pervades and determines the entire field of intelligibility, the root of this conjuncture, however, is not so easily brought into focus. As much as conservative political forces in the United States condemn the multitudes of undocumented immigrants already in the country—while ceaselessly proposing legislation to eliminate illegal entry by criminalizing their unlawful presence in the territory, such as the 2010 Arizona anti-immigration law S.B. 1070[32]—eradicating unlawful entry outright is never the main objective. It is now known that prior to proposing SB 1070 to the Arizona Senate, the primary architect of the bill, Senator Russell Pierce, presented a draft of the legislation at a meeting of ALEC (American Legislative Exchange Council). In attendance were representatives from an industry that would ultimately be the law's biggest beneficiary: the Corrections Corporation of America—the largest private prison company in the country.[33] What this co-operation suggests is that the "unauthorized immigrant" is not just a legal category but also a fundamentally economic one, and so legislation that takes this figure up in any kind of restrictive sense brings with it a labor-specific component, thus offering a parallel example of the double-exclusion experienced by the cartel's takeover of the migrant smuggling industry along the U.S./Mexico border as documented by Martínez.

As R. Andrés Guzmán notes in a recent article, the notion of the unauthorized immigrant in the United States is a juridical figure generated by and "internal to [the] legal system itself," a figure of exception that, while pointing to the margins of the law, constitutes in effect the very "center of immigration policy and neoliberal political economy."[34] Guzmán foregrounds the popular misconception that automatically links illegality with criminality by reminding us that, under federal law, unlawful entry is not a criminal offense but rather a civil one whose penalties are not at all commensurate:

> Indeed, while it is currently a crime to enter the country without permission, those who stay in this country without authorization (either by overstaying their visa or by staying after unauthorized entry) are *not* criminals because the violation they commit pertains to civil law, not criminal law. The assumption of criminality as self-evident is thus based upon a misconception of the consequences of legal transgression as homogenous—i.e. the idea that any "illegal" act makes one a "criminal." Against this, it is necessary that we demonstrate that the line between criminality and non-criminality is not that between a homogeneous law and its violation. This distinction, rather, is internal to the legal system itself and is historically produced.[35]

By "historically produced" Guzman contends that deportation wasn't always the automatic penalty for unauthorized entry in the United States. In fact, deportation only emerges as an enforcement measure as late as the Immigration Act of 1924, which "developed both the mechanisms and enforcement capacity for deportation."[36]

Consequently, deportation (or deportability), as a *secondary* historical and discursive attribute of unauthorized entry, is itself what animates the generalized and highly ambivalent anti-immigration/labor dialectic that underpins the contemporary economic scene that Martínez documents.[37] Yet, as we can also see, it is precisely the ascription of deportability status, and not necessarily deportation itself, that creates the conditions for generating a more exploitable, and perpetually itinerant, workforce. As suggested above, it may be that the goal of any immigration policy is not to eradicate unlawful entry outright, but simply to regulate its flow relative to regional and national labor needs. Juridically, this takes the form of inscribing the unauthorized immigrant within a relation of inclusion and exclusion:

> [The] phenomenon of undocumented immigration, as it has been constituted in the United States after the mid-1960s, is the purposeful creation of immigration policy, the function of which has been not simply to prevent or dissuade people from entering the US, but rather to structure the very inclusion of migrants *as "illegal"* by orienting the range of possibilities for entrance towards unauthorized means. Indeed, what [is] demonstrate[d] is the collusion between immigration law and sectors of capital in *producing* a labor force adequate to higher rates of exploitation through the very *inclusion* of workers as undocumented, and thus as *excluded*.[38]

What is ultimately at stake in the present discussion is the possibility that, not unlike the migrants in Mexico who, in attempting to evade state immigration enforcement, instead fall prey to the cartel's seemingly inescapable human smuggling operation, the unauthorized immigrant under U.S. federal law similarly becomes a figure of double-exclusion foundational to, and inextricable from, contemporary neoliberal economic and labor policy. In other words, as it relates to the status and conditions of itinerant labor populations produced under posthegemonic primitive accumulation, a formal symmetry develops between the sovereign exception claimed by the cartels along the migrant trail and U.S. federal law along the U.S./Mexico border.

To clarify the complexity of this issue, consider the U.S. government's original challenge to SB 1070 as an example that fully reveals the scale of this juridical exceptionality. The Department of Justice's legal complaint to the Arizona law argues that SB 1070, as a state law that "attempts to second guess federal policies and re-order federal priorities in the area of immigration enforcement and to directly regulate immigration in Arizona," is preempted by federal immigration law and therefore violates the supremacy clause of the United States Constitution (Article VI, Clause 2):

> Arizona's new state law prohibition of certain transporting, concealing, and encouraging of unlawfully present aliens is preempted by federal law, including 8 U.S.C. § 1324(a)(1)(C). This new provision is an attempt to regulate unlawful entry into the United States (through the Arizona

> border). The regulation of unlawful entry is an area from which states are definitively barred by the U.S. Constitution. Additionally, because the purpose of this law is to deter and prevent the movement of certain aliens into Arizona, the law restricts interstate commerce. Enforcement and operation of this state law provision would therefore conflict and interfere with the federal government's management of interstate commerce, and would thereby violate Article I, Section 8 of the United States Constitution. (*United States v. Arizona*, §56)[39]

On the surface, the federal government's prompt response to permanently enjoin and invalidate what many believe to be a racist and specifically anti-Mexican law in Arizona is a welcome development. However, the federal challenge to SB 1070 ultimately relies less on the question of preempting federal immigration policy, or of even violating the supremacy clause; instead, it relies mostly on removing any obstruction to itinerant labor flow throughout the country. The complaint alleges that "because the purpose of this law is to deter and prevent the movement of certain aliens into Arizona, the law restricts interstate commerce," and therefore violates the supremacy clause and a foundational premise of the Constitution—the commerce clause.[40] For the purposes of my argument, it is important to clarify the implications of this specific legal argument against the Arizona law: it argues, in effect, that SB 1070 is constitutionally invalid because, among other reasons, it restricts the flow of unauthorized immigrant labor to neighboring states and therefore interferes with interstate commerce. As stated in the complaint, "the regulation of unlawful entry is an area from which states are definitively barred by the U.S. Constitution." In short, states do not have the right to regulate unlawful entry into the United States; only the federal government has the power to do so.

This predicament raises interesting and pressing questions, including how can unlawful entry be regulated, if at all? The unauthorized immigrant, the object of unlawful entry, remains a strangely ambiguous figure without any positive quality under U.S. federal law. Conceptually, this logic seems contradictory, if not oxymoronic: the federal government insists that it alone has the power to regulate what is essentially unregulatable. As Guzmán argues, given the always incomplete and uneven estimates as to how many illegal immigrants there are in the country at any one time, this demographic or "group" category can only exist as an index of the state's fundamental "miscount."[41] As a result, the contemporary "sovereign state" can only regulate unlawful entry by either permitting it or prohibiting it in name only because what we are starting to see is that "unlawful entry" is not an irregularity at all, but rather a primary and fundamental economic necessity, which is tacitly sought, encouraged, and incentivized.

Under the Justice Department's reading, "unlawful entry" under federal law is positioned not as some juridical category to address extraordinary and unforeseeable historical influxes of peoples (like SB 1070 does), but rather as the name for a steady, continuous, and foundational economic process that underlies the entire capitalist system. These two readings of unlawful entry between the state of Arizona and the federal government could not be more divergent. However, and not unlike primitive accumulation, the seemingly ahistorical nature of "unlawful entry" as a juridical concept belies its full and active participation in framing the contemporary posthegemonic scene that Arizona has come to exemplify. Instead, what we are currently bearing witness to, and what writers like Óscar Martínez are successfully underscoring, is a labor-reproduction process that begins not along the U.S./Mexico border but rather further south, at that other doubly exceptional border that is La Bestia, which—existing in a postmigratory condition—the cartels secure and control as the major suppliers of labor to the United States. At this historical juncture, the question is no longer whether restricting unlawful entry itself interferes with federal immigration policy or whether restricting unlawful entry is economically desirable in and of itself. What we do need to consider is the extent to which contemporary, postmigrational efforts at restricting unlawful entry, as an act of and in the name of national sovereignty, has itself produced the "parallel sovereign imperium," which is threatening to destabilize Mexican and U.S. sovereignty, or whether these posthegemonic conditions are merely exposing the very fiction of sovereignty that the U.S./Mexico border itself generates.

No doubt the implications of what this discussion might mean for debates around immigration and Latino identity in the United States are far-reaching. On the one hand, it highlights the extent in which ethnic identity along La Bestia and at the U.S./Mexico border, in this case Central American identity, emerges not as some pregiven cultural trait fellow migrants bring with them, but rather is itself the historical result of forceful and violent differentiation and subalternization from other groups within a posthegemonic field of intelligibility within not only Central America and throughout Mexico, but even into the United States—a process I have been calling primitive accumulation. "Central American blood," in Martínez's words, is one particular history of posthegemonic primitive accumulation among others. It reveals to us that in the posthegemonic era ethnicity may no longer be binding in any kind of meaningful way to envision collectivity, or perhaps that ethnicity was only ever an economic category that over time was naturalized into a cultural form. In either case, to speak today of interethnic relations among Latino groups in Mexico and the United States is quite simply to speak of the relations between groups with competing histories of primitive accumulation, cases of which usually involve the subordination and exploitation of one Latino group by another, such as in *The Beast*. The point here is that these groups are ultimately differentially defined, which is to say defined only through their difference from the each other, and therefore without any sort of positive designation. The posthegemonic inversion of the social text allows one to see that the groups about whom one attempts to understand and begin to make historical and political claims are *not* defined primarily by ethnicity but rather, and perhaps most importantly, by their history of primitive accumulation.

Notes

1. See John Beverley, *Subalternity and Representation: Arguments in Cultural Theory* (Durham: Duke University Press, 1999); Gareth Williams, *The Other Side of the Popular: Neoliberalism and Subalternity in Latin America* (Durham: Duke University Press, 2002); Gareth Williams, *The Mexican Exception: Sovereignty, Police, and Democracy* (New York: Palgrave Macmillan, 2011); Brett Levinson, *Market and Thought: Meditations on the Political and Biopolitical* (New York: Fordham University Press, 2004); and Jon Beasley-Murray, *Posthegemony: Political Theory and Latin America* (Minneapolis: University of Minnesota Press, 2010). These works, emanating from the field of Latin American cultural studies, mark provocative and ever-relevant attempts to come to terms with the increasing discordance between contemporary theories of state power and the intensified historical contradictions brought about by the neoliberal restructuration of the nation-state.

2. Williams, *Other Side*, 1.

3. Williams, of course, is not alone in this observation, as he forms part of much larger conversation documenting these shifts in the global political order. In *Political Spaces and Global War*, Carlo Galli highlights much of the same phenomenon: "In the global age, modern political spatiality——the State, with its right and ability to enclose an internal sphere with order and security . . . has ceased to be fully in effect, challenged as it is by the power of economic flows and the needs of capital, which demand a new politics and which no longer allow the State to be the operative center of political reality and its interpretation" (Minneapolis: University of Minnesota Press, 2010),

157–58. Further, Michael Hardt and Antonio Negri also share in the assessment of this contemporary political conjuncture, one that they have chosen to call *Empire*: "[W]e have witnessed an irresistible and irreversible globalization of economic and cultural exchanges. Along with the global market and global circuits of production has emerged a global order, a new logic and structure of rule—in short, a new form of sovereignty. Empire is the political subject that effectively regulates these global exchanges, the sovereign power that governs the world. . . . The declining sovereignty of nation-states and their increasing inability to regulate economic and cultural exchanges is in fact one of the primary symptoms of the coming Empire" (Cambridge: Harvard University Press, 2000), xi–xii. Whether it's called postnationalization, globalization, neoliberalism, Empire, or posthegemony, such passages and terms not only highlight the general discursive consistency coalescing at the same time that these otherwise disparate works were being published—all between 2000 and 2002—but they also emphasize how much these critical analyses continue to resound now more than ever.

4. Antonio Gramsci, *Prison Notebooks*, vols. 1–3 (New York: Columbia University Press, 2011).

5. Óscar Martínez, "Los coyotes domados," *Elfaro.net*, March 24, 2014, http://www.salanegra.elfaro.net/es/201403/cronicas/15101/

6. Óscar Martínez, *The Beast: Riding the Rails and Dodging Narcos on the Migrant Trail* (New York: Verso, 2014). Originally in Spanish: *Los migrantes que no importan* (Barcelona: Icaria editorial, 2010).

7. While beyond the scope of the present discussion, it is important to acknowledge the substantial body of Marxist theory on primitive accumulation. A representative but by no means exhaustive list includes Rosa Luxemburg, *The Accumulation of Capital*, trans. Agnes Schwarzschild. London (Routledge, 2003 [1913]); Ernest Mandel, *Late Capitalism*, trans. Joris De Bres (London: NLB, 1975); Silvia Federici, *Caliban and the Witch* (Brooklyn, NY: Autonomedia, 2004); Michael Perelman, *The Invention of Capitalism: Classical Political Economy and the Secret History of Accumulation* (Durham, NC: Duke University Press, 2000); Tom Brass, *Labour Regime Change in the Twenty-First Century: Unfreedom, Capitalism and Primitive Accumulation* (Leiden: Boston: Brill, 2011); and Maria Mies (*Patriarchy and Accumulation on a World Scale: Women in the International Division of Labour* (London: Zed Books, 2014).

8. Karl Marx, *Capital: A Critique of Political Economy, Vol. 1*, trans. Ben Fowkes (New York: Penguin Books, 1990), 875.

9. Marx, *Capital*, 876.

10. Marx, *Capital*, 875.

11. Marx, *Capital*, 896.

12. Marx, *Capital*, 896.

13. Williams, *Mexican Exception*, 154.

14. I credit Pablo Dominguez Galbraith for this insight.

15. Luis Alberto Urrea, *The Devil's Highway: A True Story* (New York: Back Bay Books, 2004).

16. Martínez, *The Beast,* 1 [12]. Citations include page numbers from the Spanish edition in brackets.

17. Martínez, *The Beast,* 19 [30].

18. Martínez, *The Beast,* 23 [33].

19. Martínez, *The Beast,* 60 [71].

20. Martínez, *The Beast,* 90 [101].

21. Martínez, *The Beast,* 90 [101].

22. Martínez, *The Beast,* 91–92 [102–3].

23. Martínez, *The Beast,* 116 [128–29].

24. Martínez, *The Beast,* 118 [130].

25. Martínez characterizes the current situation for coyotes as follows: "Ten years ago, the image of the coyote as custodian started crumbling. The friendly neighbor who, for a small, reasonable sum, would take his compadre, his friend, to El Norte, is now a sullen man, covered in scars, and often a danger to his own clients. Sometimes he's even a Zeta ally, who migrants go with because there's no other choice. Sometimes he's a kidnapper, and most of the time he's a swindler. . . . The good coyote no longer has that option—to be a good coyote. He has to pay his dues to Los Zetas, or hand over human loot instead. The good coyote has to give up his reputation, relinquish the essence of his trade, abandon the routes and cantinas that once served as hangout and pickup spots" (Martínez, *The Beast,* 131–32).

26. Brass, *Labour Regime,* 136.

27. Gloria Anzaldúa, *Borderlands/La Frontera* (San Francisco: Aunt Lute Books, 1987).

28. Marx, *Capital,* 909.

29. The Secure Fence Act, U.S House Resolution 6061 (passed October 6, 2006). For more information, see http://library.uwb.edu/Static/USimmigration/2006_secure_fence_act.html

30. Martínez, *The Beast,* 53 [65].

31. The double-exclusion I am pointing to here may find its most critical representation in the juridical difference between Mexican and Central American immigrants, among others, who physically cross the border into the United States versus the descendants of Mexican communities who lived in the areas previously owned by Mexico and later ceded to the United States in the Treaty of Guadalupe Hidalgo.

32. The Support Our Law Enforcement and Safe Neighborhoods Act, Arizona SB 1070 (passed April 13, 2010).

33. http://www.npr.org/2010/10/28/130833741/prison-economics-help-drive-ariz-immigration-law

34. R. Andrés Guzmán, "Criminalization at the Edge of the Evental Site: Undocu-

mented Immigration, Mass Incarceration, and Universal Citizenship," *Theory and Event* 19.2 (2016). *Project MUSE*, muse.jhu.edu/article/614368

35. Guzmán, "Criminalization at the Edge of the Evental Site," n.p.

36. Guzman, "Criminalization at the Edge of the Evental Site," n.p.

37. Guzmán contends: "It is thus the condition of deportability, together with the state's capacity to enforce more restrictive legislation through detention and deportation, which transformed general undocumented status into a consequential and thus socially and legally significant category. While people who had avoided points of inspection certainly existed within national space before this legislation, it is with the latter that undocumented status becomes meaningful as a target of government action and significant to the lived experience of those without authorization. As such, migrant 'illegality' is not the automatic result of unauthorized entry, but rather, together with changes in immigration law that made more people eligible for and subject to deportation, it is the product of the state's enforcement capacity, which makes such a status consequential by transforming unauthorized entrants into targets of policing" (n.p.).

38. Italics in original, Guzman, "Criminalization at the Edge of the Evental Site," n.p.

39. United States v. Arizona, 703 F.Supp.2d 980 (D. Ariz. 2010) (No. CV 10–1413-PHX-SRB). https://www.justice.gov/sites/default/files/opa/legacy/2010/07/06/az-complaint.pdf

40. Article, I, Section 8, Clause 3.

41. Guzmán, "Criminalization at the Edge of the Evental Site," n. p.

CHAPTER 10

A Chicana Dystopian Novel and the Economic Realities of Their Dogs Came with Them

Edén E. Torres

Having already contributed significantly to the body of literature written by Mexican Americans, Helena María Viramontes secured her place as an essential American writer of the late twentieth and early twenty-first century with the publication of *Their Dogs Came with Them*. An intriguing and complex literary work, the novel takes readers on a difficult journey into a world that is specific in its setting—East Los Angeles in the 1960s and '70s—but often feels otherworldly. While it takes place during the height of the Chicano movement, her characters are not primarily involved in political resistance. Yet, in the sense that this novel offers readers an intimate description of life in a rather dystopian society that transcends time and space—where the results of capitalism's necessary inequalities seem magnified—it could be as timeless as any work of classic science fiction. It is this resemblance to dystopia as a genre that distinguishes the novel.

Among other themes, the novel addresses the transnational nature of Mexicanness; the social and political function of policing in racialized and poor neighborhoods; rape, homophobia, gender norms, and teenage trans life; perpetually conditional citizenship; and violence at all levels. Questions have been raised about whether or not Viramontes has created a real snapshot of the barrio or has merely repeated stereotypes, and whether or not she has an obligation to proffer a more positive portrait. Few critics have granted serious attention to the novel's representations of the state's mechanisms for disciplining the poor. There is no single protagonist here, and the environment, as a victim of corporate greed, is often as fully developed as any of the characters. Thus, they do not exemplify individual experiences as much as they symbolize the material conditions created by the profit class and its ongoing exploitation of the proletariat.

I focus here on the dystopian atmosphere Viramontes describes so vividly because the differential valuing of human life under global capitalism is on full display. The mood she creates through language, imagery, repetition and metaphor exposes not only the inescapability of the barrio but also the way in which a powerful—but largely unknowable—system exploits the residents' labor, imposes its values, and maintains strict borders through surveillance and punishment. It lays bare the violence that accompanies a lifelong struggle against inequality. In much the same way that early Chicanx authors and left-leaning filmmakers revealed the lives of farmworkers and the truth of their oppression under capitalism, Viramontes has brought this critical lens to urban environments. Her use of dystopian imagery and mysterious creatures that are sometimes real in a material sense, but just as often ethereal, encourages readers to feel as unsettled and off-balance as the characters do. It also brings into view the historical dominance and daunting nature of the economic system.

The dogs of the title, for instance, serve as a threatening and deeply unsettling element of outside control common in dystopian (and neoliberal) societies. Viramontes resurrects the history of dogs being used as militarized weapons as she ominously opens her novel with a quote from Miguel Leon-Portilla's foundational text, *The Broken Spears: The Aztec Account of the Conquest of Mexico*. As imagined and embodied creatures, the dogs represent and protect the interests of the bourgeoisie. She illuminates a link between the history of European dominance in the Americas and contemporary, state-supported institutions that continue this legacy of exploitation and oppression. The dogs are omnipresent in every corner of the society. They provide a real and a mythical barrier between the classes, thwart efforts by the poor to achieve equality, and embody the willingness of the upper classes to use violence to contain the poor.

These animals—in their state-legitimated *and* their supposedly rabid versions—are part of what has made the barrio itself an institution that functions as a kind of prison. While a formal system exists for punishment, the mythical Quarantine Authority (QA) regulates the neighborhood borders. Viramontes's East Los Angeles then acts as a coercive site for social control. It becomes a contained location where punishments and intimidating rules are constantly circulated through written and verbal warnings of the horrible consequences that may await anyone who resists, challenges, or crosses state-defined boundaries.

Dystopian literature has often been used to speculate on the future of a postapocalyptic society. Viramontes has constructed a similar representation of dehumanization and misery that occurred in the past, is still present in society, and is prophetic about the future. The world Viramontes describes is one in which no one would want to (or should have to) live. But it provides us with a lens through which to see how Chicanas/os have negotiated and are surviving disruption, discrimination, environmental destruction, irrational restrictions on their movements, and unreasonable surveillance.

Viramontes is first and foremost a creative writer with the talent to satisfy even the most discriminating lovers of literature. Yet the intrinsic and arbitrary structural unfairness of the world she illuminates stands out. Thus, like Fredric Jameson, I find a Marxist "structural diagnosis . . . perfectly consistent with contemporary . . . postmodern convictions which rule out presuppositions as to some pre-existing human nature or essence."[1] This novel and its inherent critique of social hierarchies, violence, and injustice begs readers to begin to imagine a future society in which class and the arbitrary unequal valuing of human life disappears. In that sense, it hints at what Jameson has described as a necessary gesture toward utopianism. If this is one's ultimate quest, then a focus on the political economy need not preclude an interest in psychology and how humans respond to their environments.

Dystopian novels have a history of being used to criticize capitalism and the state's role in maintaining the social order necessary for unfettered corporate operations. The genre has provided literary and cultural theorists with examples of possible outcomes for various institutional mechanisms that create desires, fears, and the need for individualistic competition, as well as what might occur when the system collapses under the weight of capitalism's excesses and contradictions. While Viramontes's novel functions in this way, I am not arguing that it actually belongs in this category of speculative fiction. Nor is it a work of fantasy, even as Viramontes does incorporate fantastical elements. Furthermore, *Dogs* cannot be said to be part of the tradition of George Orwell, Aldous Huxley, Margaret Atwood, or the more recent *Hunger Games* series by Suzanne Collins.

While it is fiction—and Viramontes does sometimes create the sensation that her characters inhabit an "other" world—the novel is actually a work of determined realism. But because we are all reading from vastly different social locations, the accuracy of her dream-like images or the meaning of a mysterious dog bite may be just as hard to perceive, decipher, or accept as are the more imaginative elements in science fiction.

While I am echoing some of the theoretical arguments made by Jameson, I am employing dystopia not as a critical construct of the imagination but as a reflection of the "postapocalypse" that some people are already living. What, then, might this work of fiction have to say about ever-expanding national and global inequalities, migration, and civil unrest in a supposedly postracial and "civil" society? While there is little in the novel to comfort or console Western, neoliberal readers, the work is telling us to recognize that the opposite of poverty is not wealth, but freedom from the inequalities and the unsafe environments that plague us. Unfortunately, capitalism can never guarantee either equality or safety.[2]

Though historically grounded, the novel creates a narrative of varying experiences with poverty and violence that expands beyond this particular location. While not the end goal, "verbally expressing pain is a necessary prelude to the collective task of diminishing" our scars and healing our wounds.[3] Such narratives are also necessary for teaching and learning how to speak out explicitly against injustice, claiming our subjectivity and becoming political actors. This telling of history through a mixture of fiction and reality is the exercise of what Emma Pérez has called the decolonial imaginary, adding a Chicana feminist political purpose to *Dogs* beyond the formulaic conventions of writing dystopias. Deep and abrupt time shifts in Viramontes's nonlinear narrative symbolize the fictive space between past, present, and future, reflecting a non-traditional view of time. But this slippage also brings into focus spaces rife with tension and sharp contradictions. Jameson claimed that it is in these voids where genuine thinking takes place. Gloria Anzaldúa similarly called attention to this fecund locale in her writing on the *nepantla* state (or state of in-betweenness), and the borderlands as spaces where critical insights always occur if we pay attention.

Viramontes forces the reader to go back and forth trying to keep track of the seemingly decontextualized and random threads she picks up and drops. But isn't this how our memory works? As we remember, sort through contradictions, reflect, and add new insights, we make meaning. This process helps readers to understand the frequently unnoticed links between personal, social, national, and global histories. Nothing worth noticing in our lives happens without these connections. How we respond in any given moment is dependent on what has come before. Our subjectivities are constructed and dependent on the narratives around us. The stories are the lenses through which we perceive, reflect, think, and ultimately are moved to change. This process of making meaning is not a solitary endeavor. Memory and storytelling, Viramontes tells us, are important for creating or solidifying a sense of community.

> The only thing they cherished, their only private property, were the stories they continued to create and re-create in a world which only gave them one to tell. And so they never tired of one another's company.[4]

Sadie Lansdale has stated that "[t]he non-linear representation of time . . . is a reaction by her characters to the trauma of being systemically disenfranchised. The visceral language . . . she uses to describe the violence of daily life reflect[s] the violence inflicted on her characters by the colonial attitudes and economic structures inherent in the 'American' system."[5] As such, the novel provides readers a framework for understanding how poor Chicanas/os remain perpetual outsiders to hegemonic society living in deteriorating and deliberately neglected urban areas, surviving when the communities they've managed to build are disrupted by violence or gentrification. Viramontes, Lansdale says, shows us how these characters "function as pieces of a machine . . . begging and dying without much apparent consequence."[6]

While Viramontes does demonstrate the way in which traditional values disappear or become distorted as characters go into survival modes of behavior, she also shows us their fortitude and resilience. However bleak the neighborhood seems, they stealthily *and* clumsily negotiate a plethora of contradictions or false choices presented them by a capitalist system: spontaneous opportunities and roadblocks (literal and emotional); conditionally crossable and closed boundaries; ideological freedoms and the reality of severe economic and political restrictions; loneliness or alienation and unbreakable kinship bonds; invisibility and constant surveillance; nurturing and punishing relationships; tenderness and violence; and, most starkly, life and death. The claim that Viramontes has failed to "build and support her culture" in creating such a depressing portrait of barrio life has been based on the supposed obligations and responsibilities of authors from historically oppressed groups. In an early review for *La Bloga*, for instance, Michael Sedano asked if authors have the freedom to represent racialized and poor neighborhoods as "dismal dioramas of doomed lives."[7] Is Viramontes creating a realistic representation at the expense of the social actors who actually inhabit this physical, historical, socioeconomic, and political landscape? Or is she consciously choosing to represent artistically this historical site as a symbolic dystopia?

While there is no evidence in interviews that Viramontes set out to produce a dystopian novel or a Marxist critique of capitalism, it is clear from her biography that she is writing about a time and place that she experienced. As a Chicana, Viramontes came of age during an era of civil rights protests; the extreme neglect and disruption of traditionally immigrant neighborhoods; the demonization of economically precarious but nevertheless functioning urban environments; the racialization of poverty and crime; as well as white flight and questions around the political efficacy of urban development. She was a witness to the sharp contradictions between the "Affluent Society" following World War II and the abject poverty that actually existed in many locales. Like many baby boomers, she lived through the anger and active discontent that arose among people who had been excluded from the growth of the "New Class" created through college educations and white-collar professions. The narrative indicates that she is conscious of the way in which the restoration of land values primarily benefited speculators while it ultimately destroyed affordable housing, disrupted important socioeconomic relationships, and dispersed various calls for revolution. The novel is fiction. But it also engages with history and the larger socioeconomic and political landscape that shaped the author's aesthetics and her worldview.

Unlike many narratives of the destitute, which are meant to be consumed by middle-class audiences and thus highlight the stark differences between the classes, Viramontes's novel creates a complex portrait of the poor that focuses on the diversity within the barrio through a myriad of characters and experiences. Conversely, she makes the middle and upper classes outside the barrio marginal to the novel's primary stories, rendering the bourgeoisie as uniform and wholly separate. Even as middle- and upper-class life remains relatively unknown to her characters, their economic interests are omnipresent. They are represented through the various machines or institutions that make the neighborhood a place of containment, stagnation, and death, as Tranquilina, one of the novel's main characters, realizes after coming back to the barrio after years away:

> Whole residential blocks had been gutted . . . abruptly dead—ended. . . . The streets Mama remembered had once connected . . . neighbors of different nationalities. . . . To the west, La Pelota Panadería on Soto Street crossed Canter's Kosher Deli on Brooklyn Avenue, which crossed Pol's

> Chinese Kitchen on Pacific Boulevard. . . . But now the freeways amputated the streets into stumped dead ends.[8]

Here we see the way that the neighborhood has gone from a place of vitality—where small, locally owned businesses served the community harmoniously—to a place of "dead ends." While the passage does speak of destruction, it also describes a mixed neighborhood that has now been cut off by neoliberal progress. Most narratives around urban decay re-create or accept the fiction of a monocultural or monoracial neighborhood that implodes from the fault lines within it. It makes for a less complicated story, but it is rarely the truth. If this were the case, passages like the one above might be interpreted as an example of the postmodern turn toward distilling important moments of history into empty sentimentality and meaningless images of nostalgia. But Viramontes intervenes to show that this destruction is not internal (or the fault of the residents), but the result of external forces. She is clearly writing about a predominantly Mexican American barrio, and yet she is careful to show that it has also been, and may have continued to be, a self-sufficient, multicultural neighborhood. As in most dystopian fictions, readers are left to speculate about the social, political, and economic decisions made by outside forces that have left the characters in such perilous conditions.

In the passage below, we see the same juxtaposition of an idealized memory of the neighborhood and its destruction:

> Grandmother . . . realized the construction of the freeway was ridding the neighborhood of everything that was familiar . . . who lived where, who buried their children's umbilical cords or grew lemons the size of apples, done away. Grandmother thought about how carnivorous life was, how indifferent machinery teeth could be.[9]

The memory of the grandmother is not simple nostalgia, but a device to show the harmful impact of economic "progress." Her metaphorical reference to carnivorous and indifferent "machinery teeth"—imagery that can be associated with dogs—has its literal match in the construction equipment that is tearing apart the neighborhood. Viramontes places this evidence of capitalist expansion in opposition to the Mexican indigenous ritual of burying the umbilical cord near the child's home. Again, postmodern critics might see this as a random borrowing that cannibalizes past cultural practices, but mainstream readers are not meant to consume such a reference. Viramontes is not, in fact, explicit about what cultures or whose traditions are being destroyed. In not revealing cultural destruction explicitly, she directs readers to focus on the economic impact rather than on sentimentality. As Viramontes uses the word "machine" repeatedly throughout the novel, we must recognize this as a purposeful link to the exploitation of laborers, rather than as a sentimental lament. "People" she writes, "began cranking up this clunky machinery of human enterprise while others ended their workday by dawn."[10]

Why should Viramontes "pretty up" poverty as a condition of capitalism or sugarcoat the devastating results of neoliberalism in an effort to create hope or falsely represent a positive image where none can exist? She is not attempting to overemphasize social agency, or respond to stereotyping by documenting superachievers, which would only add to the myths around meritocracy. But neither does she place blame for structural problems on the people. What we see instead is what we see in many novels by writers of color and/or working-class authors: the artist's critique of a place where survival itself is not just solitary resilience or a vehicle for heroism, but a collective victory to be applauded. Like so many narratives about the horrible conditions under which some children live, the novel cries out against preventable inequalities and injustices.[11] It is often in descriptions of the neighborhood's unhealthy environment that the novel most takes on its dystopian character. The material realities under which her characters live may feel alien to some readers outside this experience. Part of the reason for this is that the effects on the working poor of capital accumulation and progress for those at the top are so often hidden from everyone. They are mystified, made into spectacle or blamed on the victims so that they effectively escape a middle- or upper-class perception. The creation of different worlds is not just about separate cultures. It is also about the manipulation of the way we come to know, interpret, or understand diversity through class exploitation, racialization, sexism, homophobia, and other socially engineered lenses.

Viramontes clearly and unapologetically wants this life to be known in more than a factual or charitable way. This does not mean pulling at our heartstrings with maudlin prose. It simply means using her art to inform and make the effects of inequality and the intractability of social location as startling and as real as they can be for outsiders. "Four freeways crossing and interchanging, looping and stacking in the Eastside, but if you didn't own a car, you were fucked. Many were, and this is something Ermila always said in her head: You're fucked."[12] This is a world where children come home with black tar on their faces and feet; where the diesel engines from construction equipment produce "black fumes" and a constant din; where smog and smoke from various sources assault their lungs; where children play in contaminated water; and where human remains are cavalierly dug up and unceremoniously tossed back into wet cement to be forgotten. This environmental degradation overlaps with one of the many characteristics of dystopias, the disappearance of the natural world from daily life. Since "the four-freeway interchange would be constructed in order to reroute 547,300 cars a day through the Eastside,"[13] the devastation does not benefit the residents of the barrio, but only those outside it.

Displacement caused by the construction of the freeways divides cohesive neighborhoods. It relocates employers and those with hope, education, and organizing savvy. It forces those with middle-class lives and experiences out of the neighborhood and leaves behind the poorest of the poor. It assaults the bodies of those left behind, and it deprives children of elder caregivers and important memories. This division of people by class, race, and ethnicity creates silos where social mobility becomes extremely limited. It also adds to the creation of separate biospheres where everyone experiences the world from a particular social location.

Together with other equally dismal adjectives, dystopian worlds have been described as places of extreme violence, constant surveillance, isolation, distrust, exploitation, and desolation. Jody Melamed, among other Marxist scholars, writes extensively of the ways in which capitalism depends on racism, demands deportability, and requires disposable labor in order to assure wealth and power for a few.[14] Mervin Bendle argues that fiction and cinema in the past several decades have continued a post–Vietnam War era fascination with apocalyptic themes.[15] The increase in the representation of dystopias has coincided with the so-called crisis of the economy in the 1970s, the growth of deregulation and neoliberal policies during the '80s and '90s, and the great recession of 2008. Viramontes reportedly wrote this novel over a decade before it was published, and it was her teenage son who revived an interest in its themes. Could this have been a reflection of the increasing importance of dystopian images to his generation as wealth has become more and more concentrated at the top?

Unlike the classics of science fiction, however, recent works have been criticized by scholars such as Bendle for teaching young readers and contemporary audiences to accept the cataclysmic outcomes of capitalism's growth and a future of life and death competition as an inevitable human evolution rather than coming to understand that these outcomes are socially engineered consequences. Such criticisms would seem to answer Fredric Jameson's questions in regard to the "death of utopia" in the twentieth century with a resounding "yes, it is dead."[16] Writers and filmmakers (and thus "we" in a generalized sense) have moved beyond the possibility of imagining utopia. Why have we settled for the considerable lack of imagination it takes to presume that dystopian landscapes destroyed by economic collapse and characterized by rather dismal existences are inevitable? Why have we failed to recognize the privilege it requires to indulge this pleasure in science fiction while ignoring the fact that for many people around the globe these conditions already exist? Why do we find such cynicism entertaining? While acknowledging the ways in which the idea of utopia has been utilized and discredited by those on both the left and the right, Jameson maintains that we should nevertheless keep trying to envision it. That, in fact, it is the only option we may have for escaping the worst of unregulated and unsustainable capitalism.

In the same way that I have always wondered why U.S. college students feel they must travel abroad to learn about poverty, food insecurity, or lack of education and meaningful employment, I have wondered why today's audiences are so drawn to speculative fiction. And, of course, why they find representations that only resemble actual inequalities so exciting. Yet it is almost impossible to imagine a blockbuster Hollywood film being made about the world Viramontes describes. There is growing consensus that audiences are being seduced by the films' gestures toward individualism, anarchy, exceptionalism, and new frontiers, or the belief that inequality is inevitable, and a rather old-fashioned triumph of good over evil, that is, the same things that have long appealed to disaffected youth, and have (not incidentally) justified capitalism's spread around the globe. But with this pleasure comes the capitulation of revolution.

If we look at some of the common characteristics of dystopian fiction, we can easily see them replicated in Viramontes's novel. It would also be hard to miss the way these traits are actually reflected in postmodern, postcolonial, and neoliberal society. In addition to the absence or destruction of the natural world mentioned above, dystopias suggest a hierarchical society with clear and intractable divisions between socioeconomic classes. One group has a standard of living that is generally much below the expectations for an ideal society. This group is being ruled from the outside with few or no democratic ideals. Strict conformity to institutional rules and social norms is expected, and there is a general belief that dissent of any kind is bad or dangerous. This certainty is fostered in the society's institutions: family, church, school, jobs, and the media. But there is also the absolute power of the state: incessant surveillance and the constant, ominous presence of the policing agency.

Bureaucratic red tape abounds. Rules are relentlessly enforced. State-funded programs spread propaganda convincing people that they should obey or risk the consequences. They also try to convince people that capitalist society is generally good, that justice exists, and that everyone gets what they deserve. This form of ideological control engenders myths around scarcity and meritocracy, and fosters or supports the existence of social categories based on prejudices. Otherwise irrational fears are induced by an official, authoritative entity that people feel they have no choice but to trust. Unlike other societies where a caste system is a commonly acknowledged practice, people in the United States rarely speak of class. We are, in fact, taught that we have a fluid society in which anyone can rise in socioeconomic terms. In narratives, we love singular heroes (and increasingly heroines) who fight for the oppressed and move them to action, but we rarely celebrate either the underclass or actual rebellions. This failure to recognize class divisions as an entrenched part of the economic system is, of course, one of the many deceits of capitalism.

The ability to rise out of poverty in the current U.S. economic system varies with one's geographical location, but it is only about 12 percent in the best of places—for example, in dynamic areas of the country like Silicon Valley. In a place like the barrios of L.A., however, one has only about a 4 percent chance of escaping from poverty. In all places—not just those where chaos and violence are part of the daily landscape—people are much more likely to fall in socioeconomic status than they are to rise.[17] But even at the higher chance of 12 percent, social mobility is never going to be the reality for the vast majority of people. Class stratification is an entrenched feature of capitalism. Can you rise? Yes. Is it likely to happen? No. Will it happen through hard work alone? No. We see a representation of this economic reality reflected in the novel when Alfonso's father tries to live the American dream by buying a house in his largely Chicano neighborhood. But that takes place "before his father lost the first of many jobs."[18] In the barrio, parents are often made "cyclically idle and indigent by an erratic economy, not by culture or character."[19] Alfonso's mother worked two jobs in order to pay the mortgage, keeping her largely absent from her son's life. The father eventually abandons the family he cannot support. Falling through the system can have sources other than the availability of steady employment and may also be tracked to the inability of the social location to provide adequate education and (re)training.

Economic ruin or wasting can also relate to a lack of health services including mental health professionals. This situation is evident in the persona of Ben, a mixed-race character with a white father, who suffers from repeated breaks with reality. Viramontes does not describe this predicament simply from the perspective of the individual suffering the mental illness, but shows us the negative effects on the whole community as she links the reality of inadequate health services to the problem of homelessness. While an assumed-to-be-superior class decides on the rules for the poor in such dystopian places, undemocratic regulations can be enforced through totalitarianism, by a respressive police force, and through internalized ideological ideals or standards. Complicity is engendered as residents of the police state adapt to immoral rules for their own survival. For example, whenever the characters arbitrarily punish one another, are unnecessarily cruel to anyone, or try to enforce a regulation that will benefit them in some way, they precede these actions with the caveat, "I didn't make the rules." Viramontes returns to this phrase at the end of the novel when Turtle, the "boy who was really a girl," cannot answer the question of why s/he has acted with such violence. "Why? Turtle forgot why. Turtle didn't know why. She didn't make the rules."[20] The effective enforcement of the rules depends on people forgetting or not paying attention to the "why" question. It also requires a system of rewards and punishments. As people are socialized to assume that some combination of hard work, fairness, and judgment will result in a reward, they also learn to accept certain levels of surveillance and supervision. For the middle class, this management may be linked to clearly understood procedures. But for the barrio residents (and those in dystopian narratives), the rules are constantly shifting and are often more punitive or preventive than they are helpful.

Public transportation and the QA, for instance, make travel to and from work an ordeal. Long-term employers are scarce and the authorities keep everyone feeling unsafe. Most jobs do not provide a livable wage, and there are more dangers than rewards for participants in the informal economy. Hard work and diligence rarely translate into worthy returns. Yet survival still depends on being evaluated and judged by often unknowable standards. What people learn under these conditions is to follow the rules, even if they make no sense or put them in danger, in order to avoid perishing. As Michel Foucault claims, people learn to "internalize the demands of power. In this way surveillance instills discipline in subjects and produces docile bodies."[21]

Viramontes is explicit about this socially constructed docility and why collective resistance isn't an option for everyone. Noting the various factions of the civil rights movements protesting at this time, she tells us that this has very little direct relevance to her characters' lives. Ermila, for instance, is aware of the political struggles related to the 1968 Blowouts, or walkouts by Chicano students, in L.A. barrio high schools, but in the novel she and her friends are only tangentially tied to the Chicano movement. In one scene, Ermila contemplates a poster related to the Young Citizens for Community Action at Garfield High School—one of the central locations for political protest in 1968. The poster reads: "**Demand, Protest, Organize**, Grievances or Grief. You decide!"[22] Though these events are considered momentous in Chicanx history scholarship, Viramontes casts them as little more than an excuse to ditch classes. Still, the author later repeats the bolded words as Ermila stands in line waiting for the QA to let her pass. Surrounded by her neighbors, the teen briefly thinks about rebellion. Viramontes then shows us the relationship between coerced consent, obeying the rules, and survival.

> What might happen if the line of people simply wrapped themselves around the QA officers like a python? **Demand, Protest, Organize.** Before the words infiltrated her thoughts, Ermila was cleared . . . and suddenly found herself running. . . . She . . . learned her lesson, magically became . . . a good girl.[23]
>
> And then? No job, no money. . . . The risk of dissent was too costly. . . . The fear of homelessness . . . guaranteed her silence. So . . . Ermila . . . rolled the fantasy of the cannon and iron balls up for another day. . . . Like someone well-schooled in the knowledge of survival.[24]

Obedience and complicity are linked to the economic reality of this time and space. Freedom of movement is regulated by the QA—a symbolic representation of the many policing agencies that control the barrio. In printed form, in Spanish and English, the QA distributes the rules and demands unquestioned compliance. Respect for its officers is a given. It should not escape anyone's notice that the QA resembles the kind of racist policing that has long occurred in urban neighborhoods, as well as the increased militarization of the United States/Mexico border.

It is clear that the QA has taken the place of what was once a cohesive neighborhood, filling the void left by the construction of the freeways and the destruction of the community. It has become the common denominator in the characters' lives. They feel cutoff and isolated from the rest of society. Viramontes writes, "The whoosh of the city's vehicles, the broken-up silence from faraway night, made her feel that they lived on an island, the freeways closing in on them like ocean waves, the tierra firma vanishing swiftly."[25] Like other creators of dystopian landscapes, Viramontes taps into one of the hallmarks of capitalist society and audiences at the turn of the century: alienation.

In dystopian settings, fear and distrust are pervasive. This causes people to resent their oppressors, but also to be suspicious of each other and any outsiders. Because they are taught to identify with the values of those in power, they may even feel repulsed by similarly oppressed members of other groups or neighborhoods. While this fear originates in the dominant system, their anger at having little say in their own lives can be misdirected in the form of horizontal hostility toward other community members who are put into competition with them over scarce resources. Ermila's grandmother, for instance, distrusts and fears the Black teacher, Miss Eastman. Influenced by spectacular media representations of the civil rights demonstrations and propaganda put out by the QA, the grandmother perceives African Americans as the metaphorical unimmunized dogs, who are out of control and might become "rabid."[26] She has begun to see Blackness through the racialized lens of a racist society and to see the teacher as a threat. Viramontes does not gloss over this ugly prejudice. She makes it clear, however, that this is not just an interpersonal bias but one that is related to the depravity of the larger society.

While the QA and other policing agencies are a primary medium of control through intimidation and humiliation, biases are important mechanisms of repression. Such social policing is bereft of due process and effectively separates people who might otherwise join together in protest against power. Criminalization processes inspire fear that individuals and their family members might be punished if they are perceived by authority as similar to other assumed rule breakers. Thus, they find ways to distance themselves, physically and emotionally, from those who are cast as lacking in morals, respectability, or dignity, lest they also be caught up in a justice system without mercy.[27] Fear, shame, neglect, and invisibility are among the "soft weapons" that the powerful can use against the working poor to manage its reserve labor force and coerce troublemakers into submission.[28]

While neighbors know better than anyone who belongs and who doesn't, ultimately the government determines legitimate citizenship. In dystopias, relegation of this task to a federal-like entity indicates that control of the local is an economic and political imperative for those in power. Yet Viramontes is careful to show that people outside the barrio are utterly reliant on the labor that is contained within it. In order to make sure wages are kept low, the whole system is contingent on laborers being kept in a state of perpetual noncitizenship, allowing for their second-class treatment no matter how long they have lived in the area.[29] It is important to note the way in which this strict and unreasonable policing of citizenship is tied to notions of "safety." Fear of the other is an absolute requirement for being able to suspend the tenets of freedom and democracy by increasing militarism. For the QA officers, there is no difference between Mexican Americans and Mexican nationals, documented or undocumented. "QA culeros were unyielding in upholding safety. . . . They considered themselves protectors of lives, procurers of security."[30]

The contemporary transnational world, where no adequate welfare system can arise but unreasonable expenditures on the military and policing are made to seem rational, parallels Viramontes's construction of power relations.[31] As Justin Akers Chacón and Mike Davis have written in *No One Is Illegal*, "Immigration law and deportation have been crafted and implemented over the years not to streamline citizenship or stop immigration but to permanently fragment the working class. The comprehensive appropriation of the state apparatus of immigration control by capital has created the 'illegal' worker, an entirely artificial construction whose sole purpose is to deprive the international 'American' working class of its democratic rights."[32]

Unlike much contemporary speculative fiction, Viramontes does not directly pose a tension between numbers or science people, on the one hand, and literary or creative people, on the other, with the former representing a kind of robotic being and the latter representing emotion and empathy. This may simply be a reflection of the specific time period she is portraying. Or it could be seen as one of the many conventions of dystopia she has avoided. Another way in which her novel differs is that unlike the majority of contemporary dystopias, *Dogs* does not imagine what the future will be like for the middle class. Her focus remains firmly on the working poor. The timeless feeling of the text implies that any postapocalyptic future will not be much different for those in the barrio. Without profound change in the whole socioeconomic system, the neighborhoods, or nations, inhabited by the poor will continue to be places of harrowing struggle. They will remain largely unknown but nevertheless feared and exploited by those who hold or seize power.

Dogs certainly reflects at least one of the timeless themes essential to dystopias and that is the notion of posthumanism.[33] While I agree with other critics that Viramontes does work toward "validating the humanity of her characters,"[34] I also think that she mimics a dystopian atmosphere designed to show us not only what blunted affect might look like, as a condition of global capitalism, but also how this goes beyond individual psychological disorders and is related to the real trauma of living daily with violence and oppression. This makes her characters representations of many lives. Rather than defining any of the characters as a thinking, feeling, self-actualizing individual in heroic opposition to the others in the barrio, she wants readers to fully understand what it means to become a socioeconomic prisoner of informal incarceration in a merciless system of inequality.

In many scenes, the characters resemble zombies, somewhere between the living and the dead. As in other dystopias, warfare is a constant. The characters have as little control over their lives as Luis Lil Lizard does in being drafted, or as Turtle does in being sent to a different kind of war. In several passages, Viramontes insinuates that the effects on the psyche are the same, drawing a direct link between state-supported war and barrio life.

> Plugs of gunfire carried over long distances and over the cinder-blocked walls. Turtle was dead tired. That was how she said this in her head, I'm dead tired. Did Luis say that? I'm dead, somewhere in 'Nam, bullets whisking by, did she just hear him?[35]

Ray, the Japanese grocer in the neighborhood, also participates in this endless war, even though he owns his grocery store and actually lives outside the barrio. Though he is afraid of the crime in the barrio, he has empathy for Turtle and seems to understand the desperation and anger that the neighborhood youth carry within them. As a victim of the Japanese internment camps during World War II, he identifies with their experiences and understands their resentment. This is a moment of hope that by sharing histories, similarly oppressed peoples may begin to form social and political alliances.

Unlike earlier classics in science fiction that were clearly anticapitalist, Viramontes comes close to mirroring the neoliberal messages present in contemporary science fiction. In books like *The Giver, Divergent,* and the *Hunger Games* trilogy, the enemies of a given community under siege are shown to be big government, the welfare state, and either evil or well-meaning, but ultimately rigid and ineffectual, leftists.

Corporate greed and corruption seem to get a pass, at least explicitly. We see this similarly represented in the obvious demonization of the QA as a part of the government; in Viramontes's critical view of the welfare system and of the social worker who delivers Ermila to her grandmother; and in the separation of the Chicana/o movement protests from the everyday reality of the barrio. Big corporations, antiunionist politicians, and greedy neocons are not so recognizable. They are present in the construction equipment, and the hundreds of thousands of cars that speed through the neighborhood every day, but only metaphorically. This is certainly not the science fiction championed by Jameson, which offered a more direct leftist critique of capitalism.

According to critic Ewan Morrison, much of contemporary science fiction seems to support the idea that human nature ultimately rules, whereas nurture does not. Thus, it supports an unrestrictive existence "with heroic individuals who are guided by the innate forces of human nature, against evil social planners."[36] This type of sci-fi fails to offer a critique of how our understanding of human nature has been, and is being, shaped by socioeconomic and political forces. In most dystopian worlds, there is a lone-wolf hero or heroine who is somehow outside the society and seems infinitely more moral than any of the other characters. Highly sensitive to injustices, this protagonist often questions the society and is constantly alert to danger. Audiences come to see this character as having an intuitive feeling that something is terribly wrong. But this person is generally without economic or political power and has few or no allies, at least in the beginning. The heroic figure can only "win" through violence and gathering loyal followers.

Fighting such trends, Viramontes does not produce a Katniss-type hero—although it might be argued that she does lean in that direction in her portrayal of Ermila. Viramontes allows Ermila a small moment of freedom when she finally speaks back to power. The particular agent she challenges happens to be from the neighborhood and remembers, if only for a moment, his familial ties to the barrio. This connection is important because it conflicts with the message of books like the *Giver*, in which the evil social structure is actually called "Community" and families have been banished from the society. Viramontes instead offers another brief glimpse of where hope might be found, and it is not in deregulation, laissez-faire politics, big government, anarchy, or a singular hero-led dystopia. Nor is it solely in the nuclear family, which is also a hegemonic institution. It is in a world where mutual history is remembered and valued; where imposed class divisions and sociopolitical positions lose their meaning; where people have learned that silence is deadly; and where solidarity is achieved.

Symbolizing the way in which oppression sometimes has very negative results for the powerful, Viramontes again uses the dogs metaphorically to show readers that once unleashed, the suppressive tactics and weapons of the system can sometimes bite back.

These unintentional and unmanageable outcomes then become the targets of increasingly inhumane violence, as those in power must always find new ways to define and maintain power relations. At one point, Viramontes refers to one of the barrio youth with the words, "his kind always traveled in packs."[37] This is an allusion to wildness, to coyotes and wolves, which differentiates them from the guard dogs employed by those in power. It is also a projection of fear that the targets of oppression will rise up to become the agents of it. The QA's notices refer to the "dogs" over which they have lost control, who have not yet been domesticated or have gone rabid. Thus, the QA claims the right to annihilate these "undomesticated mammals." It is not the author calling the barrio residents dogs. It is a metaphor for how they are seen through the fearful eyes of policing agencies. This aspect of the novel mirrors the process of criminalization and racialization of the poor during the drug wars of the 1980s. It also foreshadows various social uprisings in urban centers as police misconduct is allowed to continue unabated. As was the case with the unrest during the civil rights movements, those with power learn that capital cannot operate successfully during periods of social chaos. Their economic interest in suppressing disobedience coincides with widespread, racist fears as policing agencies are strengthened through additional resources, more personnel, and increasingly repressive methods of control.

I also see the dogs as symbolic of what happens at all levels when this becomes a self-fulfilling prophecy of power—when ignominy replaces dignity, or when viciousness takes the place of humanity. At some level, however, it does not matter who or what the dogs represent as long as we understand that all the dogs (codified weapons or rabid animals), as well as their handlers, are locked into the same system, and thus both serve the needs of power. As Viramontes writes, "No one, not the sharpshooters, the cabdrivers . . . the barefoot or slipper-clad spectators in robes, not one of them, in all their glorious hallucinatory gawking, knew who the victims were, who the perpetrators were. . . . [Nevertheless, the] sharpshooters steadied their barrels."[38]

At the tragic end of the novel, we see Tranquilina desperately trying to recover the characters' humanity. But by this time, it has become impossible for the people who inhabit this dystopian/capitalist world to draw neat lines between good and evil. The only thing that remains is absolute power.

> *We'rrrre not doggggs!* Tranquilina roared in the direction of the shooters. Stop shooting, we're not dogs! The words crashed into one another, rocketing into one big howl of pleading, demanding, a speeding blur of raging language blending in with the chaos of commands and shouts and orders and circuslike commotion coming from the shooters who stood in the darkness.[39]

Dogs exposes the capitalist system—the reality of social stratification and the economy's fictions around welfare and meritocracy. From the first chapter, surveillance is a central theme. And as readers, we too are watching. From the comfort of our favorite chair, we want to tell the characters what to do, where to go, and with whom. We want to warn them of the mistakes they are making, tell them how to get out. But the characters are not us—not the readers. The vast majority of the working poor across the United States are not these characters. But they may be more capable of understanding what might happen if, through the luck of birth, one was relegated to a racialized and classed space full of violence and deprived of stable housing, food, and health care—where the people with whom you identify most closely have no control over their community, culture, or daily life. What if you had to exist in a dystopia—in a place that has been seriously and sometimes deliberately neglected politically and economically, torn apart by various social forces, and allowed to exist in a permanent state of chaos?

Traditionally, Marxist critiques of economic and political structures often have not taken into account any notion of human desires, of culture, individual psychology, internalization, or social mirroring—all of which have more to do with social constructs than they do with some unchangeable "human nature" or the characteristics of any group. Yet, if we are to try and understand these characters' behaviors, we have to look at what might arise in a place that necessarily breeds an ethos of survival. Given this context, the characters' behaviors begin to make more sense. Like many people who live in precarious environments, the characters are conditioned by social norms, government regulations, and the agents of enforcement to behave in certain ways. There is no true rebellion, because isolated actors—according to the logic of individualism—can only misbehave. Thus, choices are habituated by a hegemonic social, economic, and political system. Some will become the "dogs" they've been conditioned to believe they must be in order to survive. This internalization leads them to reenact or re-create the original traumas they've experienced. These few come to understand resistance not in political terms, but only as vengeance and intimidation. We cannot become postcolonial or postracial if we insist on an economic system that still replicates the foundational class divisions, inequalities, and oppressive policing strategies of the conquest. It should come as no surprise to anyone that these communities are as stressed, full of resentment, and stinginess of emotion as any other community. The primary difference is that they have few resources for dealing with any of the ills that confront them. What the upper classes may see as deviant ideologies or deformation of character are really the mark of the same self-interest that infects all of us in competitive, capitalist cultures *plus* a learned instinct for survival.[40] It is, after all, these lives that are most at risk.

Throughout chapter 11, Viramontes gives us the formula for survival that Luis Lil Lizard has passed on to Turtle. These rules we are told have come straight out of a U.S. Army Field Manual, "the only book Luis ever read."[41] These are not tools for revolution. In fact, they may be more useful for adapting and complying with existing norms. This is true whether one is in a government-supported combat zone or struggling against the socioeconomic war on the poor.[42] Viramontes makes sure that readers understand that this is the only education Luis has received. Thus, he has little choice but to mirror the survival behaviors that already exist in an unjust system rather than learning a new way of being. If we can understand his predicament and begin to look for the ways that hegemonic society shapes all of our lives, then we may begin to "discern how the ethic of capitalism, and the logic of bureaucratic rationality, push people into ways of living that perpetuate economic, racial, and gender oppression,"[43] even when it is not in their best interest to do so.

Yet Viramontes makes clear that despite the many paths that lead to an ethos of survival, the majority of the residents do not act out in ways that should make them targets of the QA. They continue to resist *and* to participate in the system in very conventional ways, continuing to provide the labor necessary for accumulating wealth at the top.

> [T]hese men and women who hastened to their destinations feeling a sense of commitment, compelled to believe they held the world together with the glue of their endless sweat? They carried everything needed . . . onto the bus except laziness.[44]

Beyond dystopia, Viramontes does not predict what is to come for Ermila, nor explicitly outline an alternative utopia, as Jameson might have wanted her to do. She more often expounds on an impossible structure that has heartlessly broken so many people. Poor U.S. neighborhoods today are not different from the one she describes in *Dogs*. Dystopia is not just in our imagination. If anything, QA-like tactics and injustices have only intensified since the 1960s and 1970s. Black Lives Matter, like so many previous political movements of the past, reminds us of this. The tragedies and inhumanity that occur daily in poor communities—rural or urban, white or multiracial—have always been prophetic. As global capitalism raises the fortunes of a few, it destroys self-sufficiency and justice for others and turns whole nations into de facto barrios. Yet we forget this constantly. Writers like Viramontes help us to remember. And the urgency to remember, philosopher Maurice Blanchot has claimed, should be the real purpose of dystopian novels.

So, what do the Ermilas and the Turtles of the world have to look forward to? Surely Viramontes has more in mind than tragedy. Ermila is the one character who moves from selective mutism in the beginning of the novel, where she is the consummate silenced observer of the contradictions in the social structures, to find her resistant voice. She is the one who speaks back to the QA and successfully crosses their arbitrary line, taking the woman who has no papers with her. While we can't read the narrative too optimistically, which is a pitfall of privilege, we do need to look for clues to some better outcome. I would argue that it is primarily when the characters speak up, listen to and remember history, and act as communal beings that hope exists. When they act only out of self-interest, desire middle-class objects, or return to solitariness and silence, things go awry. It is then that they become complicit with the system that has only one story for them, and that story is not one of possibility. Ermila and her friends, however, at least imagine something other than perpetual dystopia.

> With conviction, they designed escape routes, rehearsed their breakout and hurled their futures over the roadblocks of their marooned existence. Lest they forget that silence is destructive, they pitted each other against the sorrowful and infinite solitude, each and every hour, because that's what friends por vida are for.[45]

Viramontes is a *virtuosa* of repetition, some of it deliberate and obvious. At other times, it is subtle and requires several reads before you begin to notice. Greater depth of meaning and being awestruck by her talent are among the rewards for discovering these planted seeds—many having to do with communalism and storytelling. What she is telling us about the real-life dystopias that capitalism creates is that it hasn't always been this way and that it was not created by nature. We can undo it. Perhaps we can recover a less cynical approach toward utopia, as Jameson and José Esteban Muñoz have suggested. But we must also realize, as Chicana feminist Karma Chávez has pointed out, this is not just a project of the imagination or solely located in the future. Knowledge and social locations and stories already exist, and they can move us to action, help us to understand the efficacy of coalitions between oppressed groups more fully, and inspire us to create, as implied symbolically in Viramontes's novel, "bigger magics on the other side."[46]

Notes

1. Fredric Jameson, "The Politics of Utopia," *New Left Review* 25 (January-February 2004): 37.

2. I am paraphrasing what numerous authors have said in one form or another, the most common being "The opposite of poverty is not wealth, but justice."

3. Elaine Scarry (1987), quoted in Ariana E. Vigil, *War Echoes: Gender and Militarization in U.S. Latina/o Cultural Production* (New Brunswick, NJ: Rutgers University Press, 2014), 72.

4. Helena María Viramontes, *Their Dogs Came with Them* (New York: Washington Square Press, 2007), 61–62.

5. Sadie Lansdale, "Deslenguadas: The Intersection of Physical and Structural Violence in the Work of Helena María Viramontes" (unpublished paper, Tufts University Department of English), 3.

6. Lansdale, "Deslenguadas," 24.

7. See La Bloga, https://labloga.blogspot.com/2007/08/review-their-dogs-came-with-them.html

8. Viramontes, *Dogs*, 32–33.

9. Viramontes, *Dogs*, 146.

10. Viramontes, *Dogs*, 176.

11. See Raoul S. Llévanos, "Race, Deprivation, and Immigrant Isolation: The Spatial Geography of Air-Toxic Clusters in the Continental United States," *Social Science Research* 54 (November 2015): 50–67, for a study of Latinas/os living in so-called sacrifice zones of pollution. See also Laura Pulido, "Rethinking Environmental Racism: White Privilege and Urban Development in Southern California," *Annals of the Association of American Geographers* 90.1 (March 2000): 12–40. Pulido focuses on structural racism to question why whiteness is able to protect itself from pollution whereas people of color cannot.

12. Viramontes, *Dogs*, 176.

13. Viramontes, *Dogs*, 169.

14. See Jodi Melamed, "Racial Capitalism," *Critical Ethnic Studies* 1.1 (Spring 2015): 76–85.

15. See Mervin Bendle, "Zarathustra's Revenge: The Sordid Utopia of Contemporary Science Fiction Films" (paper presented at "Imaging the Future: Utopia, Dystopia and Science Fiction," a conference at Monash University, Melbourne, Australia, December 2005).

16. On this topic, see Jameson, "Politics of Utopia," 35–54.

17. See Raj Chetty, Nathaniel Hendren, Patrick Kline, and Emmanuel Saez, "Where Is the Land of Opportunity? The Geography of Intergenerational Mobility in the United States," *The Quarterly Journal of Economics* 129.4 (January 2014): 1553–1623; Joe Pinsker, "America Is Even Less Socially Mobile Than Most Economists Thought," *Atlantic*, July 23, 2015, http//www.theatlantic.com/business/archive/2015/07/America-social-mobility-parents-income/399311/; and Isabel V. Sawhill, "Inequality and Social Mobility: Be Afraid," May 27, 2015, http://www.brookings.edu/blogs/social-mobility-memos/posts/2015/05/27-inequality-great-gatsby-curve-sawhill. Similar findings have been reported in a number of studies from the Pew Research Center.

18. Viramontes, *Dogs*, 301.

19. Justin Akers Chacón and Mike Davis, *No One Is Illegal: Fighting Racism and State Violence on the Mexico Border* (Chicago: Haymarket Books, 2006), 187.

20. Viramontes, *Dogs*, 324.

21. See quote by Foucault in Leo Chávez, *The Latino Threat Narrative* (Stanford: Stanford University Press, 2008). Foucault was referring to prisoners, while Chávez is referring to Mexican immigrants and poor Mexican Americans. I would argue that the community Viramontes describes shares many features of the prison. Also, the poor, prisoners, and immigrants without documents share the condition of being perceived as improper citizens.

22. Viramontes, *Dogs*, 49.

23. Viramontes, *Dogs*, 64.

24. Viramontes, *Dogs*, 64–65.

25. Viramontes, *Dogs*, 316–17.

26. It is interesting to note that Viramontes ties this prejudice on the grandmother's part to the images of Blacks she has seen on the "green" television screen. Throughout the novel, the color green repeatedly symbolizes technology, money, and progress.

27. See Rosemary Hennessy's work on police responses to labor organizing, *Fires on the Border: The Passionate Politics of Labor Organizing on the Mexican Frontera* (Minneapolis: University of Minnesota, 2013).

28. This idea of "soft weapons" in the political economy is also from Hennessy's book.

29. See Martha Menchaca, *The Politics of Dependency: U.S. Reliance on Mexican Oil and Farm Labor* (Austin: University of Texas Press, 2016).

30. Viramontes, *Dogs*, 288.

31. Chacón and Davis, *No One Is Illegal*, 198.

32. Chacón and Davis, *No One Is Illegal*, 199.

33. See Tully Barnett, "Margaret Atwood's *Oryx and Crake, 2003 Dystopian Nightmare of a Novel*" (paper presented at "Imaging the Future: Utopia, Dystopia and Science Fiction," a conference at Monash University, Melbourne, Australia, December 2005).

34. Lansdale, "Deslenguadas," 3.

35. Lansdale, "Deslenguadas," 235.

36. Ewan Morrison, "YA Dystopias Teach Children to Submit to the Free Market, Not Fight Authority," *Guardian*, September 1, 2014; https://www.theguardian.com/books/2014/sep/01/ya-dystopias-children-free-market-hunger-games-the-giver-divergent

37. Viramontes, *Dogs*, 256.

38. Viramontes, *Dogs*, 324.

39. Viramontes, *Dogs*, 324.

40. See Theodor Adorno and Max Horkheimer, *Dialectic of Enlightenment* (Stanford: Stanford University Press, 2002), 22–23; and Jameson, "Politics of Utopia," 8.

41. Viramontes, *Dogs*, 229.

42. See Joe Soss, Richard C. Fording, and Sanford R. Schram, *Disciplining the Poor: Neoliberal Paternalism and the Persistent Power of Race* (Chicago: University of Chicago, 2011), for more on how the capitalist system fails the poor yet demands and engenders compliance.

43. See Stephen D. Brookfield, *The Power of Critical Theory for Adult Learning and Teaching* (New York: Open University Press, 2005), ix.

44. Viramontes, *Dogs*, 177.

45. Viramontes, *Dogs*, 62.

46. Viramontes, *Dogs*, 47.

CHAPTER 11

Mass Incarceration and the Critique of Capitalism

A Working-Class Viewpoint in Ronald Ruiz's *Happy Birthday Jesús*

Marcial González

Unlike the narrators of bourgeois novels who not only describe their worlds from expansive viewpoints but also confidently and somewhat arrogantly assume the privilege to do so, the narrators of working-class novels—and especially working-class ethnic novels—often view the world from dark, restrictive, isolated spaces. Recall, for example, the first-person narrator in Ralph Ellison's *Invisible Man* narrating his story from the seclusion of a coal cellar, or Tomás Rivera's unnamed protagonist in *. . . y no se lo tragó la tierra,* who reconstructs a year's worth of action in that novel almost entirely from the crawl space beneath a house. Similarly, the reticent narrator in Ronald Ruiz's 1994 antiprison novel *Happy Birthday Jesús* tells much of his story from the isolation of a prison cell, deprived of light, sound, and human contact—or from a state of insanity. Moreover, he fails to understand how the social institutions of family, church, school, race, and law have determined his life and have led him directly on a path to prison. In this chapter, I examine how *Happy Birthday Jesús,* narrated from such an extremely limited viewpoint, can nevertheless convey a sense of the social totality that condemns the protagonist Jesús long before he is even born. To do this, I address a cluster of related issues, first discussing the working-class implications of the novel's point of view, then commenting on the political causes of mass incarceration in the United States, before analyzing some of the specific narrative strategies employed in the novel, including time, structure, and surveillance. Drawing on a Marxist interpretive approach, I argue that, despite its limited viewpoint, *Happy Birthday Jesús* offers a far-reaching critique of capitalism's reliance on race, religion, familial dysfunction, and mass incarceration as mechanisms of social control and class domination.

A WORKING-CLASS POINT OF VIEW

Happy Birthday Jesús is a difficult novel to read, not because the language and the narrative structure are overly complex, but because of its graphic depictions of violence, sexual aggression, racism, and child abuse. "This is not a novel for the squeamish or the faint-of-heart," writes Alan Ryan. "Many of its pages paint unnerving scenes of nightmarish violence, as psychologically repulsive as they are physically repugnant. But what might otherwise be merely shocking is written here with such burning conviction, and with such obviously dead-on accuracy, that it casts a dazzling light on a portion of our reality rarely seen so clearly."[1] Ryan is referring to the realities of child abuse, sexual assault, and prison. The novel's protagonist and narrator is Jesús Olivas, a Chicano farmworker raised in Fresno, California circa the 1940s and early 1950s by his grandmother, Soledad—a religious fanatic who abuses and tortures him physically and psychologically. She punishes him, for example, by forcing him to wear a diaper while lying in a large makeshift crib and sucking on a baby bottle well into his teenage years. The grandmother's abuse is carried out with the help of Father Galván, a priest from the local Catholic church who sanctions her actions through his religious practices and beliefs.

Jesús grows up under constant surveillance through his interaction with various social institutions: the family, the church, the school, paid labor, and eventually the criminal justice system in its most extreme form—the maximum-security prison. In response to the physical and psychological repression to which he is subjected, Jesús grows up weak and timid, but also terribly angry—a time bomb waiting to explode. When he turns eighteen he rebels by attacking Father Galván, attempting to kill him, but he succeeds only in maiming him. Forced to stand trial before a racist court, and represented by an incompetent public defender, Jesús is sentenced to serve time in San Quentin Prison, where on his first night he is raped by a fellow prisoner. Later, the same prisoner sells him to a group of inmates, subjecting him to the physical torment and psychological devastation of repeated gang rape. Eventually he fights back against his abuser, castrating him, an act for which he receives a longer sentence. In all, he spends about twenty years in prison, most of it in solitary confinement. Upon his release, after a successful legal appeal, he returns to his hometown, where his grandmother and Father Galván are now long deceased. He goes to the local Catholic church, kills a young priest he has never seen before, mutilates the priest's body, smears the altar with excrement, and burns down the building.

My summary of *Happy Birthday Jesús* traces the main events of the novel, but it does not do justice to the power of the language and the shocking images that remain in the minds of readers long after reading it. The novel personalizes the brutal reality of Jesús's experiences, but without sentimentalizing or moralizing them. As Ryan writes, "Ruiz illuminates Jesús and his world without ever suggesting that we excuse him."[2] The point I want to emphasize, however, is not that the novel possesses shock value, but that, despite problems with the narrator's point of view, it nevertheless achieves a sense of completeness and closure. This is so because the novel displays a desperate desire to break out of the confines of its contradictory point of view, a process that involves overcoming the wide separation between the narrator's limited consciousness and the social world that he attempts to comprehend and represent. *Happy Birthday Jesús* may fall short of representing reality in its totality, but in the effort to do so it produces a formal reenactment of the problem of representation as such, as dramatized by Jesús himself who cannot speak but who nevertheless narrates a 314-page novel.

Late in the novel, after he has been in prison for fifteen years, a sympathetic fellow prisoner tells him, "you've got to talk, Jess. . . . You'll never get out of this fucking place if you don't talk. And you can talk. I know you can."[3] Jesús's urgent desire to speak accentuates his predicament in attempting to narrate an experience that vehemently resists narration. Theodor Adorno once wrote that the Holocaust cannot be explained rationally because the unspeakable events that took place in the Holocaust were not rational. "What the Nazis did to the Jews," Adorno writes, "was unspeakable: language has no word for it."[4] Similarly, we could say that the atrocities that take place in prisons cannot always be adequately represented with rational language because what takes place there is not always rational. Like Jesús, who cannot speak to his attorneys to tell them the truth of what has happened to him, language fails us in our attempts to speak the truth of what takes place behind bars—and yet, for Jesús, his story must be told. As Adorno writes, "Today [the position of the narrator] is marked by a paradox: it is no longer possible to tell a story, but the form of the novel requires narration."[5] Adorno's paradox pointedly describes the problem of the narrator in *Happy Birthday Jesús*. Despite his inability to speak, Jesús expresses an almost obsessive desire to talk: "I tried talking," he explains, "talking out loud. But something kept getting stuck in my throat. It seemed to hold my tongue. The only sound I could make was a dry gasping sound. . . . I tried harder. My throat got sore. I spat blood twice."[6]

Thematically, Jesús is unable to speak because of the abuse he suffered at home, in church, and in prison. But structurally, his inability to speak creates a conflict between Jesus's muteness and the fact that he nevertheless narrates an entire novel about his experiences. This structural conflict potentially places in doubt the reliability of the narrator and the events he describes, hindering our efforts to read the novel literally or realistically. On the one hand, Jesús, as the central character, is uneducated and lacks the cognitive skills to comprehend events as they unfold around him. At times, he has great difficulty understanding what other characters are saying when they speak to him. On the other hand, as the narrator, he reproduces eloquent dialogue and speeches by articulate characters, such as the trial judge, the district attorney, some of the jurors, and Father Martínez, who at one point soliloquizes for ten pages without interruption.[7] Jesús narrates the entire novel after he has been released from prison, reflecting back on the previous thirty-something years of his life. By all accounts, any person who experiences what Jesús goes through while in prison would be either dead or totally insane. Yet Jesús narrates his story calmly, collectedly, and lucidly. It would be easy to dismiss the problematic narrator in *Happy Birthday Jesús* as a characteristic flaw of a first novel that perhaps should have been written in the third person rather than in the voice of a nearly mute protagonist. This structural contradiction, however, radiates with symbolic significance that sheds light on the social and aesthetic reach of the novel. In short, Jesús's predicament parallels the social situation of the working class which has an urgent need to narrate its experiences and to voice its views on social realities but often finds itself silenced by the barriers of economic hardship, racism, gender discrimination, state repression, and ideological conditioning. *Happy Birthday Jesús* is not unique in dramatizing the internal contradictoriness of narrative form through the medium of a naïve or problematic narrator. Problems with narrators are common to all modern novels in a variety of ways depending on the particulars of the novel in question and the social substance of its representations. But these problems become sharper and more complex in novels narrated from the perspective of racialized working-class subjects because of the constraints imposed on them as a result of the aforementioned social barriers.

To clarify the issues at stake in my reading of *Happy Birthday Jesús*, it would help to reflect on an argument that David Carr makes in *Time, Narrative, and History*. Carr addresses the theoretical problems at stake in analyzing the way narrative structures convey meaning about society and history. He is a philosopher of history, not a literary theorist, but his work is nevertheless valuable for thinking about representation in literary narratives, and even though he is not a Marxist, his analysis of narrative structure and experience can be considered materialist. As a philosopher, he takes a position that mediates opposing camps in debates about the capacity of narratives to represent history. On the one hand, he opposes positivist philosophers, such as Maurice Mandelbaum and Leon Goldstein, who argue that history is a science and that narratives of history are structured in the actual events of the past. The positivists seek to disclose the truthfulness of events as they occurred in the past through a close examination of documents, statements, monuments, and ruins. One of the problems with the positivist approach, however, is that historians have tended to underestimate their own complicity with the narratives they produce, which is to say that the history might be full of the biases and ideological viewpoints of the historian himself or herself. On the other hand, Carr also distances himself from what he calls the "narrativist" conception of history, represented by theorists such as Louis Mink and Hayden White.[8] This camp argues that narratives about history are not structured in a way that faithfully mimics the structure of history itself, but that historians (like fiction writers) impose imaginary structures on events and, in so doing, determine to some degree the significance of those events.

According to Mink, "narrative form in history, as in fiction, is an artifice, the product of individual imagination."[9] Mink summarizes the narrativist argument with three propositions: "That the world is not given to us in the form of well-made stories . . . that we make [or invent] such stories . . . and that we give [those stories] referentiality by imagining that in them the world speaks itself."[10] For Carr, the problem with the narrativist position—aside from the fact that it seems to suffer from a severe "allergy to the problem of truth"[11]—is that it runs the risk of turning "all the firm ground historians usually stand on . . . into a swamp of relativism and subjectivity"[12] by denying the possibility of knowing any concrete aspects of history with certainty.

The arguments of the positivists and the narrativists "can be interpreted as the philosophical mirror image"[13] of one another, inasmuch as each camp places the historian in a precarious, no-win situation: either absolute truth or no truth at all. Carr seeks to develop a theory of narrative that does not completely sever the relation between history and narrative structure in the manner of the narrativists, but he also wants to avoid returning to the uncritical, reifying positions of the positivists. Countering the narrativist position, he argues that narrative structures are not arbitrary but are rooted in material practices. A relation does in fact exist between human experience and narrative structure because narratives draw on and thus reproduce the logic of everyday human experiences. In the most basic sense, narratives, like our actions, have a beginning, a middle, and an end. "[N]arrative," Carr argues, "is our primary (though not our only) way of organizing our experience of time, and understood in this sense it can elucidate our pre-theoretical past."[14] That is to say, our experiences in the past—before they are ever contemplated, theorized, or narrativized—profoundly influence the way consciousness and language are structured. By extension, those structures make their way into narratives, which are logically then full of historical content, or, to use Carr's term, "historicity." He argues that "in a naïve and prescientific way the historical past is [always] there for all of us, that it *figures* in our ordinary view of things, whether we are historians or not."[15] Thus, what we learn from historiography—and by extension, what we learn from fiction—has as much if not more to do with the historicity embedded in the very structures and texture of these narratives as it does with the substance of the stories narrated. Drawing on Carr's conception of historicity for the interpretation of literature, we could say that the narrator in *Happy Birthday Jesús* conveys a sense of the social totality not because his representation of the social world is accurate, complete, compelling, or even coherent, but because Jesús represents a social being who has lived in and experienced history. Thus, the structure and content of his narrative are filled with the historicity of his social class experiences, and in turn they bear the imprint of society in its totality, whether or not Jesús is able to comprehend the significance of his story—and even if, as a character, he cannot speak.

Carr's theory of narrative, especially his concept of "historicity," is highly suggestive for the interpretation of literary narratives from a materialist perspective. His theory, however, remains limited for analyzing the specific viewpoints of working-class ethnic novels, such as *Happy Birthday Jesús*, because it does not take into account the categories of race, gender, ethnicity, and, least of all, class in determining the problematics of narrative structures. For an analysis of a working-class viewpoint, we can turn to (for starters) a Marxist theorist such as Georg Lukács, who theorizes working-class consciousness and its relation to narrative point of view. For Lukács, what is unique about working-class consciousness is that it "represents an *aspiration towards society in its totality* regardless of whether this aspiration remains conscious or . . . unconscious for the moment."[16] In a capitalist society, working-class consciousness (as in Ruiz's novel) does not necessarily or automatically represent the social totality. Rather, it *aspires toward* such a representation, which implies that working-class consciousness is contradictory—on one side, determined by the reified forms of thought prevalent in capitalism and, on the other side, possessive of the potential and the need to overcome those forms of thought.

Lukács draws a distinction between bourgeois consciousness and working-class consciousness based on their fundamental relation to capitalism. Bourgeois consciousness, in his view, exists in a world of abstractions aimed at justifying its own privileged position. It assumes ownership of knowledge about the world, primarily for the purpose of maintaining class power, and it tends to universalize systems, events, and actions as if they were part of an already-determined, unchangeable historical process in which capitalism is naturalized and considered to be a system that will exist forever. By contrast, the privileged nature of a working-class standpoint lies, paradoxically, not in a more expansive or more complete comprehension of reality than that of its bourgeois counterpart, but rather, in a narrower and more limited viewpoint, one that has greater access to the concrete (to the immediacy of class-based practices), and one that has experienced *en carne propia* the urgency to change the status quo. To explain this point, Lukács refers to the working class as the "identical subject-object of history": it is an "object" because it sells its labor as a commodity, and through this process the working class itself becomes commodified and objectified; it is a "subject" because it is capable of developing a consciousness of itself as an object—as a commodity. Working-class consciousness is, in effect, the "consciousness of the commodity,"[17] which amounts to the same thing as saying the *self-consciousness of the working class*. For Lukács, the significance of working-class self-consciousness is that "*the act of consciousness* [thus] *overthrows the objective form of its object*."[18] Stated differently, working-class consciousness "is itself nothing but the contradictions of history that have become conscious"[19] of themselves, which is the precondition for social transformation. It is the transformational potential of working-class self-consciousness that creates not the inevitability but the conditions of possibility for a subject that overcomes the constraints of its own alienation, or objectification. Capitalist consciousness does not possess this potential because it is not in its interest to recognize, much less to resolve, the contradictions of capitalist society. It is, however, possible for the working class "to discover that it is itself the *subject* of this process even though it is in chains and is for the time being unconscious of the fact."[20] Similarly, Jesús lacks awareness of how his subjectivity remains imprisoned by capitalist society, but his existence as a working-class subject, and his experience with the concreteness of class exploitation and racism, creates the necessity and thus the possibility for a critical class-based consciousness.

Lukács certainly does not have the final word on all problems related to consciousness and narrative structures, and his theories have been challenged by Marxists and non-Marxists alike for privileging the possibility of a critical working-class consciousness. But his concept of a working-class standpoint, if nothing else, offers us a way of thinking (and posing the right questions) about the specificity of working-class narratives, their distinctive particularities as a genre, and the various devices they employ to convey a sense of history despite their limited viewpoints. Before discussing the specific mechanisms at work in *Happy Birthday Jesús*, however, it will prove useful at this point to contextualize Ruiz's novel by discussing the emergence of the prison-industrial complex and the proliferation of mass incarceration in the United States, a development that lies at the heart of both capitalism and Jesús's narrative.

NEOLIBERALISM AND MASS INCARCERATION

Ronald Ruiz has known prisoners like Jesús personally. He is a retired attorney, having practiced law for forty years in Northern California. For most of his career as a criminal defense attorney, he specialized in high-profile capital cases—multiple murders, child molestation, and organized crime.[21] Despite Ruiz's familiarity with the experiences of hard-core convicts, the significance of the novel surpasses the personal knowledge he brings to Jesús's story; it draws its historical substance from (and conveys the social contradictions of) actual sociopolitical developments in the United States related to the recurring economic crises of capitalism in the contemporary period. Since the mid-1970s, a period commonly associated with the dominance of neoliberalism, the recurrent crises of capitalism have become more severe, increasingly detrimental to the lives of the middle and working classes, and exponentially more difficult to resolve. Consequently, all aspects of social life—and by extension, all forms of cultural production, including Ruiz's *Happy Birthday Jesús*—can be understood to one degree or another as thematic or formal expressions of capitalist crisis.

The capitalist state has responded to these periodic economic crises in a number of ways, but two of the responses merit mentioning here because they have been among the most devastating for the working class, poor people, and racial/ethnic minorities. The first is the implementation of neoliberal economic policies, which include allowing goods and capital to move freely across borders with so-called free trade agreements; eliminating price controls; easing (and in some cases, cancelling) environmental protections; systematically dismantling government programs for the poor; privatizing state-run services, properties, and utilities; lowering tax rates for corporations; and terminating the expectation that the state is meant to serve as a safety net for the public good. These policies are primarily aimed at deregulating capitalism and making the working class pay (through various forms of austerity) for the profit losses resulting from capitalism's recurring economic crises. The result of neoliberalism for working people has tended toward the loss of millions of jobs in manufacturing and other areas of work; the destruction of unions and workers' rights; the decline in real wages and standards of living; cutbacks in education, health, and other services; a crumbling infrastructure, including roads, bridges, water supplies, and public utilities; fewer jobs for college and high school graduates; and shorter life spans due to higher rates of stress-related illness and the absence of an adequate health care system.

The second response, which is more immediately relevant for my interpretation of *Happy Birthday Jesús*, has been the mass incarceration of a significant percentage of the U.S. population, especially Blacks and Latinos/Latinas. The building of a prison-industrial complex in this country is intricately connected to capitalist crisis and the emergence of neoliberalism. Sociologist William I. Robinson points out that the transition from the so-called Golden Age of capitalism (the early 1940s to the late 1960s) to neoliberalism brought with it "a shift from social welfare to social control or police states."[22] As a result, since 1982, the United States has experienced an explosion in the number of persons serving time in prison or jail.

Consider the following statistics. There are now more than 2.3 million inmates in the United States, housed in "1,719 state prisons, 102 federal prisons, 942 juvenile correctional facilities, 3,283 local jails, and 79 Indian Country jails, as well as in military prisons, immigration detention facilities, civil commitment centers, and prisons in the U.S. territories."[23] The United States has more people in prison and a higher number of prisoners per capita than any other country in the world. Embarrassingly, it has more prisons and jails than colleges and universities.[24] It has half a million more people in jail than does China, even though China has five times the population of the United States.[25] Between 1982 and 2010, "the U.S. penal population soared from 300,000 to close to 2.5 million."[26] Not only did the United States come to have the highest incarceration rate in the world, but it now "had a larger percentage of its black population caged than did South Africa at the height of apartheid—and, in fact, more black people were under the control of the penal system in 2010 than were enslaved in 1850, on the eve of the U.S. Civil War."[27] California alone has one of the biggest prison systems in the Western industrialized world. Despite the modest reduction of the state's prison population, resulting from the passage of Proposition 47 in 2014, California still had almost 129,000[28] prisoners housed in thirty-three state prisons as of June, 2015. Maintaining jails and prisons cost California $10.2 billion in 2015–16, or 9 percent of the state's budget and its fastest growing expense item.[29] Since 1984, one California State University campus and one University of California campus have been built.[30] During that same period, the state "has completed twenty-three major new prisons . . . at a cost of $280-$350 million dollars apiece. The state had previously built only twelve prisons between 1852 and 1964."[31] In 1985, there were 7,570 prison guards in California. By 1990, the number of prison guards had doubled to 14,249. By 1994, the number had almost quadrupled to 25,547.[32] Not surprisingly, given the racial implications and influences of the criminal justice system, Blacks make up 7.2 percent of California's population but an astonishing 29 percent of the state's prison population; Latinos/Latinas constitute about 37 percent of the state's demographics and 41 percent of those in prison; and whites comprise approximately 42 percent of California's population and 23 percent of the prison population.[33]

Given these startling statistics, the question must be posed: Why has the capitalist state insisted on sending so many working-class men and women—especially Blacks and Latinos/Latinas—to prison? The most obvious answer to this question is the economy. Prisons have always been about punishing or penalizing people, but in the past forty years they have become increasingly integrated into the economic infrastructure. Today prisons function not only to punish people; they also operate to make profits, especially for corporations that exploit prison labor. The economic reality behind the privatization of prisons in the United States, a booming industry, should not be underestimated, given that privatization is a cornerstone of neoliberalism. The prison-for-profit model is similar to the charter school model—bodies equal profit. The American Civil Liberties Union (ACLU) describes the private prison industry in the United States as a "moral failure" not only for reaping huge profits from incarceration,[34] but for lobbying Congress to stiffen sentencing laws so that prisoners will spend longer terms in prison, resulting in greater profits for the corporation. Somewhat cynically, CoreCivic, formerly the Corrections Corporation of America (CCA)[35] and the largest private prison company in the United States, claimed that "[t]he demand for our facilities and services could be adversely affected by . . . leniency in conviction or parole standards and sentencing practices."[36] Inmates housed in for-profit prisons "increased by approximately 1600% between 1990 and 2009," and CCA and the GEO Group, another private prison company behemoth, "received nearly $3 billion dollars in revenue" in 2010.[37] But it is not only the contractors that run the private prisons that make huge profits from incarceration; companies that provide services and products to the prisons also rake in massive rewards. For example, "the prison phone industry . . . earn[s] an estimated $1.2 billion per year"[38] charging exorbitant prices to prisoners for calling home to their families. Corizon Health, a company that specializes in providing health services to prisoners, pockets "$1.4 billion in annual revenue," while also having to defend some "six hundred and sixty malpractice lawsuits over the past five years," according to the ACLU.[39] Additionally, the "Prison Policy Initiative, a nonprofit criminal-justice think tank, estimates that commissary companies earn $1.6 billion per year," selling food, toiletries, and other small items at "five times the retail price" to prisoners.[40] Mass incarceration reaps huge profits for corporations that lack a moral compass and a sense of humanity, but the function of prisons in the capitalist state is not only economic but ideological and political.

The strategy of incarcerating massive numbers of people has served multiple political purposes, three of which are important to point out. First, mass incarceration removes surplus labor from the population. Prisons function as a safety valve for capitalism's increasingly large pool of unemployed workers who either cannot find a decent job or have simply given up hope of becoming employable. Putting workers in prison reduces unemployment rates, giving the false impression that the economy is strong and satisfies the needs of everyone. Second, with discontent brewing because of neoliberal cutbacks and wage reductions, mass incarceration tends to contain and control the possibility of "unrest, spontaneous rebellion, and organized political mobilization among the structurally unemployed and marginalized."[41] And third, the capitalist state aims to create a "moral panic" mainly among the white population by demonizing and criminalizing racial minorities in an effort to split the working class. Thus, the state strategy of caging an obscene number of people also has severe racist implications. The capitalist state has been largely successful in meeting these goals.

Additionally, the state has attempted to make all of us, to one degree or another, complicit with a culture of mass incarceration. As early as 1971, Bob Dylan wrote and sang about the dangers for a society in accepting the carceral state passively: "Sometimes I think this whole world / Is one big prison yard. / Some of us are prisoners. / The rest of us are guards. / Lord, Lord! They cut George Jackson down."[42] Dylan's song implicitly condemns the state for the political assassination of George Jackson, a young man who was not politicized when he was sentenced to prison for robbery at the age of twenty. In prison, he became a political activist, a cofounder of the Black Guerrilla Family, and a Marxist. But the song also implicates those who passively accept the injustices of prison, comparing everyone not incarcerated to guards or active agents of the state. Dylan's song suggests that as long as so many people are in prison, the rest of us can never really be entirely free. His point is not unlike the argument Marx made about the United States in the mid-nineteenth century—that "labour in a white skin cannot emancipate itself where it is branded in a black skin,"[43] or that workers could never be free as long as slavery existed. Likewise, we could say that we are condemning ourselves to a form of ideological confinement if we become indifferent to the fact that the state continues to incarcerate hundreds of thousands of misguided men, women, and youth, or if we become insensitive to the reality of living in a carceral state—or what Franz Kafka once referred to as a "penal colony." If we remain passive in the face of repression, then tragically we have become complicit with that repression.

Mass incarceration and capitalist crisis, then, form the social backdrop or historical context that drives the structures and themes in Ronald Ruiz's

Happy Birthday Jesús. Generally speaking, racialized working-class groups have been deeply affected by the experiences of social repression and mass incarceration, and these experiences have become internalized, thematically and formally, in the art, literature, and music produced by some members of these groups. One example of this internalization in *Happy Birthday Jesús* is the novel's conception of time and its relation to the concept of totality.

TIME AND NARRATIVE STRUCTURE

In the early pages of the novel, Jesús stands on a mountain range looking down at California's great San Joaquin Valley and remembers the "coldness and timelessness" of the fog "down there" in the valley, where he had lived as a child. "It was there" all the time: an omnipresent, foggy timelessness, suggesting the inseparability of past and present.[44] Literally, the "fog" limits Jesús's ability to see clearly at a distance; figuratively, however, it hinders both his recollection of history and his consciousness of the present. This opening scene produces a kind of dark, spatiotemporal ubiquity: the past was not something that was long gone, left behind on the path of history, but rather "it was there" all the time.

Happy Birthday Jesús is intricately concerned with time—not only with thematic representations of time, as in "doing time" or losing a sense of time while locked in isolation, but also with time in relation to a dialectical conception of history. If Carr is correct in stating that "narrative is our primary . . . way of organizing our experience of time," then *Happy Birthday Jesús* organizes a conception of time that aspires toward totality and a working-class standpoint in the Lukacsian-Marxian sense. Through the use of various structural devices, Ruiz complicates the notion of time in the novel, beginning with the fact that it is not a linear narrative but is constructed as a series of flashbacks and flashbacks-within-flashbacks. This narrative approach allows Jesús to reconstruct his experiences from the time of his early childhood until his late thirties, but the actual "now time" of the narrative, the time it takes Jesús to tell his story, begins just a couple of days before it ends so that the bulk of the novel backtracks to fill the short span between beginning and end with intelligible historical content. The narrative structure conveys a conception of time as the accumulation of experiences contained within a narrowly defined frame. Or, we might think of time in the novel as a totality of events from the past that comes to bear on any given moment of the present—a dialectical conception of time that engages the immediate and the mediated, the particular and the universal. In the temporal logic of the novel, the present is always determined by (and stands as the expression of) the long history of causal events from the past—that is, the past now distilled in the immediacy of the present. Thus, we cannot understand the full significance of an event (whether in actuality or in a fictional text) without grasping its historicity, or the effects resulting from its social determinations. With this conception of time, we would not be incorrect to think of the novel as having a synecdochic structure, one in which each part of the narrative is an expression of the whole and in which the whole grants access to a critical comprehension of the individual parts, including the causes of events and the motives of the characters.

The narrative structure of *Happy Birthday Jesús* formulates a conception of time that is less akin to what Walter Benjamin calls "homogeneous, empty time" than it is to his concept of "messianic time." He defines the former as chronological or calendrical time in which time is a constant trajectory, independent of human experience; it keeps on rolling whether humans are present or not. From this perspective, time is not structured by the actions of humans but marks and measures those actions within an abstract universal dimension. Homogeneous, empty time implies a conception of history (and, by extension, of literary narratives) that follows a sequential logic along a singular continuum. By contrast, Benjamin defines messianic time as "the present, which . . . comprises the entire history of mankind in an enormous abridgment [that] coincides exactly with the stature which the history of mankind has in the universe."[45] For Benjamin, human experience is not merely measured by time but, on the contrary, determines time. Plus, with his dialectical concept of messianic time, we can think of time as a concentrated composite of the totality of our past, present, and future experiences rather than as an empty, inanimate, dehumanized marker of events. Messianic time implies a conception of history (and of literary narratives) that collapses or blurs the distinction between past and present; events from the past are thus not isolated from their effects in the present but constitute the historicity of those effects. With Jesús, for example, his past "was there" all the time.

We often think of a novel's meaning as being produced by the unfolding of events and the resolution of conflict following a logic of cause and effect, or by the linear-temporal trajectory of the story, whether or not the events are presented in chronological order. *Happy Birthday Jesús,* however, subsumes that kind of logic to a strategy that prioritizes structural tension in conjunction with a dialectical conception of time. Ruiz employs an array of storytelling devices that convey meaning by emphasizing structural tensions rather than linear rationality, or by conceptualizing the synchronic as an expression of the diachronic. These devices include parallelisms, reversals, and juxtaposition. The novel conveys significance by repeatedly comparing and contrasting images, concepts, names, objects, sentence structures, and the actions and thoughts of characters. For example, Jesús has the same name as Jesus Christ, despite his animosity toward religion and God, and Soledad bears the name of both a California prison and Chole, a prostitute who befriends Jesús. (Chole is short for Soledad.) The narrative draws a parallel between the extreme methods that Jesús's grandmother uses to discipline him when he is a child and the torture he receives in prison years later when placed in "the hole." In effect, the novel compares the repression that takes place in the family, as a social institution, to that of the criminal justice system.[46] The novel juxtaposes the way Soledad's eyes penetrate Jesús to the penetration that he will later experience while being raped in prison.[47] "It was her eyes. . . . They were eyes that seemed to see into every part of me. . . . They would strip me, and scare me, and convince me with their fierceness."[48]

Jesús's grandmother, the church, and the legal system all nurture his feelings of guilt. Fearing he has committed the mortal sin of sacrilege by not confessing to his sins before eating the host, a sacramental bread that symbolizes the Resurrected Christ, Jesús pukes after going to Holy Communion. This moment recalls an earlier scene where a young white man who is raped in jail also pukes; together, the two scenes suggest a comparison between rape and indoctrinated religion. Moreover, Ruiz's description of eating the host in the Communion scene utilizes language that evokes the imagery of a forced oral sex act.

> I was shaking. I expected some kind of thunder or blast just as the host reached my lips, but it didn't come and I swallowed hard and the host went down. And even as it was going down, He [i.e., God] started struggling and fighting and kicking all that filth in my soul. My stomach hurt; the pain was sharp. He was twisting it and knotting it as He struggled. I felt hot. I wanted to puke. . . . I could feel Him and my whole stomach in my throat. I swallowed and kept swallowing.[49]

The Communion scene draws stark parallels between Catholicism and sexuality, institutionalized religion and the legal system, and the agony of coerced confession that takes place in either institution. However, rather than serving as a form of catharsis, or a cleansing of the soul, confession serves to internalize Jesús's feelings of guilt more deeply and to consolidate his subjectivity as inherently criminal and morally corrupt.

My discussion of various comparisons and juxtaposing relations in this section of the chapter aims to disclose the logic of narrative signification and time at work in the novel—a logic that draws on a conception of time as wholistic and dependent on human experience, and one that strives to show the interconnectedness of the various component parts of the narrative, as well as the integration of past and present. Consequently, the novel produces a viewpoint that draws as much from its structural logic as from its thematic content to surpass the limited consciousness of the working-class narrator in a manner that ends up aspiring toward a social totality. Whereas the logic of messianic time guides our attention toward the novel's totalizing inclinations and its structural apparatus, *Happy Birthday Jesús* also unleashes a scathing critique of surveillance as one of the most effective means of social control in contemporary capitalist society.

WATCHING AND BEING WATCHED

There are many examples of surveillance, or watching, in *Happy Birthday Jesús*. Soledad watches Jesús from behind a slightly cracked door while isolating him in a separate room for punishment. Jesús feels that God is constantly watching him, causing him to suffer from anxiety and panic attacks. Late in the novel, the prison guard captain controls prisoners in the "rehabilitation unit" by watching them without being seen—and by establishing a system in which the prisoners cannot know at any given moment whether or not they are being watched. The motif of watching in the novel can be interpreted in a number of ways. Watching is related to issues of visibility and invisibility, seeing and not seeing, consciousness and the unconscious. The control that God exerts on Jesús by constantly watching him parallels the gaze of his grandmother, the judgmental eyes of the jurors in the courtroom, and the vigilance of the guards in prison. *Happy Birthday Jesús* makes readers watch what they would rather not see, and it turns readers into jurors—watching and passing judgment on Jesús, and on the novel itself for its graphic depictions of sexual violence. The novel also parallels watching and ideology. In thinking about the various forms of corporal punishment his grandmother would inflict upon him, Jesús admits, "For as long as I could remember, she did these things to me. Often I thought I knew why, but I never could understand how she was able to do it and get away with it."[50] Jesús wonders how his grandmother, a small woman, could control and dominate him so forcefully and completely. To draw an apt comparison, we could ask how, in a hypothetical country, a relatively small ruling class, or a regime that represents a small fraction of the population, can maintain control over the masses of oppressed people. Why don't the people just rise up and seize power? This question can be answered in part with an explanation of how ideology works by getting people to act in ways that stand against their own class interests, and the answer would also shed light on Jesús's reason for failing to rebel against his grandmother.

Watching in *Happy Birthday Jesús* illuminates the manner in which surveillance functions as a form of social control. Here, of course, we cannot help but recall Michel Foucault's well-known concept of "panopticism." In *Discipline and Punish: The Birth of the Prison*, Foucault formulates a theory of social control based on a study of European prisons in which he draws on the work of Jeremy Bentham, an architectural philosopher who conceptualized a type of prison called the "Panopticon" in the late eighteenth century. Bentham's design allowed for a prison guard to watch all the prisoners housed in a particular unit without the prisoners being able to see the official or each other, thus establishing a "sentiment of invisible omniscience."[51] Foucault drew on Bentham's work not only to analyze the conceptual designs of physical institutional spaces (schools, hospitals, military bases, factories, and prisons), but to theorize the manner in which modern societies "discipline" subjects with incessant methods of observation and surveillance based on the concepts of "visibility" (people know they are possibly being watched) and "unverifiability" (they cannot know with certainty if they are being watched at any given moment).[52] Foucault refers to his theory of surveillance-based discipline as "panopticism."

Foucault's works have been hugely popular in the humanities and social sciences for good reason, considering that so many of his ideas ring true, but his related theories of panopticism and power are also potentially problematic in some ways. For example, he formulates a critique of power, but he also defends its function as a social force, stating that "we must cease once and for all to describe the effects of power in negative terms: it 'excludes,' it 'represses,' it 'censors,' it 'abstracts,' it 'masks,' it 'conceals.' In fact, power produces; it produces reality; it produces domains of objects and rituals of truth."[53] Additionally, power purportedly operates all by itself; it is like a self-propelled "machine" that never stops. For Foucault, power is decentralized and "disindividualized." It does not need a ruling class, an army, a police force, or a head of state to be effective. Panopticism "assures an infinitesimal distribution of the power relations"[54] among groups and individuals in society, essentially making everyone contributors to the technologies of power that disempower us. The problem with this way of thinking, especially for anyone committed to fighting for social change, is that it becomes exceedingly difficult, if not impossible, to formulate a strategy against power when you cannot identify power's material source and political center of gravity. Capitalism remains absolved of its causal connection to social inequality and human suffering, to class power and powerlessness, while our attention is directed to a democratized form of power where everyone is culpable. Further, Foucault proclaims that panopticism is "a functional mechanism that must improve the exercise of power by making it lighter, more rapid, more effective, a design of subtle coercion for a society to come."[55] Here, he seems to be imagining the withering away of extreme forms of repression, such as those found in the Security Housing Units of maximum security prisons or at Guantanamo, replaced by the automated, decentered, subtlety of panoptic machines of discipline and control. The proliferation of prisons in the United States contradicts or at least seriously problematizes Foucault's forecast of a less coercive, more consensual form of punishment. Granted, he wrote *Discipline and Punish* before the rapid expansion of the prison-industrial complex in the 1980s, and he focused his study on prisons in Europe not the United States. Nevertheless, his theory of social control and power poses problems for a contemporary critique of neoliberal capitalism and mass incarceration. Despite the difficulties with some aspects of Foucault's theories of power, his concept of panopticism remains remarkably useful for reading a novel like *Happy Birthday Jesús* because it explains the profound effectiveness of surveillance in disciplining individuals, and it resonates with the novel's many references to "watching" as a form of psychological and social control.

Foucault's panopticism not only depends on visible and unverifiable surveillance but it also requires the observed subject to internalize the gaze of the watcher. Once Jesús has internalized the real or imagined watcher's gaze, the watcher no longer actually needs to be present. Even in the watcher's absence, the vigilance and surveillance continue. Referring to the control his grandmother had over him, and her particular methods of surveillance, Jesús states, "No matter what I did or where I went, she was there. . . . I saw her as they dragged me into the police car. Watching. No tears, no screams, no words, nothing. Watching, the way she always did. . . . She was everywhere. I could never get rid of her."[56] In a more detrimental example of surveillance, Jesús links the act of watching with the psychology of racism.

> I remembered the way the white people used to look at me on the streets. It was something in their eyes. . . . It took just a glimpse to see it and to know it. But I could have never described it or explained it to anyone who wasn't a Mexican. They knew. We never talked about it, we just accepted it. . . . We were forever ready to admit it. All they had to do was look at us and we confessed right on the spot, in an instant, without speaking a word. There is something that is bad about me and there doesn't seem to be anything I can do about it.[57]

In his ideologically deluded mind, Jesús fears the gaze of all white people, and being looked at by any white person triggers his own internalized understanding of the racialized gaze of the other, or what he believes to be "the way white people used to look at [him]." Thus, with Jesús racism has become an effective method of social and psychological control, not because all white people who look at him are racist, but because he does not possess the ability to distinguish between who is racist and who is not. The fact that he has experienced racism creates a condition of visibility (he knows some white people are racist) and unverifiability (he cannot tell the racists from the non-racists.) This conflicted condition points to a sharp internal struggle taking place within Jesús himself. On the one hand, he has internalized the gaze of racism. On the other hand, he refuses to acknowledge recognition of that gaze. To draw this section to a close, we can conclude that Jesús resists—even if unconsciously—the interpellated subjectivity associated with the watchful eyes of the jurors as representatives of the legal system; the eyes of his grandmother as the quintessential figure of the family; the vigilance of Father Galvan as the flag bearer of religion; and the omniscience of God himself as emblematic of the social totality.

THE FINAL ACT

There are weaknesses in *Happy Birthday Jesús* that must be acknowledged, including a problematic first-person point of view, as discussed above; the use of offensive language, especially in regard to race and religion; the gratuitous depiction of sexual violence; and, most notably, the representation of gender. The novel's depictions of women as whores and religious fanatics, and of men as animalistic and prone to violence, are troubling. Chicano literature written by male writers has sometimes been criticized for depicting Latina women shallowly as suffering mothers, domestic housewives, and healers, on the one hand, or as witches and tragic dark women, on the other. *Happy Birthday Jesús* leaves itself open to this kind of criticism in its construction of female characters, almost to the point of exaggeration. The scene in which Chole buys Jesús a cake for his eighteenth birthday is particularly depressing and repulsive, especially because she had been the only character up to that point to show affection for Jesús and to care for him. In turn, he denigrates and abuses her, and he tries to mutilate her body. To some extent, Jesús redeems himself late in the novel. After killing the priest and burning down the church, he sets out to look for her, and he finds her in a decrepit and catatonic state. The novel then ends with Jesús declaring, "'I got them for us, Chole. I got them.' But she didn't answer or nod or nothing, and I started to cry, and I held her, and I kissed her, and I said, 'Chole, I love you.'" It's a touching conclusion, one that recognizes Chole's humanity and speaks to Jesús's capacity to love. But is it too little too late? Can the violence that Jesús commits against Chole ever be undone?

Without dismissing the novel's weaknesses, we can also confidently recognize its strengths, even in its treatment of gender and sexuality. The novel provides an in-depth psychological study of the repression of Chicano male sexuality, a noteworthy accomplishment given that Chicana writers before 1994 had been far more willing to write about sexuality than their male counterparts. Importantly, *Happy Birthday Jesús* does not isolate the repression of male sexuality from other social categories but shows its interconnection with religion, the family, race, labor, and the criminal justice system. In some respects, the novel can also be read as a critique of misogyny and homophobia via its depictions of prison rape. Terry A. Kupers, who writes extensively about prisons and mass incarceration, argues that "homophobia and misogyny are two sides of the same coin" and posits that "male inadequacy," perceived or real, "is the link between these two concurrent phenomenon" in prison. The male rapists in prison will assault other men who they consider weak and vulnerable, traits that they associate with femininity and homosexuality. Thus, the attacks against these men are, in effect, attacks against the symbolic substitutes for women and gays. Kupers calls this kind of behavior "toxic masculinity."[58] When Jesús retaliates against one of his rapists in prison, castrating him, in a sense he commits a socially symbolic act not only against "toxic masculinity" but against misogyny and homophobia as well.

Despite the extremely dark representation of mass incarceration in the novel and the terribly grim depiction of Jesús's life and outcome, *Happy Birthday Jesús* nevertheless casts an optimistic view, however slim, about the possibility of social change by suggesting that state repression under capitalism can never be total because sooner or later human beings will revolt in conscious or unconscious—organized or spontaneous—ways against their oppressive conditions. In this case, the odds against Jesús are nearly insurmountable, lacking as he is in physical and mental abilities, but he nevertheless rebels at the end of the novel by killing a priest and burning down the church. Read literally, Jesús's solitary, depraved form of rebellion is politically problematic because it represents an individual act rather than collective action and because Jesús targets an innocent man instead of his actual abusers. But by reading the narrative figuratively, we can interpret his final moment as a socially symbolic act that surpasses his individuality. Unlike his earlier acts of violence in the novel, which are impulsive and reactionary, his final act is deliberate and intentional. It represents Jesús's attempt to become a socially conscious human being in his effort to take control of his own life. Thus (in a warped sort of way) his final act is an act of freedom. The killing of the priest, for Jesús, is synonymous with the killing of God, which can be understood as his felt need to annihilate the Althusserian "Subject with a capital S,"[59] or the cumulative social determinations in a capitalist society, in order to free himself from the prison-house of interpellation.[60] Unlike the lawyers and the jurors at Jesús's trial, who cannot understand the link between actions and their causes, Jesús displays intentionality in his final act because he has identified the source of his formation as a contradictory subject.

David Carr observes that "only from the perspective of the end [of a narrative] do the beginning and the middle make sense."[61] It would be hard to dispute this logical assertion, but Carr's observation can also be inverted and it will be just as significant, if not more so, for our interpretation of the novel. That is, the end (or Jesús's final act) becomes intelligible only from the perspective of everything that has come before it and everything that implicitly will follow long after the novel's conclusion. To understand the act in this way is to grasp the full meaning of the novel in terms of Benjamin's messianic time—in terms of a qualitative, revolutionary Marxist way of thinking about history, social relations, and the causes of events under capitalism. Moreover, the final dramatic moment of the novel firmly establishes the making of a working-class point of view that is at once in all its contradictory complexities both limited in its comprehension of the social world *and* representative of "an aspiration toward society in its totality."[62] This moment, however, cannot be comprehended as such without being privy to everything that has come before it—class exploitation, racism, familial dysfunction, misogyny, homophobia, religious ideology, neoliberalism, and mass incarceration—that is to say, without being exposed to the historicity of Jesús's final act.

Notes

1. Alan Ryan, "To Be Young, Troubled, and Latino," *San Jose Mercury News*, April 17, 1994.

2. Ryan, "To Be Young."

3. Ronald Ruiz, *Happy Birthday Jesús* (Houston: Arte Público Press, 1994), 301.

4. Theodor Adorno, "Messages in a Bottle," in *Mapping Ideology*, ed. Slavoj Žižek (New York: Verso, 1994), 35.

5. Theodor Adorno, "The Position of the Narrator in the Contemporary Novel," in *Notes to Literature, Volume I* (New York: Columbia University Press, 1991), 30.

6. Ruiz, *HBJ*, 302–3.

7. Ruiz, *HBJ*, 146–55.

8. Even though I find value in Carr's argument about positivists and narrativists, I do not think all historians can be easily pigeonholed into such restrictive categories. Hayden White, for example, writes convincingly that "Marxists do not study the past in order to reconstruct what happened in it, in the sense of determining what events occurred at specific times and places. They study history in order to derive the laws of historical dynamics." See Hayden White, *The Content and the Form: Narrative Discourse and Historical Representation* (Baltimore: Johns Hopkins University Press, 1987), 142.

9. David Carr, *Time, Narrative, and History* (Bloomington: Indiana University Press, 1991), 10.

10. Carr, *Time*, 12.

11. Chris Lorenz, "Historical Knowledge and Historical Reality: A Plea for 'Internal Realism,'" *History and Theory* 33:3 (1994): 306.

12. Lorenz, "Historical Knowledge and Historical Reality," 302.

13. Lorenz, "Historical Knowledge and Historical Reality," 305.

14. Carr, *Time*, 4–5.

15. Carr, *Time*, 3.

16. Georg Lukács, *History and Class Consciousness: Studies in Marxist Dialectics*, trans. Rodney Livingstone (Cambridge, MA: MIT Press, 1971), 174.

17. Lukács, *History and Class Consciousness*, 178.

18. Lukács, *History and Class Consciousness*, 178.

19. Lukács, *History and Class Consciousness*, 178.

20. Lukács, *History and Class Consciousness*, 181.

21. For an in-depth description of his experiences as an attorney, see Ruiz's self-published memoir *A Lawyer* (2012), available from Amazon Digital Services.

22. William I. Robinson, *Global Capitalism and the Crisis of Humanity* (New York: Cambridge University Press, 2014), 164.

23. "Mass Incarceration: The Whole Pie 2016," Prison Policy Initiative, accessed November 8, 2016, https://www.prisonpolicy.org/reports/pie2016.html

24. Tom Jackman, "Mass Reduction of California Prison Population Didn't Cause Rise in Crime, Two Studies Find," *Washington Post*, May 18, 2016, accessed November 8, 2016, https://www.washingtonpost.com/news/true-crime/wp/2016/05/18/mass-release-of-california-prisoners-didnt-cause-rise-in-crime-two-studies-find/?utm_term=.cf47227af92e

25. John Greenberg, "Bernie Sanders: The United States Has 'More People in Jail Than Any Other Country on Earth,'" *Politifact*, October 13, 2015, accessed November 8, 2016. http://www.politifact.com/truth-o-meter/statements/2015/oct/13/bernie-s/bernie-sanders-united-states-has-more-people-jail-/

26. Robinson, *Global Capitalism*, 183.

27. Robinson, *Global Capitalism*, 183.

28 California Department of Corrections and Rehabilitation, Office of Research, "Fall 2015 Population Projections," January 2016: v and 3.

29. The top five charges for which Californians are sentenced to prison are 1. Possession of a controlled substance; 2. Possession of a controlled substance for sale; 3. Robbery; 4. Sale of a controlled substance; and 5. Second degree burglary. Obviously, thousands of individuals are sent to prison when they would be better served by a drug rehabilitation center or a job that pays a decent wage.

30. Saki Knafo, "Prison-Industrial Complex? Maybe It's Time for a Schools-Industrial Complex," *Huffington Post*, August 31, 2013; http://www.huffingtonpost.com/2013/08/30/california-prisons-schools_n_3839190.html

31. Ruth Wilson Gilmore, *Golden Gulag: Prisons, Surplus, Crisis, and Opposition in Globalizing California* (Berkeley: University of California Press, 2007), 7.

32. Aaron McDaniels, *Truth between the Lies* (Bloomington, IN: Xlibris, 2016). Kindle ed., chapter 39.

33. Department of Corrections and Rehabilitation, State of California, "Prison Census Data as of June 30, 2013," (September 2013), 7.

34. ACLU, "Banking on Bondage: Private Prisons and Mass Incarceration," accessed January 11, 2017, https://www.aclu.org/banking-bondage-private-prisons-and-mass-incarceration

35. Facing intense public pressure for its questionable financial policies, political influences, and treatment of prisoners, the Correctional Corporation of America changed its name to CoreCivic in October 2016. See David Boucher, "CCA Changes Name to CoreCivic Amid Ongoing Scrutiny," *Tennessean*, October 28, 2016, http://www.tennessean.com/story/news/2016/10/28/cca-changes-name-amid-ongoing-scrutiny/92883274/

36. ACLU, "Banking on Bondage." Quoted from the 2010 Annual Report filed with the Securities and Exchange Commission.

37. ACLU, "Banking on Bondage."

38. Eric Markowitz, "Making Profits on the Captive Prison Market," *New Yorker*, September 4, 2016; accessed February 11, 2017, http://www.newyorker.com/business/currency/making-profits-on-the-captive-prison-market

39. Markowitz, "Making Profits."

40. Markowitz, "Making Profits."

41. Robinson, *Global Capitalism*, 180.

42. Bob Dylan, "George Jackson," 1971, Ram's Horn Music; renewed 1999, Ram's Horn Music.

43. Karl Marx, *Capital: A Critique of Political Economy, Vol. 1*, trans. Ben Fowkes (New York: Penguin Books, 1990), 414.

44. Ruiz, *Happy Birthday Jesús*, 7.

45. Walter Benjamin, *Illuminations: Essays and Reflections*, ed. Hannah Arendt (New York: Schocken Books, 1968), 263.

46. Ruiz, *Happy Birthday Jesús*, 22.

47. Ruiz, *Happy Birthday Jesús*, 23.

48. Ruiz, *Happy Birthday Jesús*, 23.

49. Ruiz, *Happy Birthday Jesús*, 51.

50. Ruiz, *Happy Birthday Jesús*, 23.

51. Jeremy Bentham, *The Panopticon Writings*, ed. Miran Božovič (London: Verso, 1995), 29–95.

52. Michel Foucault, *Discipline and Punish: The Birth of the Prison* (New York: Vintage Books, 1995), 201.

53. Foucault, *Discipline and Punish*, 194.

54. Foucault, *Discipline and Punish*, 216.

55. Foucault, *Discipline and Punish*, 209.

56. Ruiz, *Happy Birthday Jesús*, 85.

57. Ruiz, *Happy Birthday Jesús*, 115.

58. Terry A. Kupers, "The Role of Misogyny and Homophobia in Prison Sexual Abuse," *UCLA Women's Law Journal* 18.1 (2010): 108–9. It's important to clarify that not all forms of masculinity are "toxic."

59. See Louis Althusser, *Lenin and Philosophy*, trans. Ben Brewster (New York: Monthly Review Press, 1971), 177–83.

60. Vincent Pérez similarly writes that "[v]iolence in *Happy Birthday Jesús* becomes a form of symbolic action, an expression of Jesús's nihilistic repudiation of the church and its complicity with institutions that are at war with a segment of his own community." See "'Running' and Resistance: Nihilism and Cultural Memory in Urban Narratives," *MELUS* 25.2 (Summer 2000): 142.

61. Carr, *Time*, 7.

62. Lukács, *History and Class Consciousness*, 174.

Bibliography

Adorno, Theodor. "Messages in a Bottle." In *Mapping Ideology*, edited by Slavoj Žižek, 34–45. New York: Verso, 1994.

Adorno, Theodor. "The Position of the Narrator in the Contemporary Novel." In *Notes to Literature, Volume I*, 30–36. New York: Columbia University Press, 1991.

Alarcón, Norma. "Conjugations: The Insurrection of Subjugated Knowledges and Exclusionary Practices." *Chicana/Latina Studies* 13.2 (Spring 2014): 202–24.

Albarrán, Elena Jackson. "Guerrilla Warplay: The Infantilization of War in Latin American Popular Culture." *Studies in Latin American Popular Culture* 24 (2005): 70.

Alexander, Amy. "Whither Black San Francisco: A Story in Pictures." *San Francisco Weekly*, February 25, 2015. http://archives.sfweekly.com/san-francisco/african-american-san-francisco-diversity-black-san-francisco/Content?oid=3434520

Alexander, Michelle. *The New Jim Crow: Mass Incarceration in the Age of Colorblindness*. Rev. ed. New York: New Press, 2012.

Alperin, Josh. "Public Housing: Historical Essay." *Shaping San Francisco's Digital Archive @ Found SF*. Accessed August 31, 2016. http://www.foundsf.org/index.php?title=PUBLIC_HOUSING

Althusser. Louis. *Lenin and Philosophy*. Translated by Ben Brewster. New York: Monthly Review Press, 1971.

American Civil Liberties Union (ACLU). "Banking on Bondage: Private Prisons and Mass Incarceration." https://www.aclu.org/banking-bondage-private-prisons-and-mass-incarceration

Anaya, Rudolfo. *Alburquerque*. Albuquerque: University of New Mexico Press, 1992.

Anaya, Rudolfo. *Jemez Spring*. Albuquerque: University of New Mexico Press, 2005.

Angus, Ian. "When Did the Anthropocene Begin and Why Does It Matter." *Monthly Review* 67.4 (September 2015). http://monthlyreview.org/2015/09/01/when-did-the-anthropocene-beginand-why-does-it-matter/

Anzaldúa, Gloria. *Borderlands/La Frontera*. San Francisco: Aunt Lute Books, 1987.

Anzaldúa, Gloria, and Cherríe Moraga, ed. *This Bridge Called My Back: Writings by Radical Women of Color*. 4th ed. New York: SUNY Press, 2015.

Arce, William. "Landscapes of Trauma: The Transnational Dislocation of Vietnam's War Trauma in Alfredo Vea's *Gods Go Begging*." In *Re-Framing the Transnational Turn in American Studies*, edited by Winfried Fluck, Donald E. Pease, and John Carlos Rowe, 97–118. Hanover, NH: Dartmouth College Press, 2011.

Arrighi, Giovanni. *The Long Twentieth Century: Money, Power and the Origins of Our Times*. New York: Verso, 2010.

Badiou, Alain. *Logics of Worlds: Being and Event II*. Translated by Alberto Toscano. London: Continuum, 2009.

Badiou, Alain. "The Subject and Infinity." In *Conditions*, translated by Steven Corcoran, 211–27. New York: Continuum, 2008.

Bataille, Georges. *Visions of Excess: Selected Writings 1927–1939*. Minneapolis: University of Minnesota, 1985.

BAYCAT. "Public Housing on Potrero Hill: A Timeline." *Potrero Hill Archives Project*. Accessed August 31, 2016. http://www.potreroarchives.com/Archives/Public_Housing_video.html

Beasley-Murray, Jon. *Posthegemony: Political Theory and Latin America*. Minneapolis: University of Minnesota Press, 2010.

The Believer. "An Interview with Sergio de la Pava." October 3, 2012. Accessed May 2, 2016. http://logger.believermag.com/post/32817533978/an-interview-with-sergio-de-la-pava

Bendle, Mervin. "Zarathustra's Revenge: The Sordid Utopia of Contemporary Science Fiction Films." A paper presented at the "Imagining the Future: Utopia, Dystopia and Science Fiction" conference, Monash University, Melbourne, Australia, December 2005.

Benjamin, Walter. *Illuminations: Essays and Reflections*. Edited by Hannah Arendt. New York: Schocken Books, 1968.

Bentham, Jeremy. *The Panopticon Writings*. Edited by Miran Božovič. London: Verso, 1995.

Berzon, Alexandra. "A Place in Town That Will Not Die: Shipbuilding's Heyday Gone with Two World Wars, but Dry Docks Survive at Pier 70." *SF Gate*, July 3, 2005. http://www.sfgate.com/opinion/article/A-place-in-town-that-will-not-die-2657857.php#photo-2135039

Beverley, John. *Subalternity and Representation: Arguments in Cultural Theory*. Durham: Duke University Press, 1999.

Bhaskar, Roy. *Dialectic: The Pulse of Freedom*. New York: Verso Books, 1993.

Bhaskar, Roy. *A Realist Theory of Science*. London: Verso, 1975.

Biggers, Jeff. "More Than Measuring Up: An Interview with Alfredo Véa." *Bloomsbury Review* 20.1 (January–February 2000): 5.

Blackwell, Maylei, Laura Biggs, and Mignonette Chiu. "Transnational Feminisms Roundtable." Special issue of *Frontiers: A Journal of Women Studies* 36.3 (2015): 1–24.

Blasing, Mutlu Konuk. *Lyric Poetry: The Pain and the Pleasure of Words*. Princeton: Princeton University Press, 2007.

Boon, Marcus. *In Praise of Copying*. Cambridge: Harvard University Press, 2010.

Borzutzky, Daniel. *The Book of Interfering Bodies*. Callicoon, NY: Nightboat, 2011.

Borzutzky, Daniel. *In the Murmurs of the Rotten Carcass Economy*. Callicoon, NY: Nightboat, 2015.

Borzutzky, Daniel. *The Performance of Becoming Human*. Brooklyn: Brooklyn Arts, 2016.

Borzutzky, Daniel. *Lake Michigan*. Pittsburgh: University of Pittsburgh Press, 2018.

Boucher, David. "CCA Changes Name to CoreCivic amid Ongoing Scrutiny." *Tennessean*. October 28, 2016. http://www.tennessean.com/story/news/2016/10/28/cca-changes-name-amid-ongoing-scrutiny/92883274/

Brass, Tom. *Labour Regime Change in the Twenty-First Century: Unfreedom, Capitalism and Primitive Accumulation*. Leiden: Brill, 2011.

Brookfield, Stephen D. *The Power of Critical Theory for Adult Learning and Teaching*. New York: Open University Press, 2005.

Broussard, Albert S. *Black San Francisco: The Struggle for Racial Equality in the West, 1900–1954*. Lawrence: University Press of Kansas, 1993.

Brown, Rembert. "Genius: A Conversation with *Hamilton* Maestro Lin-Manuel Miranda." *Skewed & Reviewed*, September 29, 2015. Accessed January 7, 2016. http://grantland.com/hollywood-prospectus/genius-a-conversation-with-hamilton-maestro-lin-manuel-miranda/

Brown, Wendy. "Neoliberalism and the End of Liberal Democracy." In *Edgework: Critical Essays on Knowledge and Politics*, 37–59. Princeton: Princeton University Press, 2005.

Cabeza de Baca, Fabiola. *We Fed Them Cactus*. Albuquerque: University of New Mexico Press, 1954.

California Department of Corrections and Rehabilitation. Office of Research. "Fall 2015 Population Projections." January 2016. v and 3.

Callinicos, Alex. *Imperialism and Global Political Economy*. Cambridge: Polity Press, 2009.

Callinicos, Alex. *The Resources of Critique*. Malden, MA: Polity Press, 2006.

Camp, Jordan T. *Incarcerating the Crisis: Freedom Struggles and the Rise of the Neoliberal State*. Berkeley: University of California Press, 2016.

Cantú, Roberto. "Alfredo Véa Jr." In *Latino and Latina Writers*, vol. 2, edited by Alan West-Durán, María Herrera-Sobek, and César A. Salgado, 511–25. New York: Scribner's, 2004.

Carr, David. *Time, Narrative, and History*. Bloomington: Indiana University Press, 1991.

Caruth, Cathy. "Afterword: Turning Back to Literature." *PMLA* 125.4 (October 2010): 1087–95.

Castillo, Ana. *The Guardians*. New York: Random House, 2007.

Castillo, Ana. *So Far from God*. New York: W. W. Norton, 1993.

Chabram-Dernersesian, Angie. "Bucking Tradition: Sci Fi with a Chicana/o Latina/o Twist." *Confluencia* 26.1 (2010): 192–94.

Chacón, Justin Akers, and Mike Davis. *No One Is Illegal: Fighting Racism and State Violence on the Mexico Border*. Chicago: Haymarket Books, 2006.

Chávez, Leo. *The Latino Threat Narrative*. Stanford: Stanford University Press, 2008.

Chetty, Raj, Nathaniel Hendren, Patrick Kline, and Emmanuel Saez. "Where Is the Land of Opportunity? The Geography of Intergenerational Mobility in the United States." *Quarterly Journal of Economics* 129.4 (2014): 1553–1623.

Chicago Women's Liberation Union. "Socialist Feminism: A Strategy for the Women's Movement, 1972." http://www.historyisaweapon.com/defcon1/chisocfem.html

Chinchilla, Norma. "Marxism, Feminism, and the Struggle for Democracy in Latin America." In *Materialist Feminism: A Reader in Class, Difference, and Women's Lives*, edited by Rosemary Hennessy and Chrys Ingraham. New York: Routledge, 1997.

Chow, Rey. *The Protestant Ethnic and the Spirit of Capitalism*. New York: Columbia University Press, 2002.

Chrostowska, S. D. "Thought Woken by Memory: Adorno's Circuitous Path to Utopia." *New German Critique* 40.1 (2013): 93–117.

Combahee River Collective. "A Black Feminist Statement." In *Capitalism, Patriarchy, and the Case for Socialist Feminism*, edited by Zillah R. Eisenstein, 362–72. New York: Monthly Review, 1978. Republished in Gloria Anzaldúa and Cherríe Moraga, eds., *This Bridge Called My Back: Writings by Radical Women of Color* (1981), 210–18.

Crespy, David. "A Nuyorican Absurdist: Pedro Pietri and His Plays of Happy Subversion." *Latin American Theatre Review* 45.2 (2012): 25–43.

Cruz, Angie. *Let It Rain Coffee*. New York: Simon and Schuster, 2005.

Culture Clash. *Oh, Wild West! The California Plays*. New York: Theatre Communications Group, 2011.

Cutler, John Alba. "Disappeared Men: Chicana/o Authenticity and the American War in Viet Nam." *American Literature* 81.3 (2009): 583–611.

Damon, Maria. *Postliterary America: From Bagel Shop Jazz to Micropoetries*. Iowa City: University of Iowa Press, 2011.

Dávila, Arlene. *Barrio Dreams: Puerto Ricans, Latinos, and the Neoliberal City*. Berkeley: University of California Press, 2004.

Davis, Angela Y. *Abolition Democracy: Beyond Empire, Prisons, and Torture*. New York: Seven Stories, 2005.

Davis, Mike. *City of Quartz: Excavating the Future in Los Angeles*. New York: Vintage Books, 1992.

De Angelis, Massimo. "Separating the Doing and the Deed: Capital and the Continuous Character of Enclosures." *Historical Materialism* 12.2 (2004): 57–87.

Debord, Guy. "The Decline and Fall of the Spectacle-Commodity Economy." In *Situationist International Anthology*, edited and translated by Ken Knabb. Berkeley: Bureau of Public Secrets, 1981.

Delany, Samuel. *The Jewel-Hinged Jaw: Notes on the Language of Science Fiction*. Middletown: Wesleyan University Press, 2009.

de la Pava, Sergio. *A Naked Singularity*. Chicago: University of Chicago Press, 2012.

de la Torre, Mónica. *Public Domain*. New York: Roof Books, 2008.

Del Castillo, Adelaida R., ed. *Between Borders: Essays on Mexicana/ Chicana History*. Moorpark, CA: Floricanto Press, 1990.

Department of Corrections and Rehabilitation, State of California. "Prison Census Data as of June 30, 2013." September 2013.

Derksen, Jeff. *Annihilated Time: Poetry and Other Politics*. Vancouver: Talonbooks, 2009.

Dilanian, Ken, William M. Arkin, and Robert Windrem. "U.S. Urged Ecuador to Act against WikiLeaks Leader Assange." *Nbcnews.com*, October 20, 2016. Accessed February 4, 2017. http://www.nbcnews.com/news/us-news/u-s-urged-ecuador-act-against-assange-n669271

Dowdy, Michael. *Broken Souths: Latina/o Poetic Responses to Neoliberalism and Globalization*. Tucson: University of Arizona Press, 2013.

Duarte, Stella Pope. *Let Their Spirits Dance*. New York: Harper/Perennial, 2002.

Duménil, Gerard, and Dominique Lévy. "Costs and Benefits of Neoliberalism: A Class Analysis." *Review of International Political Economy* 8.4 (Winter 2001): 578–607.

Duménil, Gerard, and Dominique Lévy. "The Nature and Contradictions of Neoliberalism." In *Socialist Register 2002: A World of Contradictions*, edited by Leo Panitch and Colin Leys, 43–71. London: Merlin Press, 2001.

Duménil, Gerard, and Dominique Lévy. "The Neoliberal (Counter-)Revolution." In *Neoliberalism: A Critical Reader*, edited by Alfredo Saad-Filho and Deborah Johnston, 9–19. London: Pluto, 2005.

Dylan, Bob. "George Jackson." Ram's Horn Music, 1971. Renewed by Ram's Horn Music, 1999.

Economist. "Tu casa es mi casa." March 13, 2015. http://www.economist.com/blogs/graphicdetail/2015/03/daily-chart-5

Eisenstein, Zillah R. *Capitalism Patriarchy and the Case for Socialist Feminism*. New York: Monthly Review, 1978.

Elizondo, Sergio. *Muerte en una estrella/ Shooting Star*. Translated by Rosaura Sánchez and Beatrice Pita. Houston: Arte Público Press, 2014.

Farrington, Dana. "Photographing Puerto Rican New York, with a 'Sympathetic Eye.'" *National Public Radio*, October 26, 2013. Accessed January 28, 2016. http://www.npr.org/sections/codeswitch/2013/10/26/231704827/photographing-puerto-rican-new-york-with-a-sympathetic-eye

Federici, Silvia. *Caliban and the Witch*. Brooklyn, NY: Autonomedia, 2004.

Federici, Silvia. *Revolution at Point Zero: Housework, Reproduction, and Feminist Struggle*. Oakland, CA: PM Press, 2012.

Fisher, Mark. *Capitalist Realism: Is There No Alternative?* Winchester, UK: Zero Books, 2009.

Flores, Juan. *From Bomba to Hi-Hop: Puerto Rican Culture and Latino Identity*. New York: Columbia University Press, 2000.

Foster, John Bellamy. *Marx's Ecology: Materialism and Nature*. New York: Monthly Review Press, 2000.

Foucault, Michel. *Discipline and Punish: The Birth of the Prison.* Translated by Alan Sheridan. New York: Vintage, 1995.

Fregoso, Rosa Linda, and Angie C. Chabram. "Chicana/o Cultural Representations: Reframing Alternative Critical Discourses." *Cultural Studies* 4.3 (October 1990): 203–12.

Fricke, Jim, and Charlie Ahearn. *Yes Yes Y'all: The Experience Music Project Oral History of Hip-Hop's First Decade.* Cambridge, MA: Da Capo Press, 2002.

Furman, Jill. Introduction to *In the Heights* by Manuel-Lin Miranda and Quiara Alegría Hudes, ix–xiv. Milwaukee: Applause Theatre & Cinema Books, 2013.

Gallego, Carlos. *Chicana/o Subjectivity and the Politics of Identity: Between Recognition and Revolution.* New York: Palgrave Macmillan, 2011.

Galli, Carlo. *Political Spaces and Global War.* Translated by Elisabeth Fay. Minneapolis: University of Minnesota Press, 2010.

Galvin, Rachel. "Poetry Is Theft." *Comparative Literature Studies* 51.1 (2014): 18–54.

García, Rupert. "The New within Tradition." Introduction to *Lotería Cards,* by Juan Felipe Herrera. San Francisco: City Lights, 1999.

Gavin, Patrick. "Cornel West: Obama a 'War Criminal.'" *Politico,* February 15, 2013. Accesssed February 4, 2017. http://www.politico.com/story/2013/02/cornel-west-obama-a-war-criminal-087702

Geoghegan, Vincent. "Remembering the Future." In *Not Yet: Reconsidering Ernst Bloch,* edited by Jamie Owen Daniel and Tom Moylan, 15–32. London: Verso, 1997.

Gilmore, Ruth Wilson. *Golden Gulag: Prisons, Surplus, Crisis, and Opposition in Globalizing California.* Berkeley: University of California Press, 2007.

Gilmore, Ruth Wilson, and Craig Gilmore. "Beyond Bratton." In *Policing the Planet: Why the Policing Crisis Led to Black Lives Matter,* edited by Jordan T. Camp and Christina Heatherton, 173–99. London: Verso, 2016.

Glissant, Édouard. *Poetics of Relation.* Translated by Betsy Wing. Ann Arbor: University of Michigan Press, 1997.

Goldman, Emma. *Red Emma Speaks: An Emma Goldman Reader*. 3rd ed. Edited by Alix Kates Shulman. New York: Humanity Books, 1998.

González, Genaro. "Un Hijo del Sol." In *The Chicano*, edited by Edward Simmen, 308–16. New York: New American Library, 1971.

González, Jovita, and Eve Raleigh. *Caballero, a Historical Novel*. College Station: Texas A&M University Press, 1996.

González, Marcial. *Chicano Novels and the Politics of Form: Race, Class, and Reification*. Ann Arbor: University of Michigan Press, 2009.

González, Marcial. "The Future as Form: Undoing the Categorical Separation of Class and Gender in Ana Castillo's *Sapogonia*." In *Class and the Making of American Literature: Created Unequal*, edited by Andrew Lawson. New York: Routledge, 2014.

Gramsci, Antonio. *Prison Notebooks, Vols. 1–3*. Translated by Joseph Buttigieg and Antonio Callari. New York: Columbia University Press, 2011.

Greenberg, John. "Bernie Sanders: The United States Has 'More People in Jail Than Any Other Country on Earth.'" *Politifact*, October 13, 2015. http://www.politifact.com/truth-o-meter/statements/2015/oct/13/bernie-s/bernie-sanders-united-states-has-more-people-jail-/

Greene, Alexis. "No Place Like Home: Quiara Alegría Hudes Tells a Philadelphia Story All Her Own." *Theatre Communications Group*, October 2008. Accessed January 4, 2016. https://www.tcg.org/publications/at/oct08/hudes.cfm

Grosfoguel, Ramón. *Colonial Subjects: Puerto Ricans in a Global Perspective*. Berkeley: University of California Press, 2003.

Gumbrecht, Hans Ulrich. "Shall We Continue to Write Histories of Literature?" *New Literary History* 39 (2008): 519–32.

Guzmán, R. Andrés. "Criminalization at the Edge of the Evental Site: Undocumented Immigration, Mass Incarceration, and Universal Citizenship." *Theory & Event* 19.2 (2016).

Hall, Stuart. "The Neoliberal Revolution." *Soundings: A Journal of Politics and Culture* 48 (Summer 2011): 9–27.

Hamilton, Patrick L. *Of Space and Mind: Cognitive Mappings of Contemporary Chicano/a Fiction*. Austin: University of Texas Press, 2011.

Hardt, Michael, and Antonio Negri. *Empire*. Cambridge: Harvard University Press, 2000.

Harootunian, Harry. "Piercing the Present with the Past: Reflections on Massimiliano Tomba's *Marx's Temporalities*." *Historical Materialism* 23.4 (2015): 60–74.

Harvey, David. *A Brief History of Neoliberalism*. New York: Oxford University Press, 2005.

Harvey, David. "*Commonwealth*: An Exchange." *Artforum* 48.3 (November 2009): 214.

Harvey, David. *The Condition of Postmodernity*. Cambridge: Blackwell, 1990.

Harvey, David. *The New Imperialism*. Oxford: Oxford University Press, 2003.

Harvey, David. *The Urban Experience*. Baltimore: Johns Hopkins University Press, 1989.

Hennessy, Rosemary. *Fires on the Border: The Passionate Politics of Labor Organizing on the Mexican Frontera*. Minneapolis: University of Minnesota Press, 2013.

Herrera, Juan Felipe. *Lotería Cards and Fortune Poems: A Book of Lives*. Linocuts by Artemio Rodríguez. San Francisco: City Lights, 1999.

Hiatt, Brian. "'Hamilton': Meet the Man behind Broadway's Hip-Hop Masterpiece." *Rolling Stone*, September 29, 2015. Accessed January 7, 2016. http://www.rollingstone.com/culture/features/hamilton-meet-the-man-behind-broadways-hip-hop-masterpiece-20150929?page=2

Hinojosa, Rolando. *Generaciones y semblanzas*. Berkeley: Justa Publications, 1977.

Hofler, Robert. "The Groundbreakers: Legit." *Variety*, October 9, 2008, A23.

Horkheimer, Max, and Theodor Adorno. *Dialectic of Enlightenment*. Stanford: Stanford University Press, 2002.

Insko, Jeffrey. "Prospects for the Present." *American Literary History* 26.4 (2014): 1–13.

International Consortium of Investigative Journalists. "The Panama Papers: Politicians, Criminals, and the Rouge Industry That Hides Their Cash." Accessed February 4, 2017. https://panamapapers.icij.org/

Jackman, Tom. "Mass Reduction of California Prison Population Didn't Cause Rise in Crime, Two Studies Find." *Washington Post*, May 18, 2016.

Jameson, Fredric. *The Antinomies of Realism*. London: Verso, 2013.

Jameson, Fredric. "Culture and Finance Capital." In *The Jameson Reader*, edited by Michael Hardt and Kathi Weeks, 255–74. Malden, MA: Blackwell, 2000.

Jameson, Fredric. "The End of Temporality." *Critical Inquiry* 29.4 (2003): 695–718.

Jameson, Fredric. *The Ideologies of Theory, Vol. 1*. Minneapolis: University of Minnesota Press, 1988.

Jameson, Fredric. "New Literary History after the End of the New." *New Literary History* 39 (2008): 375–87.

Jameson, Fredric. *The Political Unconscious: Narrative as a Socially Symbolic Act*. Ithaca, NY: Cornell University Press, 1981.

Jameson, Fredric. "The Politics of Utopia." *New Left Review* 25 (January–February 2004): 35–54.

Jameson, Fredric. *Postmodernism, or The Cultural Logic of Late Capitalism*. Durham: Duke University Press, 1992.

Jameson, Fredric. *The Seeds of Time*. New York: Columbia University Press, 1994.

Jameson, Fredric. *Valences of the Dialectic*. New York: Verso, 2009.

Kaplan, Abraham. "Obscenity as an Esthetic Category." *Law and Contemporary Problems* 20.4 (Fall 1955): 544–59.

Katznelson, Ira. *When Affirmative Action Was White: An Untold History of Racial Inequality in Twentieth-Century America*. New York: W. W. Norton, 2005.

Kaufmann, David. "Thanks for the Memory: Bloch, Benjamin, and the Philosophy of History." In *Not Yet: Reconsidering Ernst Bloch*, edited by Jamie Owen Daniel and Tom Moylan, 33–52. London: Verso, 1997.

Kelly, Stuart. "A Naked Singularity by Sergio de la Pava—Review." *Guardian*, August 29, 2013. Accessed May 2, 2016. http://www.theguardian.com/books/2013/aug/29/naked-singularity-sergio-pava-review

King, Martin Luther, Jr. "The Crisis in America's Cities: An Analysis of

Social Disorder and a Plan of Action against Poverty, Discrimination and Racism in Urban America." Speech, Southern Christian Leadership Conference, Atlanta, GA, August 15, 1967, 1–6. King Center. Accessed August 29, 2016. http://www.thekingcenter.org/archive/document/crisis-americas-cities

Klein, Naomi. *The Shock Doctrine: The Rise of Disaster Capitalism*. New York: Metropolitan Books, 2007.

Knafo, Saki. "Prison-Industrial Complex? Maybe It's Time for a Schools-Industrial Complex." *Huffington Post*, August 31, 2013. http://www.huffingtonpost.com/2013/08/30/california-prisons-schools_n_3839190.html

Kupers, Terry A. "The Role of Misogyny and Homophobia in Prison Sexual Abuse." *UCLA Women's Law Journal* 18.1 (2010): 108–9.

Land, Nick. "Trump's Warsaw Uprising." *Jacobite*, July 12, 2017. Accessed July 16, 2017. https://jacobitemag.com/2017/07/12/trumps-warsaw-uprising/

Lansdale, Sadie. "Deslenguadas: The Intersection of Physical and Structural Violence in the Work of Helena María Viramontes." Unpublished paper, Tufts University, Department of English.

Larsen, Neil. *Determinations: Essays on Theory, Narrative and Nation in the Americas*. London: Verso, 2001.

Lederer, Emil. "The Economic Doctrine of National Socialism." *Annals of the American Academy of Political and Social Science* 191 (May 1937): 219–25.

Levinson, Brett. *Market and Thought: Meditations on the Political and Biopolitical*. New York: Fordham University Press, 2004.

Lewis, Michael. *The Big Short: Inside the Doomsday Machine*. New York: W. W. Norton, 2011.

Limón, Graciela. *The River Flows North*. Houston: Arte Público Press, 2009.

Limón, José E. *Dancing with the Devil: Society and Cultural Poetics in Mexican-American South Texas*. Madison: University of Wisconsin Press, 1994.

Linenthal, Peter, et al. *Images of America: San Francisco's Potrero Hill*. Charleston, SC: Arcadia Publishing, 2005.

Llévanos, Raoul S. "Race, Deprivation, and Immigrant Isolation: The Spatial Geography of Air-Toxic Clusters in the Continental United States." *Social Science Research* 54 (November 2015): 50–67.

Lorenz, Chris. "Historical Knowledge and Historical Reality: A Plea for 'Internal Realism.'" *History and Theory* 33.3 (1994): 297–327.

Lucas, Ashley. "Prisoners on the Great White Way: *Short Eyes* and *Zoot Suit* as the First US Latina/o Plays on Broadway." *Latin American Theatre Review* 43.1 (2009): 121–35.

Lukács, Georg. *History and Class Consciousness: Studies in Marxist Dialectics*. Translated by Rodney Livingstone. Cambridge, MA: MIT Press, 1971.

Luna, Jennie, and Martha Galeana, "Remembering Coyolxauhqui as a Birthing Text." *Regeneración Tlacuilolli: UCLA Raza Studies Journal* 2.1 (June 2016): 7–32.

Luxemburg, Rosa. *The Accumulation of Capital*. Translated by Agnes Schwarzschild. London: Routledge, 2003 [1913].

Maguire, Emily A. "'The Shuffle of the City Finally Becomes Us': The Corporality of Place in the Poetry of Urayoán Noel." *ASAP/Journal* 2.1 (2017): 172.

Malm, Andreas. *Fossil Capital: The Rise of Steam Power and the Roots of Global Warming*. London: Verso, 2016.

Mandel, Ernest. *Late Capitalism*. New York: Verso Classics, 1999.

Marcuse, Herbert. *Eros and Civilization: A Philosophical Inquiry into Freud*. Boston: Beacon Press, 1974.

Marcuse, Herbert. *An Essay on Liberation*. Boston: Beacon Press, 1971.

Marcuse, Herbert. *One-Dimensional Man: Studies in the Ideology of Advanced Industrial Society*. Boston: Beacon Press, 1991.

Markowitz, Eric. "Making Profits on the Captive Prison Market." *New Yorker*, September 4, 2016. http://www.newyorker.com/business/currency/making-profits-on-the-captive-prison-market

Martínez, Óscar. *The Beast: Riding the Rails and Dodging Narcos on the Migrant Trail*. Translated by Daniela Maria Ugaz and John Washington. New York: Verso, 2014.

Martínez, Óscar. "Los Coyotes Domados." *Elfaro.net*. http://www.salanegra.elfaro.net/es/201403/cronicas/15101/

Marx, Karl. *Capital: A Critique of Political Economy, Volume I*. Edited by

Frederick Engels. Translated by Samuel Moore and Edward Aveling. New York: International Publishers, 1974.

Marx, Karl. *Capital: A Critique of Political Economy, Volume 1*. Translated by Ben Fowkes. New York: Penguin Books, 1990.

Marx, Karl. *A Contribution to the Critique of Political Economy*. Translated by W. W. Ryazanskaya. New York: International Publishers, 1970.

Marx, Karl. *Grundrisse*. New York: Vintage Books, 1973.

Mathias, Christopher. "NYPD Stop and Frisk: 15 Shocking Facts about a Controversial Program." *Huffington Post*, May 15, 2012. Accessed May 23, 2016. http://www.huffingtonpost.com/2012/05/13/nypd-stop-and-frisks-15-shocking-facts_n_1513362.html

McDaniels, Aaron. *Truth between the Lies*. Bloomington, IN: Xlibris, 2016. Kindle ed., chapter 39.

McSweeney, Joyelle. *The Necropastoral: Poetry, Media, Occults*. Ann Arbor: University of Michigan Press, 2015.

Melamed, Jodi. "Racial Capitalism." *Critical Ethnic Studies* 1.1 (Spring 2015): 76–85.

Menchaca, Martha. *The Politics of Dependency: U.S. Reliance on Mexican Oil and Farm Labor*. Austin: University of Texas Press, 2016.

Midnight Notes Collective. "The New Enclosures." *Midnight Notes* 10 (1990).

Mies, Maria. *Patriarchy and Accumulation on a World Scale: Women in the International Division of Labour*. London: Zed Books, 2014.

Miller, Todd. *Border Patrol Nation: Dispatches from the Front Lines of Homeland Security*. San Francisco: City Lights Books, 2014.

Miranda, Lin-Manuel, and Quiara Alegría Hudes. *In the Heights*. Milwaukee: Applause Theatre & Cinema Books, 2013.

Miranda, Marie "Keta." "Re-Membering Emotion: Bigotes and the Unblocking of Memories." *Chicana/Latina Studies* 13.2 (Spring 2014): 186–200.

Moore, Jason W. *Capitalism in the Web of Life: Ecology and the Accumulation of Capital*. London: Verso, 2015.

Moraga, Cherríe. *Heroes and Saints*. Albuquerque: West End Press, 1994.

Moraga, Cherríe. *Watsonville/Circle in the Dirt*. Albuquerque: West End Press, 1996.

Moraga, Cherríe. *A Xicana Codex of Changing Consciousness Writings, 2000–2010*. Durham: Duke University Press, 2011.

Morrison, Ewan. "YA Dystopias Teach Children to Submit to the Free Market, Not Fight Authority." *Guardian*, September 1, 2014. https://www.theguardian.com/books/2014/sep/01/ya-dystopias-children-free-market-hunger-games-the-giver-divergent

Morton, Carlos. *The Many Deaths of Danny Rosales*. Houston: Arte Público Press, 1983.

Nealon, Christopher. *The Matter of Capital: Poetry and Crisis in the American Century*. Cambridge: Harvard University Press, 2011.

Nericcio, William Anthony. *Tex{t}-Mex: Seductive Hallucinations of the "Mexican" in America*. Austin: University of Texas Press, 2007.

Nilges, Mathias. "Fictions of Neoliberalism: Contemporary Realism and the Temporality of Postmodernism's Ends." In *Neoliberalism and Contemporary Literary Culture*, edited by Rachel Greenwald-Smith and Mitchum Huehls, 105–21. Baltimore: Johns Hopkins University Press, 2017.

Nilges, Mathias. "Finance Capital and the Time of the Novel, or Money without Narrative Qualities." *TOPIA* 30–31 (Spring 2014): 31–46.

Nilges, Mathias. "Neoliberalism and the Time of the Novel." *Textual Practice* 29.2 (2015): 357–77.

Noel, Urayoán. *Buzzing Hemisphere/Rumor Hemisférico*. Tucson: University of Arizona Press, 2015.

Noel, Urayoán. *Hi-Density Politics*. Buffalo: BlazeVOX, 2010.

Noel, Urayoán. *In Visible Movement: Nuyorican Poetry from the Sixties to Slam*. Iowa City: University of Iowa Press, 2014.

Noel, Urayoán. *Kool Logic/La Lógica Kool*. Tempe, AZ: Bilingual Press, 2005.

Noel, Urayoán. *Las Flores del Mall*. Brooklyn: Ediciones Alamala, 2000.

Olguín, B. V. "*Barrios of the World Unite!* Regionalism, Transnationalism, and Internationalism in Tejano War Poetry from the Mexican Revolution to World War II." In *Left of the Color Line: Race, Radicalism, and Twentieth-Century Literature of the United States*, edited by Bill V. Mullen and James Smethurst, 107–39. Chapel Hill: University of North Carolina Press, 2003.

Olguín, B. V. "Caballeros and Indians: Mexican American Whiteness, Hegemonic Mestizaje, and Ambivalent Indigeneity in Proto-Chicana/o Autobiographical Discourse, 1858–2008." *MELUS* 38.1 (Spring 2013): 30–49.

Oxford English Dictionary, Third Edition, 2006. Accessed February 4, 2017. http://www.oed.com

Paredes, Américo. *George Washington Gómez*. Houston: Arte Público Press, 1990.

Penrose, Roger. *The Road to Reality: A Complete Guide to the Laws of the Universe*. New York: A. A. Knopf, 2005.

Perelman, Michael. *The Invention of Capitalism: Classical Political Economy and the Secret History of Accumulation*. Durham, NC: Duke University Press, 2000.

Pérez, Emma. *The Decolonial Imaginary: Writing Chicanas into History*. Bloomington: Indiana University Press, 1999.

Pérez, Emma. "'A La Mujer': A Critique of the Partido Liberal Mexicano's Gender Ideology on Women." In *Between Borders: Essays on Mexicana/Chicana History*, edited by Adelaida R. Del Castillo, 459–82. Moorpark, CA: Floricanto Press, 1990.

Pérez, Emma. "Sexuality and Discourse: Notes from a Chicana Survivor." In *Chicana Lesbians: The Girls Our Mothers Warned Us About*, edited by Carla Trujillo. Berkeley: Third Women Press, 1991.

Pérez, Emma. "Speaking from the Margin: Uninvited Discourse on Sexuality and Power." In *Building with Our Hands: New Directions in Chicana Studies*, edited by Adela de la Torre and Beatríz M. Pesquera. Berkeley: University of California Press, 1993.

Pérez, Vincent. "'Running' and Resistance: Nihilism and Cultural Memory in Urban Narratives." *MELUS* 25.2 (Summer 2000): 133–46.

Pietri, Pedro. *Pedro Petri: Selected Poetry*. Edited by Juan Flores and Pedro López Adorno. San Francisco: City Lights Books, 2015.

Piñero, Miguel. *La Bodega Sold Dreams*. Houston: Arte Público Press, 1985.

Pinsker, Joe. "America Is Even Less Socially Mobile Than Most Economists Thought." *Atlantic*, July 23, 2015. http//www.theatlantic.com/business/archive/2015/07/America-social-mobility-parents-income/399311/

Potts, Kathleen. "Water by the Spoonful. Interview with Quiara Alegría Hudes." *Guernica*, July 2, 2012. Accessed January 4, 2016. https://www.guernicamag.com/interviews/water-by-the-spoonful/

Prison Policy Initiative. "Mass Incarceration: The Whole Pie 2016." https://www.prisonpolicy.org/reports/pie2016.html

Pulido, Laura. "Rethinking Environmental Racism: White Privilege and Urban Development in Southern California." *Annals of the Association of American Geographers* 90.1 (March 2000).

Quiñónez, Ernesto. *Changó's Fire*. New York: Harper Collins, 2004.

Rancière, Jacques. "In What Time Do We Live?" *Politica Comun* 4 (2013).

Ransby, Barbara. "U.S.: The Black Poor and the Politics of Expendability." *Race & Class* 38.2 (October 1996): 1–12.

Rivera, Alex, dir. *Sleep Dealer*. 2008. Film.

Rivera, Lysa. "Future Histories and Cyborg Labor: Reading Borderlands Science Fiction after NAFTA." *Science Fiction Studies* 39.3 (2012): 415–36.

Rivera, Tomás. "The Salamanders." In *Tomás Rivera: The Complete Works*, edited by Julián Olivares, 223–225. Houston: Arte Público Press, 1991.

Rivera, Tomás. . . . *y no se lo tragó la tierra / . . . And the Earth Did Not Devour Him*. Houston: Arte Público Press, 2015.

Robertson, Campbell. "You're 27. Here Are Millions to Stage Your Musical." *New York Times*, February 18, 2007, A9.

Robinson, William I. *Global Capitalism and the Crisis of Humanity*. New York: Cambridge University Press, 2014.

Román, Elda María. *Race and Upward Mobility: Seeking, Gatekeeping, and Other Class Strategies in Postwar America*. Redwood City, CA: Stanford University Press, 2017.

Ruiz, Ronald. *Happy Birthday Jesús*. Houston: Arte Público Press, 1994.

Ruiz, Ronald. *A Lawyer*. Amazon Digital Services, 2012.

Rustin, Susanna. "Sergio De La Pava: 'My Book's Not Perfect, but It's What I Set Out to Do. I Wanted It to Have a Propulsive, Angry Core.'" *Guardian*, June 27, 2014. Accessed May 2, 2016. http://www.theguardian.com/books/2014/jun/27/sergio-de-la-pava-naked-singularity-interview

Ryan, Alan. "To Be Young, Troubled, and Latino." *San Jose Mercury News*, April 17, 1994.

Saldívar, Ramón. *Chicano Narrative: The Dialectics of Difference*. Madison: University of Wisconsin Press, 1990.

Sánchez, Rosaura. *Chicano Discourse: Socio-historic Perspectives*. New York: Newbury House, 1983.

Sánchez, Rosaura, and Beatrice Pita. *Lunar Braceros*. San Diego: Calaca Press, 2009.

Sánchez, Rosaura, and Beatrice Pita. *Lunar Braceros: 2125–2148*. New York: BookMobile, 2012. Kindle ed.

Sandoval-Sánchez, Alberto. "An Octopus with Many Legs: U.S. Latino Theater and Its Diversity." In *José, Can You See? Latinos On and Off Broadway*, 103–23. Madison: University of Wisconsin Press, 1999.

Santina, Don. "Ethnic Cleansing in San Francisco." *Counterpunch*, September 29, 2007. http://www.counterpunch.org/2007/09/29/ethnic-cleansing-in-san-francisco/

Sawhill, Isabel V. "Inequality and Social Mobility: Be Afraid." May 27, 2015. http://www.brookings.edu/blogs/social-mobility-memos/posts/2015/05/27-inequality-great-gatsby-curve-sawhill

Schroeder, Jeanne Lorraine. *The Triumph of Venus: The Erotics of the Market*. Berkeley: University of California Press, 2004.

Singley, Catherine. "Fractures in the Foundation: The Latino Worker's Experience in an Era of Declining Job Quality." Washington, DC: National Council of La Raza, 2009. http://publications.nclr.org/handle/123456789/1211

Smith, Neil. "Giuliani Time: The Revanchist 1990s." *Social Text* 57 (Winter 1998): 1–20.

Soss, Joe, Richard C. Fording, and Sanford R. Schram. *Disciplining the Poor: Neoliberal Paternalism and the Persistent Power of Race*. Chicago: University of Chicago Press, 2011.

Spahr, Juliana. *The Transformation*. Berkeley: Atelos, 2007.

Squires, Gregory D. *Capital and Communities in Black and White: The Intersections of Race, Class, and Uneven Development*. Albany: State University of New York Press, 1994.

Swaine, Jon, Oliver Laughland, Jamiles Lartey, and Ciara McCarthy. "Young Black Men Killed by U.S. Police at Highest Rate in Year of 1,134 Deaths." *Guardian*, December 31, 2015. https://www.theguardian.com/us-news/2015/dec/31/the-counted-police-killings-2015-young-black-men

Taibbi, Matt. *Griftopia: Bubble Machines, Vampire Squids, and the Long Con That Is Breaking America*. New York: Spiegel & Grau, 2010.

Tejada, Roberto. *Full Foreground*. Tucson: University of Arizona Press, 2012.

Tejid@s Junt@s: Workers, Students, and the Movement for Alta Gracia. https://vimeo.com/40438513

THNKR. "*Les Mis* Inspires Creator of *In the Heights!*" *YouTube*, January 17, 2013. Accessed January 7, 2016. https://www.youtube.com/watch?v=aewv9UKEYkk

Thompson, Peter. "Ernst Bloch, *Ungleichzeitigkeit* and the Philosophy of Being and Time." *New German Critique* 42.2 (2015): 49–64.

Tobar, Hector. *The Tattooed Soldier*. New York: Penguin Books, 1998.

Tomba, Massimiliano. "Marx's Temporal Bridges and Other Pathways." *Historical Materialism* 23.4 (2015): 75–91.

Toscano, Rodrigo. *Deck of Deeds*. Denver: Counterpath, 2012.

United States Congress. *The 9/11 Commission Report: Final Report of the National Commission on Terrorist Attacks Upon the United States*. Authorized by President George W. Bush. 2004.

Urrea, Luis Alberto. *The Devil's Highway: A True Story*. New York: Back Bay Books, 2004.

Vallejo, César. *The Complete Poetry: A Bilingual Edition*. Translated by Clayton Eshleman. Berkeley: University of California Press, 2007.

Véa, Alfredo. *Gods Go Begging*. New York: Plume, 2000 [1999].

Véa, Alfredo. *The Silver Cloud Café*. New York: Dutton, 1996.

Viego, Antonio. *Dead Subjects: Towards a Politics of Loss in Latino Studies*. Durham, NC: Duke University Press, 2007.

Vigil, Ariana E. *War Echoes: Gender and Militarization in U.S. Latina/o Cultural Production*. New Brunswick, NJ: Rutgers University Press, 2014.

Villa, Raúl Homero. *Barrio-Logos: Space and Place in Urban Chicano Literature and Culture*. Austin: University of Texas Press, 2000.

Viramontes, Helena María. *Their Dogs Came with Them*. New York: Washington Square Press, 2007.

Viramontes, Helena María. *Under the Feet of Jesus*. New York: Penguin, 1995.

Wacquant, Loïc. "From Slavery to Mass Incarceration: Rethinking the 'Race Question' in the U.S." *New Left Review* 13 (2002): 41–60.

Wacquant, Loïc. "The New 'Peculiar Institution': On the Prison as Surrogate Ghetto." *Theoretical Criminology* 4.3 (2000): 377–89.

Wacquant, Loïc. *Punishing the Poor: The Neoliberal Government of Social Insecurity*. Durham: Duke University Press, 2009.

Wacquant, Loïc. "Three Pernicious Premises in the Study of the American Ghetto." *International Journal of Urban and Regional Research* 21.2 (1997): 341–53.

Wajcman, Judy. *Pressed for Time: The Acceleration of Life in Digital Capitalism*. Chicago: University of Chicago Press, 2014.

Wall, Catherine E. "Review of *Lotería Cards*, by Juan Felipe Herrera." *World Literature Today* 75.1 (2001): 120.

Wallace, Anthony F. C. *The Long Bitter Trail*. New York: Hill and Wang, 1993.

Weber, David J. *Foreigners in Their Native Land*. Albuquerque: University of New Mexico Press, 1973.

White, Hayden. *The Content and the Form: Narrative Discourse and Historical Representation*. Baltimore: Johns Hopkins University Press, 1987.

Williams, Brian J. "'In This Same Shamble of Strewn Bone': *Gods Go Begging* and the Community of Loss." *Critique: Studies in Contemporary Fiction* 54.3 (2013): 316–34.

Williams, Gareth. *The Mexican Exception: Sovereignty, Police, and Democracy*. New York: Palgrave Macmillan, 2011.

Williams, Gareth. *The Other Side of the Popular: Neoliberalism and Subalternity in Latin America*. Durham: Duke University Press, 2002.

Williams, Raymond. *Culture and Materialism: Selected Essays*. London: Verso, 2006.

Wilson, Annasue McCleave. "Fighting for Justice." *Publishers Weekly*, April 13, 2012. Accessed May 2, 2016. http://www.publishersweekly.com/pw/by-topic/authors/interviews/article/51486-fighting-for-justice-pw-talks-with-sergio-de-la-pava.html

Wilson, Scott Bryan. "A Naked Singularity by Sergio de la Pava." *Quarterly Conversation*, October 4, 2010. Accessed May 2, 2016. http://quarterly-conversation.com/a-naked-singularity-by-sergio-de-la-pava

Wilson, William Julius. *When Work Disappears: The World of the New Urban Poor*. New York: Alfred A. Knopf, 1996.

Wood, James. "James Woods' Classic Takedown of Faux-Dickensian 'Hysterical Realism.'" *New Republic,* July 24, 2000. Accessed May 5, 2016. https://newrepublic.com/article/61361/human-all-too-inhuman

Yu, Timothy. *Race and the Avant-Garde: Experimental and Asian American Poetry since 1965.* Stanford: Stanford University Press, 2010.

Zipes, Jack. "Traces of Hope: The Non-synchronicity of Ernst Bloch." In *Not Yet: Reconsidering Ernst Bloch,* edited by Jamie Owen Daniel and Tom Moylan, 1–14. London: Verso, 1997.

Žižek, Slavoj. *Absolute Recoil: Towards a New Foundation of Dialectical Materialism.* New York: Verso, 2014.

Žižek, Slavoj. "RSA ANIMATE: First as Tragedy, Then as Farce." *YouTube,* July 28, 2010. Accessed February 4, 2017. https://www.youtube.com/watch?v=hpAMbpQ8J7g

Žižek, Slavoj. *The Sublime Object of Ideology.* 2nd ed. New York: Verso, 2008.

Contributors

Abraham Acosta is Associate Professor of Latin American Cultural Studies at the University of Arizona. His research traverses the critical realities of contemporary multilingual contexts, where assumptions of power, knowledge, and capital crosshatch with historical translations of cultural difference. His book, *Thresholds of Illiteracy: Theory, Latin America, and the Crisis of Resistance* (2014), was published by Fordham University Press.

Michael Dowdy is Associate Professor of English at the University of South Carolina. He is the author of *Broken Souths: Latina/o Poetic Responses to Neoliberalism and Globalization* (2013) and *American Political Poetry in the 21st Century* (2007). His forthcoming book of poetry, *Urbilly*, won the 2017 Main Street Rag Poetry Book Award.

Carlos Gallego is Associate Professor of English at St. Olaf College. He is the author of *Chicana/o Subjectivity and the Politics of Identity: Between Recognition and Revolution* (2011). In addition to several published articles in academic journals and book collections, he has edited a special issue of the *Arizona Quarterly* on contemporary approaches to Chicano/a literature.

Marcial González is Associate Professor of English at the University of California, Berkeley. He is the author of *Chicano Novels and the Politics of Form: Race, Class, and Reification* (2009). His research interests include Chicano/a literature, labor movements, and Marxist theory. As a former farm labor organizer, he supports the ongoing fight against racism, fascism, and class exploitation.

R. Andrés Guzmán is Assistant Professor of Spanish and Portuguese at Indiana University, Bloomington. His research interests include political economy, Latina/o and Latin American literature and culture, philosophy, and political theory. He has published articles in *Theory & Event*, *CR: The New Centennial Review*, *Journal of Latin American Cultural Studies*, and the *Arizona Journal of Hispanic Cultural Studies*.

Dennis López is Associate Professor of English at California State University, Long Beach. His teaching and research focus on Chican@ and Latin@ literature, U.S. ethnic literature, and U.S. radical protest literatures. His scholarship has appeared in *MELUS*, *College Literature*, *Science and Society*, and *American Studies*.

Elena Machado Sáez is Professor of English at Bucknell University. She is the author of *Market Aesthetics: The Purchase of the Past in Caribbean Diasporic Fiction* (2015), and coauthor, with Raphael Dalleo, of *The Latino/a Canon and the Emergence of Post-Sixties Literature* (2007). She teaches courses in U.S. Latino/a literature, Caribbean literature, American literature, and theater performance studies.

Marcelle Maese is Assistant Professor of English at the University of San Diego. Her publications include "'But It Should Begin in El Paso': Civil Identities, Immigrant 'World'-Traveling, and Pilgrimage Form in John Rechy's *City of Night*" in *Arizona Quarterly* (2014), and "Toward Planetary Decolonial Feminisms" in *qui parle* (2010).

Mathias Nilges is Associate Professor of English at St. Francis Xavier University, Canada. He is the coeditor of *Literary Materialisms* (2013), *Marxism and the Critique of Value* (2014), *The Contemporaneity of Modernism* (2016), and *Literature and the Global Contemporary* (2017). He has published on American literature and culture, critical theory, and literary history.

Beatrice Pita is a Lecturer in Spanish in the Department of Literature at the University of California, San Diego. She is coeditor, with Rosaura Sánchez, of *Conflicts of Interest: The Letters of María Amparo Ruiz de Burton*, and the coauthor, with Sánchez, of the introductions to Ruiz de Burton's *Who Would Have Thought It?* and *The Squatter and the Don*, and the sci-fi novel, *Lunar Braceros* (2009).

Rosaura Sánchez is Professor of Literature at the University of California, San Diego. Her publications include *Telling Identities: The Californio Testimonios* (1995), *Chicano Discourse: A Socio-Historic Perspective* (1984), a number of essays on settler colonialism, xenophobia, Rudolfo Anaya, Chicana literature, Américo Paredes, Ruiz de Burton, and other topics, and short stories collected in *He Walked in and Sat Down and Other Stories* (2000).

Edén E. Torres is Associate Professor of Gender, Women, and Sexuality Studies, and Chicano/Latino Studies, at the University of Minnesota. She has served two terms as Chair of the Department of Chicano and Latino Studies, and has won two prestigious awards for excellence in teaching. Her publications include *Chicana without Apology: The New Chicana Cultural Studies* (2003).

Index